P9-ASE-766

THE WORLD'S
LIGHTHOUSES
FROM ANCIENT TIMES
TO 1820

D. Alan Stevenson

DOVER PUBLICATIONS, INC.
Mineola, New York

Bibliographical Note

This Dover edition, first published in 2002, is an unabridged republication of the work originally published by Oxford University Press, London, in 1959 under the title *The World's Lighthouses Before 1820.*

Library of Congress Cataloging-in-Publication Data

Stevenson, David, 1815–1886.
    [World's lighthouses before 1820]
    The world's lighthouses from ancient times to 1820 / D. Alan Stevenson.
        p. cm.
    Originally published: The world's lighthouses before 1820. London : New York ; Oxford University Press, 1959.
    ISBN 0-486-41824-3 (pbk.)
     1. Lighthouses—History. I. Title.

VK1015 .S7 2002
387.1'55'09—dc21

                                                   2001047326

Manufactured in the United States of America
Dover Publications, Inc., 31 East 2nd Street, Mineola, N.Y. 11501

FOREWORD

The purpose of this book is to record facts about seamarks and to arrange them in Sections, with some explanation, to show the transition from the wood fires of Antiquity to the reflector lights of 1819. As each country was developing its lighthouses independently the narrative cannot be continuous and closely woven.

PART ONE describes seamarks before 1690 when technical progress began, and then lists chronologically the more interesting attempts at improvement before 1820. PART TWO elaborates particular periods and episodes. To PART THREE there have been banished the details of illumination. The 16 Sections are independent but cross-references and footnotes have been avoided by occasional repetition of facts. Paragraph titles should enable readers to avoid what interests them least.

Another Section might have been included to cover 18th-century European lighthouses and earlier German and Dutch seamarks but it would have added little to the tale of development. That the lighthouses of the British Isles are set forth more fully than are those of other countries is accidental in so far as more information about them has been preserved, and deliberate because their sea-structures after 1698 and their lights between 1786 and 1820 were more advanced than those elsewhere.

The answer to the probable criticism that the book contains too many dates, dimensions and details is that it would lose coherence without a substantial framework of chronology, that publications relating to seamarks bristle with conflicting dates, and that descriptions of lighthouses in only general terms would be valueless and confusing.

A search for details of fire beacons which I began over 40 years ago led gradually, as sources of information were discovered and examined, to setting up as a distant target the preparation of a history of lighthouses. This project could only proceed slowly as business interests permitted but a few years ago the aim was set anew, libraries and museums in Britain and abroad were searched for more information, and friends engaged in lighthouse affairs supplied particulars of their countries' lights. From the facts thus assembled a summary might have been prepared with little trouble, but it was evident that a detailed account should have more permanent worth. This volume carries the account from Antiquity to 1820, a year that offers a convenient break in the narrative as it follows the completion of the Bell Rock tower (the last of the great isolated lighthouses to be constructed before steam-vessels were available to lighten the transport of building materials) and precedes the introduction by Fresnel of the dioptric system of sea-lighting. I hope to complete the account from 1820 to 1960 and to include particulars of lights made over 100 years ago, but now obsolete, which I saw in nightly use shortly after 1901.

The facts on which this book is based have been drawn largely from unpublished records such as were accumulated by my family during its connection with lighthouse engineering since 1786, and from old books which, apart from those noted in the text, are now inaccessible to the general reader. It is difficult to find contemporary pictures of early seamarks except those of a few lighthouses which attracted many artists. But each Section includes several

Foreword

contemporary illustrations which together form a fairly representative pictorial record of seamarks over the period of the book. Only when special points require mention are they referred to specifically in the text.

I am grateful for information from many quarters, especially from Captain W. R. Chaplin of Trinity House, London, Sven Öberg of the Swedish Lighthouse Service, A. D. H. Martin of the Irish Lighthouse Service, and the Lighthouse Services of France and the United States of America; and I owe much to the researches of Howard Fox, John Whormby of Trinity House, Henri Wallon of Rouen, George R. Putnam of Washington, Commander P. E. B. Sinding of Copenhagen and Hilmer Carlsson of Stockholm. I am indebted also to the artists and draughtsmen, many of whose names are unknown, who pictured the sea-marks of their times and to Miss Jean Brown for copying numerous drafts, Lady Henderson and my daughter Mrs. Rhoda Shepherd for improving and correcting proofs, Francis Inglis for photography, Hislop and Day for block-making, P. Neill Fraser for printing-trials, T. R. Marshall for copies and the Oxford University Press for advice in production.

Well-deserved tributes have often been paid to the designers, builders and keepers of early lighthouses but it has escaped notice how much seamen owe to the projectors or proposers of the lighthouses, to the designers and manufacturers of the lighting apparatus, and not least to the men who relieved the keepers and carried supplies by land and sea often in conditions of hardship and danger. I should be glad if this study of early seamarks were to arouse appreciation and admiration of the efforts and achievements of many men some of whose names are little-known but to whose initiative and courage all seafarers are deeply indebted. In striving to satisfy the navigational needs of their times they laid the foundations for the advancement of sea-lighting to its present state of high efficiency. As a descendant of Thomas Smith and Robert Stevenson I have endeavoured, in describing their work in these pages, to be as fair in assessing its merit as in describing the work of others.

I should welcome any further original information about lighthouses and additional pictures and I invite intimation of any errors in the text. If I obtain sufficient new material to warrant the issue of a Supplement this shall be done, and purchasers are invited to write to me, care of the Oxford University Press, for further information about this.

In describing the construction of the Bell Rock lighthouse in detail, I cannot overlook the statements made by the Rennie family which are sometimes quoted in the Press: it has seemed best to deal with this matter separately in the Appendix.

I am responsible for all the views expressed, except where stated otherwise.

MARCH 1959

22 GLENCAIRN CRESCENT,
EDINBURGH

ACKNOWLEDGMENTS

Grateful thanks for information and assistance of much value in the preparation of this book are offered to the following Lighthouse Services: England (Trinity House, London); Scotland (Commissioners of Northern Lighthouses); Ireland (Commissioners of Irish Lighthouses); Canada; Denmark; Finland; France (Service des Phares et Balises); Holland; Sweden; United States of America (U.S. Coast Guard); Clyde Lighthouses Trust and Belfast Harbour Commission; to the following individuals and institutions in Great Britain: The Admiralty Library; James Alexander; Dr. J. Bartholomew; Professor A. J. Beattie; Charles M. Beckett; James D. Boyd; Bristol Public Library; The British Museum; F. G. G. Carr; Cassell & Co.; R. & R. Clark; Miss R. M. Clay; Captain W. R. Colbeck, R.N.R.; Mrs. Trenchard Cox; O. G. S. Crawford; A. A. Cumming; Miss M. Hope Dodds; A. Donaldson; Major A. A. Dorrien-Smith; Edinburgh Public Libraries; Edinburgh University Library; Essex County Council; Glasgow Art Galleries; Mrs. Z. Groundes-Peace; L. Hall; E. G. Hatton; N. D. Lessells; H. W. Liddell; Liverpool Public Libraries; Dr. C. A. Malcolm; Commander Hilary Mead, R.N.; Dr. Henry W. Meikle; Mitchell Library, Glasgow; Donald G. Moir; The National Library of Scotland; The National Maritime Museum; W. T. O'Dea; The Parker Gallery; Captain G. L. Parnell, R.N.; The Phaidon Press; R. W. Plenderleith; Price's Patent Candle Co.; The Public Records Office; John S. Rees; The Royal Geographical Society; The Royal Scottish Geographical Society; The Royal Scottish Museum; The Royal Society; The Royal Society of Edinburgh; The Royal Society of Arts; The Signet Library; R. A. Skelton; The Society of Antiquaries of London; The Society of Antiquaries of Scotland; K. C. Sutton-Jones; The Town Clerk of Glasgow; The Town Clerk of Liverpool; Trinity House, Newcastle; Tynemouth Public Library; Miss H. M. Wallis; A. G. Watson; E. Cuthbert Woods; William Young; and to the following individuals and institutions abroad: Dr. E. Aghib, Milan; Bancroft Library, California; Mrs. T. W. Blanchard, Boston; Professor A. Bodin, La Flèche; The Bostonian Society; Commander A. E. Carlson, U.S.C.G.; Mademoiselle S. Clermonté, Paris; Didier Costes, Paris; G. A. Cox, Amsterdam; Antonio Dias Affonso, Lisbon; P. J. G. van Diggelen, Scheveningen; Commander A. Gomes Ramos, Lisbon; Dr. A. W. Lang, E. Friesland; Gordon J. Laycock, Melbourne; J. F. Lenoire, Bordeaux; The Mariners' Museum, Newport News; The Musée de la Marine, Paris; The N.H. Scheepvaart Museum, Amsterdam; Rear Admiral C. A. Park, U.S.C.G.; Forsten Petersson, Stockholm; A. Maclaine Pont, Amsterdam; The Rijks Museum, Amsterdam; André de Rouville, Paris; The Royal Library, Copenhagen; Commander P. E. B. Sinding, Copenhagen; Fitz-Henry Smith, Jr., Boston; A. G. de Sousa, Lisbon; Captain Sakari Tainio, Helsinki; B. G. Teuber, Leipzig; University of Michigan Library; Norman Wilson, Ottawa; The Boston Marine Society, U.S.A.

CONTENTS

PART ONE. A GENERAL ACCOUNT OF LIGHTHOUSES BEFORE 1820

PART TWO. A FULLER ACCOUNT OF CERTAIN LIGHTHOUSES

Contents

PART THREE. ILLUMINATION OF EARLY LIGHTHOUSES

ILLUSTRATIONS

Illustrations

Illustrations

Illustrations

Illustrations

PART THREE

Illustrations

APPENDIX

MAPS

*The illustration on the title-page is of an eighteenth-century
fire beacon (Foster)*

OBSERVATIONS ON EARLY LIGHTHOUSES

As the key to navigation without which ships cannot in safety reach their intended ports, seamarks have a value that has been recognised from the first days of sea-venture and has not diminished with the passing of the centuries. In particular, the call for more and better lighthouses is unceasing and science, which was first applied effectively shortly after 1780 to enhance the brilliancy of their lights, now provides acoustic and radio signals which extend their service to shipping.

The gradual increase in numbers and power of navigation lights up to 1820 has continued to the present day. Since 1819 the number of coastal lighthouses has multiplied a hundredfold and the maximum power of their lights a thousandfold. Indeed, the power of the single most powerful light of 1819 exceeded the combined powers of all the navigation lights of 1780 and that of 1959 exceeds the combined powers of all those of 1819.

In Britain the extent of common knowledge of early lighthouses is usually limited to the inclusion of the Pharos of Alexandria among the Seven Wonders of the World and to awareness of the difficulties experienced in building the towers on the Eddystone Rocks. The popular impression of old navigation lights is romantic—monks lighting tapers to guide sailors through the storm and fire beacons set ablaze on headlands with flames streaming to the skies. But only so far as the facts now presented speak for themselves does this book either touch on the romance that attaches to the towers battered by the waves, the lightships tossing at their moorings and the lonely keepers often exposed to the perils of transport across wintry seas, or link lighthouses to the complicated background of sea affairs of which they are a facet.

DEFINITION OF *LIGHTHOUSE*

In Britain before 1600 a lighthouse was termed a pharos. Samuel Johnson defined it in 1755 as 'an high building at the top of which lights are hung to guide ships at sea', a description that applied to only two lighthouses in England, one at the Spurn Point and the other maintained for several years at the North Foreland. Earlier, less specific but more curious definitions were 'a vehicle of light' and 'a machine ministerial to the more commodious or conspicuous exhibition of the light'.

But like *ship* and *harbour*, the term *lighthouse* cannot be defined exactly and the apparently simple and obvious definition as 'a structure bearing a light to assist navigation' is too wide: the varieties of navigation lights extend from the simple hand-lantern which guides a boat to its haven or indicates a particular state of the tide, to the elaborate sea-tower of the present day giving powerful light-flashes as well as other signals. Some towers with outlines that are supposed to denote a lighthouse bear a light of little power or value for shipping while other structures without resemblance to the accepted lighthouse-form exhibit powerful lights of great importance. So one cannot draw a sharp line of demarcation between powers of lights or types of structures and must just accept the fact that to some extent the term *lighthouse* is used arbitrarily.

In this book the word is applied both to towers of the accepted lighthouse-form and to structures bearing any light, however feeble, that is intended to serve general navigation. The latter may be called coastal lighthouses. A group of 2 or 3 lighted towers on the same site is reckoned as one lighthouse. An Authority or a Government Department providing lighthouses usually includes in its charge all other seamarks and signals for navigation.

Lights marking harbour entrances have always had importance for vessels when out of course or seeking shelter; in such circumstances every identifiable light gives the full service of a coastal lighthouse.

The British lighthouse patents stipulated that lights should be shown during darkness on every night throughout the year, a provision that was strictly maintained, but in some countries lights were not exhibited with such regularity, by instructions or through neglect. In northern Europe they were discontinued by rule during the summer months when the nights were short.

LIGHTS MORE IMPORTANT THAN STRUCTURES

In all accounts of early lighthouses it is the structure that receives attention: scant notice is taken of their lighting, although that was the essential purpose of their establishment. Only by knowledge of their lights is it possible to understand the part which they played in navigation or to assess the value of a particular lighthouse. Perhaps when details of lighting were available they were supposed to be too technical for the comprehension and interest of the general reader; but today he is familiar with complicated mechanical and scientific appliances and so should find no difficulty in understanding the simple optical apparatus fitted in lighthouses before 1820.

REFLECTORS AND LENSES

If the actions of the various kinds of optical apparatus illustrated below are kept in mind, descriptions of early lights will be readily understood.

Figure 1 gives an impression of the action of reflectors and a lens in collecting the rays of light which they intercept from a candle flame or another illuminant (set at their focus) and in directing them to the seaman (supposed to be at a position to the right of the diagram). The spherical reflector returns the rays to the flame, so is of little benefit to the seaman. But both the parabolic reflector and the lens (indicated by the arrow L) benefit him greatly, as they collect and direct seawards all the rays falling upon them, thus emitting concentrated beams of light perhaps several hundred times that of the candle. The extent of concentration will depend on many considerations such as the area of the reflector or the lens. The dotted arrows indicate the passage of light-rays.

For simplicity of explanation, only the rays from the focus are shown in the diagram. As all illuminants are of considerable size, their extreme edges emit ex-focal rays which give the maximum divergence and cause reflectors and lenses to produce conical beams of light as shown in figure 184 and diagram 185e.

L ↓

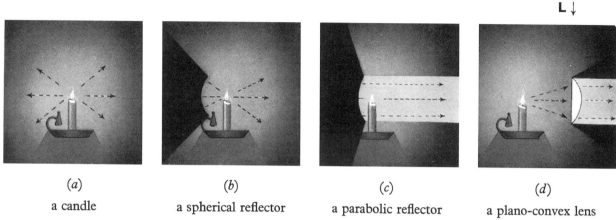

(a)   (b)   (c)   (d)

a candle   a spherical reflector   a parabolic reflector   a plano-convex lens

1. Action of reflectors and lens in collecting and directing light-rays

THE VALUE OF A LIGHTHOUSE

Expressed shortly, the value of a lighthouse depends on its light and its position, its service as a daylight beacon being of less importance.

The light should offer distinction from its neighbours and be of a candlepower sufficient to penetrate poor visibility to the desired extent. Between 1780 and 1819 it became possible to fulfil both conditions to a certain degree but few Authorities were aware of these advances and fewer put them into practice.

As for position, it has been appreciated from ancient times that a light must be raised high above sea-level to give the necessary geographical range. But occasionally the mistake has been made of choosing a site so high that the light is frequently shrouded in mist. The difficulties involved in setting a light on the actual point of danger were tackled first in 1698 at the Eddystone and then in 1731 at the Nore. In each case a light was placed boldly in the track of vessels, the one on a sunken rock and the other at the fringe of a sandbank.

IDENTIFICATION OF LIGHTS

The avoidance of a wreck and the survival of a ship's company may depend on quick recognition of a landfall or a lighthouse. Before 1820 telescopes were not uncommon in ships but spectacles were worn rarely even by landsmen. No law barred from their calling mariners who suffered from defective eyesight or hearing, so the sailor with the sharpest eyes among the crew must often have been summoned on deck to view breakers, rocks or the glimmer of a light and answer the urgent questions on which their lives depended—'is that land on the larboard quarter?' or 'what is that light ahead?'

Identification of a sea-light from its neighbours is one of the problems constantly facing navigators: before 1781 all coastal lighthouses throughout the world showed fixed lights so mistakes of identification were frequent and wrecks resulted. From that year the revolving light with a chosen period of revolution was available to offer distinction between lighthouses but, as always, the latest advances in any field can rarely be applied speedily in all countries. Sailors' tales about lights travelled quickly enough but, as Lighthouse Authorities rarely exchanged information and few manufacturers could supply an optical apparatus, adoption of the revolving light was slow. In 1800 less than a dozen lighthouses in the world showed revolving or moving lights and some 170 showed fixed lights, while in 1819 the corresponding numbers were 35 and 219. Seamen liked fixed lights for taking bearings but, fortunately for seafarers, people with technical knowledge of varieties of sea-lights pressed the extensive adoption of revolving lights not only for better identification but also for the longer range in poor atmospheric visibility which their more powerful beams could give.

LIGHTS AND ATMOSPHERIC VISIBILITY

Gradually since 1819, and even markedly since 1900, the candlepowers of all lights used on land and sea have been increased enormously and it is now almost impossible to imagine the extremely low powers of the navigation lights of the 18th century, when it was considered sufficient to provide the fluctuating illumination from a coal fire to guide a ship many miles away and the feeble glow from one candle (transmitted through a pane of coarse glass or a sheet of horn) to mark a harbour entrance.

It may well be asked whether ships before 1820 got much advantage from navigation lights of such low power. The answer is that in good visibility lights of low power may be as useful to navigation as are those of high power but that in poor visibility they are obscured and have no value.

Although in 1959 lighthouses are provided with powerful lights and devices giving guidance in other ways than directly to the navigator's eye, poor visibility remains the most deadly enemy of shipping and causes many strandings and collisions yearly despite the fitting of radar and other aids on vessels. In 1819 the only means of guiding ships past dangers when fog obliterated lights were by the frequent tolling of bells on lightships and at half-a-dozen lighthouses and, rarely, by the firing of guns or rockets.

ESTIMATED POWERS OF LIGHTS

One cannot assess the candlepower of the light-beam actually emitted from any lighthouse except on the assumption that the optical apparatus is in perfect condition as when it was originally fitted. That assumption was unjustified in many countries before 1820, as it would be at any ill-kept lighthouse to-day. At the early lights a keeper or his supervisor, if one were appointed, could through carelessness or lack of knowledge in the absence of training mar a light however well-designed and well-constructed by keeping it badly, letting it get out of repair or adjusting it incorrectly. An alteration of a fraction of an inch in placing a reflector relative to its lamp or of a couple of degrees in its inclination would reduce materially the original power of the light emitted towards the navigator by an amount that can hardly be estimated. The unsatisfactory state of the optical apparatus at the South Rock in 1812 was an instance of bad keeping and disrepair which occurred unfortunately after the contract for its maintenance had lapsed and before the new responsible engineer was in full control. This instance was not unique: few keepers knew when repairs were necessary and supervisors rarely understood the simple laws of optics and were seldom instructed to make periodical inspections of lighthouses.

Observations on Early Lighthouses

SUCCESSES AND FAILURES OF DEVELOPMENTS

The more interesting developments of seamarks are chronicled in this book but it is hoped that criticism has not been too forthright either in describing those that failed, such as the spherical reflector lights in France and the lens-reflector lights in the United States of America, or in referring to the continuance of the coal-fire lights in northern Europe up to 1858 and the reluctance of Trinity House to erect lighthouses before 1816.

In the construction of early lighthouses the outstanding tragedies were those overtaking de Foix at Cordouan (where the disappearance of the island was the main cause of delaying the showing of a light until 26 years after he signed the building contract) and Winstanley at the Eddystone (where the sea swept his tower off the Rock during an unparalleled storm). Yet each of these audacious builders set a notable milestone along the path of progress. At the Eddystone, too, it was Rudyerd who evolved from layers of wood and stones the most astonishing of sea-towers which endured for 47 years, while at the Smalls Whiteside produced with perfect economy of material a beacon of a design which avoided the full force of the waves and is frequently adopted in principle to this day. The towers erected by Smeaton at the Eddystone and Robert Stevenson at the Bell Rock are famous as sea-structures but Rogers's enterprise in raising a more simple tower at the South Rock has rarely been noted. A great novelty in its day, among structures carrying a light, was Avery's adventurous lightship at the Nore.

The story of lighthouse illumination has not been told fully hitherto. Its main interest begins soon after 1780 with Argand's discovery of an excellent lamp which showed the way to good lighting, Norberg's invention of the revolving light and Rogers's first use of a lens for a sea-light. Teulère gains sympathy for the surprising condemnation of his reflector apparatus which should have produced the most splendid light-beam of the period. Bordier-Marcet too, in spite of his exceptional understanding of lamps and reflectors, achieved little success. Sangrain and Lewis made bad lights which were imposed on seamen for upwards of 60 and 25 years respectively. Hutchinson, Ezekiel Walker, Smith and Robinson made good lights before 1800, while Lenoir and Stevenson can claim credit for fitting the best optical apparatuses in lighthouses before 1820.

WRECKS AND LIGHTHOUSES

Between 1793 and 1829 the number of wrecks occurring annually on the British shores, then the best-lighted in the world, was very large: the average of 550 increased to 800 in 1833, the tonnage of merchant vessels being some 110. On the French coasts the number of wrecks averaged 163 between 1816 and 1823 and dropped to 59 during the next 8 years. A comparison of these figures alone would indicate that the best-lighted shores drew most wrecks, but it would be a mistake to draw such a conclusion. The full facts show that more lighthouses and more identifiable and powerful lights would have reduced the numbers of wrecks in all countries. The greater losses round the British Isles were amply accounted for by the larger volume of shipping engaged in these waters and the more numerous points of danger.

Despite a high standard of seamanship, sharpened continuously by hard experience, most of the casualties might be ascribed to the difficulties of handling the sailing-craft of the period in storms, fog and darkness, and to the state of navigation. Only the larger vessels were equipped with navigational instruments other than an inferior compass and a sounding line and carried the somewhat crude sea-charts and pilotage books then published.

Wreckers plied their murderous business of showing false lights on remote coasts as in Cornwall, Wales and the Orkney islands in Britain, and Brittany in France. Their usual procedure was to drive an ass bearing 2 lanterns along the shore, to represent a vessel in motion and so lure a ship to destruction among the near rocks and shoals. Occasionally they displayed a light on a headland, hoping that it would be mistaken for a navigation light established elsewhere.

OLD TOWERS AND LIGHTS

Judging from visits paid to many old lighthouses or their sites in Europe and America, about a quarter of the early masonry or brick towers still continue their seaward vigil, some bearing new lanterns and powerful lights and others incorporated in later buildings; but examples of their original optical apparatus can rarely be found.

PART ONE

A GENERAL ACCOUNT
OF
LIGHTHOUSES
BEFORE
1820

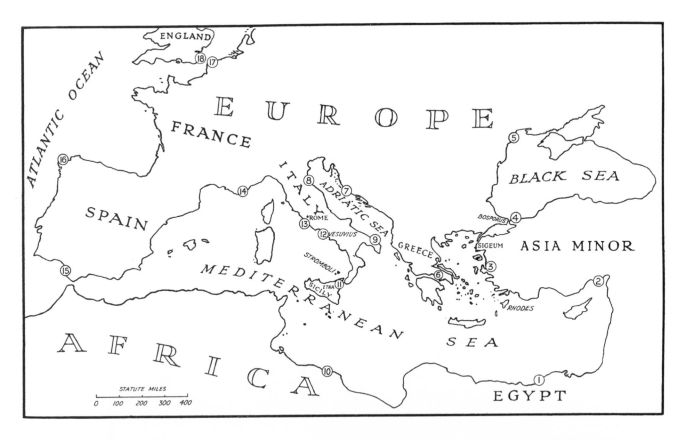

MAP SHOWING THE SITES OF 18 REPUTED ANCIENT NAVIGATION LIGHTS

1. Alexandria
2. Aegae
3. Smyrna
4. Chrysopolis
5. Neoptolomeia
6. Corinth

7. Zara
8. Ravenna
9. Brindisi
10. Lepcis Magna
11. Messina
12. Capri

13. Ostia
14. Frejus
15. Caepio
16. Corunna
17. Boulogne
18. Dover

I

LIGHTHOUSES OF ANTIQUITY

2. A lighthouse on an early Christian sarcophagus in the Lateran, Rome (Garucci)

(a) On a sea-chart of 1763

(b) According to Huril c. 1870

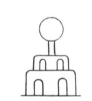

(d) A contemporary
representation on the
Peutinger Table

(e) A representation
of 1800

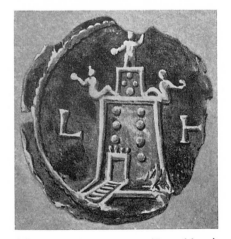

(c) According to Ebers c. 1890

(f) On a coin c. 150 A.D. (Donaldson)

3. IMPRESSIONS OF THE PHAROS OF ALEXANDRIA

I. LIGHTHOUSES OF ANTIQUITY

The first use of seamarks cannot yet be placed earlier than 300 B.C. when the Egyptians erected the Pharos of Alexandria. Of lighthouses which served shipping between that date and 300 A.D., some 200 representations have been found and about 30 lighthouses have been identified at particular sites within the Roman Empire. Their illumination came from wood fires and torches burning in the open. When the Empire dissolved, references to seamarks ceased.

There is no doubt that the earliest seamarks were *beacons*, either cairns of stones or wooden spars set up on the shore, on rocks and on sandbanks, and *buoys* made of pieces of wood anchored by a rope tied to a stone and dropped on the sea-bed. These simple types are used still at small harbours and along coasts in many parts of the world: they serve well as warnings to boats of dangers that are not obvious, such as rocks and shelves lying just below the water surface. Dom Bernard de Montfaucon, who published in 1724 a many-volumed encyclopædia of classical art entitled *L'Antiquité Expliqué*, reproduced an early representation of a primitive port where a beacon of stones and timber is associated with a quay and boats. More elaborate beacons such as masts or pillars with top-marks of various shapes fulfil many navigation requirements admirably and are used in all countries at the present time.

EARLY FIRE BEACONS

Fears of storms and of adverse winds and the peril of shipwreck upon hostile shores retarded the development of early navigation. Probably the first fires to help local boats were lighted on the shore or on the towers built to defend the entrances to ports. To show lights every night would mark a port for attack so, as now, they were exhibited only in times of peace.

Early sailors in the Mediterranean Sea must have benefited much from the direct blaze, the reflection from the clouds and the smoke from Etna, Stromboli and Vesuvius, which gave direction to ships at a considerable distance and, indeed, served as lighthouses. Possibly the idea of setting a fire and smoke on a height so that it could be seen from afar originated in the flaming summits of these volcanoes.

The first definite event in the history of seamarks is the construction of the Pharos of Alexandria in the 3rd century B.C. Authentic records of that period bear out the splendour of that building and acclaim the advantage to shipping of the fire of wood that burned on its top. It seems unlikely that the construction of a lighthouse of such tremendous proportions and the maintenance of its great fire would have been contemplated had not lighthouses already proved of value to ships, and persistent penetration into the mists of Antiquity may yet reveal earlier instances of navigation lights.

4. A beacon marking an early port (Montfaucon)

5. A reputed pharos at Cronus in Sicily (Lajeune)

FABULOUS LIGHTHOUSES

In the 18th century, the study of mythology was a necessary part of a liberal education and antiquaries, when interpreting the past, did not hesitate to draw freely on their imagination when facts were not obvious. To the less credulous, the Cyclops, the monstrous cannibals each with one huge eye, who, it was believed, dwelt in Sicily or in the depths of Etna where they manufactured lightning and thunder-bolts for Zeus, were fanciful allusions to actual lighthouses.

SIGEUM PILLAR

Many modern writers have accepted, with apparently little question, statements that about 1300 B.C. the Trojans maintained a lighthouse at Sigeum, near Troy, in the north-west corner of Asia Minor, and that Homer alluded to lighthouses about 800 B.C. These statements are incorrect.

The Sigeum story is based on an account by Montfaucon in 1721 of a tablet dating from about 50 B.C. which was discovered in Rome in the 17th century. It depicted a pillar, with a squat conical top, which he illustrated. An inscription on the tablet explained that the outline accorded with a description by Lesches, a poet of about 1200 B.C. whose writings have long been lost. Montfaucon, who wrote in French, called the pillar a *phare* but as he used the word *phare* to indicate not only a lighthouse or beacon carrying fire but also the unlighted stone-and-timber beacon shown in his representation of an early port, it is clear that he did not intend to give the impression that the Sigeum tower carried a light: he concluded from its proximity to the coast that it served as a navigation beacon. More recently the pillar has been explained as a symbol for the tomb of Achilles, certainly not as supporting the idea of an early lighthouse having been established at Sigeum.

6

HOMER'S REFERENCES TO LIGHTS

The suggestion that Homer alluded to lighthouses in both the *Iliad* and the *Odyssey* appeared first during the 19th century but examination of the Greek texts shows that it cannot be substantiated. The passage referred to most often in this connection is one in Book XIX of the *Iliad* which has been interpreted as describing Achilles' polished shield as being so bright that its reflection resembled the flash of a beacon fire or lighthouse. The translation from the Greek text is as follows: 'As when from the sea, sailors see the light of a fire that burns high on the mountains in a lonely steading, while, against their will, the breezes carry them over the fishy sea away from their own folk; so, from Achilles' shield, bright and beautifully engraved, the light streamed to heaven.' Other translations of the passage, such as George Chapman's robust version of 1616, offer no support to the idea that Homer referred to lighthouses, though the following lines by Alexander Pope, who sought about 1720 to reproduce Homer's masterpiece in a poem in English and was unfettered by a call for an exact translation, may have been responsible unintentionally for the suggestion of a lighthouse:

> 'So to night-wandering sailors, pale with fears,
> Wide o'er the wat'ry waste a light appears,
> Which on the far-seen mountain blazing high,
> Streams from some lonely watch-tower to the sky.'

THE COLOSSUS OF RHODES

Most lists of the Seven Wonders of the World include the Colossus of Rhodes. This bronze figure of Apollo, over 100′ high, which the sculptor Chares took several years to construct, stood near a harbour in the island of Rhodes in the eastern Mediterranean. The Greeks, who were exacting critics of sculpture, thought highly of this statue which endured

6. Sigeum pillar as copied by Montfaucon from the Iliac tablet

7. The Colossus of Rhodes on a sea-chart *c.* 1640

8. A boy fishing off the Pharos of Ostia on a Roman relief

56 years and was cast down by an earthquake about 224 B.C. A traveller in the 1st century A.D. described the strengthening blocks of stone which he had seen within the broken limbs. About 700 A.D. three hundred tons of its metal were sold as scrap and transported to Alexandria. Not until the 16th century was a story put about that the figure bestrode the harbour entrance so that ships in full sail could pass between its legs. Such a proceeding is not impossible, as these vessels were very small, but statements that navigation lights were kept burning in its eyes or that it held a flaming beacon in one hand are less probable. Indeed, there is no evidence to justify inclusion of the Colossus among ancient lighthouses.

THE PHAROS OF ALEXANDRIA

But the authenticity as a lighthouse of the Pharos of Alexandria in Egypt is beyond question, and by its fame the word *pharos* or *pharus* came to be adopted by the Romans and Greeks, modified slightly in all languages derived from Latin, to denote a beacon, though not necessarily one bearing a light—hence *phare*, *farol* and *faro*.

Despite numerous references in ancient times to the Pharos of Alexandria, it has not been possible to determine its dimensions, as contemporary writers are lacking in details. Medieval records are contradictory. But modern archæologists believe that it rose about 450′ from a base of 100′ square. The shores of Egypt are low-lying and, for sufficient geographical range, the light required to be raised. To a seaman's eye 15′ above sea-level, the height of 450′ would give a range of 29 miles and 50′ more or less would alter the range by 1·5 miles. A tower of 200′ would give a range of 21 miles.

After many years spent in preparing materials, the lighthouse was completed about 280 B.C. on the island of Pharos at the west entrance of Alexandria harbour. The building consisted of several storeys of white stone contracting in diameter towards the top where the fire burned at night, perhaps in a kind of lantern or with a roof to shield the flames from rain. The collection, payment and transport of fuel and lifting it to the top of the tower must have presented difficulties, perhaps solved easily by slave labour. Recent drawings, based largely on measurements taken on the spot in 1165 A.D. by an Arabian observer, considered reliable, show a tower of three storeys, the bottom being square in section, the middle octagonal and the top circular. The geographer, Edrisi, who visited the tower about 1150, before its destruction, described how the stones were strapped together by metal ties and declared that it was reduced in diameter as it rose upwards until at the top its pinnacle could be clasped by a man's arms. The stairs were well-lighted by windows. Many attempts have been made to depict the Pharos according to the information available. Such reconstructions are shown in figures 3 (*a*), (*b*), (*c*) and (*e*). The Peutinger Table from which figure 3 (*d*) is taken was a copy made about 1300 of an early MS. The copper coin in figure 3 (*f*) was issued in Alexandria about 150 A.D. The letters indicate the year of minting and the assay.

The lantern on its top was destroyed about the 8th century, but much of the tower survived in its original form until about 1200, when it was overthrown by an earthquake. Its remains were visible as late as 1350. The fact that it endured as a great mass of stone for some 1600 years gives the impression that it may have been a structure even larger than the dimensions suggested by archæologists. The ancients considered it a stupendous work and during many centuries geographers and historians included it in their differing lists of the Seven Wonders. To be bracketed therein with the Great Pyramid which contained ninety million cubic feet of stone, a quantity calculated as sufficient for building a wall round the French coasts, gives assurance that it was indeed of vast size and not merely the largest building in Alexandria.

Pliny, who perished in 79 A.D. while attempting to view closely the eruption of Vesuvius that overwhelmed Pompeii, refers thus to the Pharos (according to a translator of 1601): 'Over and above the Pyramides abovesaid, a great name there is of a tower built by one of the kings of Aegypt within the Island Pharos, and it keepeth and commaundeth the haven of Alexandria, which tower (they say) cost eight hundred talents the building. And here, because I would omit nothing worth the writing, I cannot but note the singular magnanimitie of kind Ptolome, who permitted Sostratus of Gnidos (the master workeman and architect) to grave his owne name in this building. The use of this watch-tower is to shew light as a lanthorne, and give direction in the night season to ships, for to enter the haven, and where they shall avoid barrs and Shelves.' A different version of this story is that on top of that inscription on stone, Sostratus fixed plaster on which he cut Ptolemy's name, knowing that in a few years the plaster would disintegrate and the concealed inscription with his own name would be revealed. Pliny adds that some mariners found the lighthouse misleading: 'This is the daunger onely, lest when many lights in this lanterne meet together, they should be taken for a star in the Skie, for that afar off such lights appears unto sailors in manner of a star.'

In the course of its long existence the Pharos was the subject of many absurd stories, such as that from it enemy vessels could be detected at distances several hundred miles. The magic power which produced such an extraordinary effect was supposed to lie within a mirror on the top of the tower and it is certainly not impossible that a kind of *camera obscura* could be constructed with mirrors which would show ships at a distance of 25 miles. According to another story, the tower contained mirrors which made its fire visible to ships at a distance of 100 miles. But though mirrors could increase the candle-power of oil lamps, if such were used, and extend their effective range to a degree that would appear astounding to the ancients, they could not extend the direct visibility of either a wood fire or an oil lamp beyond the geographical range limited by the height of the tower. Perhaps the reflection in the sky of the lighthouse fire during some uncommon atmospheric condition accounted for the phenomenon. No writer who mentions the mirrors appears to have seen them: it was said that they had been destroyed by 'the intriguing arts of the Christians' or had been seized and removed while the captain of the port was attending a feast on board a vessel pretending to be friendly.

THE PHAROS OF OSTIA

The best-known lighthouse of Antiquity, after the Pharos of Alexandria, was the pharos of Ostia, which had only one-quarter of its height. It, too, consisted of several storeys which diminished in diameter towards the top and consequently it is impossible to distinguish by shape alone between representations of the two lighthouses. Nor does the apparent height of a pharos provide a clue to its identity: the Romans were not bound by tradition to use the same scale when depicting adjacent objects.

Ostia being the port of Rome and the chief centre of over-seas trade, its pharos became ultimately of more importance to navigation than that of Alexandria. As completed by the Emperor Claudius about 50 A.D., Ostia ranked as one of the finest harbours built by Roman engineers. An island breakwater covered the entrance between two long piers, with the pharos in its centre, decorated with various orders of architecture and containing rooms and

9. A mosaic pavement at Ostia depicts its lighthouse which is similar to the pharos shown in figure 15

staircases designed for the care and defence of the port. Surrounding the lighthouse, galleries, raised high above the sea, commanded the approaches. A huge statue of the Emperor fronted the tower and the whole produced an imposing effect on navigators. After nightfall, the fire lighted on the top of the lighthouse could be seen afar by the seamen bringing cargoes from all quarters into the heart of the empire.

PHARI IN SPAIN

A pharos at Caepio in Spain, the forerunner of the present lighthouse of Chipiona, is described by the geographer Strabo about 20 B.C. as standing on a rock washed on all sides by the sea and resembling the Pharos of Alexandria. He said that this beacon preserved vessels from the sunken rocks and shallows at the mouth of the river Guadalquivir.

The more famous lighthouse of Corunna near Ferrol on the north-west coast of Spain is recorded in the 4th or 5th century A.D. as being useful for ships sailing to England. It was built by either the Phoenicians or the Romans and has been called by various names, such as the *Tower of Hercules* and the *Iron Tower* or *Tour de Fer*, the latter possibly due to confusion of *fer* (French for iron) with *faro* (Spanish for lighthouse) or with Ferrol. The poet Southey recorded a tradition that Hercules founded the tower and that by his magic art he 'composed a lamp burning continually day and night without putting of anything thereto, which burned afterwards the space of 300 years. Moreover, upon the pinnacle or top of the tower he made an image of copper looking into the sea, and gave him in his hand a looking-glass having such virtue' that hostile warships could be detected as they approached. But, according to the story, an enemy, knowing this, camouflaged his galleys with green boughs so that only trees appeared in the glass: thus he seized the tower without warning and destroyed the lamp and mirror.

OTHER ROMAN PHARI

After the completion of the Pharos of Alexandria, seafaring increased as Rome expanded and enforced peace in the known world: ports were constructed on the European and African shores of the Mediterranean and phari were established as far away as the Black Sea and the Atlantic. Some thirty lighthouses are known definitely to have been in service before 400 A.D.—that is, before the Roman Empire began to decline.

About 40 A.D. the Emperor Caligula, having brought his army through Gaul or France, arrived at the Straits of Dover. There he assembled his men in battle array on the Gallic shore and in his crazy manner proclaimed a *Victory* over Neptune. He ordered his soldiers to adorn their helmets with shells and seaweed as the spoils of the ocean and apparently directed that a tower should be raised on which a fire should be kept burning to assist navigation. This tower is supposed to be the one at Boulogne which was known subsequently as the Tour d'Ordre. Several Roman medals depict an individual departing by sea from the neighbourhood of a lighthouse similar to those of Alexandria and Ostia. One such medal of about 185 A.D. has been identified as showing the Emperor Commodus embarking on an expedition to Britain with the lighthouse of Boulogne as the point of departure, having made sacrifices to the gods to obtain success.

Some 20 miles across the channel from Boulogne lies Dover in England where one or possibly two towers, some distance apart, were constructed about the same time and of similar materials. At least one of the towers has been accepted generally as an ancient lighthouse, but its considerable distance from the shore suggests that the purpose of the towers of Dover and Boulogne may have been rather for signalling between the Roman provinces of Britain and Gaul. The upper part of the 80′ Dover tower is medieval and it stands about 400′ above the sea.

FALSE LIGHTS

The misuse of lights to cause wrecks, which persisted on the shores of civilised countries until a century ago, was an early form of outrage practised on seamen, as is instanced by the story known as the *stratagem of Nauplius*, an argonaut, who displayed fires in a wrong position at Caphareus in Euboea, to represent the lights of vessels, and thus misled and wrecked a Greek fleet returning from Troy.

MIRRORS

As the ancients understood many properties of mirrors, it is not impossible that they used them to intensify the lights from oil lamps, perhaps in lighthouses. Certainly several marvellous tales concern the use of mirrors in lighthouses.

A Roman historian declared that about 212 B.C., during the siege of Syracuse, Archimedes destroyed an enemy fleet by using mirrors at the distance of an arrow's flight to direct and concentrate the sun's heat rays on the ships' timbers, thus setting them on fire. It was announced in 1747 that the French naturalist, Buffon, had reconstructed these *burning-glasses*

10. The Pharos of Ostia on a sea-chart of 1575 with an oil lantern of that date

11. The top of a Roman lamp shows a *bucina* or sea-shell being blown from a ship approaching a lighthouse

as used by Archimedes. He made a large wooden frame to mount about 150 flat pieces of looking-glass about 4″ square. Each had 3 screws for adjustment 'to meet the sun' but his difficulty lay in making the images in the mirrors coincide. When most of them were directed to his satisfaction, at a distance of 60′ he could melt silver-plate and at 150′ he set

12. A lighthouse on a Roman sarcophagus

13. The pharos of Boulogne on a medal of Commodus

14. Timber piles protect from the waves a pharos lit by a torch, probably at Centum Cellae, 106 A.D.

tarred wood on fire.   He hoped to increase the effective distance to 900′ but seems not to have proceeded further with the experiment.   In the United States of America in 1958 intense heat was produced by similar instruments—5000° Fah. at the focus of a huge concave mirror of 180 pieces which received the flash from a heliostat 40′ by 36′, formed by 355 plane mirrors.

15. A ship and a lighthouse appear on the tomb of Firma Victora, a Roman lady aged 65 (Garucci)

It was much more difficult, by means of mirrors, to produce fire at a distance than to increase the intensity of a navigation light.   If the first operation was within the capacity of the ancients, the second certainly was.

CONSTRUCTION OF PHARI

Records of ancient beacons and lighthouses are confined to the mention of their sites and general observations as to their construction.   The more important bore fires of wood or torches burning in the open air or perhaps under a roof for protection from rain and wind. The lesser lights may have burned candles or oil lamps in a lantern glazed with sheets of horn or skin, or thinned oyster-shells.   Glass panes were used after the 1st century A.D.

Lighthouses figure on ancient Roman sculptures, mosaics, medals and coins.   A tower with flames spouting from its top often represented a lighthouse or a port though it did not always represent a particular one.   The appearance of these symbols carved on the stonework of a building does not prove its antiquity, since they are found sometimes on the walls of medieval churches and on 19th-century buildings.

II

MEDIEVAL LIGHTHOUSES

Tour d'Ordre
ore dun Siège
de Boulogne
Gravé en 1549

16. The tower of Boulogne in 1549

(b) A view on a sea-chart
of 1568 (Domingo Olives)

(c) On a sea-chart c. 1764

(a) A sectional elevation
drawn in 1832

(d) A view of Genoa c. 1650

17. IMPRESSIONS OF THE LANTERNA OF GENOA BUILT IN 1544

II. MEDIEVAL LIGHTHOUSES

After the passing of the Dark Ages, sea-lights were established anew in Europe, commencing about 1100 A.D. at the entrances to Italian ports. Their illumination was given by oil lamps or candles sheltered in lanterns but in northern Europe coal fires burning in the open were preferred. Contemporary accounts of the tall Lanterna of Genoa, lighted in 1544, encouraged the establishment of more lighthouses throughout Europe. Before 1586 the navigable channels of Dutch and German rivers were marked by beacons and buoys which by shape and colour directed ships to port or starboard.

Between about 400 and 1100 A.D. a gap in lighthouse history followed the collapse of Rome. Europe lost the cohesion which had been achieved by a central Government, sea-communications were interrupted and shipping declined. Ports retained only local trade and, being left each to defend its own interest, learned anew the lesson that a harbour light exhibited every night assisted ill-disposed neighbours in an attack. Further, one can assume that coastal lighthouses beyond their walls were discontinued, from the difficulty and cost of maintenance.

After 1100, as law and order followed the emergence of national States from the turbulence of the Dark Ages, trade pushed out gradually beyond the immediate neighbour-hood of the ports in the Mediterranean, the North Sea and the Baltic and resulted in increasing transport by sea with the provision of better harbours and navigational equipment, including seamarks. Ports set up and maintained their own lights; but in France the Government took an interest in the isolated Cordouan lighthouse, considering that it assisted general trade and not merely the trade of Bordeaux.

Over 30 lights of value for coastal trade are known to have been exhibited regularly in Europe before 1600 and it is likely that research in various countries might nearly double that number if one included lights of value chiefly for marking harbours. References to these early seamarks appear in records, such as charters dealing with the land on which they stood, accounts showing costs of erection and upkeep, and agreements or enactments for levying dues, appointing lightkeepers and providing for fuel and repairs. After 1500, references to lighthouses occur in books of travel, pilotage directions and sea-charts.

As in Antiquity, a lighthouse consisted usually of a stone tower burning wood, coal or torches in a grate on its summit in the open air, or of a tower or pole on which a keeper hoisted an iron basket containing burning coal or pitch. Sometimes moveable or built-in lanterns with windows of horn or thick glass protected oil lamps or candles. The cost of maintaining these lighthouses was often considerable: stocks of fuel had to be obtained and transported, and attendants had to be paid for the arduous task of keeping fires bright by stacking, stirring and blowing during the night and for frequent trimming of the wicks of oil lamps and snuffing of candles. The oil lamps, smoky and difficult to regulate, unless one were content to show only a tiny flame of which the total light value was small, bore little resemblance to the lamps introduced in 1782. The candles also differed greatly from their modern types. In northern Europe, where the nights of summer were short, the fires were not kindled for several months of the year.

A General Account of Lighthouses before 1820

ITALY

MELORIA AND LEGHORN

At Meloria in Italy about 1157 the Pisans established the first lighthouse to be recorded in this era. It was destroyed and re-built several times during their unceasing wars with the Genoans, until in 1304 they replaced it by a lighthouse on an isolated rock at Leghorn. About 1350 the poet Petrarch wrote of this tall tower and of the weary sailor lifting his eyes to the port's twin lights, and about 1500 Leonardo da Vinci showed in his highly-detailed maps the principal lighthouse with three other towers off the harbour, which also figured in mosaics and engravings.

MESSINA, VENICE AND TINO

In 1194 a lighthouse guided navigators through the Strait of Messina, ever frequented by shipping. In Venice a decree of the Senate in August 1312 authorised the erection of a magnificent pharos on the tower of St. Nicholas and in 1350 a lesser light topped the porch of St. Erasmus. The Tino lighthouse in the Gulf of Spezia originated in a scheme of defence against the pirates infesting that part of the coast. Churches in the little Italian seaports contain pictures representing lighthouses concerned in incidents when seamen were saved from shipwreck.

GENOA

The most celebrated of all Italian lighthouses, the Lanterna of Genoa, dates from before 1161. In that year ships paid dues for a fire or light displayed on the headland: 'pro igne faciendo in capite fari'. References to this Capo di Faro or Lighthouse Point go back in details to 1166. Probably the earliest tower on the Point formed part of the city's defences. The Lanterna is usually depicted as displaying flags or shapes to direct ships entering the port. Alternatively, the lightkeepers made smoke-signals on top of the tower by burning straw and, later, pitch and tar. Antonio Colombo, uncle of the Columbus who crossed the Atlantic in 1492–98, was keeper of the light in 1449. No doubt this uncle's connection with the sea, a break-away from the family's traditional occupation of weaving, led to Christopher's interest in sea affairs. The lantern often suffered damage in wars and in 1544 the tower had to be re-built completely. Two pillars 30' and 23' square, each over 100' high, were then set one upon the other to form the present imposing tower which in 1959 still serves as an important seamark for leading-in vessels from a distance as well as for coastal traffic. Oil lamps provided its first illumination and they were increased in number during storms. Its great height made it liable to serious damage by lightning. Various measures thought likely to avert the danger were adopted in vain, such as cutting pious inscriptions on the walls and erecting a statue of St. Christopher. Benjamin Franklin introduced the lightning-rod or conductor in America in 1752 and its use was soon extended to Europe, Smeaton fitting a rod at the Eddystone in 1759. But religious scruples delayed its adoption at Genoa until 1778 when they abated sufficiently to allow it to be fitted at the Lanterna. This tower of 1544 has always been noted for its conspicuous situation at the edge of the sea, its impressive design and unusual height. 17th-century pictures show it to bear an excellent lantern in which from time to time experiments with lamps, wicks and glazing were carried out; so one can well believe it to have been one of the most efficient lighthouses of those times and undoubtedly its fame encouraged the use of lighthouses in other seas. Its vaulted construction is remarkable: such a design would be avoided by a

18. An oil navigation light at Venice *c.* 1400

19. A Mediterranean lighthouse according to Rubens *c.* 1610

modern architect. But the fashion in the Middle Ages, particularly in Italy and Germany, of erecting tall towers in cities—Perugia boasted seven hundred towers, several rising to 200'—gave ample experience to the designers of such buildings, and the endurance of the Lanterna which has stood unaltered for over 400 years is a dramatic proof of the skill of its designer and builders.

TURKEY

About 1550 an explorer from western Europe, crossing to Asia Minor, observed in the Bosphorus a navigation light contained in an octagonal tower with small windows which he described as of 'christian design', the glasses being jointed with lead. He warned navigators to beware of false or misleading lights with a similar aspect that were set up occasionally by wreckers elsewhere in the vicinity. In 1595 another traveller described the same lighthouse as 'a turret of stone 120 steps high having a great glass lanthorne in the top, four yards in diameter and three in height, with a great copper pan in the midst to hold oil, with twenty lights in it'.

SPAIN

Looking to the leading part taken in maritime exploration by Portugal and Spain, it is to be expected that these countries' headlands and harbours would have been marked by fires or lights around 1500, but none have been noted apart from the great tower of Corunna which appears in maps and charts before 1600, though not all show distinctly that it carried a light. The cartographers who marked it as a lighthouse may have been content to assume that it still bore the traditional light of Roman times and it is to be noted that it may well have done so before 1500. Corunna was the port used by pilgrims, some carried in ships from England, who voyaged to the celebrated shrine of St. James at Santiago de Compostela, 30 miles from Corunna. To these vessels a light on the ancient Tour de Fer would be helpful. A Spanish poem quoted in 1549 refers to its occupation by a witch whose magic spell prevented anyone who mounted the staircase from finding his way down, an excellent story to keep off intruders but perhaps indicating that it did not serve then as a lighthouse. It is likely that the tower had some use in defence.

FRANCE

EARLY SEAMARKS

In 1397 a statute of Richard II obliged ships proceeding from England to Calais, fishing-boats excepted, to carry stones as ballast for the urgent repair of the piers and 'les beekenes devant le port' which had been weakened 'par les hydouses concourses et rages de la meer'.

Lights were noted at the ancient port of Aigues-Mortes in the Mediterranean during the early Crusades, about 1100 and 1246, and at the Tour des Castillans at the Groing de

20. The Corunna light-house from a 13th-century map

21. A 19th-century representation of an early English navigation beacon

Caux for the rendezvous of the Spanish fleets about 1364. Dieppe had a light in 1389, Havre in 1540. Arundel, La Chaume, showed a light first in the 13th century, and one was raised on the castle tower occasionally from 1593. It proved so useful that in 1702, in return for authority to levy dues, the owners of the castle provided a larger lantern with glazing inserted between its iron bars and an oil lamp with large wicks. For 30 years after 1445 a navigation light was shown from a tower at La Rochelle: a round turret carried a stone lantern of 6 windows surmounted by an elegant spire and containing a thick wax candle as the illuminant. Harfleur was probably the site of the Caux light. Groing de Caux was a tiny village no longer in existence, situated between Cap de la Hève and Harfleur. By order of the French king and following trade agreements with Spain, its inhabitants were bound to tend the light or fire on the tower.

Medieval Lighthouses

BOULOGNE

It is said that about 800 A.D. the Emperor Charlemagne ordered the repair of Caligula's tower at Boulogne, and the showing of lights from it. This building figures often in the incessant wars between the English and the French, when it probably had a considerable military value, and it is supposed to have carried navigation lights at different times before 1600. Its former name of Tour d'Ordre or d'Odre was long believed to be a corruption of *turris ardens* or *burning tower* but etymologists consider now that *Odre* is derived from a Celtic word meaning *shore*. To Elizabethan seamen it stood as the *Old Man of Bullen*. It came to an end without warning at noon on 29th July 1644 when it collapsed with a thunderous roar; the cliff on which it stood had crumbled away and the materials composing it had been removed gradually for the construction of other buildings. No vestige remains, but measurements taken before its fall show it to have been octagonal in plan and built in 12 diminishing stages to a height of 124', each side of the lowest and the highest stages being 40' and 5' broad respectively. Possibly to assist in defence a door was set at each angle of every stage, 96 doors in all. The prospect of the tower was remarkable: it was constructed with red bricks and grey and yellow stones arranged in layers, giving a striking blending of colours. The tower enclosed 3 or 4 vaulted chambers and an internal stair led to the open platform at the top. In 1545 the English Privy Council instructed Sir Thomas Palmer, the 'Captayne of the Olde Man', as to 'the ordering of the Owlde Man as well touching the fortification as the saufkeping of the same'.

CORDOUAN

It is certain that before 1550 a lighthouse existed on the islet of Cordouan which lay off the entrance to the river Gironde and some 5 miles from land, amidst currents and shifting sandbanks highly dangerous to sailing-vessels. Charlemagne, again, is credited with having founded a chapel on the islet, stipulating that from its tower trumpets should sound to warn shipping, presumably on dark nights and in fog. According to a charter of 1409, a chapel and a tower, containing equipment 'necessary for the safety of ships', had been erected on the island by Edward, the English Black Prince, about 1370 and, to pay for its upkeep, a tax had been levied on all passing vessels carrying wine from Bordeaux. As the buildings had been damaged extensively by tempest, wind and water the tax was doubled and shipmasters were ordered to pay it to Galfredus de Lasparre, a hermit or priest who dwelt therein and whose predecessor received the previous tax. The document did not mention a light, but a lighthouse was shown clearly on the earliest sea-charts and it continued in service until 1612, when the famous tower designed by Louis de Foix took its place.

ENGLAND

A lack of coastal lighthouses in England before 1600 is surprising; only one, at Tynemouth, is known. The reputed Roman lighthouses at Dover appear to have been long-disused and 16th-century antiquarians who wrote of one of them as 'a beacon to assist nocturnal navigation' and 'a pharos for the comfort of sailors' seem merely to be repeating a tradition. About 1540 Leland, the chronicler, found it out of service: 'on the toppe of the hye clive . . . a ruine of a tower the which hath been as a pharos or a mark to shypes on the se'. Its remains are substantial still, a rare example of a Roman building in Britain. Its base was square, each side measuring 14′.

ST. CATHERINE'S

A small light was set up at St. Catherine's on the Isle of Wight about 1323 by Walter de Godyton. He erected a chapel and added an endowment for a priest to say Masses for his family and to exhibit lights at night to warn ships from approaching too near this dangerous coast, both purposes being fulfilled until about 1530 when the Reformation swept away the endowment. Neither the present lighthouse tower, lighted in March 1840, nor the chapel of which the ruins remain, held these ancient lights.

SPURN POINT

It is recorded about 1427 that Richard Reedbarowe, a hermit living at Ravenspurne or Spurn Point, 'havying compassion and pitee of the Cristen poeple that ofte tymes are there perisched . . . hath begunne in weye of charite, in Salvacon of Cristen poeple, Godes and Marchaundises comying into Humbre, to make a Toure to be uppon day light a redy Bekyn, wheryn shall be light gevyng by nyght, to alle the Vesselx that comyn into the seid Ryver of Humbre'. Finding that his venture could not be 'brought to an ende withouten grete cost' he petitioned the King for help, which was granted in the form of a permit to levy tolls on vessels for 10 years, a tax which the merchants and shipmasters of Hull had already agreed to pay.

ILFRACOMBE

Of a visit to Cape Cornwall near Land's End, Leland observed, also in about 1540: 'There is at this point a chapel of St. Nicholas and a pharos for light for ships sailing by night in those quarters' but it is likely that he referred to the chapel at Ilfracombe in Devon which was dedicated to St. Nicholas, a saint who was specially venerated by sailors and fishermen: in England over 370 chapels were dedicated to him. The existence of a light at Ilfracombe is confirmed by a Catholic Indulgence of 40 days granted in 1522 by the Bishop of Exeter towards the maintenance, on the roof of the chapel set high on the cliff, of a light described in the document in Latin as like a twinkling star shining nightly throughout the winter, its beam leading to safety in the harbour seamen venturing amid the waves of the open sea and facing death during storms. Though such lights, tended by priests or hermits and maintained by alms, must have been inexpensive and of little power (probably a tiny oil lamp provided a flame less than a candle's), yet in these times, when all lights were feeble and navigation lights were rare, their value to seamen in indicating a haven might be very precious.

NORTH SHIELDS AND TYNEMOUTH

A good deal of information is available about early lights at North Shields and Tyne-mouth which are close together. At North Shields two towers were built in 1540 by the Trinity House of Newcastle, under a charter of 1536 from Henry VIII who authorised the levy of dues for their maintenance. It provided that the members of this Corporation, which existed in 1492, might 'found, build, make and frame of stone, lime and sand, by the best ways and means that they knew or can, two towers' for the safety of 'our subjects and others, being in our alliance, coming to the said town and port . . . with a perpetual light to be nightly maintained'. Though intended partly for defence, the towers indicated the navigable channel of the river Tyne to a seaman when he kept them in line. Accounts for their upkeep in 1541 include an item of four shillings and three pence for 34 lbs. of candles. The number of candles burned at each lighthouse was increased to two in 1613. In 1658–9 one of the towers was rebuilt in wood, so that it could be moved easily to mark the deep channel between the shifting sandbanks. The towers were rebuilt in 1727 and burned 3 candles in place of 2. In 1736 copper reflectors were set behind the candles, but particulars are not recorded. In 1744 the firing of guns near the low lighthouse by Government troops was complained of by the Newcastle Trinity House: probably the vibration cracked the lantern panes. Oil lamps were installed in 1773. The towers were re-built in 1805–8 and lighted in May 1810.

A happy instance of the charity of the Newcastle Trinity House occurred in June 1716 when Roger Heaton, who was employed to light and extinguish the candles at the North Shields towers at certain states of the tide, became incapable in body and mind. A girl who looked after him took over his duties but the Corporation appointed a successor, not considering it 'fitt or safe to commit such a great charge to the care of a woman though never so ingenious and watchfull'. A letter from the Clerk of the Fraternity shows much kindliness: 'Honest Roger! Be not discouraged because John Dobbins is commanded to take care of the lights. He will be no detriment to you but rather a help; and though your maid be a fine ingenious carefull lass, yet it doth not stand with the honour of the Trinity House to leave so great a charge to the management of a woman. . . . Do not feare but our masters will take care of you as long as you live.' There are indeed many interesting associations of this body with lighthouses. It continues to manage unlighted seamarks from its ancient House on the old quay at Newcastle. One of its rooms is decorated with a profusion of models of sea-monsters, real and fabulous, suspended by chains from the ceiling.

A coal fire at Tynemouth castle seems to have been the earliest British lighthouse with any pretension to serve coastal navigation. It was established probably by Crown patent after 1540: in 1581 there was a reference to 'the keeping of a continuous light in the night season . . . as in former times had been'. In 1746 the fire was partially screened from the wind.

LYNN CROSS

About 1550, John Puttock, a hermit, is credited with erecting near Hunstanton a wooden beacon over 100′ high, long-known as Lenne Crutch, or Lynn Cross, to direct ships entering the Wash.

THE GOODWIN SANDS

Towards the end of the 16th century a petition to Queen Elizabeth sought her consent to an ambitious scheme which, if it had been practicable, would have benefited general navigation greatly: namely, the erection of a lighthouse on the dreaded Goodwin sands in the English Channel off Kent, ever a trap to shipping. The petitioner, Gowen Smith, proposed that as soon as he had erected a 'fyrme and staide beacon to shewe his fyre by night' and had delivered to the Queen 'grasse, herbe or flower' grown upon the sands which he would reclaim, he should receive a payment of £1,000 from her Treasury and authority to collect tolls from ships to pay for the maintenance of the light.

REPUTED LIGHTHOUSES

Several places on the British coasts such as Holywell in Wales offer traditions of navigation lights maintained by priests and monks. Most of these tales are baseless: some towers supposed to have served as seamarks were intended to show warning fires on invasion. Others were not situated in positions helpful for navigation, such as Arundel church spire which was supposed wrongly to have facilitated entry to Littlehampton harbour several miles distant. It has been stated that a sea-chart by Richard Poulter of 1584 shows an early light at South Foreland but on examination of the document at the British Museum the words relied on for proof appear to be YE FANE and not YE FARE or YE PHARE. In 1387 a hermit was recorded as dwelling on this headland but there was no mention of lights.

In rejecting a story that an ancient light existed at Richborough, John Lewis wrote with point in 1723: 'The Romans knew better than to build a Pharos or Light-house for the use of shipping on a low flat ground where it was impossible the Ships which sailed in the Channel could be at all the better for it.'

Flamborough Head is said to have been crowned by a navigation light in medieval times but as the contemporary sea traffic would have been insufficient to justify the expense of exhibiting a light every night the assertion must be denied.

The danger from fire to shipping and surrounding buildings makes suspect all reports of English sea-lights consisting of open braziers burning wood, coal or pitch being set at harbours or on the tops of church towers. This risk to shipping was noted at Portpatrick harbour in 1789. In some instances it is merely the application of the architectural term *lantern*, denoting the unglazed upper part of the stone tower, which gives rise to traditions of navigation lights at these churches. Without glazing, an oil lamp would have insufficient shelter from wind and it would be obscured from various directions by the stone pillars.

When a navigation light had to be established from a tower surrounded by buildings, the usual arrangement was to hang a small horn-lantern containing an oil lamp or a candle outside the tower on the seaward side. For example, at the former port of Rye a lantern was suspended from the old Ypres tower, but this proved ineffective and another was 'hung out o' nights on the south-west corner of the church for a guide to vessels entering the port'.

SCOTLAND

ABERDEEN

In 1566 Aberdeen Town Council decided to erect a *gryt bowat* or great portable lantern on the east gable of St. Ninian's chapel to direct ships to the harbour entrance. It would contain 3 flaming oil lamps, to be lighted from 1st September to 31st March. For its upkeep the Council instituted an elaborate system of dues to be levied on ships, on lighters ferrying goods between ship and shore, and on goods imported and exported, and they also appointed a person specially to make the collection.

LEITH

The accounts of the town of Edinburgh show that a beacon at Leith harbour entrance existed before 1552–3 when several entries occur, as follows: 'to sax men that labourit two dayis in the redding [repairing] of the bekyn and the casting [heaping] of the stanis [stones] thairto agane, ilk [each] man XXs, [20s.] in the day' and 'efter the bekyn being brokin be ane Inglis schip, the maister payit the hale expensis in the upsetting theirof except xxiiijs [24s.]'.   The Scots pound was then worth some twenty pence in English money.

Local legend is persistent as to a navigation light having been shown from St. Anthony's chapel on the slope of Arthur's Seat at Edinburgh, but a glance at a sea-chart indicates that if a typical medieval light consisting of a couple of candles were shown from a window of the chapel which is $1\frac{1}{2}$ miles inland it would not have been of the slightest benefit to a mariner.

THE BELL ROCK

A Scots antiquarian recorded in the 16th century a tradition of a bell without a light having been set up on the Inchcape or Bell Rock, which lies in the North Sea about 11 miles off the east coast of Scotland: 'On this great hidden rock . . . there was a bell fixed upon a tree or timber which rang continually, being moved by the sea, giving notice to the saylers of the danger.   This bell or clocke was put there and maintained by the Abbot of Arbroath and being taken down by a sea pirate, a yeare thereafter, he perished upon the same rocke with ship and goodes, in the righteous judgment of God.'   About 1815 Robert Southey turned the tale into a poem, long popular for recitation by school-children in Scotland.   It is obvious that if this form of seamark had been actually erected and found to work satis-factorily, it would have been extended to many other rocks where a warning to ships was sorely needed.   Regretfully one must deny the Abbot's ability to establish a bell-signal on the rock but he may have made an attempt to do so.   It has been said that the Abbot might have been John Gedy who ruled the Benedictine Monastery of Arbroath in the 14th century and built the harbour under an indenture dated 2nd April 1394.

IRELAND

Two early lights were recorded in the south of Ireland.   The earliest was shown from Hook tower at the east entrance to Waterford harbour.   Tradition suggests that it was built about 810 by Rosa Macrue, sister of a chieftain named Strongbow, to guide her sons back to Ireland.   About 1245 the warden and chaplains of the monastery of St. Saviour Rendeuan are credited with building the tower and maintaining upon it a light to warn sailors.   The other Irish lighthouse is said to have been built at Youghal about 1190 by Maurice Fitzgerald who put it into the care of the nuns of St. Anne's convent, which he endowed.   They arranged for the burning of torches to guide ships into the harbour, a practice that ceased in 1542 when the convent was dissolved but was renewed later.

HOLLAND AND BELGIUM

In Holland about 1280 two lighted beacons marked the mouth of the river Maas and for their upkeep the town of Brielle had authority to levy taxes on seafarers, a right that continued until 1836. The keepers lighted or stoked the fires until they could detect a particular distant mark in the morning light. In the 16th century the Dutch erected beacons at Goeree and Terschelling, and set a fire upon a restored church tower at Brandaris in 1593, where it served until about 1750.

In Belgium lighthouses marked Nieuport harbour entrance: two are believed to have been erected in 1284. Fire destroyed one of these, a wooden tower known as the Groote Vierboete in 1413, and a stone tower took its place. A charter of 1366 refers to 'nouvelles lumières et vierbotes si comme souloient estre en vieulx temps' at Dunkirk, Ostend and Blankenbergh, the *vierbotes* being huts showing lights. In 1475 mention is made of repairs carried out at the lighthouses of Dieppe, Ostend and Blankenbergh.

N.E. EUROPE AND THE BALTIC

One finds in Germany and in the Baltic the most extensive use of seamarks before 1600. Political conditions favoured trading by water along rivers and coasts, and the long winter nights made lighthouses welcome. The German States evolved methods of

22. In 1586 Waghenaer described a buoyage system adopted in
Holland and Friesland

directing ships in navigable channels by shapes and colours of beacons and buoys and Waghenaer described in his atlas of 1586 a buoyage system enforced in Dutch rivers. As early as 1066 buoys guided ships through the river Weser channels and the German coasts had no lack of unlighted beacons.

Several lighthouses originated as wood fires lighted on headlands and foreshores to direct the herring fisheries. Among them was Falsterbo, at the eastern entrance to the Baltic. Here the city of Lübeck established about 1202 what is claimed to be the first lighthouse proper of northern Europe. It was lighted each October for the winter season.

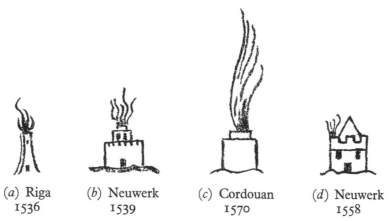

(*a*) Riga   (*b*) Neuwerk   (*c*) Cordouan   (*d*) Neuwerk
    1536   1539   1570   1558

23. 16th-century navigation beacons depicted on maps and charts

The Gollenberg light at Coslin in Pomerania is recorded about 1532 as consisting of several lamps or candles in front of a polished *becken*, a term which might apply to a plane or a concave mirror or to a glazed lantern.

24. A portion of Olaus Magnus's 16th-century map shows lighthouses in Germany at Neuwerk, Travemünde, Wismar, Warnemünde and Hiddensoe (seen from left to right)

Well-known 13th-century lights include those at Travemünde and Wismar in Germany and another in the vicinity of Copenhagen. Several lighthouses established in that region in the succeeding centuries were intended not so much to assist coastal navigation as to mark the entrances to harbours and river estuaries. The famous map, the *Carta Marina* of

Bishop Olaus Magnus of 1539, besides depicting fabulous sea-monsters, shows one light-house at Neuwerk at the mouth of the river Elbe and seven others on the south shores of the Baltic between Lübeck and Riga.

At least 15 lights had been established along the Scandinavian and German coasts by 1600 and this comparatively large number, which made the area the best-lighted in the world, was due to the influence of the powerful Hanseatic League which had cherished the great medieval trading lands served by the German rivers and had extended its influence to Holland. Probably the sea-channel from the Baltic to the North Sea had become the most important navigation route up to 1550: Denmark, which controlled both sides of the Sound and the Kattegat, had undertaken about 1350 to maintain lighthouses along their shores.

NORWAY AND GREENLAND

A map of about 1530 has a curious reference to a compass erected by two freebooters on the coast of Greenland to warn mariners of a dangerous rock. Probably it consisted of a post or beacon with a wooden arm pointing to the danger, of the same type as one which in 1590 Robert Norman in *The Safegarde of Saylers* described in directions to enter the haven of Longe or Lyngor in Norway: 'there lyes a round drye rocke before it and there stands as it were a Beacon with a Barrell on it, keepe well on that . . . and at the entering in on sterboorde [starboard] is a hand that pointes you to holde off from that place'.

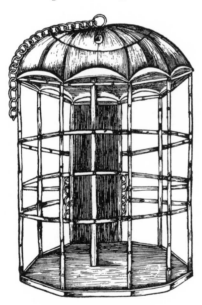

25. A lantern believed to have been used at Warnemünde in the 15th century

26. A German lighthouse shown on a woodblock of 1572, possibly at Warnemünde

LIGHTHOUSES 1590 TO 1690

27. A 17th-century lighthouse probably in Germany (Zeeman)

28. Cordouan lighthouse from Chatillon's drawing *c.* 1612, showing the former tower and timber piling to prevent erosion of the island by the sea

III. LIGHTHOUSES 1590 TO 1690

In this period many navigation lights were established in Europe and were used occasionally in India and Japan. More coal fires were set up and lanterns were improved, but no notable advance was made in the illumination or the construction of towers. The outstanding event was the completion about 1612 after extraordinary troubles of the magnificent lighthouse of Cordouan in France.

ITALY

The existence of numerous sovereign States in the peninsula of Italy encouraged the establishment of lighthouses chiefly at their ports, where the sea-trading interests of each State were served most directly. Excellent towers were raised at several ports in the 17th century, the illuminants being candles and lamps. The fame of the Lanterna of Genoa continued to spread and this tower as well as the lighthouse at Messina figured prominently on maps and sea-charts. John Evelyn, the diarist, toured Italy in 1644 and expressed surprise at the 'incredible' height of the Lanterna and noted the 'divers fanales and sconces' at Leghorn.

EGYPT AND TURKEY

Travellers in the Near East made drawings of lighthouses at Damietta in the Nile delta and in the Bosphorus. These were lights from oil lamps which at Damietta seem to have been hoisted in a small lantern on top of a tower by a lever as in a *vippefyr*.

FRANCE

Cordouan

The lighthouse on the small islet of Cordouan near Bordeaux requiring repair in 1581, Henri III instructed the engineer-architect Louis de Foix to visit it and report what should be done. De Foix had an unusually extensive experience in engineering works: he had been employed as an assistant architect in building the Escorial Palace near Madrid and, in France and abroad, had constructed water-works, bridges and fortifications, had trained rivers and protected their banks, and had even made clocks. He estimated the cost of repairing the tower at 50,000 *écus-soleils*. As this sum was higher than expected, the King considered alternative proposals and decided to build an entirely new lighthouse of outstanding aspect. He approved of the design prepared by de Foix who contracted in March 1584 to carry it out in two years, according to a model in wood which he deposited with the Maire of Bordeaux. The price would be 38,000 *écus*, worth about 400,000 francs or £16,000 in 1914.

The splendour of de Foix's design accorded with the French tradition that buildings erected by public funds should be a credit to the period of their construction and excite the admiration of posterity. Several engravings taken from a drawing made in 1612 by the celebrated architect Claude Chatillon show the completed lighthouse. They differ in minor details of ornaments and in the surrounding decoration of whimsies—ships, whales and cupids—but the main architectural features appear similarly in all as also do the island of Cordouan, the former tower and out-buildings.

Essentially the building was shaped like a barrel. It contained two vaulted rooms—a great hall 52′ in diameter called the King's room and a spacious chapel above it. The principal dome carried an open *lantern* (in the architectural sense) which was crowned by a turret enclosing the fire and tapering to a tall chimney shaft. The stone pillars of the turret blocked the fire entirely in several directions and at one time panes of coarse glass were set between the pillars to form windows and to shelter the flames. The internal staircase was

29. Messina lighthouse in 1674 (Jollain)

30. A 17th-century Italian lighthouse, probably off Leghorn

31. A reputed lighthouse at Damietta, Egypt, in 1678

enclosed in a separate shaft to exclude dirt from the main building while the keepers carried up the billets of oak wood to the grate.

Externally the building was decorated to the utmost possible extent, which was successful in breaking-up its rather unattractive outline. Four parapets provided views from different floors and a profusion of pillars and windows, both real and false, offered countless opportunities for ornament, none of which was lost. The treatment of the interior was excellent and is a delight to behold. The trouble of building a plain lighthouse on an island several miles from land is considerable enough, but the vaulting and ornamentation specified by de Foix caused far more trouble for the masons than at any other lighthouse. His initial drawings and measurements required to be highly-detailed and every stone had to be cut with great precision, presumably on shore, ready to be set into its place when brought to the island; elaborate records were necessary.

The operations proceeded extremely slowly. By 1595 with 80 men at work, the building became visible from the land and in the following year it had been raised to the third storey. Seven horses were kept ashore to move the masonry at the yard and 6 boats manned by 27 seamen provided transport between island and shore. De Foix's signature on a contract dated 1600 to supply 60 barrels of wine for 90 workmen shows that the works were proceeding on a considerable scale. In 1602 de Foix disappeared without trace: he had met political and religious difficulties, had run into debt, suffered imprisonment and was overwhelmed by adversity. His son Pierre continued the works but he too had to abandon them in 1606 when the cost had exceeded thrice the contract price. Their foreman François Beusher, a skilled mason, entered into a new contract and succeeded in completing the structure in 1610 sufficiently to show a navigation fire. Only 4 years later was it protected completely from the sea.

In view of the low prices of these times it must have appeared when the contract was signed that the agreed sum would ensure success, particularly with such an expert engineer

32. Cordouan from a map *c.* 1650

33. Signatures of de Foix and Beusher on a contract of 1600

in charge of the work. When signing the contract, de Foix failed to assess the uncertainties of tides and weather and likely delays of sea-transport: his estimate of two years as the time required to complete such an unprecedented work might have applied perhaps to building the structure on land. But his chief trouble was brought about by the disappearance of the island itself—an amazing phenomenon, because for so many years it had afforded a residence to the hermits and other persons in charge of the beacon fire. A wall and parapet begun in 1595 to encircle the tower succeeded in saving it from destruction by the sea. Its original diameter was increased substantially by Beusher in 1606–10, and this protecting-rampart was enlarged to 135′ before 1753 when it incorporated extensive stores for fuel and quarters for the lightkeepers who no longer lived in de Foix's structure.

When it became clear that his tower might be exposed to direct sea-action, de Foix must have suffered intense distress and despair, but as the foundations became more threatened he accepted the challenge with a bold heart and caused a poem to be composed extolling the work among the Wonders of the World because it would be built below the sea:

> 'Bâtir dessus la terre, est-ce une chose rare?
> Mais qui jamais a vu bâtir dessus la mer?'

His epitaph, composed by himself and engraved in letters of gold on a marble slab set in the tower, cursed the gods representing the elements for the evil they had done to him, and defied them to injure his splendid work further by their fire and water. The gods reacted with violence: in 1612 Jove's lightning struck the tower and hurled into the sea the top portion for a height of 25', while Neptune's waves eroded the base so severely that Chatillon was sent to list the damage and specify repairs. He had to undertake works of preservation immediately or the structure would have been undermined in a few tides.

Chatillon's drawing shows that timber piling had been driven close to de Foix's tower, no doubt designed by Beusher or Chatillon. Clearly its purpose was to close a breach by the sea between the lighthouse and the island. The architect's inclusion in this drawing of

34. A cross-section of Cordouan before 1727 showing the corkscrew staircase for carrying wood to the fire

such practical details as the piling, along with working-sheds and dwellings, shows that the drawing was made with care and completeness and confirms that a large extent of the island remained intact in 1612. Probably before 1665, when the engineer Dominique spent three years in effecting what were extensive repairs of the lighthouse, all vestiges of the island had disappeared.

Despite the removal of the upper part of the structure, partly in 1717 and completely in 1788 when, as described in Section XII, Teulère re-built it to a new design with less decoration, sufficient of de Foix's structure remains today, internally as well as externally, to indicate its original magnificence and beauty of craftsmanship. Much of the exterior ornamentation has gone, having crumbled away from the action of salt spray caught in the crevices of the soft white masonry.

The altered tower, which is still used for a lighthouse, is seen to stand now on a small plateau of bare rock below the level of high-water. The plateau is surrounded by a sand-bank of which a large area is exposed at low tides. Landings are effected in calm weather by small boats proceeding up to the base of the parapet wall or to the edge of the sandbank some distance away, according to the state of the tide. It is due entirely to the well-designed protective parapet that encircles its base that the lighthouse has withstood the ocean's fury for nearly 350 years. It may seem surprising that this time-proved design of a lighthouse with a protective parapet or saucer has not been adopted for other towers built on similar low-lying wave-swept rocks: but the circumstances requiring such a design have not been met elsewhere.

The French engineer Belidor in criticising in 1753 the placing of a highly-ornamented structure in so unsuitable a situation, was unfair to de Foix who could not foresee that the apparently-substantial island of Cordouan on which it would be set should vanish into the sea in the course of his operations. His ability and experience in hydraulic engineering would have prevented him from exposing the carefully-cut edges of the external masonry of, say, the pillared entrance of the tower to sea-action, even with the waves curbed by the enlarged parapet shown in Chatillon's drawing. No architect proud of his skill would spoil his design so completely by concealing the handsome base, an essential part of the outline, behind a large parapet which, when the structure is seen from the surface of the sea as intended, mars it completely. Chatillon recognised this fact by his choice of an unnatural elevation for his drawing which produced a view that might be glimpsed only by a seabird in flight.

OTHER FRENCH LIGHTHOUSES

Towards the close of the century, four more lighthouses of importance were set up in France—Chassiron and Baleines on the islands of Ré and Oléron, close to the naval base of

35. Calcedonia port light in 1678

36. The reputed light at Havana in 1671 showing chains to close the port

35

La Rochelle, Cap Fréhel near St. Malo, and Stiff on Ushant close to the naval base of Brest. Chassiron, begun in 1679 and lighted in 1682, proved cheaper to maintain than had been estimated so, without increasing the dues, Baleines lighthouse was established in 1686. The design of both towers is attributed to Augier. Because seamen complained of the dimness of their oil lamps, coal or wood fires were substituted as their illuminants in 1733, Chassiron having two grates, one set 2 to 3 metres above the other, as a distinction from Cordouan; and Baleines, 27 metres high, having a fire inside a glazed lantern with thick stone pillars that, as at Cordouan, obstructed the light in as many directions.

The first lighthouse set up near St. Malo about 1667 proved to be too far inland, so it was discontinued and supplanted about 1695 by a tower at Fréhel, and at the same time a lighthouse was built at Stiff. Both structures consisted of twin circular towers, keyed into one another and communicating at each floor. The wider tower, 13′ in diameter and 60′ high, contained the lightkeepers' quarters and stores. The narrower tower contained the staircase and carried the fire grate at its top. As might be expected, the designer Vauban, the famous builder of fortresses, provided walls of massive masonry. By the use of these twin towers he excluded from the lightkeepers' quarters, as at Cordouan, the dirt and wet consequent on servicing the fire burning on the open top.

At first, Cap Fréhel may have been lit by coal, but torches were used about 1730: its twin towers endure to this day. At Stiff coal burned in a chauffer in the open air, and by treaty with England, France undertook to exhibit the light for 8 months of the year, in war as in peace, 'to serve humanity in general'.

ENGLAND

At this time, according to an English treatise, maritime law cast a stern eye on the exhibition of false lights and other outrages upon seamen—'the preventing of Help to such shipwreckt Persons, was punish'd with the same suffering as a Murderer. The like for those that shall put forth any treacherous Lanthorn or light, with Intention to subject them to Danger or Shipwrack, was punished with Death. And though no Harm happens, yet he may be punished: Hence it is, that Fishers are forbidden to fish in the Night, for fear of betraying Sailers.'

Of all countries, England between 1600 and 1700 showed the greatest increase in the number of coastal lighthouses, from 1 to about 14, all on the east and south coasts. This increase reflected her rapidly expanding sea-trade coupled with a wider though qualified recognition of the advantage of lights in preventing shipwrecks.

The influences affecting the establishment and management of lighthouses in England involved not only the Crown and Trinity House but also the personal interests of individuals to such a remarkable extent from 1600 to about 1800 that the subject must be dealt with in detail in Sections VII, IX and XV.

SCOTLAND

For centuries, strong ties of trading and friendship had bound Scotland to France, Holland and the Baltic countries, and such apprehensions as were felt in England from the proximity of possible enemies and pirates across the narrow Straits of Dover and the North

Sea had no place in the minds of the Scots. Despite the Union of the Crowns they had not lost their view of England rather than the continental countries as a possible foe; she was indeed the most recent one. A proposal for a lighthouse would be treated entirely as a business proposition and the question which arose in England at the Lizard about 1620, of exposing the coast to foreigners, was not raised in Scotland.

Though James VI, who became King of Scotland in 1587 and King of England in 1603 on Queen Elizabeth's death, had moved with his Court to London, Scotland retained her own Parliament. The Charters and Acts held by Trinity House had no force in Scotland and the independent Government in Edinburgh could examine freely any proposal for a lighthouse within that Kingdom. In this period lighthouses were established on the May island and at Buddonness.

ISLE OF MAY 1636

The situation of the May island at the entrance of the Firth of Forth in the North Sea served admirably for a lighthouse to benefit the overseas trade of Scotland which flowed almost entirely through her east coast ports. In 1630 Charles I, who had succeeded his father James VI, remitted from London to his Scots Privy Council in Edinburgh a petition for erecting a lighthouse on the May island and instructed it to consider the means of maintaining a lighthouse, if one should be necessary, and, if there be a willingness 'in such of our subjects as [are] most interested to pay such a dewtie' as it considered necessary, to draw up a patent specifying the number of years and how the duty should be levied, and either to send the document to him for signature or to append his seal in Edinburgh. The Council summoned the magistrates of interested ports to appear and express their opinion. Because of opposition the proposal languished until 1635 when the King informed the Council that he had received another numerously-signed petition for lights on the May that might prevent the frequent losses of lives and goods of his subjects and strangers at the entry of the Firth of Forth, especially in the night time, and directed it again to interview persons interested and, if it should find lights necessary for the public good, to hasten issue of a patent to Charles Geddes and John Cunningham, owner of the island and holder of a Court appointment, to entitle them to erect and maintain a light on a spot to be selected by experienced seamen, and to fix a reasonable duty. The Council appointed a committee to interview merchants and shipowners. It reported that 'the best and greatest part' of the witnesses approved of the proposal, while 'few and these not verie considerable, doe oppose the same without giving a reason'.

In 1636 the Scots Council granted a patent for the light to James Maxwell and John and Alexander Cunningham for 19 years at a rental of one thousand pounds 'in coin of this realm', equalling £84 in sterling, the deed being a lengthy document in Latin referring to a *domus luminaria sive lichthous*, a 'house of lights'. The Convention of Burghs, an ancient organisation which represented the chief Scots towns and had considerable control over their citizens, did not approve of the terms but it came to an agreement with the patentees in 1639 and passed an Act of its own which the Scots Parliament confirmed in 1641. This stipulated that for the remaining 14 years, extended later, the duty should be less than granted in the patent and should not be levied during the summer months. In return for the consequent reduction in the expected revenue, the Convention undertook to give the patentees lists of ships owned locally and of their tonnages and to assist in collecting dues at the ports. In undertaking to establish and maintain a lighthouse on this exposed island, the patentees benefited their country's trade greatly.

As at Cordouan, maintenance of this light, 6 miles from the mainland, was difficult—coals being brought by boat, landed on exposed rocky shelves and carried on the back of the keeper across the island to the massive square tower 40′ high. Most of the coal-fire lighthouses of north-west Europe imported coals from the Forth estuary. The lighthouse on the May seems to have consumed more fuel than any other, suitable coals being cheap in the neighbourhood. This large consumption entailed exceptionally heavy labour for the lightkeeper and for the seamen bringing fuel to the island.

The arched masonry tower had a top paved with stone slabs on which stood an iron grate. The builder Alexander Cunningham was lost by shipwreck on returning to Fife during a winter's storm which lasted only half-an-hour, a circumstance which was considered peculiar. Ten years later, some old women of Crail in Fife, the nearest haven, confessed that they had brought it about with the help of the devil. The incident was set to Latin verse by Alexander Scott, a professor of St. Andrews University. He referred to the May island bearing her safety light between the Carr Rock, which destroyed ships, and the high cliffs of the Bass Rock off the south shore of the Firth. This star light which Cunningham had set upon the waters had made the heavenly stars jealous because his fire equalled theirs. Scott continued thus:

> 'Obscuri cecidere alii, et volvuntur in undis,
> Mors eadem, ast tumuli non erat aequus honos,
> Hinc, quoniam multos servasti lumine cives,
> Civica te in coeli luce corona beat.'

This verse related that though Cunningham perished by drowning like many seafarers, the waves did him honour by bearing his body to the shore whereas others remained tossing upon the ocean, and concluded by addressing his spirit: 'since by your lighthouse you saved the lives of many citizens of this world, you are rewarded with a crown as a citizen of Heaven'.

Charles Geddes, one of the original applicants for the patent, composed the following chronogram in the form of a Latin distich:

Flamina ne noceant , neu flumina , Lumina Maja
PrabVIt, & MeDIIs InsVLa LVXIt aqVIs.

which might be translated freely as: 'unless prevented by wind and sea, the light of May will shine brightly amid the waters'. The Roman numerals of the second line indicate the year of construction of the lighthouse, that is, 1636.

BUDDONNESS *c.* 1660

About 1660, two lights were shown in maps on the north side of the river Tay entrance. Their purpose was to mark the deep channel over the bar and it is possible that they were erected about 1600. One tower was designed to be moved as the channel shifted. The cost of repair of these wooden structures often exceeded the income. About 1687 the Scots

Privy Council extended to the Dundee Town Council or to the Trinity House of Dundee authority to levy dues for the improvement of these candle lights. In the same year four pints of oil were purchased to make a trial of two lamps but the test was not successful. In 1695 the dues collected amounted only to 182 pounds Scots, equal to £15 of English money.

IRELAND

Though in 1664 a Frenchman noted that torches were lighted to guide ships into Youghal harbour, it is likely that this renewal of the practice of the previous century had ceased some years before he wrote and that the Hook tower at Waterford also had been discontinued as a lighthouse, perhaps in consequence of the Spanish schemes to invade

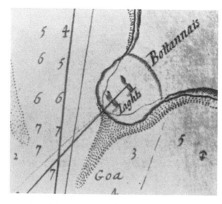

37. Buddonness lights (*c.* 1693) which guided Dundee ships over the Tay bar

38. The lighthouse at Loop Head in Ireland *c.* 1690

south Ireland. In 1659 the Trinity House of London, or the Commission which replaced it during the Commonwealth, resolved that a lighthouse was necessary upon the Hoth or Howth at Dublin; and in 1668 Trinity House reported that lighthouses would be useful at Dublin, Wexford, Waterford and Youghal.

It appears that 5 coal-fire lighthouses were erected in Ireland before 1700, the coals being imported from Scotland. A patent to establish 6 lighthouses was granted by Charles II to Sir Robert Reading soon after 1664 and he lighted the first about 1668. The 6 included 2 at Howth (one 'to mark the land' and the other 'to come over the bar' at Dublin), one near Kinsale, one at Hook, and another at the entrance to Belfast Lough on the peninsula of Magee or on Copeland island. Evidently the sixth was set upon Loop Head at the entrance to the river Shannon, as a lighthouse is shown here on sea-charts of 1689 along with others at Howth and on the Old Head of Kinsale. The light authorised at Dublin bar was not established, a perch to the south of the entrance and a buoy to the north being considered sufficient.

In collecting dues for the upkeep of his lighthouses, Reading spread his net more extensively than his patent allowed and gave the objectors to lighthouses an opportunity to point out the unreliability of the blaze from a coal fire.

In 1670 the masters and owners of ships in Chester, Liverpool and adjacent ports complained to Parliament that Reading's agents exacted not only fees upon a trading vessel's tonnage, but also unauthorised impositions of a levy of twelve pence on each passenger and a yearly toll on fishing-boats. The town of Liverpool sent a letter to Sir Gilbert Ireland, its member of Parliament, asking him to support a general complaint against Reading's lighthouses. It was signed by Thomas Johnson the Mayor, and Councillors Andoe, Corkey, Sturzaker and Bickersteth and stated that 'those light houses will be no benefit to our Mariners, but a hurt and Expose them to more danger if [they] trust to them, and also be a very great and unnecessary burden and charge to them'. The Parliamentary Committee of Grievances decided that Reading's patent formed 'a common grievance' and advised the King to annul it. Probably Reading withdrew his illegal charges. He seems to have retained his rights: in 1671 he applied to the Government in Dublin for payment of £500 per annum in accordance with the agreement which he made with the Crown when he established his lighthouses. In 1704 he surrendered the patent.

HOLLAND

The lighthouses at Terschelling and Brandaris remained of good service and others are believed to have been erected before 1636 at Urk, Hindeloopen, Vlieland, Scheveningen and Zanddijk. A type of firehut termed *vuurboet*, similar to those established earlier at Nieuport, showed lights about 1670 from the higher dunes at Bergen aan Zee, Vijk aan Zee and Callantsoog. They burned first wood and then coal. In 1613 local herring-fishers contracted to contribute money for the maintenance of a *vuurboet* at Egmond aan Zee, and at Petten the local Council in 1641 decreed that a percentage of the fish brought to port should be sold in the market to maintain their *vuurboeten*. On such low coasts, church towers carrying oil lamps made excellent seamarks.

39. The landing of the English at Terschelling in Holland in 1666. The beacon may have been a grate holding a fire

40. Brandaris lighthouse in Holland in 1666

GERMANY

Lighthouses erected on the North Sea islands included Wangerooge in 1602 and Heligoland about 1630. The State of Oldenberg set up the former at the instigation of Bremen: but lanterns containing oil lamps, placed at three corners of the tower, gave such poor illumination that they had to be replaced by coal fires which had peculiar periods of exhibition, from Michaelmas until Christmas and from Shrove Tuesday until Easter, thus excluding periods of short nights in summer and of frozen navigation in winter. In 1687 a new tower at Wangerooge, 38′ high, carried a coal fire in an iron basket. The Heligoland coal fire burned in the open and from its central position in the sea it was of great advantage to general navigation.

The use of buoys and beacons to mark the navigable channels of rivers and estuaries was extended. Buoys, moored in line with prominent buildings or beacons on shore, defined safe channels. A chart of the river Ems in 1642 shows that the town of Emden provided an elaborate display of seamarks incorporating this system. Lines of wooden posts indicated the edges of sandbanks, mostly on the starboard hand approaching from the sea, and buoys marked the fairways. These wooden buoys, shaped like cones and hooped with iron, were moored with chains attached to the pointed ends and had large stones as anchors.

DENMARK AND SCANDINAVIA

At the Danish lighthouses of Anholt, Skagen (Scaw), Falsterbo and Nidingen in 1624–9, Jens Pedersen Groves introduced a new type of structure consisting of a timber lever arrangement called a *vippefyr* or swape, which hoisted a brazier of burning coals quickly into the air, thus easing the work of the keepers.

Sweden maintained 5 lighthouses by 1700, 4 burning coal in open grates. As a distinction from other navigation fires, 2 towers each with an open fire had been erected at Nidingen in 1624 by Denmark. By the Peace Conferences of Brönsebro in 1645 and Roskilde in 1658 these towers passed to Sweden along with the lighthouses of Kullen and

41. Howth light near Dublin
c. 1693

42. Landsort lighthouse
in Sweden in 1669

43. The vippefyr at
the Scaw c. 1650
(Resen)

Falsterbo. The latter had been an occasional fire but henceforth it was lit nightly. Kullen may have been a reflector light for a time and the evidence seems conclusive that reflectors were used at Landsort, south of Stockholm, from about 1669 to 1671 and at Örskär, in the Gulf of Bothnia, from 1687. But no contemporary descriptions of the reflectors remain: oil lamps would be the illuminants. According to an inspection report of August 1736, the lantern of Örskär contained 12 lamps burning rape oil and 6 metal mirrors of 24″ diameter: these may have comprised the apparatus of 1687.

In 1651 a man named Gardiner received permission to erect a lighted beacon at Landsort but it was withdrawn next year as the Swedish Admiralty took over all coastal lights. They gave Gardiner 600 dalers as compensation for his lantern. In 1658 another individual, Van der Hagen, received authority to erect a tower here and a light seems to have been shown regularly from 1669. In 1671 a stone tower with an open coal fire replaced the wooden tower, which had been burnt down.

The Norwegian lighthouses of Lindesnes (the Naze) and Ferder were established in 1655 and 1697. A second lighthouse was erected at the Naze. In November 1708 the Trinity House of London, in response to an enquiry from Norway, expressed the opinion that a lighthouse was unnecessary as the shore was very high and well seen. This was a rare early instance of international consultation regarding lighthouses.

INDIA AND JAPAN

An account of India in 1639 mentions a Portuguese navigation light at Goa harbour entrance—'a Rock upon which is erected a tower, in Form of a Redoubt, which in the Night-time serves for a Beacon to Mariners'.

Ogilby's account of an Embassy to Japan in 1669 in a barque 'seeming more like a prison than a ship because none could stand upright in it' mentions, as a seamark to be seen 8 leagues off at sea, a high mast at the fort of Pulicat north of Madras in India, which carried a flag '500 yards long'! In Japan he found seamarks in use. They were timber beacons carrying lanterns.

AMERICA

There are inconclusive references to lights at Havana in Cuba and at Coutejuba in Brazil. From 1673–4 fire beacons at Point Allerton are recorded in much detail at the sea-approaches to Boston, Massachusetts, but their purpose is believed to have been rather to warn the town of approaching shipping than to serve as seamarks. Dutch seamen noted before 1700 a conspicuous watch-tower as an excellent beacon for identifying this part of the coast.

IV

PROGRESS 1690 TO 1782

44. An 18th-century Mediterranean lighthouse (Ozanne)

45. A Mediterranean lighthouse *c.* 1750 (Vernet)

IV. PROGRESS 1690 TO 1782

Remarkable improvements in lighthouse structures and lighting were achieved in this period. In England, the first towers exposed directly to wave-action were erected on the Eddystone Rocks, a piled beacon was set on the Smalls Rocks, and lightships were moored at sandbanks; in Sweden, parabolic reflector lights, oscillating lights, and ultimately in 1781 the world's first revolving light were exhibited to the mariner. The number of coal-fire beacons reached its maximum but oil lamps served the majority of sea-lights. North America established its first lighthouse, probably in 1716.

THE FIRST WAVE-SWEPT LIGHTHOUSES 1696–1708

These years cover the erection of the first towers in the world that were exposed fully to the force of the sea, when three lighthouses in succession were set upon a tiny peak among the Eddystone Rocks, 13 miles off the south-west coast of England. The erection by Henry Winstanley of the first two towers was the greatest challenge yet offered to the ungauged stroke of the waves, and the third tower designed by John Rudyerd was perhaps the most curious lighthouse ever built, from its remarkable construction of stone cased in timber. Each is described in Section VIII.

THE FIRST AMERICAN LIGHTHOUSE 1716

The lighthouse established on the small island of Little Brewster off Boston, Massachusetts, is the earliest sea-light to be recorded in America. Its tall masonry tower of excellent design carried a glazed lantern containing oil lamps. It is described in Section XI.

DISTINGUISHING LIGHTHOUSES BY ROCKETS 1716

To distinguish the Scilly lighthouse from others and thus to reduce the frequency of wrecks in the vicinity, William Whiston proposed 'that a Ball of Light or Fire be thrown up from St. Mary's, the principal of the English Isles of Scilly every Mid-night and three Times more every Night, to be proportioned as the Necessities of Navigation shall require. That the Mortar and Ball be such as may afford Light above a Degree of a great Circle, or 60 geographical Miles; and the Sound heard above one Third of the same Distance, both which we know from Experience may certainly be done. And that the Proposer and his Assistants may be enabled, by a small Duty upon the tonnage of Ships, or otherwise, as to the Wisdom of the Parliament shall seem meet, to set about the same Design immediately for the Advantage of this Nation and the common Benefit of Mankind.' Though Whiston's scheme was not adopted then, systems of firing rockets to aid navigation by light and sound have been carried out subsequently: for instance, from the Mersey lightships around 1830. Whiston had proposed in 1714 to provide seamen with information of their longitude by discharging rockets simultaneously from vessels anchored in particular positions.

ALTERATIONS AT CORDOUAN 1717–27

The burning of a wood fire nightly since 1612 gradually injured the stonework at Cordouan lighthouse to such an extent that the upper part of the tower had to be removed in 1717 and rebuilt with the grate set at a lower level. At the same time coals displaced wood as the fuel. But navigators objected to the change, as lowering the grate reduced the geographical range of the fire. They remained dissatisfied until 1727 when an iron lantern was put up over the grate which protected the fire from the weather and resulted in a brighter and steadier blaze. Another real benefit came from the lantern's thin vertical bars which offered less obstruction to the light than did the former masonry pillars. In addition, polished metal sheets in the form of an inverted cone were placed above the grate with the object of reflecting the glow of the fire, but they proved useless for that purpose as their newly-cleaned surfaces always became covered with soot shortly after lighting the fire.

TRIPLE LIGHTHOUSES 1724

Another attempt to distinguish a lighthouse from others was made at the Casquets, formidable Rocks lying off the north-west of the Channel Islands, by the erection of a group of three coal fires placed close together, each in a lantern on a separate tower. The importance of the site in the navigation of the English Channel had required quick identification at night. Enclosing the fires within glass lanterns afforded some assistance to the keeper in his Sisyphean task of maintaining all the fires at the same intensity. This seems to be the only instance of three separate lights being erected in a group as a distinction for a lighthouse. It is described in Section IX.

THE FIRST LIGHTSHIPS 1731–98

By the persistence of private adventurers in England who established lightships at the Nore in 1731 and at the Dudgeon in 1736, seamen benefited greatly in navigating through the adjacent sandbanks. In all, six more lightships were established before 1800: one in the channel to Dublin harbour before 1740, one off the Eddystone Rocks as a temporary seamark from 1756 to 1759 while Smeaton built his tower there, and four off south-east England at the sandbanks of Owers, Newarp, Goodwin and Sunk between 1788 and 1798. Not until after 1800 were lightships tried in other countries.

It is impossible to over-emphasise either the value of these early lightships in preventing wrecks, or the danger to which their crews were exposed from being run into and breaking adrift. They are described chiefly in Section IX.

PARABOLIC REFLECTORS 1738

In 1737 lightning destroyed the 148' high red masonry tower at Örskär in Sweden in the south of the Gulf of Bothnia. A letter from the King dated 2nd January 1738 ordered that it should be replaced by a stone tower 113' high, with a glass lantern to contain 5 mirrors of polished steel which were to be 'burning mirrors . . . with a parabolic line'. This recognition of the correct curve for lighthouse mirrors was unfortunately of no avail in obtaining the strongest possible light from the lamps: it was noted on 17th May 1768 that the lamps, numbering 10, had been placed, not one at the focus of each reflector, but one on each side of it, thus not concentrating the light and so losing the benefit of the designer's scientific knowledge. It is possible that the unlighted sectors between the narrow beams of light which resulted from placing one lamp exactly at the focus of each mirror had been found objectionable by navigators and that diffusion of light by setting lamps ex-focally had provided a partial cure. Probably a cluster of 5 wicks or lamps was fitted to each reflector eventually.

BELLS ON BUOYS 1750

A proposal to mark the dangerous Wolf Rock in the English Channel, 8 miles south of Land's End, had been put to Trinity House, perhaps before this date. A buoy would be moored 'in such a manner that it should swing clear of the Rock, carrying a Bell upon it,

46. The pier light of Har-
lingen in Holland *c.* 1730
(Vanderhaan)

47. Enkhuisen light in
Holland *c.* 1725

48. Brielle lighthouse in Holland in
1749

so as to ring by the motion of the waves, and to give notice of danger; but this jingling scheme (of buoy bells upon the English coasts for alarming us) was not accepted, on a supposition that the fishermen (not approving the musick) would remove the bells when they catched no fish'. Though the excellent suggestion was not acted on at that time, it is possible that bell buoys were established elsewhere by 1819: they were much in use in the latter half of the 19th century in all parts of the world and many are still in service.

A LAND LIGHTHOUSE 1751

From the earliest times a lamp or candle stuck in the window of a house guided a man to his home and there are several instances in England before 1600 of lights being shown nightly from churches and other buildings to direct travellers over moorlands. A late example is Dunstan Pillar, or *Lincoln lighthouse*, which gave guidance across a heath between Lincoln and Sleaford. In 1751 Francis Dashwood erected this square tower 92' high, as a land lighthouse, and topped it by a lantern raising it another 15'. In 1810 a statue of George III was substituted for the disused lantern and this in turn was removed about 1940 as a possible danger to aircraft. This curiosity in lighthouses, being so far from the sea coast, offered no service to shipping.

LIGHT OCCULTED BY SCREEN 1753

The traders in Turku in Finland, then Swedish territory, introduced a novelty in lighting when in 1753 they established a lighthouse at Utö at the north entrance to the Gulf of Finland. This islet lies on the southern edge of the extensive archipelago of the Åland islands. The tower, 24' high and shaped like a cone, was constructed of quarried stones and boulders and bore a glazed lantern. A pole projecting from the side of the tower carried an iron bucket which, every night, burned coals continuously in the open air. This formed the main fire and it was visible round the sea horizon. The lantern contained a subsidiary light consisting of a cluster of candles and a screen or reflector which was turned

49. Dunstan Pillar erected in 1751 to guide travellers over a moor in England

50. Utö lighthouse in 1753, on a medal struck in 1946 to commemorate the 250th anniversary of the Finnish Pilotage Service (Sailo)

abruptly by hand every 15 minutes to light first one and then the other of two navigable channels 56° 15′ apart. Thus, alternately, ships in one channel saw this subsidiary light while those in the other channel could not see it. A few years after erection of the tower, the light in the lantern was described as coming from 6 lamps each with 2 wicks, hanging from the ceiling, with 4 tinned mirrors behind.

The benefit of the arrangement to occult the light lay in economy of oil and not in distinction from other lighthouses. Though the screen or reflector cost 800 out of the total capital expenditure of 19,280 silver thalers, the apparatus is stated to have been extremely primitive and unpractical. But interest arises from its being an early instance of occulting a sea-light.

SEAMARKS DEFINED 1755

The definitions of seamarks which Dr. Samuel Johnson gave in his celebrated dictionary of 1755 might be noted. He accented the last syllable of *lighthouse*.

Beacon: 'marks erected, or lights made in the night, to direct navigators in their courses and warn them from rocks, shallows and sandbanks.'

Buoy :   'a piece of cork or wood floating on the water, tied to a weight at the bottom.'

Lighthouse : 'an high building at the top of which lights are hung to guide ships at sea.'

Pharos :   'a lighthouse—a lantern from the shore to direct sailors.'

THE FIRST STONE SEA-TOWER 1756–9

After the destruction by fire in 1755 of Rudyerd's lighthouse on the Eddystone Rocks, John Smeaton (1724–92) designed a tower to consist entirely of stone, a choice of material resulting from a study of the advantages and defects of the previous Eddystone lighthouses. This stone tower, described in Section VIII, was the first to be exposed directly to the ocean, and was an achievement in construction much in advance of contemporary navigation lighting. Until 1810 its light came from merely 24 candles.

OSCILLATING LIGHT 1757

Jonas Norberg (1711–83), known sometimes as Johan Nordqvist, an assistant at the State Model Museum in Stockholm, introduced novelties in sea-lights which seem to have been developments of the occulted light of Utö. In 1757 he showed the first oscillating light from the Swedish lighthouse of Korsö.

In 1746 a red stone tower, 71' high, had been erected at Korsö but it was not lighted until 1750 when polished brass reflectors were fitted in the lantern. It seems not to have been approved, for in 1753 a Royal patent, as in England, authorised the erection of a new lighthouse and the collection of dues for its maintenance. The patent directed that, in order to be different from the open coal fire at Landsort lighthouse some 45 miles away, the light should consist of 4 'well-cut concave reflectors' each with a lamp. This new tower, 86' high, was completed in 1757 and the light was described as given by 2 large lanterns 24' apart, each holding 2 gilded reflectors. Every 4 minutes the 2 lanterns were turned to and fro horizontally by machinery, thus giving flashes which varied in timing according to the direction of the observer. A contemporary view of this tower shows that the two lanterns on its balcony were turned by rods connected to clockwork placed within the central lantern, which housed only that machinery. Ships saw the lights gradually coming into view and disappearing into darkness. The Swedish Government purchased the lighthouse patent in 1833 and a more modern light was installed in 1847.

Before fitting his apparatus, Norberg tested parabolic mirrors over a distance of 14 miles near Stockholm, keeping one candle in focus automatically, probably by the old device of a wire spring.

WRECK-LIGHTING 1762–5

Though the marking of wrecks by buoys in the open sea was carried out in England by Trinity House before 1700, and in particular in that year at the wreck of the *Carlisle* man-of-war in the Downs which was extremely dangerous to ships desirous of anchoring, the lighting of wrecks was probably not attempted until in 1762 the frigate *Hermione* was wrecked at Galleons Reach in the Thames whereby the navigation was 'greatly amazed, obstructed, and rendered more dangerous and precarious'. A person named Winn had appreciated the advantage of indicating to shipping at night exactly where the wreck lay in the channel and he moored a boat with a light close to. For this beneficial service he demanded a toll of 1 shilling from each vessel passing. Trinity House, in objecting to the

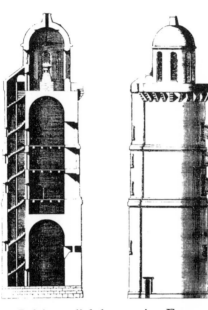

51. Baleines lighthouse in France *c.* 1740. Thick pillars obstructed the light from oil lamps set on the central pedestal in the lantern

52. The French lighthouse of Port-Vendres *c.* 1780 (L'Espinasse)

charge, claimed that its 'good and charitable purposes . . . were likely to be defeated' by his action, but recognised the excellence of the mark and settled the matter by buying Winn's lightvessel for £205, a sum fixed by arbitration.

Fog Bell 1766

The idea of helping shipping by sound signals in fog seems still to have been a novelty. A large bell, cast specially, was set up at Nidingen lighthouses in the Kattegat and foreign newspapers reported it as a curiosity.

Improved Oscillating Light 1769

After Norberg criticised the Örskär light in his report of 1768 which is referred to in Section XVI, he was instructed to improve it, which he did by arranging, within its large wooden lantern, small lanterns or reflectors, probably 5 in number, each with a lamp. Together they were turned by clockwork gradually to and fro somewhat as at Korsö. No doubt his purpose in moving the reflectors was to overcome their small divergence and ensure that the light was visible over the whole sector desired. Thus he increased their arc of visibility from about 17° to 65°. The lantern with Norberg's apparatus was replaced in 1852 by a metal lantern containing revolving mirrors with argand lamps.

REFLECTORS AT LIVERPOOL 1772

The earliest recorded use of reflectors in British lighthouses was at Liverpool. It has been stated frequently that William Hutchinson, the dockmaster, introduced them into the lighthouses built at that port in 1763 after he had seen the result of a wager laid at a convivial meeting. One of the party undertook to read a newspaper by the light of a farthing candle, perhaps 30′ distant, and did so by holding behind it a wooden bowl lined with putty, to give a parabolic shape, in which he embedded small facets of ordinary looking-glass.

Hutchinson published in 1777 a description of the reflectors then used at Liverpool, and it is known that he sent one reflector to Rouen in 1774 along with an account of reflector lights. The only earlier reference to the Liverpool reflectors that has been discovered by local historians is an entry in a Minute of Liverpool Town Council dated 1st July 1772 ordering payment of 'the sum of twenty guineas to Mr. Halden for his invention of the reflecting lights fixed up in the lighthouses in this port and to be paid to him by Mr. Gerrard in full for all his demands on the Trustees of the said duties'. The name of Halden is otherwise quite unknown in connection with lighthouses. But the Holden family are famous for their investigations of the tides at Liverpool which they based on a long series of tidal levels observed by Hutchinson, with whom they were close friends. In his book, he credits the Holdens and many other persons with improvements and useful information in connection with sea affairs. As he does that so freely and as it is against his apparent character that he should withhold from the Holdens any credit to which they might be entitled, it is hard to believe that any important part in proposing reflectors for the lighthouses was taken by them. His book of 1777 states merely 'We have made and had in use here at Liverpool, reflectors . . . .'. In September 1789 George Holden was awarded 10 guineas by the Town Council for drawing up a Table of tidal predictions for the port and was commissioned to revise it annually for the same sum. No award to Hutchinson appears in any of the Council Minutes and one might well suppose that the clerk made a slip in entering the name of Halden in the Minute of July 1772, and that it was Hutchinson and not a Halden or a Holden who received the award for the reflectors. It is certain, however, that before 1774 Hutchinson had expert knowledge of the manufacture and the properties of parabolic reflectors: his book shows the correctness of his views.

The date of the first use of parabolic reflectors at Liverpool cannot confidently be placed earlier than 1772. A letter from the Pilot Office to an Admiralty surveyor dated 6th December 1771 stated that the lights 'are allowed by all Seamen using the port by much to exceed any lights in Europe that they have seen', and concluded, 'yet another great improvement is very near ready for execution'. This may well allude to the imminent introduction of reflectors.

The parabolic reflectors fitted at Liverpool and attributed to Hutchinson were of two types. The smallest reflectors, of 3′ diameter and 12″ focus with a wick 3″ broad, were formed of tinned plates soldered together. The larger reflectors, of $5\frac{1}{2}′$, $7\frac{1}{2}′$ and 12′ diameter, consisted of a wood frame of parabolic shape, covered with a film of plaster to which facets of mirror glass adhered. The 12′ reflector had a focus of 3′ and a wick 14″ broad. So large a mirror was never fitted at another early sea-light. The proportions of unusually long focus and wide wick offered an excellent reflector system, besides keeping the reflectors away from the smoke of the crude lamps. But the low intensity of their flames made the large reflectors less effective than was to be expected.

DESIGN OF FRENCH LIGHTHOUSES 1773

When the Rouen Chamber of Commerce applied in 1773 to the French Government for its sanction to the establishment of four new lighthouses in Normandy, it was informed that the architecture should be of a higher standard than intended: the towers should reflect the genius of the Age.

  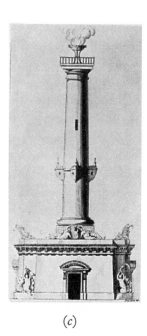

(a)　　　　　　　　(b)　　　　　　　　(c)

53. Designs by Penseron for lighthouses in the Seine estuary

A few years later, an architect, Pierre Penseron, published designs for beautiful towers which were never carried out, as they envisaged the burning of an open fire on the summits and this type of illumination had become obsolete in France.

Perhaps because of the Government's expression of opinion in 1773, coupled with the splendid example of the architectural masterpiece of Cordouan, many French lighthouses constructed subsequently have been of outstanding beauty in design.

SPHERICAL REFLECTORS *c.* 1773–80

The success of spherical reflectors for lighting the streets of Paris after 1766 encouraged Tortille Sangrain, their manufacturer, to offer them for sea-lights, and experiments made in 1773 led the French Minister of Marine to suppose that they might be useful for that purpose. Before 1778 they were fitted at St. Mathieu lighthouse near the naval base of Brest, to the number of 60 mirrors arranged in 4 horizontal tiers. They were small, being less than 200 mm. or 8″ square. Each had one tiny oil lamp. In 1779–80, to save expense, spherical reflectors replaced coal fires at four lighthouses in Normandy, 16 mirrors over 500 mm. square being arranged in two tiers. The crude lamps of the lower tier had 3 wicks and those of the upper 2.

Spherical mirrors reflect rays of light not to the horizon but to the flames at their centres as described in Section XVI. French seamen soon discovered that these reflectors had little effect in strengthening the light from the lamps and they desired a return to coal fires. But the reflectors were retained largely because of the convenience and cheapness of the system of reflectors and oil lamps, and as war with Britain interfered with the import of coals. No country other than France adopted spherical reflectors. In 1835 the last of them was removed from the lighthouse of Gatteville at Barfleur.

TESTS OF COAL FIRES AND REFLECTORS 1774

Before choosing an illuminant for the new lighthouses in Normandy, the Rouen Chamber of Commerce carried out comparative tests of an open coal fire, a spherical metal reflector from Sangrain and a parabolic reflector from Hutchinson, and made trials of French, Spanish and British coals. An open fire from British coal appeared to be best suited to the requirements and probably was the right choice from the three alternatives but, as related in Section XII, it led to 5 years of trouble for the Chamber.

SMEATON'S COAL FIRE 1776

For 80 years the coal swape lights at the Spurn satisfied seamen making the entrance to the Humber, but by 1766 the sands in the estuary had shifted so much that the navigable channel was far distant from the lights. John Angell, a relative of the first patentee, declined to move them and shut himself in his house and refused to discuss the problem. But his partner Leonard Thompson, who had a quarter-share in the ownership, agreed to Trinity House promoting an Act of Parliament to authorise the building of lighthouses in better positions.

54. Korsö lighthouse in Sweden in 1757 with two external turning lanterns

55. Neuwerk lighthouse in Germany in 1751

When the Act was obtained, Trinity House instructed John Smeaton to visit Spurn Point. On his recommendation, two temporary lights, 250 yards apart, were erected in 1767, both swapes as before, with the coal buckets hoisted 50′ and 35′ above ground level. A paved path 3′ wide with a handrail at each side guided the keepers when passing between them at night. To provide for a possible further shifting of the sands, the larger temporary swape was set on rollers so that it could be moved according as the navigable channel shifted.

On 5th September 1776 his two brick towers 90′ and 50′ high which had been capped by 'inclosed lanterns for fire lights' were lighted. The novel design of their grates, good ventilation of the lanterns and excellent means for raising coals and removing cinders would justify a claim that they were the first scientific coal-burning lighthouses. The chief improvement, as described in Section XVI, consisted of a shallow grate with a controlled supply of air which kept the layer of coals at a whiter or more luminous heat than had been achieved previously with coal fires, but it is likely that the small-capacity grate required too continuous an attendance by the lightkeepers. Not until July 1819 were these two coal fires replaced by oil lamps and parabolic reflectors.

Smeaton recorded that his new lighthouses on their first exhibition gave 'an amazing light to the entire satisfaction of all beholders' and that 'vessels going round the Point in a dark night have the shades of their masts and ropes cast upon their decks'.

THE FIRST PILE LIGHTHOUSE 1776–8

The Smalls lighthouse, erected on sea-swept Rocks in the Irish Channel some 21 miles from land, is of outstanding interest not so much because of the difficulty of setting a lighthouse on such an exposed site, as on account of the novel type of beacon designed and constructed by Henry Whiteside, a young musical-instrument maker of Liverpool. It is described in Section VIII. The idea of erecting a seamark on these rocks originated with John Phillips, assistant dockmaster at Liverpool. He planned a fixed white light to show all round the horizon with a range of 12 miles, surmounted by a fixed green light which would be visible from particular directions at short range, and thus would guide vessels through channels close to the main Rock.

EZEKIEL WALKER'S REFLECTOR *c.* 1776

After fire destroyed the rear lighthouse at Hunstanton in England about 1776, the tower which replaced it was topped by a glazed lantern containing one reflector with an oil lamp instead of the coal fire. An account of 1781 says that the 'light is thrown out by a lamp of oil which plays upon a great variety of pieces of glass artfully disposed, by which the flame from the lamp is multiplied and reflected and is to be clearly distinguished at sea at a distance of seven leagues. By this construction the light is constant and certain, whereas the seamen were sometimes obliged to awaken the old gentleman at the former lighthouse with a shot, to put him in mind his fire wanted blowing.'

Ezekiel Walker, a philosopher of Lynn, designed this reflector light but his numerous scientific papers do not include a reference to the subject. It is unlikely that he was unaware of Liverpool's earlier use of reflectors for sea-lights. Bearing in mind the type of reflector which Thomas Smith produced in 1787 after discussions with Walker as described in Section X, one might assume that the Hunstanton reflector was parabolic and formed of facets of mirror glass set in a plaster mould. This accords with the description of 1781.

WILLIAM HUTCHINSON'S BOOK OF 1777

The first printed account of parabolic reflectors as used in lighthouses is found in Hutchinson's *Treatise on Practical Seamanship* published in 1777, which includes observations on lighthouses, proposals for their improvement and engravings of reflectors.

Hutchinson was one of the most colourful figures that have appeared in lighthouse affairs. He went to sea as a lad and on one occasion when his vessel was wrecked and the crew were faced with starvation, only the timely appearance of another ship saved them from recourse to cannibalism: to this gruesome end Hutchinson's life had been forfeited by lot. In 1758 he proposed to resume his former command of a Liverpool privateer 'to curb the insolence of Thurot's French squadron' which molested British shipping. The venture was supported by the town's merchants who promised to indemnify the vessel's owners and advanced to each seaman five guineas, exclusive of a share of the booty to be seized from their intended prey. But when the ship was got ready for sea, the scheme fell through: of the 207 seamen who signed on, only 28 reported for duty. Another of Hutchinson's enterprises was to provide the Liverpool market with live fish.

His book is a collection of observations on a variety of matters based on his life-long experience at sea, including the navigation and care of a ship, attack and defence, and the health of seamen. In the course of remarks on religion, as practised in the merchantmen trading to the East, he held the East India Company to be 'highly blamable, in shamefully rating those large ships only at 499 tons, in order to avoid the expense of a Clergyman and the penalty of the law for not carrying one'. The regulation applied to ships above 500 tons.

He described the Liverpool lighthouse reflectors as looking 'like a blaze as big as the reflectors themselves, to people in that quarter nearly facing them, by the angle of reflection being equal to the angle of incident'. The lights had successfully 'stood the test of fair trial' despite their detractors, 'as there always will be to new things, commonly calling them new whims'. He illustrated the parabolic curve and recommended that the copper lamp should have its oil cistern at the back of the reflector so as not to obstruct the light, and that the width of the burners holding the wicks should be 'proportional in their bigness to the reflectors'. He advised a careful choice of oil on which 'the goodness of the lights greatly depends'. He observed that the huge Liverpool reflector of 12′ diameter gave little reflected light within 3 points on each side of the axis, 'but the blaze of the lamps can be seen . . . above half of the compass clear of the edge of the reflector, which illuminates greatly the atmosphere fronting them'.

For a light to be seen further round the compass than 90° he would place one reflector towards each quarter, with pipes radiating from a central cistern to carry oil to the lamps. This was the arrangement adopted at the Smalls. But he believed that the most effective arrangement would be to set 'a parcel of lamps' with reflectors of 11″ diameter and 4″ focus, in rows upon shelves close to the windows of a lantern, the upper row nearest and those below a little behind, to avoid smoking the upper reflectors. Very modestly, he limited his recommendations to his actual experience, and says of his proposed arrangement of lamps and reflectors, 'the advantage that would be gained, wants to be confirmed by experiment'.

His book contains a new proposal to distinguish lighthouses by exhibiting different numbers of lights from windows in the same tower, and he had experimented to find the vertical spacing necessary. He mentions that it was intended at one of the Liverpool lighthouses to throw up fire balls, like Whiston's rockets, when a vessel was seen in distress, to alarm the port into sending help. The ball 'sparkling in the air' would give comfort to the distressed persons and assurance that their plight was observed.

56. A Mediterranean lighthouse in 1772 (Vernet)

57. Algiers light in 1776 (Bazire)

Hutchinson advocated circular lanterns for lighthouses with large plate-glass windows and narrow vertical bars so as not to obstruct the light, a large opening in the roof with cover to emit the smoke and a 'large vane to traverse freely with the wind'. In general, he urged that 'no pains or expence should be spared to make lighthouses as perfect as possible as many valuable lives and great property often depends upon the certainty of seeing these lights at a sufficient and proper distance. . . . To with-hold whatever contrivance, or the best materials that can make them the most perfect, as far as the fund which is to support them will afford, should be looked upon as an act of great villainy.'

SPANGLE LIGHT 1777-8

A Minute of the Elder Brethren of Trinity House dated 2nd August 1777 records that they 'ordered that a reflector be made in London and put up at Lowestoft by way of experiment, and the opinion of persons concerned in navigation be collected'. A contemporary local account states that at the upper lighthouse they discontinued the coal fire and fitted in its place a glass lantern 7′ high and 6′ in diameter within which a cylinder covered with 4,000 small mirrors reflected the light from 126 oil lamps: the light was brilliant and visible 20 miles to sea.

In 1778 a London newspaper gave prominence to 'a very ingenious contrivance' lately finished by cabinet-makers in Aldersgate Street as a substitute for the fire grate on top of a lighthouse. In the centre of a large lantern of iron and brass they set a cylinder as a reservoir for oil which flowed through pipes to a horizontal circular hollow tube, placed midway between the cylinder and the lantern panes, and containing many oil burners. Probably wicks projected from holes in the top of the tube. The central cylinder was 'covered with small square mirrors fix'd close to each other; by which means such a Magnificent light is reflected as will (it is supposed) be seen twenty miles at sea. A very considerable expense will be saved by the above contrivance as, it is said, a gallon of Oil will be equal to three Chaldrons of Coal . . . the Effect is Amazingly Grand'.

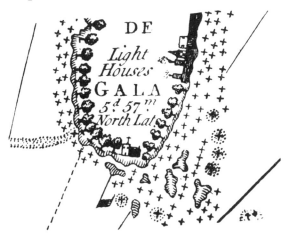

58. This Dutch sea-chart of 1788 shows two lights in Ceylon. In the Far East lighthouses were established in 1760 in the Pescadores islands and in 1771 in Kamchatka

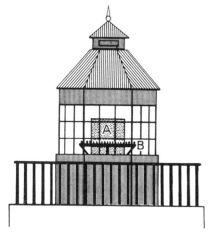

59. In this reconstruction of the Lowestoft spangle light of 1778 (more substantial than the original) A marks the central oil container covered with 4,000 tiny mirrors and B marks the circular tube with 126 wick burners

It is difficult to resist the conclusion that the reflector light tried by Trinity House at Lowestoft was this apparatus or a similar contraption. Mariners would soon recognise the futility of this sparkling affair. Apart from the difficulty to the lightkeeper of managing so many lamps, practically no light would be directed usefully to shipping. The twinkle of the numerous mirrors would be bright and attractive in a confined space but the rays of light which they reflected would be dissipated in all directions, upwards and downwards. The tiny pieces of mirror served merely as spangles and a better result would have been obtained at the lighthouse if they had been removed and the lamps alone clustered in the centre of the lantern.

REFLECTORS FOR CASQUETS AND PORTLAND 1778–80

The Minutes of Trinity House show that the Elder Brethren ordered reflectors and copper lamps between 1778 and 1780 for Casquets and Portland lighthouses, but no particulars are recorded nor is it known whether they were fitted at these places.

THE FIRST REVOLVING LIGHT 1781

One of the most notable milestones in the history of lighthouse optics was reached when Norberg installed at Carlsten lighthouse near Marstrand in Sweden the first revolving light in the world. This emitted flashes at regular intervals by an arrangement of oil lamps and reflectors attached to a vertical axis and rotated by clockwork. The official Stockholm paper *Post och Inrikes Tigningar* of 15th February 1781 published a *Notice to Mariners* announcing the establishment of the lighthouse, having 6 burning-mirrors moved by clockwork and revolved in 5 minutes: thus giving a variable light of 6 strong and 3 weaker flashes or intervals of light at an elevation of some 260' measured from sea-level to centre of the mirrors. The light would be shown from the 1st August 1781, and in future years from that date until 1st May, like the other Swedish lights in the Kattegat.

From a distance the light showed one strong flash every 50 seconds. In addition, one at least of the lamp flames was always visible and provided the weaker light mentioned in the *Notice* which was apparent to seamen close to, who might not perceive the strong flashes from the reflectors which, from the considerable height of the lantern and the small vertical divergence, might pass over their vessels. The system of revolving optical apparatus which Norberg introduced is fitted now at most lighthouses throughout the world and it would be difficult to exaggerate the importance of his invention to navigation. Figure 168 shows his apparatus.

V

PROGRESS 1782 to 1800

60. An earthquake destroyed two lighthouses at Messina on 5th February 1783. The engraver shows Scylla and Charybdis, the rock and the whirlpool dreaded by the ancient mariners

61. Cordouan tower as re-built by Teulère in 1790
with a modern lantern (Labat)

V. PROGRESS 1782 TO 1800

The invention by Argand in 1782 of an oil lamp which gave a steady smokeless flame was one of the most important events in lighthouse history, though only in England was this lamp used before 1800 in its proper form for sea-lighting. In this period England and Scotland adopted parabolic reflectors as the standard illumination of their coastal lighthouses; France, England and Ireland introduced revolving lights of considerable power; and England and Ireland fitted lens lights. The most important structure was the South Rock lighthouse.

SPHERICAL REFLECTORS AT CORDOUAN 1782

Obtaining coal and transporting it by sea to the rocky shelves of Cordouan had always been troublesome and by 1780 had become extremely expensive. The Government Departments in Paris welcomed the economy achieved from replacing coal fires by spherical reflectors and oil lamps at the lighthouse of St. Mathieu and at those in Normandy, and invited Tortille Sangrain to visit Cordouan and state his price for replacing its coal fire by a reflector light. His tender was accepted and, accordingly, Bitry's open lantern of 1727 was removed and a new metal lantern, completely glazed, to hold no fewer than 80 tiny silvered spherical reflectors each with an oil lamp was set on top of the tower.

The light was exhibited in November 1782 and was condemned at once by seamen who complained of its poor visibility. The keepers also had difficulty in attending to the multitude of smoky lamps. As described in Section XII Joseph Teulère, one of the engineers at the fortress of Bordeaux who had charge of Cordouan, was directed from Paris to examine the new light; he pointed out its defects to Sangrain who fitted larger spherical reflectors, but the seamen remained dissatisfied and demanded a return to the coal fire. Their objections were well-founded: the spherical reflectors did little more than obstruct the light from the lamps but were nevertheless retained until 1790 when a better light could be procured.

ARGAND'S SMOKELESS LAMP *c*. 1782

Hitherto, all oil lamps and candles in use at lighthouses, besides requiring trimming several times nightly, gave out smoke which, though sometimes invisible in the air, was deposited ultimately on the mirrors and lantern panes as a film of soot consisting of particles of unburnt carbon, which resulted from imperfect combustion due to lack of oxygen or air in the hot portion of the flame above the wick.

Ami Argand, a scientific philosopher born in Geneva in 1755, discovered a cure for this trouble and evolved a comparatively smokeless oil lamp which gave a steady flame and a more intense light than was obtainable previously. His invention improved lighthouse illumination and soon brought immense social and economic benefit to western Europe.

The special feature of Argand's lamp consisted of two vertical concentric tubes of thin brass, about 1″ in diameter and separated slightly, the space between them holding a cylindrical cotton wick. Air passed upwards through the inner tube as well as outside the outer

61

tube and this double air current playing on both sides of the lighted wick ensured an even temperature and good combustion of the oil.

A part of the complete lamp that assisted combustion was a circular glass chimney closely surrounding the outer tube and the wick. Discovery of its advantage was accidental. Argand's brother was reaching across a table for a broken neck of a flask which he happened to place over the lamp flame. 'Immediately it rose with brilliancy. My brother started from his seat in ecstasy, rushed upon me with a transport of joy and embraced me with rapture.' Argand is credited also with adding a screw to alter the level of the wick. A further development made by Lange, one of his rivals in improving lamps, was a contraction of the chimney above the wick, which drove the air inwards to the flame, giving an even more intense light. By about 1815 the lamp gave light worth 7 to 8 candles.

An improvement after 1820 was a *spreader*, a small metal piece shaped like a mushroom or a circular T, which was set above the centre of the tubes and below the chimney contraction. This drove the flame outwards towards the glass and increased the combustion even more. About 1840, when the lamp with its single circular wick had received all these improvements, its power was rated at 10 candles.

Argand made his discovery about 1781 while seeking to improve the lighting of a distillery which he had established near Montpellier in France. In 1783 he took his lamp to Paris, hoping to arrange for its manufacture on a large scale. There he assisted the Montgolfier brothers in their famous balloon trials: they thought that the lamp would provide heating during the air-flights. Several of Argand's companions in this enterprise afterwards claimed some of the credit for perfecting the lamp. In 1784 he brought a specimen lamp to London and arranged for its production in England by a manufacturer named Hunter, and in 1785 he began to make lamps at Gex in France. When his workshops were destroyed during the French Revolution of 1789 he retired to Geneva and occupied himself with designing reflectors suitable for lighting streets, factories, churches and houses.

The success of these double-air-current lamps in France and England increased the demand for sperm oil after 1784 and whale-hunters suddenly found prosperity. But the Revolution and the subsequent wars with Britain soon cut off the supply of that oil to France and ruined her fisheries, and recourse was had to colza oil obtained locally from crushing the seeds of a wild cabbage. The outcome was surprising: cultivation of this plant on an increasing scale proved of great benefit to French agriculture. The only adjustment required in the argand lamp, in changing from sperm to colza oil, was a thicker wick. After 1845 colza oil was introduced into the British lighthouses as being the most suitable oil for their lamps.

Despite assistance from influential friends, Argand failed to get adequate protection for his wonderful invention and Quinquet and other lamp-makers in France produced lamps to his design from which no financial benefit accrued to him or his family. A petition presented to the British Government in 1793 suggested that he should be rewarded: it had been signed in England by 10 firms interested in the whale-fisheries, by 8 proprietors of workshops which profited from making his lamps and by George Robinson *pourvoyeur et surveillant* of sea-lights to Trinity House and Greenwich Hospital. But a grant was not forthcoming and Argand died in poverty in Geneva in 1803. The petitioners declared that Argand's invention prevented shipwrecks on dangerous coasts, as only by using his lamp in a reflector could excessive smoke be avoided and a strong beam of light be obtained.

Argand lamps were first adopted for lighthouses by Trinity House at Portland in 1789 and by 1820 they had been installed at some 50 coastal lighthouses in Britain and Ireland, but at few lighthouses elsewhere. They were in use at many lighthouses about 1880 but wick lamps are found now at only a few lighthouses and these are of little importance.

FRENCH TRIALS OF LIGHTS 1783–8

The hostile attitude which seamen took up towards Sangrain's spherical reflector light at Cordouan, coupled with Teulère's account of its defects, induced the French Minister of Marine in 1785 to order an investigation into lighthouse illumination: probably it was carried out by Teulère and the philosopher Borda. Since 1783 various proposals for new types of lights had been put forward in France and the officials concerned with lighthouses were aware that a revolving light had been established at Carlsten in Sweden in 1781.

Teulère was credited with making a novel proposal in 1783 which was that 24 parabolic reflectors of 22″ diameter and 5″ focal distance should be arranged round a circle and rotated by clockwork in a lantern. He intended to give not a flashing light, but a continuous light which would fluctuate in intensity. To seamen it would not appear to be occulted or eclipsed except at a long distance or during poor visibility. From every direction the maximum light would be seen as each reflector came into view and no ship would find herself in the arc of darkness that occurred between reflectors. But the idea was not considered valuable and the apparatus was not constructed.

Some of the suggestions for new types of sea-lights were associated with Dieppe where Muletin, a clock-maker, designed in 1783 some undescribed revolving apparatus to produce lights with variable timing so that a mariner, watch in hand, could identify each lighthouse. Borda is said to have tried out in 1784 a revolving light using 5 reflectors. Le Moyne, Maire of Dieppe and Agent-Général des Pêches, experimented also, and Argand carried out tests which may have included revolving lights and lights waving or oscillating horizontally. Finally, a Journal recorded in 1787 that experiments which had been made at Dieppe in May would be repeated in the following November with an apparatus consisting of 3 revolving reflectors which, if fitted at a lighthouse, would give strong beams of light and sure identification from other lighthouses, or if fitted at a harbour would, in some undisclosed manner, give tidal information and assure mariners of making the harbour entrance in safety.

Accounts of these proposals and trials are confused, but it is certain that Argand's lamp was tested at Dieppe and that observations of revolving apparatus resulted in a recommendation to the Minister that a revolving light should be constructed for Cordouan: its preparation began in 1788.

BEACONS AT SANDBANKS 1784

A novel attempt to meet the difficulties of founding tall beacons at the edges of sandbanks was made by J. Pickernell in 1784. He designed an egg-shaped boat 35′ long and 25′ broad with a 65′ mast which carried a barrel-top surmounted by a 4′ arrow for a wind-vane. The vessel, containing 8 stone blocks each weighing $4\frac{1}{2}$ tons which were built-in during her construction on the river Thames, was towed out and sunk at the Gunfleet Hook, an exposed turning-point at a sandbank in the Thames estuary. The chief weakness of the design lay in the connection of the mast at its foot, but this was met to some extent by multiple fixings. The problem of keeping the mast upright after the vessel settled in the shifting sand remained unsolved, but even with its sloping mast Pickernell's seamark served a useful purpose in the Thames for many years. But his idea was not a success.

CORUNNA LIGHTED 1784–6

The ancient tower of Corunna seems to have been long without a light, but it appears again in lighthouse history about 1780 when the need for a lighthouse at this prominent point was felt greatly by ships of many nations. The British and Dutch consuls resident in Corunna petitioned the Spanish Government to put it into use as a lighthouse, the cost of repairs to be met by dues on ships entering the port. The tower was then 132' high and 31' square with 3 stone floors and its roof showed markings believed to have resulted from the use of navigation fires over a long period. The encircling stone stair had been demolished to provide building material for houses in the neighbourhood. The consuls' request was granted; a wooden staircase was constructed inside and lights were set in two turrets at the top. A more complete repair, begun in 1797, was commemorated by inscriptions in Latin and Spanish placed over the entrance.

CONTROL OF SCOTTISH LIGHTHOUSES 1786

The increase of seafaring round the Scottish coasts led to the establishment in 1786 of an independent Board of Trustees to erect and manage 4 lighthouses. This Board was probably the first Authority in the world to be established with the sole duty of managing a number of lighthouses on a national basis. The Trustees were lawyers and magistrates of the chief Scottish towns. Though they had no connection with sea affairs they formed the right opinion as to the most suitable lighting apparatus and did not hesitate to instal it at their first lighthouses: namely, parabolic reflectors arranged in circular tiers. Their

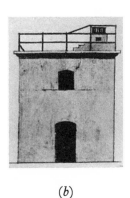

(a)   (b)   (c)

62. Lighthouses at (*a*) the Scaw in 1789, (*b*) Lindesnes in 1797, and (*c*) Falsterbo in 1792 (Martü). They lighted headlands in Denmark, Norway and Sweden

fixed lights gave so much satisfaction that seamen called for more lighthouses of the same type. By 1819 the Board, with the title after 1798 of *Commissioners for the Northern Lighthouses*, had established 12 lighthouses, and its jurisdiction had been extended to include the Isle of Man. The constitution of the Commission remains unchanged since 1786 and its members draw no payment for their services.

Their first lighthouse at Kinnaird Head, in which the reflectors were bunched together to avoid the usual dark sectors between them, held the most powerful fixed light of its time, for even distribution of light over a wide arc.

TRINITY HOUSE AND LIGHTHOUSES 1786

It is difficult to assess the attitude of Trinity House towards the English coastal lighthouses at this time. Judging by its actions and not by its protestations, the determination of the Corporation to erect lighthouses had never been strong: before 1806, whenever possible, it had passed on to lessees the duty of erecting them.

In 1786 it controlled lighthouses at 4 places: at Caister and Lowestoft (both managed in virtue of its local buoyage dues), and at Winterton and Scilly (both erected by the Corporation to thwart individuals keen to profit from dues under Crown patents). In 1786 failure of negotiations with a prospective lessee forced the Corporation to build lights at Needles and Hurst, a proceeding that might indicate that the Brethren would thenceforth be prepared to erect coastal lights. But any such expectation would have been misplaced for, though they obtained patents for 6 new lighthouses between 1786 and 1819, they passed 3 to lessees as formerly (Longships, Mumbles and Burnham), and erected 3 themselves (Happisburgh, Flamborough and South Stack). As the Happisburgh lights replaced the old lights at Caister and so could not be passed on to a lessee, it may be considered that Flamborough, erected in 1806, was the first lighthouse to be established freely by Trinity House. The Corporation reverted to its former procedure in 1815 when it established lighthouses at Burnham and passed them on to a lessee. Yet after 1786 the Brethren did not hesitate to take over the management of lighthouses when the leases expired and they even went out of their way to take over management of Longships and Farnes where the leases had several years to run. Perhaps the reason for leasing lighthouses as soon as they received the patents was simply that the Brethren did not wish to divert large sums of money from their charities to meet the capital costs of building them; when the periods of the leases expired, the lighthouses would fall into their possession, under the patents, without any payments by them. The circumstances of lightships were entirely different.

There can be no doubt that in 1786 Trinity House took a keen interest in lighting apparatus. The Brethren must have been aware of the excellence of the argand lamp which was manufactured in London but they were undecided on the merits of reflectors, as to which their own experience had been unsatisfactory. The spangle light which they installed at Lowestoft in 1778 had been a failure and the reflectors, of which particulars are not known, which they ordered in 1779–80 for Casquets, Portland and Lowestoft had also turned out ill—one can conclude that this was so from no mention of the results in their Minutes, from no repetition of the orders, and from official statements in 1818 and 1835 on behalf of the Corporation that the introduction of parabolic reflectors and argands into the English lighthouses originated not from its own experiences before 1786 but from a visit to French lighthouses and from subsequent tests of reflectors in England. It was well known that parabolic reflectors had served satisfactorily for lighting channels at Liverpool since 1772 and at Hunstanton since 1778: it is likely that the Brethren did not believe that such reflectors, which lighted only narrow arcs, could be arranged to light a wide horizon adequately, without producing arcs of darkness which might mislead navigators.

TRINITY HOUSE VISIT TO FRANCE *c.* 1787

Doubtless the usual careful scrutiny of happenings on the French coast revealed to the British Government the tests of lights that were taking place at Dieppe. Whenever the news reached Trinity House its representatives crossed the Channel to see the reflectors and argand lamps on trial. A full contemporary account of the proceedings was lost when the House was destroyed by fire on 30th December 1940 as a result of the bombing of London. Even the date of the visit and the names of the lights viewed do not appear in the Elder Brethren's Minutes which have been preserved, but it is recorded elsewhere that they installed reflectors and argand lamps first at the Portland lighthouses in 1788–9 after a series of tests in England extending over two years which followed a visit to France, so one would suppose that the visit took place in 1787. That what the deputation viewed was a trial of a revolving light at Dieppe, probably the apparatus under test in 1787, is supported by Teulère's statement in 1803 that, in designing the Scilly light of 1790, the English had copied a little revolving light at Dieppe harbour; and by the fact that argand-type lamps were on trial there and were not used at any of the French coastal lighthouses before 1790.

TRINITY HOUSE TRIALS OF LIGHTS 1787–9

What the Elder Brethren saw on their French visit induced them immediately to carry out experiments with reflectors and lamps. They erected a temporary beacon at Shooter's Hill, Blackheath, near London and, after completion of their own tests there, they invited, probably by newspaper advertisement, any persons with proposals for improved lighting to send apparatus for test. In response to this invitation Thomas Rogers submitted a lens light. The best apparatus was then transferred to the Portland lighthouses where tests were resumed under practical conditions for sea-lights. No record exists of any of the tests.

The apparatus fitted subsequently at Trinity House lighthouses included parabolic, conical and *square* reflectors, and lenses. The square reflectors were plates of mirror glass either flat or shaped to some peculiar curve according to the fancy of the inexpert designer: such ineffective reflectors were tried at other navigation lights.

CORDOUAN ALTERATIONS 1788–90

When investigating the complaints about Sangrain's reflectors at Cordouan, Teulère came to the conclusion that the light was too low for the range required. To raise it would involve a radical reconstruction of the lighthouse and this expensive operation was decided on in the knowledge that extensive repairs to its stonework were necessary and could conveniently be carried out at the same time. Accordingly, Teulère removed the upper half of the structure and re-built it to a simpler design chosen in Paris after consideration of

several alternatives. The large apartments designed by de Foix remained unaltered
Much skill was shown in harmonising the new tower with the original base from which part
of the elaborate ornamentation was removed because it too was decayed.

ROGERS'S LENS LIGHT 1788–9

In 1791 William Hutchinson published an account of the first use of a lens at a lighthouse. He stated that, having heard that Trinity House offered its Blackheath tower for
experiments, Thomas Rogers 'got reflectors blown in one piece of glass to their form and
by a new method silvered over the convex side with silver leaf, made them very bright good
reflectors, and had what I call a large circular patent lamp, three inches diameter, consequently, the wick nine inches round, stands at the focus of the reflector, and before it is a

(a)   (b)

63. Lighthouses in 1782 at (a) Scio and (b) Metelin in the east Mediterranean (Dawburn)

plain convex lense of solid glass twenty-one inches diameter and five inches and half-inch
thick in the focus, which makes the light answer the principle of the Magic lantern upon an
enlarged scale'. His reflectors were then only 12″ in diameter but he intended to make
them 18″. 'He reckoned he would not lose one ray of light from going through his lenses.'
Rogers's system of a plano-convex lens with reflector has the technical description of
catadioptric. He used the lens to collect and concentrate many of the rays which escape
from the front of a lamp and used the reflector to collect and return to the flame the rays
falling upon it from the back of the lamp. Clearly his reflector was spherical, though
no contemporary account mentions its type of curve. It cannot have added more than
10 per cent. to the light passing through his lens, which was thick in the centre and
absorbed much of the light falling upon it from the flame.
As the Brethren left Rogers's catadioptric light in operation at Portland high lighthouse
when they finished their tests there, it is clear that they approved of his arrangement.
Drummond mentions, however, as explained in Section XVI, that when they substituted
an argand of 1″ diameter wick for Rogers's lamp of 3″ diameter wick they found that they
had reduced the divergence so much that they had to replace his spherical reflector by a
parabolic one. His patent lamp had not been so satisfactory as an argand lamp.
Robert Stevenson noted at Portland in 1801 that Rogers's lenses were incorporated in
alternate lantern panes and were intended to distinguish the lighthouse from others, not

to give a powerful light. After Portland, Rogers fitted them in 1790 at Howth near Dublin where, according to Hutchinson, 'the report of them seems incredible and to very great advantage in hazy and foggy weather', at the Hook tower in 1791, at North Foreland in 1792 and at other coastal and harbour lighthouses in Ireland. All his lights were removed from the Irish lighthouses about 1812 and replaced by better types. They were kept in use at Portland after 1818 and at North Foreland until 1834.

Augustin Fresnel, whose production in 1823 of a dioptric or lenticular light is one of the most important events in the history of lighthouses, mentions in a scientific *mémoire* of 1822 which describes his light that 'il existe, en effet, un phare lenticulaire en Angleterre'. This was the lighthouse at North Foreland. Fresnel added that he did not have precise details of that light except that its flash was of little brilliancy, perhaps due to the great thickness of the lenses which he understood was 20 mm. or 8″. Actually the thickness was 5″ whereas the thickness of the lens at the centre of a modern 1st-order or a 2nd-order lenticular light is under 1·5″.

In 1786 Thomas Rogers described himself as a glass-cutter of the parish of St. Mary-le-Strand in the liberty of Westminster. In that year he was granted a patent in England and Berwick-upon-Tweed for a method of attaching by varnish or glue to looking-glasses and furniture, glass outlines or cut-outs representing flowers and leaves.

Reflector and Argand Lights 1789–99

Trinity House did not instal Rogers's catadioptric light except at Portland high light-house. Elsewhere it fitted metal parabolic reflectors of 18″ or 20½″ diameter with argand lamps and pressed the patentees and lessees of the English private lighthouses to fit similar apparatus. Howard supplied it for Dungeness, Robinson probably elsewhere. By 1799 parabolic reflectors and argands had been fitted at various dates at the following 11 English lighthouses, making the south and south-east coasts of England the best-lighted in the world:

TRINITY HOUSE LIGHTS	PRIVATE LIGHTS
1789 Portland	1791 Winterton
1790 Casquets	1792 Dungeness
1790 Scilly	1793 South Foreland
1791 Happisburgh	1793 Orfordness
1792 Cromer	1795 Longships
1796 Lowestoft	

Control of U.S.A. Lighthouses 1789

By an Act dated 7th August 1789 the first United States Congress took over from the former Colonies their coastal lighthouses and agreed to maintain them thereafter. The number of lighthouses is sometimes given as 8, but the 12 that were established at various dates previously, as described in Section XI, seem to have been transferred:

1716 Boston	1767 Charleston
1746 Brant Point	1768 Gurnet, Plymouth
1749 Beaver Tail	1771 Portsmouth
1761 New London	1771 Cape Ann
1764 Sandy Hook	1784 Great Point
1765 Cape Henlopen	1788 Newburyport

In all, 24 lighthouses were established by 1800. Congress placed the lights under the control of the Secretary of the Treasury and gave him authority to erect others. He attended to the lighthouse business personally at his office but obtained the approval of the

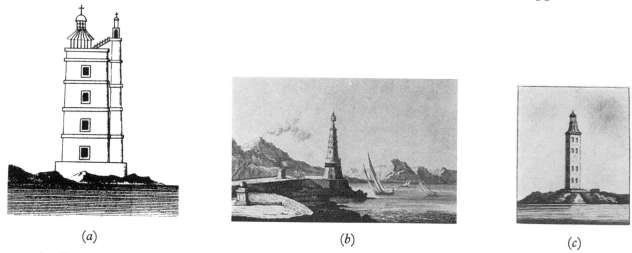

(*a*)   (*b*)   (*c*)

64. European lighthouses shortly before 1800: (*a*) Chassiron in France, (*b*) Naples and (*c*) Corunna

President before taking any important action concerning them. In 1792 control passed to the Commissioner of Revenue but returned to the Secretary of the Treasury in 1802. In 1813 it passed again to the Commissioner of Revenue and on 1st July 1820 it was transferred to the Fifth Auditor of the Treasury with the management of 55 lighthouses. In 1851 a new Lighthouse Service was established, which was answerable to the Treasury.

FRENCH AND ENGLISH REVOLVING LIGHTS 1790

The most valuable results of the French and English trials of lights before 1789 were the establishment of revolving lights in 1790: at Cordouan in France in August and at the Scilly Isles in England in October. At Cordouan 4 metal parabolic reflectors of 32″ diameter were set vertically on each of 3 sides of a rotating frame and at the Scillies 7 metal reflectors of probably 18″ diameter were arranged somewhat similarly with parabolic reflectors at two sides, and conical reflectors which gave a poor light at the other. Each flash or period of light was emitted from 22·4 square feet of parabolic reflecting surface at Cordouan and from 12·46 square feet at the Scilly Isles. On these figures, if the lamps and focal distance had been identical, the flashes should have been 80 per cent. more powerful at Cordouan. Apart from a small harbour light shown from Dieppe some time between 1791 and 1799, no other revolving light was constructed in France until 1818, by which date 18 were established in Great Britain and Ireland.

The Scilly apparatus was probably somewhat 'rough and ready' in construction but it gave a good result, whereas the Cordouan apparatus was disappointing, perhaps being too ambitious and not so practical. A French account of the time describes the Scilly light incorrectly as consisting of two rows of 8 reflectors of 30″ diameter 'dont la fabrication est si soignée que chacun d'eux a coûté 50 livres sterlings'. Robinson charged high prices but probably not as much as this.

REFUGES FOR SAILORS 1791

In 1791 a stone beacon was constructed at Duon in France purely for navigational needs, and the opportunity was taken to fit it as a refuge for ship-wrecked sailors. The idea that beacons erected round the coasts and furnished with boxes of food and clothing might help sailors was current particularly in England about 1830–50, but it was extremely unlikely that they would be of the slightest practical use for that purpose.

POLHEIMER'S COAL FIRE 1792

Commencing in 1788, Anders Polheimer, who had interests in coal-mining, investigated the operation of the coal-burning Swedish lighthouses of Nidingen, Kullen, Falsterbo and Grönskär, and then devised a new form of grate which he fitted first at Kullen in the summer of 1792. He left it open to the air, as was usual in Sweden, but he provided that the light-keeper could regulate the fire in the grate by means of a door set in the space between the walls. When this was opened a strong draught passing upwards through a pipe induced a brighter and more uniform blaze from the coals. Before and after installing the new grate the keepers at Kullen recorded nightly the quantity of coals burned, the weather conditions and the direction and force of the wind. The records revealed that the economy resulting from the alteration was merely proportional to the reduction in the size of the grate, but seamen enjoyed a better beacon fire.

BEACONS ON EXPOSED ROCKS 1795

As described in Section IX, Trinity House in 1791 leased the Wolf Rock near Lands End to Henry Smith for the erection of a lighthouse, but as he came to the conclusion that he could not carry out such a difficult work the Brethren agreed that, instead, he should erect a lighthouse on the higher Longships Rock and beacons on the low-lying Wolf and Rundlestone Rocks, all in the same area. A tower was soon established on the Longships to the design of the Trinity House architect, and on the Wolf Rock Smith undertook to set a

(a)

(b)

65. English harbour lights shortly before 1800: (a) the tower housing the south pier light at Sunderland (the rear tower was erected on the north pier in 1803) and (b) the Ramsgate light

wrought-iron mast 20' high and 4" in diameter with 6 stays, surmounted by a metal model of a wolf, but the beacon which he put up in 1795 was slightly less substantial than had been specified. Though it offered little resistant surface to the waves, the sea carried it away immediately. His mast on the Rundlestone met a similar fate. It was not surprising that Smith had under-estimated the force of the sea: the difficulty and expense of erecting permanent beacons on these exposed Rocks was confirmed 40 years later. For the Wolf Rock, James Walker designed a beacon consisting of a concrete core enclosed within iron plates and having a base 16' in diameter and a height of 16'. It would be founded at half-tide. With an average of $30\frac{1}{4}$ working hours obtained over 5 seasons, the beacon was completed successfully by John Thorburn in 1840 at a cost of £11,298. At the Rundlestone Rock, the small area of the foundation allowed fixture of an iron mast 6" in diameter. After two masts had been destroyed by ships and a third washed away by the seas, Walker abandoned the project and marked the Rock by a buoy.

SOUTH ROCK LIGHTHOUSE 1793-7

By fitting his lens lights into Howth lighthouse Thomas Rogers got an introduction before 1790 to the Authority controlling the Irish lighthouses. In 1792 he severed his connection with George Robinson and decided to remain in Ireland where he erected lighthouses and obtained a contract for managing them.

His originality extended from the practical introduction of the lens into lighthouses to the design of lighthouse towers.

The most interesting lighthouse that he built was the Kilwarlin tower on the South Rock, a reef in the Irish Channel, 3 miles off the coast and near the entrance to Loch Strangford. This lighthouse might fairly be named 'the forgotten lighthouse'. Mention of it is omitted from most books referring to seamarks, largely because its lighting was discontinued in 1877 when the lightkeepers were removed. But it deserves notice as one of the small number of lighthouses built before 1820 whose towers were exposed directly to the waves. In design and construction it owed little to the Eddystone towers.

The tower was built of stone and was reinforced by vertical iron rods connecting iron plates built-in as the structure rose, a novel method of reinforcement that was adopted afterwards, with modifications, in somewhat similar structures. The operations described in Section X were begun in 1793 and were concluded in 1797.

VI

PROGRESS 1800 TO 1820

AND

A SURVEY OF SEAMARKS IN 1819

66. An imaginary scene *c.* 1810 with ships being driven ashore. The lighthouse is like
Smeaton's Eddystone and would be too elaborate for such a harbour entrance

67. Macquarie lighthouse in Australia constructed in 1817, from a painting by
Sainson *c*. 1830.   The base of the parapet on the top of the tower may have been
circular and the diameter of the lantern larger than 6′ 6″ as was recorded

VI. PROGRESS 1800 TO 1820

In this period, reflecting apparatus was improved and new types of lights were evolved. The advance in lighting was most marked in the British Isles where argand lamps, revolving lights and coloured beams were fitted extensively. In France, scientists and manufacturers endeavoured to produce lamps giving more light and to calculate the candlepower of lighthouse beams. The Bell Rock lighthouse was the most notable structure.

THIEVILLE'S PRISMATIC SEGMENTS 1800

When one reads that prisms and lenses 'might be adopted with great advantage for lighthouses erected on the sea coasts, by directing their foci in such a manner that they should be perceptible to a great distance at sea in every point and that no point should be left dark', one would suppose that the writer understood thoroughly the dioptric system of illuminating lighthouses. Yet Count Thieville, who wrote these words in 1800, seems to have had no contact with lighthouse illumination and to have lacked knowledge of optics as well as incentive to turn his words into effect. Before 1791 he and Smethurst had been rivals in lighting London thoroughfares: their oil lamps illumined Sloane Street and Westminster Bridge. They endeavoured by trial and error to utilise the refractive qualities of cut-glass with the object of reducing the numbers of lamps required to light a particular area. Cutting facets on glass cylinders and bottles and thus producing what Thieville termed *prismatic segments* and setting them with *bull's eye* lenses 2″ or 3″ in diameter in front of oil lamps to concentrate patches of light upon walls and pavements was the limit of his suggestion and achievement in dioptric lighting, and his diagrams do not show a full understanding of the passage of light-rays through glass.

GAS FROM WOOD 1800

A system of distilling gas from wood and burning it in the lantern from crude jets at the ends of pipes was introduced at Porkkala lighthouse in Finland in 1800. Figures of costs supported the claim that this system of lighting was economical, but it received no general application to lighthouses. Probably gas-making caused too much labour for the lightkeepers.

BI-CATOPTRIC REFLECTOR 1802

One of the last incidents of Argand's life was his demonstration to Danish Government envoys at Geneva in September 1802 of his lamp set at the focus of a reflector which was partly a paraboloid and partly an ellipsoid. He hoped to obtain for a sea-light the advantage of the first curve in condensing the light into a narrow beam and that of the second in increasing the angle of spread. Arrangements for a trial at sea were abandoned after his death in 1803.

BORDIER-MARCET'S REFLECTORS 1802–33

About 1802 J. A. Bordier-Marcet re-built Argand's workshops in Paris and began the construction of lamps and reflectors of different shapes and of excellent workmanship which met with a ready sale for lighting streets and interiors of buildings.   He effected no improvement of the argand lamp but his mind was filled to overflowing with novel ideas for utilising the light-reflecting properties of the parabola.   Ceaselessly up to 1833, he demonstrated his apparatus at Expositions and bombarded municipal and maritime Authorities and the public at large in France and abroad with pamphlets and press-notices about reflectors. He designed for marine lights three ingenious variations of the parabolic reflector combined with the argand lamp, of which, for lack of better apparatus, two had a limited success in France.   If a powerful lamp had been at his disposal, it is likely that he would have produced reflecting lights unequalled in power for years to come, which would have changed the course of lighthouse illumination towards catoptric apparatus (with mirrors) and away from dioptric apparatus (with lenses and prisms) to which it was directed by Fresnel.   Bordier-Marcet gave the following names to the sea-lights which he invented:

> *fanal à double effet*, produced in 1808,
> *fanal sidéral*, produced in 1809, and
> *fanal à double aspect*, produced in 1823 but never used for coast lighting.

As soon as the Napoleonic wars ended, he offered his apparatus to Trinity House with a claim that he could supply lights superior to those at the English lighthouses.   In December 1816 the Corporation acknowledged his descriptions of the *fanal à double effet* and the *fanal sidéral* and, in sending him 25 guineas, stated that in the opinion of all seamen the English lights were so excellent that their improvement was neither required nor possible.   The Corporation added that if his apparatus were so superior, as he claimed it to be, why had it not been adopted for many French lighthouses?   Bordier-Marcet commented 'les Anglais specialement sont très vain de leurs phares' and regretted that his communication to the Brethren had been translated so poorly into English that half of it must have been incomprehensible to them.   He supposed that they had not understood his proposals.

Aware that he alone had produced variations of the parabolic reflector and declaring that his inventions had assured for reflectors 'the sceptre in marine lighting', Bordier-Marcet announced in 1818 that he had, in consequence, given France the leadership in lighthouse optics.   But in 1823 he had to acknowledge that the beam of the newly-produced lenticular light of Fresnel combined with a multiple-wick lamp had surpassed in power that of the finest reflector lights in France.   However, despite the dawn of the dioptric system, he endeavoured still to compete against it by producing his *fanal à double aspect*, a clever arrangement of reflectors without practical merit.   About 1830 he constructed a *fanal sidéral* of giant proportions with a diameter of 1·95 metres and having a cluster of 27 argand lamps around the focus.   The French Lighthouse Commission viewed this huge apparatus but did not adopt it, deciding that Fresnel's dioptric light gave better illumination from less oil.

Bordier-Marcet's designs are illustrated in Section XVI.

RED AND WHITE FLASHES 1806

For the illumination of a new lighthouse on Flamborough Head in England, Trinity House introduced a colour characteristic said to have been suggested by Benjamin Milne, Customs agent at Bridlington. His inventiveness extended to a proposal to harness the energy of a neighbouring rill of water to rotate reflectors at the lighthouse, but that part of his scheme was turned down as impracticable. Establishment of this lighthouse followed a campaign by Milne who pressed seamen and merchants throughout Britain to subscribe towards the cost.

The Flamborough light was made red and white revolving, the first use of colour in this way. A rotating vertical axle carried 21 parabolic reflectors, 7 on each of the 3 sides of the frame. Red glass covered all the reflectors on one side. Thus one red beam or flash succeeded two white beams and produced a striking characteristic; but the red glass absorbed so much of the light that the normal range of the coloured beam was reduced to about 56 per cent. of that of the white ones. Beyond 12 miles distance, only the white beams were perceptible and then only in good visibility.

Robinson had great difficulty in obtaining whole sheets of red glass of $20\frac{1}{2}''$ diameter and it was said that he applied to most of the glass-makers in England before he could procure *flashed* glass, which had been heated after the colouring chemicals were applied to a surface: the colour had not been mixed throughout the *pot-metal*.

ROBINSON'S LENSES *c.* 1806

When Robert Stevenson and one of his foremen visited Flamborough lighthouse in September and December 1809 they noticed that Robinson had placed a lens $4\frac{1}{2}''$ in diameter in front of the flame of each argand lamp. Winslow Lewis saw similar lenses at the South Stack lighthouse which was lighted in February 1809. It is not known who designed them: probably the idea was taken from Rogers's lenses. The lenses were too small and thick to be useful and they were soon removed from both lighthouses. The same foreman visited the new lighthouses at the Farnes in April 1810 and noted that lenses were not fitted there.

HYDROGEN GAS LIGHTS 1806

The well-known Birmingham engineering firm of Boulton and Watt, of which James Watt of steam-engine fame was one of the founders, hoped to produce a light from burning hydrogen in the air that would be suitable for lighthouses and, probably in association with Captain Huddart, the hydrographer, carried out experiments throughout this year but they did not achieve success.

LIGHTSHIP LANTERNS 1807

When mooring a lightship temporarily at the Bell Rock in 1807 Stevenson designed lanterns to encircle the masts and to be lowered to the deck for the servicing of the lamps. This arrangement was an improvement on the practice of suspending lanterns from cumbrous yards or frames, which he found in use in the English lightships. His lanterns contained a ring of 10 small *agitable* oil lamps each with a cotton-thread wick and a tiny parabolic reflector of $3''$ focus. He recorded that the lights then shown from lightships, including his own, were feeble and lacking in the candlepower that the situations required.

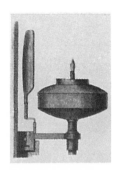

68. Stevenson's agitable lamp with parabolic reflector had a candlepower of 10. It was unaffected by the rolling of the Bell Rock lightship

69. The Nore lightship in February 1809 when the *Thames Smack* of Dundee ran on the Nore sand. Her captain and crew deserted the ship and 4 women passengers, unwilling to get up the shrouds, were swept off by the waves before help came

LIGHTSHIPS OUTWITH THE BRITISH ISLES 1807–19

In the autumn of 1807 a large hanging-lantern with a supply of oil was sent out by Trinity House to Denmark in charge of an artificer familiar with the English lightships. He assisted in the conversion of the fireship *Fury* into a lightship and she was moored 6 miles N.N.W. from the Scaw to aid the British fleet operating in Danish waters. But she failed to hold that exposed position and was withdrawn after a month. A Danish drawing of that year shows a *vippefyr* on a lightship, which may be the same vessel; a pole pivoted on the mast 20' above the water-line was raised by a pulley to an angle of 45° so that the lantern was suspended 45' above the water.

About 1812 a lightship was moored on the London Chest shoal at the east end of the Gulf of Finland and in 1815 lightships were tried in Germany and were soon established permanently in the Elbe and Weser estuaries.

Before 1817 a lightship was moored at the entrance to the river Hughli in India with a lantern containing 8 reflector lights arranged in a circle, as in the Bell Rock temporary vessel. She was moored by 14" tarred coir cables and a 14-cwt wood-stocked anchor, but she broke adrift frequently.

The difficulty and expense of mooring and provisioning a lightship, the exposure and danger to which her crew was exposed, and the comparatively miserable light of under 50 candlepower, the utmost that she could exhibit, made all countries reluctant to establish such seamarks.

FANAL À DOUBLE EFFET 1808

Bordier-Marcet exhibited at the Institut de France in 1808 a bi-catoptric light, somewhat similar to the apparatus demonstrated by Argand in 1802: it also was built up of a paraboloid and an ellipsoid. On its trial as a sea-light at Havre the result was unsatisfactory, as the compromise of merging two different curves in the design halved the concentration of light obtainable from a complete parabolic reflector without gaining sufficient compensation from the wider spread of weak light from the elliptic portion. Haudry, the engineer of the port, suggested a combination of a paraboloid and a cone, one of the shapes used at the Scilly light of 1790, and observed there to be imperfect in 1801, but Bordier-Marcet rightly rejected it, knowing that it would be unsuitable for a sea-light.

Instead, he designed a new type of reflector which he named *fanal à double effet*. This apparatus consisted of 2 conjoined reflectors, one encircling the other, with 2 argand lamps set on the common axis about 9″ apart horizontally. Each reflector emitted along that line,

70. The pharillon or lighthouse of Alexandria in 1801 (Willyams)

71. The lighthouse at Vera Cruz, said to be a reflector light, *c.* 1815

over the usual angle of divergence, the light falling upon it from the lamp placed at its own focus, and scattered over a larger angle the rays falling upon it from the other lamp.

The *fanal* was tested against Sangrain's spherical reflector with a flat-wick lamp and, having proved the immense advantage of the parabolic reflectors of which it consisted, was fitted at La Hève in 1811 and after 1819 at other French lighthouses. Its evident superiority to Sangrain's apparatus blinded the observers to the defects in its design: these remained undetected in France until Fresnel pointed them out in 1819.

FANAL SIDÉRAL 1809

Bordier-Marcet's next parabolic light, which he named *fanal sidéral* or *star-lantern*, consisted of two circular reflecting metal plates, one arranged above a flame and the other below it. The flame was in the centre. They were shaped to show a parabolic curve in all horizontal directions. This was the first optical apparatus that was capable of spreading light equally round the horizon. It condensed or concentrated a large part of the vertical light and reflected it horizontally towards the seaman.

The first of these *fanaux* was tried at Honfleur in 1809 and the seamen, finding it so excellent, called it *notre salut* or *our salvation*. This admirable contrivance increased tenfold the power of the argand flame, to some 70 candles. It was used with much benefit at French harbours: at 16 by 1829. In 1889 several of these apparatuses were still in service.

STEVENSON'S EXPERIMENTS *c.* 1809–11

Robert Stevenson observed Flamborough light from the sea in 1809 and, recognising the advantage of its colour distinction, carried out two series of experiments with many colours, using as light-filters coloured fluids sealed between sheets of white glass. He also tried red chimneys and sheets of green glass of which the first consignment was rejected as being of too poor a quality, and found red to be the best colour as an alternative to a white or natural light.   He desired to experiment with lenses and applied to Rogers without avail for one of his 22″ lenses.   In October 1810 he had 24 small lenses made in London by Pellet and Green at a cost of about £7. 10. 0, and mounted in brass rings by Lawton and Debaufer.   These were of clear glass and he ordered large lenses of red glass.   Presumably the small lenses were copies of Robinson's.   The experiments were made at Inchkeith lighthouse, of which he had a view from his house in Edinburgh, but as he did not fit lenses at a lighthouse one can assume that he found them useless.

DISTANCE CALCULATIONS FROM LIGHTHOUSES 1810

A rule by which navigators might obtain their distances from lights by observing their relative brightness was devised by Andrew Mackay, a teacher of navigation.   In 1810 he published a formula involving logarithms, for estimating the position of a ship from observations of two lights of known intensities 'and thereby, perhaps [to] prevent some of those fatal consequences which too often appear'.   Unfortunately at that date, tables showing the intensities of lighthouse lights were not issued to seamen, but even if lists had been available, it would have been impossible to estimate, by the visual comparison demanded, the relative brightness of different lights.   So Mackay's idea, however excellent in theory, proved impracticable.   He took into account the law of optics which states that the candle-power of a light varies inversely as the square of its distance from the observer.

LEWIS'S CATADIOPTRIC LIGHTS 1810

A remarkable story in lighthouse history is that of Winslow Lewis, a retired sea-captain, who sold to the United States Government in 1812 a patent for lights incorporating a lens and a mirror and, in addition, obtained a contract to install his apparatus in all its light-houses.   Further, the Treasury appointed him to supervise them.   The reason for this business success was entirely financial: he undertook to save much money by halving the quantity of oil which they consumed.   Such an attractive proposition dazzled the American Treasury and blinded it to the possibility that the lights might suffer.

Lewis took the idea from Robinson's lens lights which he observed at the South Stack lighthouse in England.   Some years elapsed before American navigators appreciated fully the worthlessness of the lenses which he fitted and voiced their condemnation of his lights.   The offending apparatus was removed gradually.

Lewis's patent had the title of *a reflecting and magnifying lantern;* details are unknown as the patent records were destroyed by fire.   He was born near Cape Cod in 1770 and died in 1850.   In the war of 1812 he commanded the Sea Fencibles at Boston where he owned a rope-works and served on the local Council.

BELL ROCK LIGHTHOUSE 1807–11

The year 1811 saw the exhibition of a light upon the Inchcape or Bell Rock, a reef 11 miles off the Scottish coast, the most difficult situation yet chosen for a lighthouse.   Below highwater there had to be deposited 25 times the amount of stone required below that level at Smeaton's Eddystone tower, and the lowest complete course was set some 12′ lower. The light was made revolving, showing red and white beams alternately.

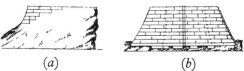

(a)   (b)

72. The bases of (a) the Eddystone and (b) the Bell Rock towers between high and low water, showing in elevation the extent of the stonework set below sea level at each lighthouse

The completion of the tower in 4 seasons was due to careful planning, ready improvisation and the continuous employment of comparatively large numbers of men and much shipping as described in Section XIII. This was the last sea-tower erected before steam-vessels were available to transport building materials. Today, unaltered and without having required repair, it stands on the Inchcape reef, serving its original purpose.

Robert Stevenson had the responsibility of making the plans and constructing the lighthouse after consultation with John Rennie before 1807.

FOG SIGNALS 1811

The mechanical operation of a fog signal may have been carried out first at the Bell Rock where the machine for revolving the reflectors of the light also operated the striking

(a)   (b)

73 (a) and (b). Italian proposals for automatic fog signals, using the wind to strike gongs and bells before 1820

of a bell every 30 seconds during fog and snow-showers. About this time the operation of bells mechanically by the wind seems to have been attempted in Italy and clockwork to be actuated by the rise and fall of the tide was designed to ring a bell at the Carr Rock beacon.

FRENCH LIGHTHOUSE COMMISSION 1811

Baron St. Holouen, a naval officer, evolved a plan in 1811 for distinguishing light-houses by a system of coloured lights. The Minister of Marine submitted it for examination to a Commission consisting of 3 naval officers, an inspector of naval construction, 3 members of the Ponts et Chaussées (the Department which carried out the public works of France) and two scientists of the Institut de France. The Commission rejected St. Holouen's proposal after tests at Meudon in 1813, but the Minister retained its members as a Board to advise him on lighthouse affairs and it gradually took over the management of the French lighthouses.

74. The lighthouse at Cadiz. The artist has reduced the size of the lantern which held a revolving apparatus. *c.* 1810

CARR ROCK BEACON 1813–21

Erecting a beacon 40′ high on a rock of small area below the level of low-water at an exposed situation was attempted at the Carr Rock, about two miles off the headland of Fife Ness in Scotland. Doubtless after completing the Bell Rock tower, Stevenson and his artificers supposed the work would be well within their capacity. The operations could be carried on only with a placid sea during the lowest tides. After most of the structure was built, a storm washed away the top, which they replaced by a weighty cast-iron cap of 8 tons surmounted by an open pyramid to a height of 29′. It was the first beacon to be founded at such a low level and this may have been the first use of cast-iron for a seamark.

FRENCH TESTS OF LAMPS AND REFLECTORS 1813–18

The French Lighthouse Commission instituted experiments with lighthouse lamps and reflectors which when extended bore valuable fruit in 1823 by the production of the famous lens light at Cordouan with its multiple-wick lamp.

In October 1813 tests began in the gardens of the Marine Dépôt in Paris of Lenoir's reflectors and argand lamps. As a result, no changes in reflectors were proposed but it was discovered that the wicks in Quinquet's lamps at Cordouan were consuming oil unnecessarily, Lenoir's short-focus reflectors being unable to concentrate into a small beam the volume of light produced by their large flames. The cause lay in the excessive diameter of the wicks. After determining the best diameter for single-wick argand lamps, the scientists Arago and Mathieu gave their attention to the design of multiple-wick lamps but, like other experimenters of the time, they were unable to overcome the effect of the excessive heat engendered, which cracked the glass chimneys, melted the metal wick-holders and boiled the oil.

THE FIRST AUSTRALIAN LIGHTHOUSE 1817

The cessation of the Napoleonic wars in 1815 freed shipping to roam the oceans and develop new trade with recently-discovered and backward countries. In consequence, the establishment of lighthouses proceeded apace and far afield. In 1817 the first important lighthouse in Australasia was established 341' above the sea at Macquarie at the entrance to Sydney harbour, then named Port Jackson.

Its circular stone tower 76' high carried an excellent lantern stated to be 15' high, containing a triangular iron frame to which were attached silvered parabolic reflectors, 3 on each side, with oil lamps 'like an ordinary hall lamp'. The frame revolved to give one flash every 100 seconds. Strangely, although it would take about 8 months to obtain duplicate parts from London, no spare reflector was supplied. The lamps consumed annually 330 gallons of the best sperm oil and the whole apparatus was made by Robinson. Three unmarried lightkeepers each receiving 70s. per month resided at the lighthouse and a superintendent receiving 5s. per day was given a separate house. They were permitted to attend church 1½ miles distant, 'two each alternate Sunday'.

The tower would form 'a monument for future ages to contemplate with pride'. It would be crowned with a frieze 'on which will be carried the four winds in *alto relievo* distributing their good and evil qualities from their drapery as they appear to fly round the tower'. Such was the curious account of the work which appeared in the *Gazette* of 20th May 1816, an Australian Journal.

SCANDINAVIAN COAL FIRE LANTERNS 1817

Though oil lamps and parabolic reflectors gave the best sea-lights at this time, the use of coal fires at lighthouses continued in Scandinavia and Denmark and their numbers increased in Sweden up to 1838. The reasons for the preference of coal fires in northern Europe are obscure: they may have been climatic. In 1817 a new type of enclosed coal fire was established at Kullen lighthouse in Sweden which was clearly advantageous over the usual open coal fire in giving a steady glow at less expense, and it was this type that was welcomed in that country.

COAL GAS LIGHTS 1818

About 1780 the *spirit of coals* or coal gas was believed to offer considerable advantages for the illumination of lighthouses and, on the suggestion of an elderly man named Champion, Trinity House spent some £500 in experiments to determine the point. But the brilliant column of light which he produced, 7″ diameter and 6′ high, was accompanied by such unreliability in exhibition that a trial at a lighthouse was not attempted.   In a later experiment, Captain Huddart found it impossible to obtain from a gas-jet as much light as he did from an argand lamp.

Trinity House took up the question of gas-lighting again about 1817 when the supply of spermaceti oil was becoming precarious.   Captain Cotton, an Elder Brother like Huddart, condemned this revived proposal to use gas and it was dropped.   He considered that its production would be uncertain and that the failure of a light 'might occasion infinite distress and loss at sea, a failure that never can occur with the argand lamp to the extent of total darkness or of much lapse of time before its renewal, when declining'.   He believed it improbable that coal gas would be used at lighthouses unless there was a failure in the supply of spermaceti oil, 'a contingency not impossible to occur . . . the whale is not so prolific

75. The flaming anchor of gas jets which was proposed
for Flatholm lighthouse *c.* 1818

as other fish'.   He added that 'independent of these reasons for not admitting this gas, it is incumbent on the Corporation to give that encouragement to the employment of seamen which the whale-fishery affords, the transit of the pit-coal from which the gas is extracted, being by barges on canals'.

The first important lighthouse to be lit by coal gas was at Salvore near Trieste which in April 1818 displayed a light obtained from treating Istrian coal.   The gas-producing plant at the lighthouse was designed by Giovanni Aldini and the project was acclaimed extensively as a wonderful enterprise.   But on the grounds of excessive expense and unreliability it was discontinued in 1824 in favour of a battery of lamps burning olive oil and without reflectors.

Aldini had been in touch with several English engineers, keen to develop coal gas-lighting.   Among them was T. S. Peckston who undertook by using gas to halve the cost of maintaining lighthouses.   He would instal a coal gas-producing plant at each lighthouse and in the lantern would set a large metal box with many holes of 1/30″ diameter.   From these, gas would emerge and the flames would unite to display in fire a different letter or sign according to a published list of lighthouses.   The box would be rotated to show the allotted sign gradually in every direction.   Dr. Wilkinson of Bath proposed to introduce Peckston's system at the Flatholm lighthouse: the sign which he had it in mind to adopt was an anchor picked out by the vivid flames.

A revolving reflector at Morro Castle lighthouse at Havana was lit by gas in 1818 but soon discontinued: the problem of supplying gas without leaks to a reflector carried on a rotating frame may have been too difficult to solve.

SYNCHRONISED REVOLVING LIGHTS 1818

In February two towers were established on sites 560′ apart on Calf island at the south end of the Isle of Man so that their line pointed the direction of a low-lying Rock extremely dangerous to navigation which was known as the Chickens. The two lanterns 375′ and 282′ above sea-level carried what were described as 'double-revolving and leading-lights without colour', which would appear in good visibility like two stars of the first magnitude at 6 to 7 leagues. Synchronisation of their revolutions was checked from time to time by the lightkeepers so that at the same instant in every direction the lights were either visible or eclipsed. This characteristic was effective as giving a clear distinction from other lighthouses, but the expense of establishing two adjacent towers each with a revolving apparatus could be justifiable only where, as in this instance, an out-lying danger or a navigable channel must be indicated by special means. The Calf towers were discontinued in 1875 when a sea-tower was constructed on the Chickens Rock.

FRESNEL JOINS FRENCH COMMISSION 1819

The urgent need to improve the French lighthouses brought about the appointment of Augustin Fresnel in 1819 as Secretary to the Commission, with the additional duty of investigating lighthouse apparatus. This French scientist, born in 1788, had made his mark already with *mémoires* on optics which demonstrated his outstanding genius.

Immediately after his appointment the Commission had an instance of his understanding of the subject. In October 1819 Bordier-Marcet's newly-completed optical apparatus for Baleines lighthouse, consisting of 10 *fanaux à double effet*, was set on the Arc de l'Etoile in Paris for observation by the members of the Commission, and they were startled by Fresnel's remark that practically the same result as was got from this double parabolic reflector and 2 lamps in a line would be obtainable merely from one ordinary parabolic reflector with two lamps set abreast—one on each side of its focus.

In the same month Fresnel put forward a proposal to construct a refracting apparatus consisting entirely of lenses and prisms and was authorised to spend 500 francs in its manufacture; with Arago he began a series of experiments with multiple-wick lamps. These trials concluded successfully in 1823 when his first lenticular apparatus with a new type of lamp shone forth from Cordouan lighthouse, with a revolving beam surpassing in power any produced before that date.

A SURVEY OF SEAMARKS IN 1819

For an assessment of seamarks in 1819 particulars are available in the countries which had the more advanced lighthouse systems; in the others, where records have disappeared or were never kept, sea-charts and pilotage books indicate the state of their navigation aids.

BEACONS

By 1820 beacons were established in most countries in large numbers which cannot be estimated. The usual forms were the spar or tower of wood and the pillar of stone, often with a topmark or painted to facilitate identification and give direction.

Difficulties beyond expectation had been experienced in establishing beacons on rocks exposed to ocean waves as on the Wolf and Rundlestone Rocks in England, Boon island in the United States and the Carr Rock in Scotland. Though these unlighted marks did not require keepers and need not be so substantial as lighthouses, their foundations had to be secure or their cost would have been in vain. Therefore their design had to ensure that they were conspicuous to the seaman yet not so large as to offer undue resistance to the sea.

BUOYS

Large numbers of buoys, the most useful of seamarks, were laid down in many countries but they were not so numerous as the beacons. In 1818 Trinity House alone maintained 75 buoys in the Thames estuary and along sandbanks off south-east England.

The diameter of the buoys rarely exceeded 5′ and they were made of wood of various shapes (can, conical or nun, and spherical) with topmarks and were coloured. Wood spars with flags or the tops of coniferous trees with cables attached to the trunks were used as buoys in the Baltic. The more expensive buoys were moored by iron chains and had large flat stones as anchors. A can buoy was cylindrical in shape and the conical buoy had the apex on top. When the can buoy heeled over it was liable to be identified as a conical buoy.

SOUND SIGNALS

During poor visibility, bells were tolled by hand on lightships and by machinery from sea-exposed towers, but they were operated at perhaps fewer than 6 shore lighthouses, as their sound was considered to be too feeble to reach passing vessels, which in fog endeavoured to keep out to sea beyond shores and rocks.

NUMBERS OF LIGHTHOUSES AND LIGHTSHIPS

Estimates of the number of lighthouses established throughout the world in 1800 were published in France in 1800 and in Germany in 1900. The French estimate suggested 100, exclusive of 30 harbour and local lights, and the German estimate was about 150 after obvious corrections. In this present book 98 coastal lighthouses and lightships are named as being established in 1800 in Sweden, France, the British Isles and the U.S.A. and with an estimate of 77 for the number established elsewhere, a world total is suggested of 175.

On these lines one is tempted to hazard the following guess at the numbers of lighthouses and lightships of value for coastal navigation established in other years:

	1600	1700	1800	1819
Sweden . . .	2	5	11	12
France . . .	1	5	16	17
England . . .	1	14	30	37
Scotland . . .	none	1	9	15
Ireland . . .	none	3	8	17
U.S.A. . . .	none	none	24	50
Elsewhere estimated .	30	38	77	106
Total estimate . .	34	66	175	254

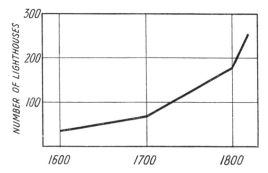

76. Graph showing the estimated increase in the number of lighthouses assisting coastal navigation between 1600 and 1820

Difficulty arises at about 10 per cent. of these lighthouses in deciding whether they should be classed as of general coastal value rather than as of local or harbour value.

After 1785 the lights in most countries improved gradually, and in western Europe rapidly, but in 1819 one must include a few lighthouses of a low standard of efficiency, as for instance the important lighthouse of Messina where the light was kept so inefficiently that *Sailing Directions* warned mariners that it could scarcely be distinguished from the torches of fishing boats. Several seamarks which were important in the earlier years became less so as navigation developed. But many local or harbour lights not included in the estimates above have always been of much value to sailing vessels which are often forced by contrary winds or storms to seek shelter in harbours and embayed positions or where local lights are visible.

It is unlikely that by 1819 the total number of seamarks of all varieties which were lighted nightly with regularity (except in summer) reached 500.

LIGHTHOUSES

Few lighthouses erected on land before 1819 had been difficult to construct, apart from trouble in transporting workmen and materials. Most towers were built of masonry varying from massive square or circular piles of plain stones in Scandinavia to buildings of more lively design with classic ornamentation in France.   Outstanding was the admirable arrangement of twin towers adopted originally at Cordouan which was repeated at half-a-dozen French wood or coal beacons: one tower contained the stairway leading to the fire grate at its open top and thus reduced the penetration by cinders and rain of the keepers' dwellings in the other tower.

Only four lighthouses seem to have been constructed to withstand directly a powerful stroke of the waves.   Three were stone towers founded on sunken Rocks (Eddystone, South Rock and Bell Rock) and the fourth (Smalls) was a cabin on wood piles.   The decision to erect them on isolated reefs, each involving an operation of great difficulty, was a recognition of the sound principle that a light should be placed at the actual point of danger if construction were practicable.   The lighthouse of Cordouan was erected on the same principle on an isolated reef but, being built on an island, was designed as a land-structure; when the island disintegrated, its tower, not designed to withstand the direct stroke of the waves, was shielded skilfully by a great circular parapet extending to 135′ in diameter and to 27′ in height, a veritable fort rising from a rocky plateau which fortunately lay just below the island's surface and offered a firm foundation.

ELEVATION OF LIGHTS

Recognition that a tower should be raised high to give a sufficient geographical range to the light had been instanced by the huge Pharos of Alexandria and the slender Lanterna of Genoa.   But the possibility that lights might be elevated so much that they would be obscured frequently by fog had seldom been considered by 1819.   Such dawning appreciation resulted in the abandonment, before it was lighted, of the lighthouse constructed in 1786 high on the cliffs at St. Catherine's in England, and in the lowering of the lighthouse at Howth in Ireland.   In Scotland, Little Cumbrae fire tower had been placed too high as well as too far from the tracks of shipping, in the vain endeavour to serve by only one light two parallel channels, one on each side of the island: it too had been re-built at a lower level.

LIGHTSHIPS

The number of lightships established in 1819 was about 17: 12 in England and others in Ireland, Russia, Germany and India.   Though their fixed lights consisted of oil lamps of under 5 candlepower which, being raised little above the water, had a geographical range of under 5 miles, the service which they rendered when stationed at the edges of sandbanks was invaluable to mariners and prevented the loss of thousands of lives.   The vessels were moored at sites where they were subject to great risk of collision and in most cases the crews led a life of hardship.

ILLUMINANTS

In 1819 half-a-dozen European lighthouses still used candle-lighting and in the Far East a few open wood fires warned ships of their positions.   Two coal fires remained in service in England, at least two in Holland and about a score in Denmark and Scandinavia, where the number of coal fires was increasing in the form of grates enclosed in lanterns.

Oil lamps were fitted at the majority of lighthouses, burning many varieties of fish and vegetable oils of which colza oil, used in France, was probably the best. Most of the lamps had flat-wicks. The true argand lamp with one circular wick and a close-fitting glass chimney was the finest illuminant available, giving a steady light of 7 candlepower, but it was fitted at few lighthouses other than 50 or more in the British Isles.

ILLUMINANTS {
- 5 *CANDLES*
- 30 *WOOD OR COAL FIRES*
- 157 *COMMON OIL LAMPS*
- 60 *ARGAND LAMPS*
- 2 *GAS*
}

Coal gas lighting had been introduced at four or five lighthouses and harbour lights in Italy, Germany and the United States, but proved disappointing.

Of the 254 lighthouses estimated to be established in 1819, 5 may have been lighted by candles, 30 by wood or coal fires, 2 by coal gas and 217 by oil lamps of which 157 were flat-wick lamps and 60 argand lamps. This estimate and those following include lightships and the numbers are proportional to the lengths of the horizontal lines of the diagrams.

OPTICAL APPARATUS

ESTIMATED NUMBERS

Possibly 165 lighthouses of the 254 had optical apparatus for concentrating the light; 103 had parabolic reflectors, 12 had spherical reflectors and 50 had Rogers's or Lewis's lenses, probably with reflectors.

TYPES OF OPTICAL APPARATUS {
- 89 *NO OPTICAL APPARATUS*
- 12 *SPHERICAL REFLECTORS*
- 103 *PARABOLIC REFLECTORS*
- 50 *LENSES WITH REFLECTORS*
}

The best lights of the period were produced by parabolic reflectors. England and Scotland adopted this form of lighting as the standard after 1785–9: in 1819 it was fitted at about 50 lighthouses in the British Isles and at many local lights. Other countries were slow to adopt it. Russia and Poland were exceptional in using it at a dozen lights and Holland installed it first on a church tower at West Kapelle in March 1818. France had parabolic reflectors at 3 lighthouses, of which one had Bordier-Marcet's peculiar design of a *fanal à double effet*, and was the only country using spherical reflectors without lenses. Reflectors were recorded before 1800 in Denmark and Norway but they were probably of little concentration. They were mentioned at Skudenaes and Hoyvaden: at Bergen one reflector was hoisted on a mast.

The lens combined with a reflector was in use at one lighthouse in England and perhaps 50 in the United States of America, but in each case the apparatus was crudely made and the light unsatisfactory to seamen.

CHARACTERS OF LIGHTS

Of the lighthouses estimated at 254 in 1819, perhaps 30 revolved, 5 oscillated or occulted and 219 showed fixed lights. Of revolving lights the British Isles exhibited 19 and France 2, while Sweden, Spain, Australia and probably Montevideo had 1 each; in the United States 5 of Lewis's lights may have revolved. Two lights oscillated in Sweden and 1 in Finland. Perhaps 2 were occulted in the United States. Of the 19 revolving lights in the British Isles 6 showed red and white beams alternately.

CHARACTERS OF LIGHTS { ——————————————————— 219 *FIXED LIGHTS*
—————— 35 *OSCILLATING AND REVOLVING LIGHTS*

The revolving lights, by emitting beams of light that had been concentrated by parabolic mirrors, were the most powerful lights of the period. Though revolving lights were welcomed by many persons because of their distinction from fixed lights and their powerful beams, yet seamen disapproved of their short flash or duration of light, coupled with the long period of darkness between flashes due to the slow rotation of the optical apparatus. At Walney, an extreme case, this rotation occupied 15 minutes giving one flash every 5 minutes. At other revolving lights the flash appeared every 2 to 5 minutes.

LIGHTS DESCRIBED TO SEAMEN

After about 1780 many Lighthouse Authorities began to assist navigators by advertisements in the Press or by printing *Notices to Mariners* before they established new lighthouses. Before 1820 the lights were often described as being like a star of a particular magnitude, from the first to the sixth, according to the impression of the describer. About 1815 Arago, Bordier-Marcet and other experimenters in France began to calculate the candlepowers of navigation lights, but about half a century elapsed before lists of lighthouses with figures representing the relative candlepowers of their lights were issued for the information of navigators. The standard of manufacture of reflecting apparatus and its condition of maintenance was so varied that such figures would have been misleading around 1819.

Occasionally it was supposed that lighthouses could be identified by the different strengths or powers of their lights, though no figures were stated. For instance in 1810 the Elder Brethren recommended that a light to be erected on a pier at Newcastle in Ireland should be 'a light of much smaller body and inferior brilliancy to the neighbouring coast lights so as to be readily distinguishable from them by vessels approaching the pier or navigating on the coast'. It is now recognised that navigators cannot be expected to distinguish or identify lighthouses by their apparent brilliancies: the varying conditions of the atmosphere render such hopes quite vain.

CANDLEPOWERS OF LIGHTS

An indication of the powers of the lights at various lighthouses can be deduced from the estimated values of lamps and reflectors stated on pages 285–6 on the assumption that the apparatus was always in perfect condition and without allowance for the obstruction of light by the astragals of the lantern and the smoking of the lamps as at Cordouan.   Although the resulting figures demonstrate the enormous advantage in power and hence in range of the revolving light over the fixed light—its additional advantage in offering a distinctive characteristic must not be overlooked—the desire of the seaman for a more powerful fixed light to show a beam of the same power in every direction persisted for many years and was achieved first in 1836.

After about 1805 the parabolic reflectors in French and British lighthouses were maintained in good condition so one can accept as relatively correct the following estimated candlepowers of the most powerful revolving and fixed lights in 1819.   The production of lights of such large candlepowers, from oil lamps giving as a service maximum the equivalent of 6 candles' worth of light, was a considerable technical achievement.

(a) *Revolving Lights*

To arrive at the power of revolving lights, the number of reflectors contributing to the beam can be multiplied by their estimated value.   For instance, at Calais in 1818 Lenoir fitted 6 reflectors of $31\frac{1}{2}''$ diameter with argand lamps.   Each reflector being valued at 4,680 candles, the beam given by 3 reflectors can be assessed at 14,040 candlepower.   At Flamborough in 1807 Robinson fitted 21 reflectors of $20\frac{1}{2}''$ diameter with argands.   As each reflector was valued at 1,980 candles the white beam formed by 7 reflectors can be assessed at 13,860 candlepower and, as the red glass of the period absorbed some 80 per cent. of the light rays, the red beam given by 7 reflectors produced a red flash of 2,772 candles. The poet Southey observed from Arbroath in 1820 that the red flash from the Bell Rock was weaker than the white one: it had less range, as was advertised to the mariner.   All revolving reflectors were parabolic except at Scilly before 1807 and each country adopted a different size as its standard.   At Carlsten each lamp probably gave less light than 3 candles.

On the same basis of calculation, a beam or flash from 4 large Lenoir reflectors with argands should have a candlepower of 18,720 but though each of the beams emitted from Cordouan came from 4 such reflectors its power was only 9,360 candles.   In July 1822 Augustin Fresnel stated: 'ce phare n'est pas plus brilliant' than French lighthouses where each beam was given by 2 large reflectors: this, he explained, was due to the axes of the 4 reflectors being set in slightly different directions in order to prolong the flashes, as desired by many seamen.

Estimated candlepowers of revolving lights and the number of
reflectors forming each beam

1781	Carlsten	500	two-thirds of a reflector
1790	Cordouan	9,360	4 reflectors
1790	Scilly	10,710 and 1,000	7 parabolic and 7 conical reflectors
1807	Scilly	19,800	10 reflectors
1807	Flamborough	13,860 and 2,772	7 white and 7 red reflectors
1811	Bell Rock	20,580 and 1,764	7 white and 3 red reflectors
1812	South Rock	14,700	5 reflectors
1815	Tuskar	13,860	7 reflectors
1816	Inchkeith	2,940	1 reflector
1816	Calais	14,040	3 reflectors

As regards the Bell Rock light, Robert Stevenson was criticised by Sir David Brewster for not equalising its red and white beams (as is the modern practice) by reducing the number of reflectors producing the white flash and increasing those producing the red flash. Had he done so, the character of the light would have been improved but its range reduced materially: probably his choice was right in the particular situation of the lighthouse and considering the optical apparatuses then available. The Bell Rock apparatus gave satisfaction for many years at Bonavista lighthouse in Newfoundland where it was set up in 1843.

(b) *Fixed Lights*

For fixed lights, only candles, lamps and *fanaux sidéraux* gave an equal light to every part of the horizon. Twenty-four candles at the Eddystone before 1810 gave a light now estimated at 67 standard candles, the argand lamp gave 7 candles or *bougies* and the *fanal sidéral* gave from 35 to 70.

Where reflectors were arranged in a circle each gave a maximum light along its axis and a minimum between two adjacent reflectors consisting of a fraction of light from each and the full light directly from 2 or more lamps. At the Eddystone in 1810 Robinson fitted twenty-four 20½″ reflectors with argands giving a maximum light of 1,980 and a minimum of perhaps 700. The reflector curves were all parabolic except at Barfleur where they were spherical. All were metal except the facet reflector at Kinnaird Head. The apparatuses at La Hève were the *fanaux à double effet*, each with 2 argands. Though these reflectors spread the light more, their wide spacing at La Hève caused dark sectors.

Estimated maximum candlepowers of fixed lights.

1780	Barfleur	30	Only one-half to one-quarter of the maximum candlepower was seen on the line between two reflectors.
1787	Kinnaird Head	1,000	
1789	Portland	1,530	
1810	Eddystone	1,980	
1814	La Hève	4,776	
1816	Isle of May	2,076	

PART TWO

A FULLER ACCOUNT
OF
CERTAIN LIGHTHOUSES

VII

ENGLISH LIGHTHOUSES 1600 TO 1690

77. Dungeness lighthouse *c.* 1690

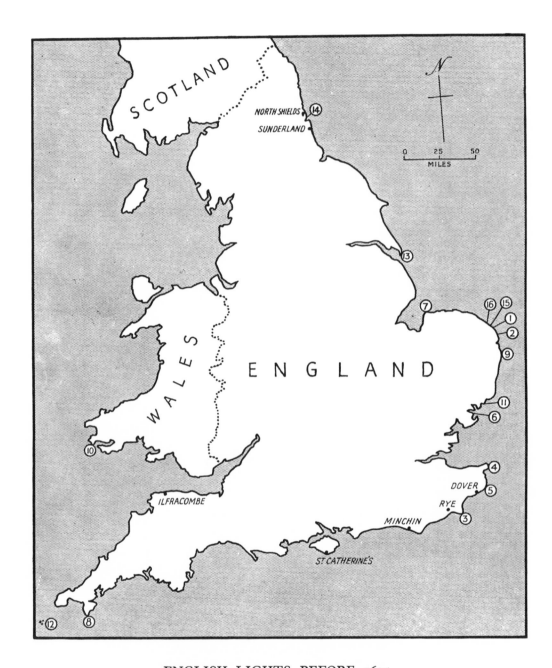

ENGLISH LIGHTS BEFORE 1695

The sites of the 16 coastal lights mentioned in the text are numbered and those of the
local or reputed ancient lights are named Corton and Milford Haven were discontinued

1. Caistor	5. South Foreland	9. Lowestoft	13. Spurn Point
2. Corton	6. Harwich	10. Milford Haven	14. Tynemouth
3. Dungeness	7. Hunstanton	11. Orfordness	15. Winterton
4. North Foreland	8. Lizard	12. Isles of Scilly	16. Wintertonness

VII. ENGLISH LIGHTHOUSES 1600 TO 1690

In 1600 the only lighthouse in England with any pretension to serve coastal shipping was at Tynemouth. Seafarers called for more lights but their proposers had both to counter the objection that beacon fires were unreliable and misled seamen and to allay apprehension that their exhibition would assist hostile attack by sea. Gradually prejudice and opposition were overcome and by 1690 lighthouses were in operation at 12 places from Berwick to Dungeness, but the south and west coasts remained unlighted except for 1 lighthouse erected in the Scilly Isles in 1680.

CAISTOR c. 1600

About 1600 the London Corporation of Trinity House first became connected with lighthouses when it took over from a builder named Bushell two lights which he had put up at Caistor, a village two miles north of Yarmouth, and probably found impossible to maintain on voluntary contributions. The buildings are described as mere wooden structures with lanterns containing two candles. The Corporation's overseer resided at Yarmouth and had difficulty in arranging for a resident of Caistor to attend to them.

In 1628 the Brethren appointed as lightkeeper, at a salary increased from £30 to £37 per annum, a man named Hill who appeared before them in London, with a recommendation from the overseer, Benjamin Cooper, who explained that he had dismissed the former lightkeeper for neglecting his duty. At the same time they strengthened the lights by exhibiting three candles, of 3 to the pound, from sunset to fair day. The low pay induced the lightkeeper to take additional work and he engaged as his substitute an old woman who lived several miles inland. In bad weather the candles remained unlighted owing to her incapacity to make the journey.

In 1663 the Corporation received a demand for payment of £3. 13. 0, a levy on the lighthouses on behalf of indigent Cavaliers, supporters of King Charles II who had been restored to the throne in 1660, but it avoided the impost by certifying that the lightkeeper, being its servant, did not hold an office and that it spent all the lighthouse profits on the relief of poor seamen and their widows. In the same year the Brethren summoned the keeper to London and after an enquiry dismissed him on account of the light not being 'put forth at one in the morning', which resulted in the loss of a ship.

By 1746 candles had given place to oil lamps. In 1790 the two Caistor lights were discontinued.

LOWESTOFT 1609

Trinity House erected a pair of lights at this harbour and lit them, about Lady Day 1609, with candles as at Caistor. The original purpose of these lights is described as 'for the direction of ships which crept by night in the dangerous passage betwixt Lowestoft and Winterton. . . . They happened to be of further use to ships crossing the sea, yet that was not their original design.'

In 1621 the Corporation sent two individuals, Geere and Cooke, who may have been

Younger Brethren, to repair the Caistor and Lowestoft lights. In 1627 it sent Walter Cooke and William Ewins to inspect the lights at Caistor and Winterton and to use their best skill in erecting a new upper light at Lowestoft. 'If the candles burned in the lanterns be too few, they may supply one or two more.'

In 1676, at a cost of £300, Trinity House rebuilt the rear or high lighthouse at Lowestoft and inscribed its heraldic Arms on the tower with a statement that it had been erected during the Mastership of Samuel Pepys, the celebrated cipher diarist, who held the office of Secretary of the Admiralty while his unbusinesslike brother John occupied the post of Secretary of Trinity House. The tower carried a coal fire burning in the open air, but within a few months of its erection (as it stood within 80 yards of the town, to which it brought a risk of fire) safety required it to be enclosed in a glass lantern, an eventuality which had been expected and so was provided for in the design of the tower.

At first the cost of maintaining the Caistor and Lowestoft lights and the buoys in their vicinity came from 'an antient prescriptive payment . . . paid and payable for time whereof the memory of man is not to the contrary'. This phrase, used in a document of about 1720, may refer to a letter of 1606 from the Privy Council to various ports, directing them to collect dues for buoys moored between Lowestoft and Winterton and to remit the proceeds to Trinity House. To remove doubts as to the legality of the collection the Crown granted successive patents, the last in 1815, authorising the levy of dues for Lowestoft lights.

In 1706 the low lighthouse, which burned candles, was given up as being useless and in danger of being undermined by the sea. But navigators called for its replacement, so in 1729 a new tower was built with a lantern which, like that of the upper lighthouse of 1676, held oil lamps.

DUNGENESS *c.* 1616

Soon after 1600 Trinity House reported against a proposal for a light at Dungeness Point and declined an invitation of the King's Privy Council to erect one. But persistence by the petitioner, Sir Edward Howard or Hayward, who held a Court appointment, met with success. Trinity House withdrew its opposition and Howard received a patent in August 1615 and marked the spot by an open coal fire. Navigators recognised its value immediately. For its maintenance the patent authorised the levy of dues on shipping for a period of fifty years. This appears to be the first British lighthouse erected solely for the benefit of general coastal navigation.

Finding the dues difficult to collect and being content with having established the lighthouse, Howard made over his rights to William Lamplough, Clerk of the Royal Kitchen, who wisely enlisted the help of the Customs officials to collect the money at the ports where they were represented. This roused the indignation of shipowners who could no longer avoid paying the charges, and they joined forces eagerly with Trinity House in promoting a Bill in Parliament to suppress the lighthouse as a nuisance to navigation from its poor light. Candles had replaced the original coal fire, doubtless from the difficulty of transporting coals to such an out-of-the-way spot. Parliament would not interfere with the patent and rejected the Bill, but warned Lamplough that a better light must be shown. Seamen complained of the distance of the lighthouse from the sea so in 1635 the patentee discontinued it and put up a tower nearer the Point with a coal fire on top.

From 1647 to 1660, during the short-lived Commonwealth, a Commission superseded Trinity House, because of its Royalist sympathies, and about 1655, for the same reason, the patentee of Dungeness lost his lighthouse, this causing much dispute thereafter as to ownership. When the owner of the ground threatened the new patentee with 'pulling down the structure' because of non-payment of rent, the latter received Government protection, in view of 'the safety of many lives and the State's ships'. The value of the lighthouse had been appreciated fully by seamen but it was often badly kept and in 1668 its light or blaze became so miserable that Trinity House, which rarely interfered with the keeping of private lights, summoned the patentee to appear before it and insisted that he must provide better illumination.

In 1746 Dungeness Point showed a coal fire still but the position of the lighthouse was complained of as being misleading: the sea had receded, leaving the tower far from the water's edge. Samuel Wyatt built the tower of 1792 which served nearly 150 years.

WINTERTON AND WINTERTONNESS *c.* 1617

Accounts of the erection of lights at Winterton are contradictory. In 1618 Trinity House claimed that it had long maintained a lighthouse there, perhaps from 1613. It may have done so without levying dues. Apparently in 1616 the Corporation discussed with the Admiralty the advisability of having a light near Winterton and shortly afterwards obtained a grant from the King's Council approving the proposal to establish one, and

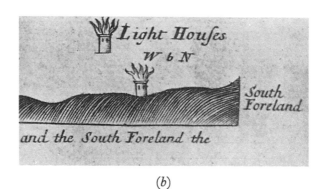

| (*a*) | (*b*) |

78. (*a*) Lowestoft and (*b*) South Foreland lighthouses from sea-charts *c.* 1690

authorising the levy of dues on ships 'having comfort of the said light'. In March 1617 Trinity House instructed 'Mr. Norreys and Mr. Geere to go to Winterton . . . and make Lighthouses there'. But opposition to this grant came from Sir William Erskine who obtained a patent in the following year. This gave to him and Sir John Meldrum, the purchaser of half his share, 'for their true, faithful and acceptable service' to the King, and 'as being the first suitors to him for erecting lighthouses near Winterton and for other good causes and considerations', authority to erect and maintain within 2 miles of Winterton village as many lighthouses with lights burning all night as might be advised by skilful seafarers trading on that coast, and restrained Trinity House from erecting or maintaining other lighthouses within that radius. Trinity House made a protest against the withdrawal of the grant but for reasons not recorded the Council brushed it aside. Erskine and Meldrum eventually held three lighthouses, one at Winterton and two at Wintertonness—the Thwart lights—some 2 miles north of the village. A second light at Winterton, erected in 1677, is referred to later in this Section.

By 1746 the Wintertonness lights had been changed to oil lamps and the Winterton light of 1617 had become an open coal fire.

LIZARD 1619

Many points of consequence in the struggle for and against the erection of lighthouses in England in the 17th century are exemplified in the case of the Lizard Point.

In 1619 Sir John Killegrew, landowner at the Lizard Point, Cornwall, a coast where the inhabitants made great profit from wrecks and even caused them by exhibiting false lights, applied for a patent for a lighthouse there along with his cousin Lord Dorchester, British Ambassador to Holland. Their mutual correspondence shows with what circumspection they went about their application. In May 1619 Thomas Locke, probably a lawyer, wrote to Dorchester thus: 'I went to the Court with Sir Jo. Killegrew, drewe his petition, brought him to Sir Christopher Perkins & he hath undertaken the suite, but it is by way of a voluntarie contribution. If it had bin by imposition it would have had verie harrd passage. . . . If the contribution shall not fall out to be answerable to the charge or his expectation, upon certificate from sea-faring men that such a seamarke is of importance . . . it will afterwards be easie to obtain an imposition but now at the first there is no good ground for it. If it should be foyled at the first it would never recover. This will be a good beginning and if it passes this way there will be a promise that no other light shall be erected neere that place.' But Trinity House opposed the petition, declaring the site to be free of outlying dangers, the channel good, and a lighthouse consequently unnecessary. Furthermore it would assist pirates and enemies desiring a landing. Locke suggested that the application would be assisted if the Dutch would offer to contribute to the upkeep of the lighthouse.

At the end of the month Killegrew obtained a patent from the Duke of Buckingham, one of the King's intimate friends, who signed as Lord High Admiral of England. Its terms entitled Killegrew, jointly with Robert Thynne, to erect a lighthouse at their own cost, to maintain it as a charity for 50 years and to accept voluntary contributions from shipping. Erection of other lighthouses near it was forbidden.

In July Killegrew began construction of a tower on his land and wrote to Dorchester in September complaining of the cost of the building and of the hostility of his neighbours, adding 'I assure yr Lp yt hath byn more chargeabell and far more Trobellsom than I expected for the inabytants neer yt think they suffer in this erection. They affirm I take awaye God's Grace from them. Their english meaning is that they now shall receve no more benifitt by shipwrack (for this will prevent yt). They have been so long used to repe by the Callamytye of the Ruin of Shipping as they clayme it Heredytorye, and hourly complayne on me. Costom breeds strange ills . . . but I hope they will now husband their Land, which their former idell Lyffe hath omitted in the assurance of their gayne by shipwreck.' Again in December he wrote that 'the Light and Tower on the Lizard is, I prayse God, finished and I presum speaks itself to most parts of Christendom . . . the light cannot be mentayned under 10sg a night'. In January 1620 he complained 'I protest I am out about this business

500 £, and yet no return. . . . I am now attempting to gett an impostion lyk the Dungenesse and other Lights in England have, but I dispair in it this time. My misfortunes meet together. . . . It must be granted that the Light is, under God, a Particular Advantage that all ships shall offten recover their owne Ports; by reson that the Light lets them know with assurance wheare they ar, and so they need nott keepe off at sea all night but direct their course home which if they should beate off at sea . . . can make Land agayne.'

In the spring of 1620 he reported that a ship had 'perished thro nott having notice that anie such light was there mentayned and the men Drunk being confessed by them that are saved. I intreat your Lp's speedye resolution whether I shall continue the light or nott for the charge lys so heavy. Without these parts contribute. . . . Neither is it possibell to gett perfect notice of whence and what the ships ar that yearly do suffer on or neer the Lizard for it is seldom that anie man escapes, and the ships split in small pieces; . . . I assure your Lp that most of the houses near the Lizard ar built with the ruins of ships. . . . I should not grone under the Burthen of this worke, where I now suffer and have littell hope of ease, but I will adventure the Landing of 50 £ worth of coles for a wynter provysion. . . . The ships that transported the 8000 soldiers from Lisbon to Dunkirk looking for the Light (which I have put out), six of the ships were near perishing . . . on the Lizard. They expressed their joy by discharging their ordinance for such a strange delivery.'

The light seems to have been extinguished for a period and then re-lit about 1621. In 1623 the King ordained that 'the tower or lighthouse should remain a lighthouse for ever on that coast' and granted the right to show a light for the duration of the longest life of Killegrew or Thynne, at a rent of £40. Local seamen and mariners differed in opinion as to its benefit. 'Discreatist and most capable ship masters' declared that it could not be seen in hazy weather, whereas in clear weather the land was visible. Trinity House continued to object that it was a great burden and much complained of, but Killegrew believed that the objection came from an inbred hatred against the Dutch, which may well have been shared by English seamen generally. The Brethren estimated that with dues of $\frac{1}{2}$d. per ton the lighthouse gave a profit of £400 per annum.

In 1624 Sir William Monson, a most distinguished naval officer with much commonsense, strongly supported maintenance of the lighthouse. 'It is most fitt seamen should be furnished with as manie other helps as can be devised. . . . There is noe man that hath layne tossing at sea some tyme but will be glad to make the land, for the good landfall is the principall thinge to find cominge for our coast . . . what a comfort a shipp in distress shall find by this light, it is to be imagined by example of a traveller on land loosinge his waie in a darke cold night, and discerning a light in a cottage or hearinge a ringe of bells, by reason of which he maie be directed. . . . The year before this, I remember Mr. Cavendish, in his retourne voyage about the world, fallinge with our Channell, somewhat shorte of the Lizard, he was taken with so great a storme that he could not make the land, and hath confessed to me, he endured more hazard and trouble in two nights uppon our coast than in his long navigation. . . . The tenth of som thousand ships that sayle that waie is not a piratt and then consider if after that proportion it were fitt to take awaie the light by which men shall receive soe much good. . . . The Piratts comming for our Coast is nott soe much to robb and spoyle as to be provided with victuals and necessaries and to make sale of their stolen goodes. . . . They run great hazard first in respect of shoare, of his Majesty's shippes and Holland men of warre . . . in a continual feare of invasion from the shore and

mutinie on board, for the condition of those people are to surprize and betraye one another.
. . . Divers other misfortunes I could collect together with the late fearful wrecks that have
been in Mounts baye, which is sufficient to prove the necessarie convenience of a Light to
be placed on the Promentarie of the Lizard, if it be carefully preserved and maintayned
with fewell as I am informed nowe it is.' But Monson's authoritative support failed to
counter the Trinity House opposition. Lack of money from dues forced Killegrew to give
up the struggle and he extinguished his light.

It is difficult to reconcile Killegrew's desire to establish a lighthouse to preserve ships
with his sentiments about wrecking. In 1627 ill-wishers in London accused him of piracy
and alleged that men under his command had removed cargo from a wreck and threatened
death to all who interfered. He informed Dorchester that he had acted thus under his
rights 'which custom and descent gave me'.

In 1630 a Killegrew relative petitioned the King for a patent for the Lizard lighthouse,
stating 'Tis a thing all seamen desire, but most strongest who wonder by what unjust
complaints soe great a benefitt is Lost. Every year many shippes are wreckt for want of it.
I am at the intreaty of all men desired to sett it up againe.' But this further petition also
failed and the tower remained lightless and derelict.

Not until 1752 did a light shine forth again from the Lizard. Passing ships contributed
compulsorily to its upkeep.

NORTH AND SOUTH FORELANDS *c.* 1634

Increasing numbers of shipwrecks on the Goodwin sands induced shipmasters in
1634 to petition for a lighthouse on the South Foreland which might give them some indication of the proximity of the sands, but Trinity House opposed it strenuously and declared
that the headland required no lights and that the imposition of a rate for their support would
be a grievance to navigation. 'In times of hostility such lights would be a means to light
an enemy to land and, in a chase by night, ships would be brought to where the King's
ships and unarmed merchantmen rode peacefully at anchor and then those pursuing vessels
might on dark nights by mistake board either frigates or merchant ships without having
time to demonstrate what she was. True, in time of hostility, the lighthouses could be put
out yet they would so far do mischief as to acquaint strangers with the coast in every point
so that in time of war, they might get through the channels by night without lights, merely
by their depths.' The Trinity House of Dover backed up the London Corporation by
objecting 'to such costly follies as lighthouses. . . . We at sea have always marks more
certain and sure than lights—high lands and soundings which we trust more than lights. . . .
The Goodwins are no more dangerous now than time out of mind they were, and lighthouses
would never lull tempests, the real cause of shipwreck. If lighthouses had been of any
service at the Forelands the Trinity House [of London] as guardians of the interests of the
shipping, would have put them there.'

Despite these objections the Privy Council gave authority to Sir John Meldrum to put
up lighthouses at South Foreland which he did about 1634, probably with oil or candle
illumination. As erection could no longer be prevented, Trinity House at last offered to
establish them but the Council replied that the offer 'comes out of time'. Under the formal
patent, extended later, Sir John secured the right to maintain *fires* at both North and South

Foreland for 50 years at a rent of £20 payable to the Crown. Though some 15 miles apart, the Forelands lighthouses always passed together under the same ownership. Two towers marked the South Foreland, one the North Foreland. All three had a chequered career and were rebuilt several times. On the destruction of the timber and plaster tower of North Foreland by fire about 1683 a temporary arrangement consisting of one candle in a lantern hoisted on a pole gave much dissatisfaction. About 1698 each light burned about 100 tons of coal every year and the use of bellows increased the glow.

Letters from the patentee to his agent at Deal between 1685 and 1700 directed him to 'let ye men at the lighthouses have a strict charge to be diligent about their fires, for wee hiar that ye *Windsor Castle* is lost upon ye South Sand Head'; also, 'Pray give all my servants at the lighthouses a strict charge to be very diligent in keeping good fires this rumbustious weather that no damage may come by their defaults.' Even the Vicar of the local church was asked to 'peep out sometimes before your going to bed to see how my lights burn and, if you find dimness, to reprove the men'. In 1690 the lightkeepers feared the attentions of the pressgang in seizing seamen for the Navy. The patentee wrote, 'The dangers yt ye lighthouse men apprehend themselves to be in from ye Press-masters proceeds I find from themselves and therefore you did very well in charging them to mind ye lights which is their proper business and leave off their fishing. Otherwise I shall suspect my concern to be neglected and thereby their disadvantage may be greater than their gains by fishing. Besides, I dont know how they can be sufficiently watchfull after sayling all ye day.' In 1698 2 lightkeepers for each light received a yearly salary of £13 with free house and fire. In 1686 difficulty is noted with the foreign money offered in payment of dues—'the outlandish money wch you sent will be no great loss. You reckon'd ye pieces of eight at 9 pounds and the 3 pieces of gold at 3 pounds 3 shillings. The pieces of eight will yield but 7 pounds.'

About 1719 the lights passed by will to the Trustees of Greenwich Hospital who, to save coal, enclosed the open fires in lanterns. At North Foreland they removed an iron grate and covered the top of the tower 8′ square 'with a sort of lanthorn with large sash lights' [windows] in which 'the fire is kept burning with the help of bellows which the light men keep blowing all night'. Probably they made a similar arrangement at the South Foreland towers. Shipping complained that the enclosed fires could not be seen sufficiently, so in 1730 the Trustees removed the lanterns and left the coal fires burning in the open air until about 1792 when they rebuilt the towers and installed oil lamps with reflectors and lenses.

Probably the longest continuous family service as lightkeepers began with the appointment of Henry Knott at the Forelands in 1730: one of his descendants retired from service with Trinity House in 1910.

ORFORDNESS *c.* 1636

Full recognition of the need for lighthouses at the entrance to the Thames estuary came surprisingly late. To the south the Forelands were conspicuous headlands, but to the north, where the land was irregular and coastal features lacking, wrecks were numerous, particularly at Orfordness where in October 1627 one night's storm destroyed thirty-two ships. Two timber sheds containing candle lights were put up on trial before 1637. As the test gave satisfaction, a patent for permanent lighthouses was granted in the same year to Gerald Gore, a London alderman, who had acquired from Meldrum (Erskine having died) the three lighthouses at Winterton and Wintertonness. He took the opportunity to cover all five lighthouses in the new patent at an inclusive annual rent of £20 to the Crown.

In 1720 the patentee pulled down the original timber structures, which were decayed, and erected two brick towers at a cost of £1,850. In 1724 the seas washed away the lower tower and it was replaced by a timber hut which was supposed to be better fitted to withstand the undermining of the beach, but it too was washed away in 1730. Two more timber lighthouses were burnt down in 1730 and 1731 so the next tower of 1733 was the fifth that had been erected since 1720. In 1746 the two Orfordness lighthouses had glass lanterns, one enclosing a coal fire and the other oil lamps.

MILFORD HAVEN c. 1662

In 1662 Trinity House approved of the erection of lighthouses at the Calf of Man, the Skerries and St. Ann's Head near Milford Haven. Only at St. Ann's was a tower with a light put up. In 1667 Parliament received a complaint 'of a Grievance on the People, by exacting an illegal Tax for maintaining a pretended Light-house at Milford Haven by colour of some Grant from His Majesty'. On investigation it was resolved that 'these Three Persons, John Man, John Morice and Isaac Morgan who have put this Patent in Execution by receiving Monies thereupon be summoned to answer the same'. The King was asked to call in the patent. This resulted in discontinuance of the light. Presumably the terms of the patent provided that dues might be paid voluntarily, as at the Lizard around 1620. Parliament's insistence on the cancellation of the patent was a misfortune for shipping, as the whole west coast of England was thus left completely unlighted until the next century. The lighthouse is marked on sea-charts published at the end of the 17th century as a tower *without fire*.

HARWICH 1665

Sir William Batten, Surveyor of the Navy and a former Deputy Master of Trinity House, established lighthouses at Harwich in 1665 under a Crown patent for 61 years at a rent of £5. Other persons had put forward the original proposal which Sir William persuaded Trinity House to resist, declaring that lighthouses were an intolerable burden on shipping. According to his friend Pepys, who censures his behaviour in this matter, he changed his mind after a visit to Harwich where he persuaded seamen to sign a petition for lights and he used his influence at Trinity House to 'certify the usefulness of it'.

He placed two lights in a line to guide vessels through a channel between sandbanks. The rear light was a coal fire, blown by bellows, set in a large window built over a road leading to the town, and the front light came from candles shown from a wooden hut on the foreshore. These structures remained unchanged for 150 years. Accounts of 1734 mention disbursements of 1s. 6d. 'for oyll and oyling the billes' [bellows] and 1s. given to the 'bloers' [blowers] to celebrate the visit of the Princess of Orange who passed through the town to take passage to Holland.

When Dutch warships entered the Thames estuary in 1667 Trinity House attempted to deceive them and wreck the vessels by altering the buoys and other marks. One of the suggestions considered was to blow up the front light at Harwich and with the utmost secrecy to set in a false position a canvas screen representing it. The measures taken seem not to have caused the extensive damage hoped for. After the enemy withdrew, navigators complained that they had cut down a group of trees long used as a seamark. In 1668 Lady Batten, who had succeeded to the patent rights, erected unlighted marks in their stead, using some of the profits from the Harwich lights 'out of a generosity to navigation'.

Later, the Government insisted on an increase in the rent and allowed the patentees to retain only two-fifths of the profits.

During the Mutiny at the Nore in 1795 Trinity House endeavoured again to impede navigation: the Elder Brethren destroyed every beacon and buoy in the Thames estuary that might assist the mutineers in taking the Fleet to sea.

HUNSTANTON *c.* 1665

In August 1663 a petition was presented to Charles II that had been signed by the Mayor of Lynn and 183 shipowners and mariners desiring the issue of a patent for the erection of lights at Hunstanton. They expressed themselves as ready to pay dues of 8d. on every 20 chalders of coal or 20 tons of other goods and suggested a charge of 1d. per ton on foreign vessels. They declared that the coast was 'much infested with many sands, not only troublesome but exceedingly dangerous to all ships passing . . . especially in the night'. The King referred the petition to Trinity House along with an endorsement expressing concern for the lives of his subjects and the encouragement of their trade. The Brethren considered then that the lights would be largely of local value and hence not of interest to themselves and gave their approval promptly on 17th October. A month later the King's warrant of consent was issued to John Knight, a Court surgeon and friend of Pepys, who had assisted the King in exile and had relatives at Lynn. The petitioners had not asked that the patent should be issued to a particular individual and probably the Council offered it to Knight as its members knew him as a responsible person. No doubt his friends had heard of the petition and urged his name as connected with the district. The formal patent was issued in June 1665, the delay being caused perhaps by negotiations for a site which had to be specified in the deed. At a cost exceeding £200 two stone towers were set in line to show the channel through the sandbanks.

With considerable repairs in view, the patentee sought an extension of the grant in 1709. Trinity House now opposed it and claimed that all lighthouses passed automatically into its hands when the original terms expired. But the Crown lawyers rejected this interpretation of its rights and granted the renewal. The legal charges and other costs of the application came to £112 and swallowed up profits and interest for three years. At this time the annual expense of maintenance of the lights came to £42. £15 went in salaries, £21 in coals for the exposed brazier of the inner light and £3 in candles for the outer light. Accounts of 1769, when the father of George Vancouver, the explorer, acted as collector of dues, showed a profit of £83 subject to cost of repairs. The profits increased to £450 in 1824. The last remaining lighthouse passed to Trinity House by purchase in 1838.

SPURN POINT *c.* 1672

Shifting banks of fine sand round Spurn Point, 20 miles below Hull, have always made navigation difficult in the Humber estuary, but no light had been exhibited in the area since the hermits' 15th-century beacon. Indeed, many seamen considered that a light would be a danger, as it could never form a reliable mark for a constantly-changing channel and fore-shore. Hull Trinity House had stated as far back as 1638 that lights at Spurn would be 'unusefull and needless' and in 1657 declared that they would be 'an inconvenience and a mischief to navigation' and believed that 'the fewer lights the more skill requ'd in pilotage'.

About 1660 several Hull shipmasters believed that any light would be better than none and despite long and violent opposition from many quarters, including on occasions the Trinity House of London, they asked Justinian Angell, the owner of land at the Point, to erect a lighthouse. As they undertook to pay dues on a voluntary basis, he erected a light about 1672 and it proved a success. He obtained a patent in 1676 with compulsory dues of $\frac{1}{4}$d. per ton, having won the support of the Trinity Houses of Newcastle and Hull by promising them annual payments of £40 to £80 from the profits. These bribes caused the London Trinity House to rue its opposition.

To mark the channel effectively two lights in line were obviously necessary, so a site for another light was marked out in September 1674 with the assistance of three Brethren of the Newcastle Trinity House, and a patent to cover erection of this light was obtained in 1678 which provided for maintenance of the two lights on dues of $\frac{1}{2}$d. per ton. When applying for this patent with authority to increase the dues, Angell produced accounts showing from November 1675 to Christmas 1677 an expenditure in maintenance of £905 and dues of £948. Eventually the new grant was given in perpetuity and consequently, as increasing trade produced a rich harvest from dues, a huge capital payment was made in 1841 when the Government purchased the outstanding lighthouse patents.

The rear Spurn light was shown originally from an octagonal brick tower 60′ high, the front light from a ground-level platform. In both cases open coal fires burned in braziers hoisted some 14′ higher by levers or swapes like the early Danish light at Anholt. The coal was expensive, being picked for quality. Newcastle lighters discharged it along the shore near the lights, and it was then carted over soft sands and sharp shingle that some-times lamed the oxen. Two lightkeepers and an overseer attended to the two fires with additional help in the winter. A lever or swape light is shown in figure 173.

During the *Great Storm* of 1703 the lightkeeper at the Spurn feared that the large tower would be blown down: its fire burned so fiercely that the iron bars melted as if they were made of lead.

CORTON 1675

Many petitioners put forward proposals for lighthouses at all parts of the English coasts during the first twenty years after Charles II's Restoration in 1660, and Trinity House duly reported on these to the Privy Council, which acted for the King.

None of the applicants for patents was so unwelcome to Trinity House as Sir John Clayton: though, according to one of its Secretaries, it succeeded in damning every scheme he put forward. His proposal that annoyed the Brethren most, covered no less than five lighthouses on four different sites—at the Farne islands off the coast of Northumberland, Flamborough Head in Yorkshire, Foulness at Cromer and Corton near Lowestoft. At Corton he proposed to erect two towers to lead ships through St. Nicolas Gatt, a passage between sandbanks. Five hundred shipmasters backed his petition. It may have been

Sir John's hope that by asking for so many lighthouses at once he might be granted at least one or two, as it would be extremely difficult for Trinity House to object to every one. However, it did so. Yet despite its opposition, Sir John with George Blake obtained a comprehensive patent in 1669 and at a cost of £3,000 erected towers at each of these four places. The patent would last for 60 years and dues were specified as 1½d. per ton for vessels when laden and 1d. when light, but payment by shipowners would be voluntary. The Crown took an annual rent of £20.

All seemed well for Clayton when he kindled the fire on one of his Corton lighthouses on 22nd September 1675. The tower was not so splendid a structure as might appear from an account in 1682 by a lawyer who, in the belief that it had been erected at the personal cost of the King and desirous of gaining the Court's favour, praised it far beyond its merits—'that most Excellent Light-house near Goldston by Yarmouth which, both for Height, curiosity and Form, is not inferior to if not Excelling all, or most, in Christendom'.

Trinity House showed considerable skill in defeating Clayton's enterprise. It discontinued one of its candle lights at Lowestoft and erected on a higher site the substantial Pepys tower already described. The crux of its plan lay in asking no dues for this light. In its new position it gave most of the advantages of Sir John's Corton lighthouse which many traders preferred, but few paid the voluntary dues which he required. The cost lay heavy upon him and in 1678 he told the King that he had collected only £60 in dues. So from lack of revenue he extinguished his light in 1678 and he could not afford to kindle fires in the towers already built at the Farnes, Flamborough and Cromer.

Recognising his defeat, Sir John offered Trinity House £100 a year to withdraw its opposition to a light at Corton, or £500 a year to approve his whole project. Such payments would have been very welcome to the Brethren for their charities and they were much tempted to accept, but finally they rejected his advances. Completion of their own fine tower influenced their decision; also a fresh proposal which he made for a light at the Scilly Isles in return for surrender to them of his patent for the five towers angered them anew.

These unlighted towers, which had value as beacons, are marked definitely as lighthouses on sea-charts after 1680 with references such as 'a Light-house but no fire kept in it' and 'a high lighthouse but doth not burn as yet'.

WINTERTON 1677

Soon after its erection about 1617, the single light at Winterton village which was maintained by Erskine and Meldrum appeared to be insufficient for navigation. In 1622 Trinity House prayed leave of the Privy Council to erect additional lighthouses there and to collect dues which had been offered by masters and owners of ships trading on that coast, but the application did not succeed: it may have been put forward in the hope of getting a cancellation of Meldrum's patent which the Corporation had opposed in 1624.

In September 1677 on a petition for a second light signed by shipmasters, and on the recommendation of the Admiralty, Trinity House erected a candle light and got a patent in 1678. The original light at Winterton remained vested in Meldrum's successors. In 1746 it was an oil light.

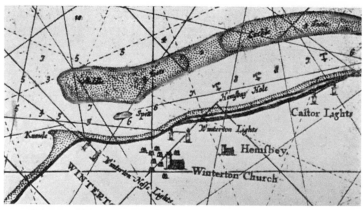

79. Caistor, Winterton and Wintertonness lighthouses from a
sea-chart *c.* 1690

ISLES OF SCILLY 1680

Trinity House obtained a patent for a light in these islands in June 1680. Contrary
to custom, this specified that the dues should be 'reasonable' and that the profits might be
devoted by the Corporation entirely to its charities. Clearly these provisions reflected
Clayton's persistence and accorded with Pepys's advice of 1676 not to seek profits.

(*a*)   (*b*)

80 (*a*) and (*b*). St. Agnes lighthouse in the Scilly Isles
c. 1740, showing tubes on the lantern roof to draw out
smoke from the coal fire

As at Winterton, work was put in hand before the patent was granted. On 14th May
1680 two of the Brethren, Captains Tiel and Bayley, proceeded to the Scilly Isles to choose
a site for a lighthouse. In August they received instructions to make the tower 'full 60′
high' before setting on the lantern which would make it 70′. A glass lantern enclosed a
coal grate and a picture about 1740 shows a curious arrangement of ventilation tubes on
the lantern roof, it being essential to adopt every means of expelling the considerable smoke
from the coal fire. On 16th October a circular letter from the Corporation informed

merchants in France, Spain and elsewhere that the lighthouse had been erected on St. Agnes island at a height of 200′ above high-water and that it would be kindled on 30th October. It remained a coal fire until 1790.

Though this light benefited the navigation of the English Channel very greatly, the reluctance of shipping to pay dues was expressed immediately by the collector appointed at Cowes who reported to Trinity House that 'the most considerable persons have joined in a clubb to obstructing of the collection for Scilly'; but his apprehensions were quelled by the Corporation's show of determination to enforce payment.

A hydrographical book described the dangers attending navigation about these islands. 'With this Mark [in the vicinity of the Bishop Rock] you run in amongst many Rocks terrible to behold . . . with the Seas alternately flying over them in white Sheets or Fleeces of that Element.'

VIII

THE EDDYSTONE AND SMALLS LIGHTHOUSES
1690 TO 1778

81. Smeaton's Eddystone lighthouse *c.* 1850 (Stanfield)

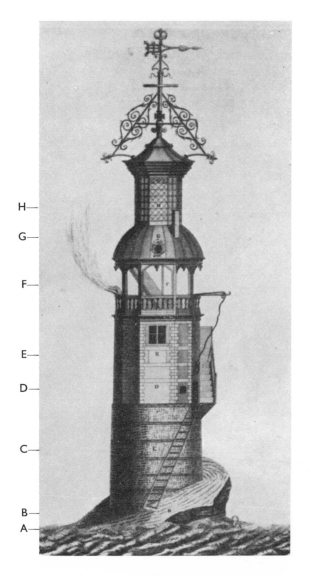

(a) 1698

(b) 1699

82 (a) and (b). Winstanley's two lighthouses on the Eddystone Rocks. The first was lighted in 1698 and the second, which replaced it, in 1699 (Roberts)

VIII. THE EDDYSTONE AND SMALLS LIGHTHOUSES
1690 TO 1778

The construction of 4 lighthouses in succession on the Eddystone Rocks by 1759 provides the most dramatic chapter in lighthouse history: in striving to withstand the force of the waves their builders showed enterprise, ingenuity and courage of a high order. The last of these towers, which was built of stone, served as the pattern for sea-exposed lighthouses erected during the next century. The simple design of the Smalls lighthouse, a cabin mounted on timber piles which offered little resistance to the waves, proved so excellent for its purpose that it is often adopted for present-day sea-works.

Among the greatest achievements of civil engineering, there must be recorded the construction of the first lighthouse tower on a rock exposed fully to the force of the sea. This was accomplished at the close of the 17th century by Henry Winstanley on the Eddystone reef which lies off the south coast of England, 9 miles from land.

The reef consists of a cluster of submarine pinnacles huddled together to form a half-mile band of danger, with the highest peak rising 3' above the level of spring tides, or some 15' above that of the corresponding low-water.

No less than five lighthouses have been built upon them, two by Winstanley in 1698 and 1699, one by John Rudyerd in 1708, another by John Smeaton in 1759 and the present tower by Sir James Douglass in 1882. From this unusual number of structures set up successively on the same spot, one might suppose that all failed except the last, but in fact each marked a successful step towards the design of a relatively permanent sea-tower.

Setting the first lighthouse, that would resist the waves and house the keepers securely, upon one of these ocean pinnacles that offered barely enough area for the base, raised many practical questions for which experience was not available to give answers. What materials could be used? What should be its shape and size? How could it be fixed to the rock? What would be its cost? Obviously some ingenious and daring person must come forward to make trial of his ideas.

It is probable that about 1700, of all underwater dangers throughout the world, the Eddystone reef shared with the extensive sandbanks off the south-east coast of England the terrible record of wrecking ships most frequently. Even at low-water during daylight little of the Eddystone reef appeared above the sea surface. Hence it formed a nearly invisible trap, dangerous particularly to vessels entering the English Channel from the west, when not sure of their position.

The need for a lighthouse was clamant but its construction seemed impracticable. In 1665 when the British Admiralty received a petition for one, and passed it for observations to Trinity House, it received the reply that a lighthouse 'could hardly be accomplished' though it was most desirable. In 1692 a certain Walter Whitfield put to Trinity House a rather nebulous proposal for securing the Eddystones from continuing 'obnoxious to navigation' and when he replied in the affirmative to the question 'whether he meant the setting of a lighthouse' upon them, the Brethren managed to obtain a Crown patent in

1694 authorising them to erect a lighthouse and collect dues, and contracted with Whitfield that he should undertake the work and share the profits equally with them. It is supposed that he made experiments at the Rocks and concluded that the work was beyond his capacity. Be that as it may, he faded out of the picture and his contract rights passed to Henry Winstanley.

WINSTANLEY'S LIGHTHOUSES 1696–9

As clerk of works at the reconstruction about 1690 of Audley End, a palatial house near Saffron Walden, Winstanley had considerable scope in handling a wide range of building materials. In addition to being an engraver of skill he was a mechanical genius, his house in Essex being full of curious and amusing contraptions, such as a chair with arms that imprisoned a sitter and an arbour on a canal bank which suddenly went afloat with its occupants. At Hyde Park Corner in London, he exhibited elaborate waterworks at stated times at an entrance charge of 1s. a head: they were advertised as a public show as late as 1709.

None knew better than Winstanley that the difficulties of fixing any structure upon the Eddystones had not been exaggerated, but the idea fired his imagination. The project seemed a worthy challenge to his ability in construction and mechanics and he felt success to be within his powers. He required financial terms more favourable than Whitfield had accepted and after lengthy negotiations with Trinity House he signed an agreement on 10th June 1696 under which he alone would receive the profits for the first 5 years after showing a light. Thereafter the Corporation and he would share them equally for 50 years.

SEASON 1696

Immediately after signing the contract Winstanley selected the highest peak of the reef for the site of the tower which he decided should be fastened to the rock by 12 long iron rods about $3\frac{1}{2}''$ diameter. Workmen were engaged, boats were chosen and he and his party set sail daily from Plymouth whenever weather seemed propitious. Occasionally the boats would remain all night off the reef. The level of the Rock made possible several hours' work on all tides. The operations were discontinued in the autumn after holes had been bored in the rock to receive the ends of the rods.

SEASON 1697

During the summer of 1697 the masons ran in the rods with lead and built round them a pillar, probably of stone, 14' in diameter and 12' high. Benefiting from its shelter, progress became faster as it rose.

The British Admiralty readily supported the venture, in the practical form of appointing a guard-ship to protect Winstanley's party and promising to provide another ship if required. But its arrangements for protection fell through in an unexpected fashion. In June 1697 the Captain of the guard-ship on duty off the reef received news of the proximity of a French merchantman. This chance of seizing a rich prize was not to be let slip, so he deserted his monotonous occupation at the Rocks and set off to capture her. By ill-luck, fog stopped the chase and prevented his return for several days, during which a French privateer approached the Rocks and sent in a boat with armed men who carried off

Winstanley to France and stripped his men and turned them adrift in their own boat. It was said that when the French King heard of the incident, he reprimanded his Ministers for the act and, declaring that he did not wage war on humanity, ordered Winstanley's release. Unfortunately for this part of the story, which may have been true, research in France revealed no confirmation. By exchange of prisoners, Winstanley returned to his work in July and the Admiralty devised a new system of protection, entailing the party's return each night to Plymouth. This delayed the operations.

SEASON 1698

Early in 1698 Winstanley enlarged the pillar to 16′ diameter and by June, with careful preparations and excellent weather, had erected the superstructure and fixed the lantern frame on top, with the wind-vane raised to 80′ above the rock. At midsummer the party decided to lodge in the tower, hoping to save the time and labour spent in passage between Plymouth and the reef. But during the first night a storm of exceptional severity for the season arose unexpectedly and no boat could approach to take them off. With little shelter and well aware of their perilous situation, they were marooned in the roofless tower for 11 days when they got ashore in a half-drowned condition. When the weather improved, undeterred by the unhappy experience, they returned to complete the lighthouse and lighted it on 14th November.

In the following months the waves over-topped the lantern and Winstanley saw that he must raise it.

SEASON 1699

In the spring of 1699 he discontinued the light and after removing the whole superstructure, doubled the mass of the core and increased the diameter to 24′, by encircling it with a ring of stones having their joints covered with hoops of metal, to bind the mass together and to guard the mortar from the wash of the sea. He enlarged the superstructure in all parts and elevated the lantern 40′ higher than the lantern of the first tower. A light was shown before the end of the year.

Winstanley considered that the time taken to complete his work was unduly long and explained that delays were caused by difficulty of transport between the reef and Plymouth, bad weather, the heavy ground-swell and the hampering action of sea and tides.

WINSTANLEY'S TWO STRUCTURES

It is not appreciated generally that two different structures had been built by Winstanley, the only part common to both being the central core and its connection to the rock. Despite a resemblance in their aspects, they differed in many features. For instance, an external ladder and stair led to a door half way up the first tower, whereas a door at rock level gave entry to the second.

In the illustration of the first tower on page 112, A marks an eye-bolt for tying up boats, and D, E and G mark the positions of storeroom, stateroom and kitchen, all of which were used for lodging the lightkeepers and any artificers making repairs. F marks an open gallery for looking-out which was supposed to allow the seas to pass through in storms. H marks the *lanthorne* with small glass panes as in windows of the period, and containing a candle light. Smoke is shown issuing from a heating-stove in the stateroom and from the kitchen chimney. The pulley would assist in raising stores.

Winstanley's second lighthouse had many new features such as the projecting cabin. In the illustration on page 112 a crane appears above the boat. It was removable when not in use, and intended to provide an easy landing of stores. The lantern of 11′ diameter, had 8 windows, fittings to hold 60 candles, and 'a great hanging lamp'. The outside gallery facilitated washing the lantern panes, ladders being placed against the ornamental candlesticks, and formed the platform for working 3 pulleys or cranes. As a defence against privateers, Winstanley provided a chute for casting down stones on an enemy attempting to enter. He repeated the open gallery of the first tower and it was said that at high tide a 6-oared boat could be lifted on a wave and carried right through it.

The first tower is depicted in a rare engraving after a picture by Jaziell Johnston. Winstanley inscribed a short account of his labours upon his engraved plate of the second tower and sold copies for 6d. at his waterworks in London, where a model of the lighthouse could be examined. Several editions of this engraving are known. Roberts engraved both views for Smeaton's *Narrative of the Building of the Eddystone Lighthouse* and it is his engravings that are reproduced in this Section.

DESTRUCTION OF WINSTANLEY'S LIGHTHOUSE

Despite public misgivings, the second tower survived 3 winters without mishap. In November 1703 it needed repairs, which Winstanley arrived at Plymouth to superintend. Gales threatened when he sailed for the reef with his men, but on his departure he assured his friends of his confidence in the stability of the tower and his desire to be present within it during the greatest storm that could arise, so that he could witness the effect of the sea. His visit to the lighthouse coincided with the occurrence of one of the most disastrous storms that ever ravaged the south of England by land and sea. On 27th November, when its fury abated, it was apparent to the townsfolk of Plymouth that the lighthouse had disappeared. No trace remained of Winstanley, his workmen or the lightkeepers. Only a few twisted rods which had tied the tower to the rock showed that it had existed.

This terrible storm made a deep impression throughout England and a London bookseller commemorated it by a bequest to provide for a *Storm Sermon* to be preached annually in a London church on the Sunday nearest to the 26th November. Contemporary literature noted the destruction of the lighthouse: one reference occurs in Farquhar's *The Beaux' Stratagem*, a play of 1707,—'going souse into the sea like the Edistone'.

WINSTANLEY'S ACHIEVEMENT

Of all works connected with the sea, the erection of this tower was one of the most daring and original ever to be attempted, and Winstanley must be honoured for his decision to build it on these wave-swept Rocks and for his ingenuity and his unflagging resolution to carry out his plan—thus flaunting the universal qualified opinion as to its impracticability. He devoted more than 4 years to his humanitarian purpose and having imbued his workers with his own enthusiasm, he met his death while sharing their labours.

The entire cost of the enterprise came from his own pocket. This amounted to nearly

£8,000, against which he received some £4,000 in dues. In view of his losses, the Government apparently granted his widow a payment of £200 and a yearly pension of £100.

Winstanley's towers have been derided on account of excessive external decoration, but criticisms as to the unsuitability of the external iron ornaments for a lighthouse on an exposed Rock can be rebutted by pointing out that his towers, both incomplete and complete, stood successfully on the Eddystone reef from 1697 to 1703 and were demolished only by the greatest recorded storm. It has been suggested too that they endured so long because peculiarities of the sea-bed surrounding the Rocks reduced the destructive effect of the waves which assaulted them during these six winters, and that these particular winters were unusually free from storms. There may be truth in both suggestions.

On examination of Roberts's engravings the eye is certainly caught at once by the ornamentation, but it offered no resistance to the waves, and less to the wind than appears at a glance. The lower parts of the towers were compact and suitable for sea-structures, and only when Winstanley designed the open galleries was he diverted from the essentials of a simple design. Their gravest defects lay in his method of fixing the core to the rock, the inadequate cohesion of the whole and the insufficient weight. Excess in ornamentation was the least important defect.

RUDYERD'S LIGHTHOUSE 1706–8

After Winstanley's tower disappeared, seamen felt the lack of a light even more keenly than before the advantages had been enjoyed; ships perished on the reef and adjacent shores.

It remained uncertain whether a tower could be designed which would endure on the Eddystones, but after Winstanley had pierced the tradition of impracticability, proposals for another lighthouse could be expected.

Trinity House still would not venture to undertake such a work but, fortunately again, men of enterprise eventually came forward, keen to put their ideas into effect. Colonel John Lovett, a Member of the Irish Parliament, and his friend John Rudyerd, a silk-mercer of Ludgate Hill, London, who in early life had experience of mechanics and building materials, decided to make the attempt. Lovett sought an investment for his wife's dowry of £5,000 and calculated that a lighthouse on the Eddystone should yield a free profit of £700 a year. The percentage return seems an inadequate compensation for the great risk.

After the destruction of the first lighthouses, Trinity House obviously had to concede to any new undertaker better terms than Winstanley accepted, so the Elder Brethren agreed with Lovett to apply for an Act of Parliament authorising the re-building and the levy of dues and to grant him a lease of their rights for 99 years at an annual rent of £100. Lovett would construct a tower and receive the whole of the free profits. The Corporation obtained the Act in the spring of 1706 and Rudyerd began work in July.

It is believed that Rudyerd made the plans. Very wisely he enlisted the services of two expert shipwrights, Smith and Norcutt, who were employed at the naval dockyard at Woolwich in fitting out men-of-war, but it is not clear whether they influenced his design. Certainly, as craftsmen, their qualifications to carry it out could not have been higher.

83. Rudyerd's lighthouse of 1708

THE DESIGN

Rudyerd, Smith and Norcutt have not received sufficient credit for their ingenuity in evolving a remarkable design and for their skill in executing it. They chose a simple outline, a cone without any projections that might catch the seas, except an outside stair and, at the top, below the lantern and 71′ above the base of the tower, a small cornice to throw off the water slightly and reduce the risk of the seas breaking the windows. The outside of the tower consisted of some 70 vertical wood planks which formed a smooth sheath enclosing horizontal layers of wood and stone. Into this huge timber frame, connected together in ship-like fashion, they packed as much stone as possible to give the necessary weight for resisting the waves. The brilliant idea of consolidating the structure by relying entirely on timber joints which the shipwrights excelled in making, avoided the difficulties with cements and mortars that Winstanley had failed to overcome. Rudyerd used more bolts than Winstanley in connecting the tower with the rock—this method of attachment by bolts would be considered inadequate at the present day—but neither this nor any other part of Rudyerd's work can be condemned, as his tower lasted satisfactorily for almost 50 years until destroyed by fire, the direct cause being the use of timber instead of metal for the lantern.

OPERATIONS IN 1706-9

In preparing the irregular rock surface and cutting rough steps to secure the 23′ 4″ diameter base of his tower, Rudyerd discovered that Winstanley's treatment of the same area had been very crude, but owing to its exposure to wave-action he had much difficulty in doing better. He bored 36 dovetailed holes up to 30″ in depth to hold the chief bolts, and 200 more to take subsidiary iron branches. The method devised to fix the bolts instanced the ingenuity that was applied to every part of the structure. Each hole was filled with tallow, the bolt placed in position and a key or wedge driven home. Red-hot pewter was then run in, which melted and drove out the tallow, and filled the crevices completely. Some 50 years later, Smeaton found that this filling had protected the bolts from corrosion so well that they appeared to have come newly from a smith's forge.

The rock being stepped and the bolts fixed, a dressed timber laid lengthwise on the

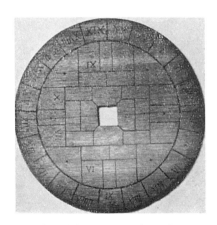

84. A miniature template showing how Rudyerd arranged the stones of one of his courses

85. A contemporary French view of Rudyerd's lighthouse (Lemprière)

119

lowest step brought it up to the level of the next step. Then 10 layers of timber laid crosswise and lengthwise alternately, brought up the foundation to a smooth platform. Upon this base came 16 circular courses of stones separated by courses of timbers which, when connected to the external timber sheathing, held the stones as if packed tightly in boxes. The arrangement of the stones in each course differed so as to break-joint. A wood mast passing through the centre guided the setting of stones and timbers. The shipwrights, who made slight changes in executing the design, fitted with great care the important wooden kerb or *cante*, shaped to the rock surface, so that it covered the junction of the rock with the vertical sheathing timbers. No other lighthouse tower has been built to such a design, with stones bound together so ingeniously by timbers.

The external staircase gave entry to the tower without breaking into the base. Its projection afforded an obstruction to the waves but it is not recorded that it was washed away. Drawings of the tower after completion show only 3 horizontal rows of windows; the 4th and lowest row had been filled up or was never fitted. Iron hoops springing from the balcony stiffened the wooden lantern. Unfortunately its vertical pillars and the bars separating the glass panes obscured much of the candle light. Rudyerd completed the tower in 1709 but he had lighted it on 28th July 1708.

HISTORY 1710–34

From the first, collecting dues from ships proved difficult. A flaw in the Act prevented their collection in Irish ports. This could be cured only by another Act. Mrs. Lovett's dowry did not suffice to cover the cost of erection and Rudyerd and others had to contribute to it. The deaths of Lovett in 1710 and of Rudyerd in 1713 forced the sale of the lease which passed for a bid of some £2,000 to business associates of the Lovetts, who formed a syndicate for this purpose, a leading part being taken by Robert Weston whose family's interest continued until the lease expired in 1807. In 1721, an average year for that period, the collection of dues amounted to £1,520 and expenses to £511. The lessees divided £1,009 without reservation of sums to cover exceptional maintenance or depreciation, which might be expected to take place since this sea-structure was built of English timbers liable to destruction by boring animals and seaweeds.

By 1723 sea-worms had damaged several of the timbers at the joints and particularly where they touched the rock. The lessees took action at once and carried out considerable repairs to the woodwork then and later under the direction of John Holland, a shipwright at the dockyard at Plymouth. He made experiments in covering the lowest timbers with copper, but failed to halt their decay. In 1734 he made a drawing of the tower in the form of an evolute which projected on the flat the entire rounded outer surface and facilitated reference to any outer plank by showing all at a glance. On the right side, he marked upwards *cante*, *timber* and *stone*, and the four floors, *storeroom*, *chamber*, *diningroom* and *cookroom*. At the base he listed timbers destroyed, shifted, renewed, coppered and leaded from 1730 to 1734. The drawing showed the scarfing and butting of the timbers.

DESTRUCTION OF RUDYERD'S LIGHTHOUSE

The end of the tower came on 2nd December 1755. About 2 a.m. the lightkeeper on watch went up to perform his half-hourly duty of snuffing the candles. He found the lantern full of smoke and his action of opening the balcony door caused a draught that set the timber dome ablaze. The keepers attempted to extinguish the fire by leather bucket, using water from a small tub kept in the lantern for such an emergency, but they failed to reach the flames by throwing water 12′ upwards, and the darkness prevented them from fetching more water from the sea, 70′ below. Quickly the fire got a grip of the tower, the flames extended downwards over their heads and drove the men from room to room until they found shelter in a cleft in the Rock under the iron ladder while burning embers and

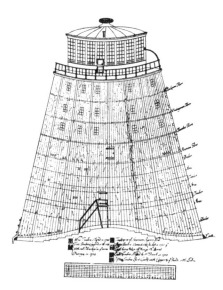

86. A conical evolute of the outside timbers of Rudyerd's tower, showing their joints and where repairs were made in different years

87. An impression *c.* 1890 of the destruction of Rudyerd's tower in 1755

red-hot bolts rained down from the glowing mass. When the fire was at its height, the conflagration was seen from Plymouth and a fishing-vessel put out to sea and reached the Rocks at 10 a.m. The ground-swell prevented it from entering the landing-gully, so each lightkeeper in turn tied a rope round his waist and was hauled to safety through the surf.

One of the lightkeepers, Henry Hall, declared that when looking upwards during their descent of the burning tower, a quantity of molten lead had fallen into his mouth and down his throat. He experienced no pain and a physician who examined him did not believe his tale, but he died 12 days later. Looking to his advanced age of 84, the cause of his death might well have been delayed shock; but the piece of lead, over 7 ounces in weight, which was found in his stomach has been preserved as a proof of the incident.

The dreadful experience at the Eddystone so terrified another of the lightkeepers that on reaching land he ran off and was not heard of again.

SMEATON'S LIGHTHOUSE 1756–9

When Rudyerd's lighthouse was destroyed, the lease had some 50 years to run and the manager of the syndicate holding it was Robert Weston whose family held 3 of the 8 shares. His associates had faith in his judgment so, being secure of their support, he could act quickly. He knew well that such an exceptional event as building upon a Rock in the sea called for ingenuity in design and execution of a type that might not be found in architects accustomed to building on land, so he applied to Lord Macclesfield, the President of the Royal Society of London, who, without hesitation, advised an approach to John Smeaton, a philosophical-instrument-maker engaged in the profession known now as civil engineering. In January 1756 Smeaton accepted the commission and in February he met Weston who described Winstanley's and Rudyerd's towers and gave him models and detailed drawings of these works which, because of his interest in the lighthouses, he had made some years previously.

Weston favoured a repetition of Rudyerd's design but assured Smeaton that any proposal which would offer more permanency would have careful consideration. From the first, Smeaton contemplated a structure entirely of stone though he faced the obvious fact that the previous tower had proved its suitability, apart from risk of fire, by lasting for almost half a century. To the criticism that a stone building could not possess the elasticity of Rudyerd's tower which swayed slightly in storms and therefore did not offer an unyielding opposition to wave-action, Smeaton replied that such elasticity was unnecessary, that the structure had suffered from lack of weight and that only the layers of heavy stone, and not all the straps and ties that the tower contained, had saved it from being upset by the sea.

Smeaton approved the accommodation provided by Rudyerd and the conical shape of his tower, but he would enlarge the base and reduce the diameter of the upper part, thus arriving at a curved form which he likened to the trunk of a tree. He rejected as inadequate the system adopted in the previous towers of connecting the stones to the rock by iron rods alone, also Rudyerd's device of containing the stones within a timber frame and Winstanley's plan of tying them to each other by encircling metal straps. To bond the stones, as in land-buildings, would increase the work to be done at the reef.

Ultimately he decided on a system of dovetailing so that the shaped stones would fit immediately without adjustment and lock together in the horizontal courses; each course would then act as one complete stone. To prevent them from sliding, stone cubes would be inserted into the stones of the courses, half in one course and half in the next, and to avoid any movement of the stones while the mortar had a chance to harden, oak trenails or pins and wedges would be driven through grooves cut vertically between the stones, and into holes bored in the course below. The upper part of the tower, at the levels where the arches of the apartments met the walls, would be tied by 2 horizontal circles of iron chains let into grooves cut in the stones.

After a month spent in considering the whole problem and preparing his preliminary design, Smeaton proceeded to Plymouth at the end of March and met Josiah Jessop, a foreman-shipwright and draughtsman at the naval dockyard, who since 1744 had supervised repairs, often extensive, of Rudyerd's tower. His knowledge and experience proved of immense value to Smeaton. The idea of a building consisting entirely of stone on such a site amazed Jessop but he agreed that the methods proposed should save much time on the Rock and reduce expense.

Smeaton attempted 10 voyages to the reef during his 6 weeks' stay at Plymouth: 6 journeys proved fruitless as the weather prevented landings. During the other 4, he spent $28\frac{1}{2}$ hours in examining the tiny area minutely and choose the same site as used by

Winstanley and Rudyerd. He tried out the effect of tools in working the rock, noted its configuration and took levels. In addition, on the mainland he visited quarries, interviewed workmen, arranged for boating and leased a workyard near Plymouth harbour.

On returning to London he informed the lessees of his decision that the lighthouse should be built of stone—granite in the foundations and outside, and softer Portland stone in the interior. He expected to complete it in four seasons but on the question of expense he stated: 'In the progress of the work we should lie so widely open to accident that I could not undertake to make any calculation of this part, which might not possibly be exceeded ten-fold.'

Looking to the small area of the Rock available as a base, he decided to humour its irregularities by cutting into it as little as possible and, to ensure his complete understanding of the work, he made with his own hands two models, the one of the existing rock surface and the other of the surface after his intended cutting with the foundation courses set upon it. With these models he demonstrated his ideas to the lessees, the Admiralty and Trinity House. All accepted his recommendations despite the public belief that 'nothing but WOOD could possibly stand upon the Eddystone'. The lessees gave Smeaton complete control of the operations and Weston arranged to supply the funds. Smeaton signed a contract for the supply of stone and appointed a clerical staff. The opening of 14 books for accounts and to check supplies indicates his careful planning.

SEASON 1756

Despite the lateness of the season, Smeaton began work in August, because even a short experience of working on the site would influence his plans for the next season. He divided the seamen and the workmen into two companies to work in turn, each under an experienced foreman-builder. When tide, weather or darkness stopped work on the Rock the company engaged returned to Plymouth with tools to be sharpened and the other company took up duty next day. On occasions a boat with materials and fresh tools could

88. An engraving of Smeaton's tower *c.* 1820

123

come out from Plymouth to lie all night in the gully against the lighthouse Rock ready for a start at daybreak. Later in the season a store-ship on which the men could take refuge was moored about a mile and a half off the reef, towards Plymouth.

To serve shipping with a temporary light and thus enable the collection of dues to be resumed, Trinity House obtained a Crown patent authorising a lightship to be established, and bought and fitted-out a vessel which was moored on 13th August some 2 miles north-west from the reef.

By November the foundation for the tower had been cut accurately into steps and dovetailed ready for the first stones to be brought out in the spring.

In December the masons began cutting the stones at Plymouth—their weight being generally one ton—and during the winter Smeaton carried out extensive experiments with cements and mortars. The stones came regularly by sea from Portland quarries to the yard at Plymouth, a journey exposed to interference by French privateers. The Admiralty's instructions to its Commissioner at Plymouth to convoy shipments of stone proved valueless, as naval protection never materialised when asked for. Fortunately, despite the war with France, the workmen suffered no interference at any time except from the British Navy in its operation of the pressgang, but the men who had been seized were released immediately.

SEASON 1757

At the beginning of June the store-ship took up her station and the second season's work began. Fenders fixed on the east side of the Rock prevented boats from fretting against it. Shears and a windlass were fixed for raising the stones directly from a boat and tested by hoisting above the Rock a heavy longboat complete with crew.

Sunday 12th June saw the first stone, weighing 2 tons, fitted in position and bedded

(a)

(b)

89 (a) and (b). Early 19th-century engraving and lithograph of Smeaton's tower. The engraving (by Prout) exaggerates the overhanging parapet which caught the waves. Its projection was reduced about 1865

in mortar with the joints coated with quick-setting plaster of Paris as a protection from the wash of the sea. Next day the masons set the other 3 stones of the 1st course. On the 15th a heavy swell carried away 5 of the 13 stones of the 2nd course but the masons at Plymouth, working day and night, cut duplicates in 2 days, which enabled that course to be completed on 30th June. Rapid progress followed. The 6th course was set by 11th August, then 3 entire courses by 30th September, when operations on the reef ceased for the season. Sometimes work had been prolonged into darkness by lighting links or torches, but one hour's work by daylight equalled two at night. At this stage, on completion of the 9th course, Smeaton had an interview at Trinity House and offered, if the Brethren should so desire, to complete the structure with timber instead of with stone, but they approved the plans which he had made already.

In December a storm drove the lightship from her moorings and tested the building severely but no damage occurred.

Season 1758

By May the last of the stones had been cut on land and a start was made at the reef. During the summer all went well and the operations proceeded apace. By the 1st October the 29th course had been set.

At that level Smeaton arranged to exhibit a temporary light on his tower and thus dispense with the lightship during the ensuing winter, and two of the workmen, who would receive double wages, undertook to live on the tower and maintain the light. But the plan fell through, as Trinity House decided that such an arrangement infringed the terms of the patent of 1756 authorising the mooring of the lightship. This decision annoyed Smeaton greatly as it made him appear to have fallen short of the enterprise shown by Winstanley and Rudyerd who lighted their towers at the end of 3 years' operations.

Season 1759

Work began earlier in the spring than usual at the Rock and the last of the cornice stones, to complete the 46th course, was set on 17th August, and on a careful measurement the pillar, now 70' high, appeared to be within one-eighth of an inch from the perpendicular—a striking proof of the masons' skill. Smeaton endeavoured to hasten the works and complete them before arrival of winter's blasts. So he ferried smiths, carpenters, glaziers and other craftsmen continuously between the Rock and the shore until his purpose was fulfilled. On 8th October the painters applied their last coat of paint and the smiths connected the lightning-rod. With stores delivered, two labourers who had seen the work through from the beginning took up the duties of lightkeepers and on the 9th October, having put up a time-piece and set it in motion, Smeaton took leave of the great stone beacon which he had devised, and came 'to an anchor in Plymouth Harbour with a flowing tide to the great joy and satisfaction of all concerned'.

For the light, which first shone forth from the tower on 16th October 1759 and released the lightship from her exposed station, Smeaton introduced no novelty but repeated the previous arrangement of 24 candles set in a chandelier, consisting of two metal rings raised and lowered by tackle, and snuffed every half-hour. When he first observed his light from a distance of 7 miles, it appeared 'very strong and bright to the naked eye, much like a star of the fourth magnitude'. He had intended to use 24 oil lamps, shaped to fit into the candle-sockets but, glass chimneys being not yet invented, the smoke from the lamps obscured the lantern-glazing, so he instructed the keepers to reserve them for emergencies.

Smeaton's tower had a height of 60' to the top of the stone cornice. Rudyerd's tower had almost the same height. The vane of Winstanley's second tower would have overtopped both.

SMEATON'S *Narrative* AND THE LATER HISTORY OF THE TOWER

Of all his engineering achievements, Smeaton took most pride in the erection of the Eddystone tower. In 1791 he published his *Narrative* and declared that writing it had given him more trouble than building the lighthouse. He had spent seven years in the preparation of the book. A curious point about it is that while the account of the operations on the reef and ashore occupies 80 pages, the description of his experiments with cements occupies as many as 21: he believed that his remarks on suitable cements for sea-works formed one of the important lessons he could offer to his fellow-engineers. His story shows that he involved himself in the most trivial details of the building operations and spared no pains to anticipate difficulties. He observed that transport had been his greatest worry, that knowledge of the previous works on the Rock and his contact with persons acquainted intimately with Rudyerd's tower had been of great value, and that his operations had been blessed by good weather.

Smeaton's lighthouse exhibited an oil and reflector light from 1810 and marked the reef until 1882 when it was replaced by a higher tower built on a lower but broader pinnacle by Sir James Douglass, then engineer of Trinity House. Smeaton's foundation had become shaky and the lantern was not high enough above the waves. The upper part of his tower with reduced cornice was removed stone by stone and re-erected on Plymouth Hoe upon a replica of the original base. There it looks southwards down the Sound to its successor flashing nightly and continuing the enterprise of Winstanley, Rudyerd and Smeaton.

THE SMALLS LIGHTHOUSE 1775-8

For ingenuity and enterprise in lighthouse-building the names of John Phillips and Henry Whiteside stand prominent.

Phillips, a Welshman whose life was shadowed by bankruptcy, became in 1770 manager of Liverpool's north dock at a salary of £60 per annum, increased in 1772 to £105. He lost his job in 1782 after a quarrel with the Mayor and died in 1783. Whiteside, born in Liverpool in 1748, started his career as apprentice to a local cooper, developed skill in wood-carving and set up business in London about 1770 as 'a maker of violins, spinettes and upright harpsichords'.

The construction of the Liverpool lighthouses in 1763-4 interested Phillips and gave him the idea of setting a lighthouse on the Smalls, one of two tiny clusters of Rocks lying close together in the Irish Sea, 21 miles off St. David's Head in Wales. In the darkness they menaced shipping, as their highest peak projected only some 12' above the highest tides. They were exposed to the short fetch of the Irish Sea and the south-west swell from the Atlantic.

As with Avery, Phillips's head was full of projects which he tried to persuade his creditors would prove profitable if only they would provide funds. In 1773 while acting as agent for the Skerries he disclosed to them a plan for setting a beacon on the Smalls, having failed to persuade the lessees of the Milford lights to finance it. On the largest of these Rocks—'always above the water, about the bigness of a Long-boat'—his lighthouse would be 'of so singular a construction as to be known from all others in the world as well by night as by day'. He did not disclose then what novel features he had in mind but he pushed on his project, and on 4th August 1774 the British Treasury granted him a lease of the Rocks. He advertised for designs and chose one submitted by Whiteside which was doubtless the simplest and cheapest. Trinity House did not oppose his plans, as the Brethren, like other persons experienced in sea affairs, believed that they were quixotic and impracticable.

WHITESIDE'S DESIGN

Whiteside had designed an octagonal house or hut of timber, 15' in diameter, perched on 9 legs or pillars, 5 of wood and 3 of cast iron, spaced round a central timber post. At the rock surface, the legs spanned 40' and the overall height was 65'. The iron pillars in lengths of 6' were bolted together and tapered from 9" at bottom to 6" at top. The thickness of the timber legs varied and the largest had a diameter of 2' 9" at the base. The house had two apartments, a living room below, divided into compartments for sleeping berths and stores, and a lightroom and lantern above.

SEASON 1775

In June 1775, after Phillips had scraped together sufficient funds to buy materials, an expedition led by Whiteside set out from a base at Solva, a small Welsh haven over 25 miles from the Smalls, with 8 miners, 1 blacksmith and 2 labourers in a cutter with the master and 2 hands, 'all employed in and upon the said expedition by John Phillips of Liverpool, to do their utmost in their several capacities to forward the same'. They were much delayed by being unable to find a suitable anchorage close to the Rocks and lost their moorings, 'the sea being turbulent, and a gale of wind coming on suddenly'. After a few days an anchorage was chosen half a mile off. It was decided to set the lighthouse upon the largest Rock of the Smalls group.

Five men were stranded on the Rock at the first attempt to work upon it: wind and sea rose suddenly and the cutter had to sheer off to avoid being wrecked. Fortunately one long rod had been securely driven into the rock to which the men could cling until the tide fell. Thereafter, standards and rings were fixed variously over the working area and gave protection from exceptional waves which might dash the men down on the rough surface.

On returning to Liverpool in October they made an affidavit before the Mayor, for the satisfaction of Phillips's creditors, in which they described their proceedings. They declared that from the 17th June when they left Liverpool until their return soon after the 5th October 'they missed no opportunity to do their utmost to accomplish the work they were sent to do: that in all this time they did not work on the Rock in the whole, more in proportion to nine days, owing to the badness of the weather, and in part of that time six of the miners made one hole, mortice or lodgment for the central pillar 18" deep, made a considerable progress in another, marked all the rest, and built a hut big enough to lodge twelve men and provision for them for 14 days, which hut they one and all apprehended will maintain its station during the next winter, that the building of this hut became a principal object with Henry Whiteside towards the close of the summer, as its being found standing on the subsequent spring will encourage the miners and others to dwell on the rock *de die in diem* and carry on their work in all weather without wishing to retreat till it is finished; that they are one and all of opinion the intended Light House may be erected in the course of a summer, perhaps in two months under the direction of the present engineer: that the violence of the sea and winds separately and united in the common effects of the

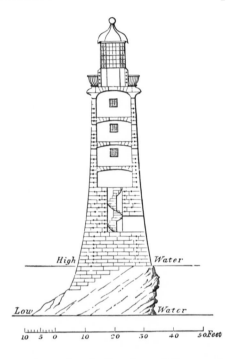

90. A sectional elevation of Smeaton's tower

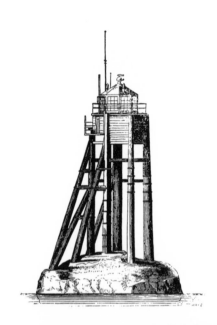

91. Whiteside's Smalls lighthouse lighted in 1776. The supports were altered on several occasions.

most tempestuous weather in this climate, cannot, they apprehend, destroy the Light House when erected, that they are led to this conclusion more decisively as five of them . . . were left on the Rock of necessity on the 26th and 27th of June last, then being at the height of a spring; and all of them have worked several times on the height of spring tides since in turbulent weathers; they are unanimous in the same opinion, as the materials whereof the hut is built, and many tools were left unsecured on the Rock for two successive springs, in both of which there were tempestuous gales and high seas; from the same premises they are severally and unitedly persuaded that they would have erected the intended Light House in course of the past summer, had they been employed as early in April last past, as they might have been'.

The impression they gave as to the exposure of the site and the difficulty of their work was much too optimistic. No doubt a few tools left on the Rock were not displaced by the waves during a particular fortnight of the summer of 1775, but the damage suffered in succeeding winters by the completed structure shows that a hut set on the Rock could not be expected to endure a winter's storms.

SEASON 1776

During the winter of 1775–6 Whiteside erected the whole structure temporarily at Solva, a fortunate decision as the iron legs proved to be faulty and he had to replace them with wood. Work was resumed on the Rock in the spring of 1776 and, thanks to the preliminary assembly when the parts were carefully fitted together, it proceeded so well that he showed lights on 1st September, a white light below and a green one above by which Phillips intended to direct shipping through the channels between the two clusters of Rocks. Doubtless this coloured light and the curious piled-structure were his promised novelties. Before leaving the Rock, the workmen excavated a hole as a cellar 10' × 6' × 6' to hold coals, and fresh water in a wooden tank.

SEASONS 1777–8

By December it was obvious that the structure was incapable of withstanding the sea forces and in January 1777 Whiteside and his blacksmith proceeded to the Smalls to repair and strengthen it. They encountered a period of severe storms. In February Williams, the local agent for Phillips, received a letter in a bottle which had drifted to the Welsh coast in a cask—one of three copies in bottles which had been tossed into the sea by Whiteside. Another bottle reached Galway Bay in west Ireland. The contents were as follows:

'Smalls February 1st 1777

To Mr. Williams,

'Sir, Being now in a most dangerous and distressed condition upon the Smalls, [we] do hereby trust Providence will bring to your hand this, which prayeth for your immediate assistance to fetch us off the Smalls before the next spring [tide] or we fear we shall perish; our water near all gone, our fire quite gone, and our house in a most melancholy manner. I doubt not but you will fetch us from here as fast as possible; we can be got off any part of the tide almost any weather. I need say no more, but remain your distressed humble servant,

Hy Whiteside'

The letter had the following postscript:

'We were distressed in a gale of wind upon the 13th of January, since when have not been able to keep any light, but we could not have kept any light above sixteen nights longer for want of oil and candles, which make us murmur and think we are forgotten.

Ed. Edwards
Geo. Adams
Jno. Price

We doubt not but that whoever takes up this will be so merciful as to cause it to be sent to Thos. Williams Esq. Trelethin near St. David's Wales.'

Even more drastic repairs and alterations became necessary after the storms, which Whiteside and his men survived, but Phillips had no funds to carry them out. He discharged the keepers and extinguished the light and made over his interest to a committee of Liverpool traders who were satisfied of the value of the light and considered that the structure merely required strengthening. They induced Trinity House to obtain an Act of Parliament in 1778 which authorised the Brethren to repair, re-build and maintain the lighthouse and to 'collect and levy reasonable duties'. In view of Phillips's services and his financial losses they granted him a lease on 3rd June 1778 for 99 years at a rent of £5. They advanced funds for strengthening the beacon by adding struts and ties and in September the white light, without the green, shone forth anew from 4 facet reflectors of 5′ 6″ diameter set back to back 90° apart, with an oil reservoir in the centre of the 4.

HISTORY AFTER 1800

Authoritative accounts of this lighthouse accept as true a tragic episode which seems to have occurred before 1801. Apparently, one of the two keepers died and the survivor, fearing that he might be suspected of murder if he committed the body to the deep, put it in a box which he made from the interior woodwork of the house, and lashed it to the lantern rail. Passing ships noticed this strange object but raised no alarm, as the light appeared as usual. Three weeks elapsed before the usual relief boat arrived to succour the unhappy survivor. Between 1801 and 1818 3 men kept the lighthouse in winter, 2 in summer.

It was noted in 1801 that the reflectors of 4′ diameter were worn out, giving a miserable light. In 1818, 18 reflectors of Trinity House type arranged in 2 tiers crowded the small lantern unduly. Their diameter was 1′ 8½″.

As a result of damage in October 1812 the keepers were withdrawn and the light was discontinued until the spring of 1813. In December Whiteside described the incident in a letter to Robert Stevenson: 'The misfortune that happened to the lightroom was at first by the sea breaking some of the windows, at which the men were so much terrify'd, thinking that if the sea and wind together came into the room at one side and no passage out at the other the top would be carried away, and without further hesitation they set to and broke the remaining windows. The room remains firm but as one of the house pillars is broken it must remain so for perhaps three months when the lights will be removed so soon as a temporary light would be more of use, and then when summer comes every other damage will be reinstated by a few men only at the time of landing the pillar. . . . It was a tremendous storm here such as cannot be remembered. The Smalls has now been up 37 years with no damage: only a few panes of glass broke sometimes. The men suffered very little hardships, only being frightened at the time of the storm. If they had stay'd there long their house would have been somewhat leaky the windows being broken. They had plenty of firing [fuel for heating] and everything they wish'd for to live upon. One of the men lived there thirteen years and they are going there again as soon as it is made tenantable.' From time to time the pillars were renewed. In 1831, the flooring and 2 sides of the cabin were forced in by the sea, the iron stove in the living-room squeezed flat and for 8 days the men cooked by the argand lamps of the light.

In 1823 Trinity House proposed to cancel the lease but considered exorbitant the sum of £148,430 at which the lessees valued their rights, the annual profit being £6,747. In 1836 the profits rose to £11,142 and the Corporation had to pay £170,468 for rights to the remaining 54 years of the lease, a capital sum fixed by a local jury.

On 7th August 1861 shipping saw a new light appear from the top of a stone lighthouse 107′ tall, built for Trinity House by Sir James Douglass and placed close to the old beacon which in 1801 had been described as a 'raft of timber rudely put together'. None the less, its survival for over 80 years is proof that Whiteside had made an admirable design. His simple method of raising a superstructure on piles, so that the sea could pass through them with but little obstruction, has been adopted since for hundreds of sea-structures. It is unnecessary that such a structure should bend to the waves as at the Smalls, where the slight movement experienced during storms struck new lightkeepers with terror.

IX

ENGLISH LIGHTHOUSES ESTABLISHED BETWEEN
1690 AND 1800

92. A typical English lighthouse in 1748 resembling the Skerries

ENGLISH LIGHTS IN 1819

The sites of the 37 coastal lights are numbered and those of the weak or local lights
mentioned in the text are named

1. Bembridge lightship
2. Burnham
3. Casquets
4. Cromer
5. Dudgeon lightship
6. Dungeness
7. Eddystone
8. Farnes
9. Flamborough
10. Flatholm

11. North Foreland
12. South Foreland
13. Galloper lightship
14. Goodwin lightship
15. Gull lightship
16. Happisburgh
17. Harwich
18. Hurst
19. Lizard

20. Longships
21. Lowestoft
22. Milford Haven
23. Needles
24. Newarp lightship
25. Nore lightship
26. Orfordness
27. Owers lightship
28. Portland

29. Isles of Scilly
30. Skerries
31. Smalls
32. Spurn
33. South Stack
34. Sunk lightship
35. Tynemouth
36. Walney
37. Winterton

IX. ENGLISH LIGHTHOUSES ESTABLISHED BETWEEN
1690 AND 1800

By 1700 the value of lighthouses was well recognised in England, so proposals to extend their service to the west coast were received with less disfavour; Trinity House obtained patents for several and granted leases to the proposers. In 1760 coal was the illuminant of 16 out of 24 coastal lighthouses but from 1788 the Elder Brethren took the lead in fitting argand lamps and parabolic reflectors at their new lighthouses and encouraged the managers of other lighthouses to take similar action, thus making the English coasts the best lighted in the world before the end of the century.

EDDYSTONE LIGHTHOUSES 1698–1759

An account of the lighthouses built on the Eddystone Rocks successively by Winstanley, Rudyerd and Smeaton is contained in Section VIII.

MILFORD HAVEN 1714

Soon after 1700 an agitation for the lighting of the west coast of England arose among sea-traders in that region, and on receiving a petition for a lighthouse at St. Ann's Head near Milford Haven, Trinity House applied to the Crown for a patent, which was granted on 15th March 1713. Dues of 1d. per ton would be paid compulsorily by British ships and 2d. by strangers. The Corporation agreed to lease its patent rights to Joseph Allen, described in the deed as the first proposer and the owner of the headland. He undertook to erect two lighthouses, keep them in repair and leave peaceably in 99 years when the lease expired. Trinity House set aside for the relief of its poor the rent of £10 payable by Allen. On 24th June 1714, before the lease was signed, Allen had erected the towers close to the lighthouse that had been disused since 1667 and kindled coal fires on their tops.

As this was the first lighting of the west coast, it might be supposed that one coal fire would suffice. But the possibility that ships approaching England from the south or the west might proceed too far to the north and mistake a single fire at St. Ann's Head for the fire of the Scilly Isles was probably the reason for setting up two lighthouses.

On 20th June 1800, reflectors with argand lamps in glazed lanterns replaced the coal fires, the lessees having accepted the views of Trinity House that the change would benefit navigation. The Corporation carried out the alterations at a cost of £2,600, which was repaid out of the dues, and thereafter undertook the management of the lights for an annual charge of £140.

On expiry of the lease in 1813–14 the lights reverted to the Corporation with the net profits, which amounted for the year 1815 to £5,339. In 1820 the cost of collecting the dues amounted to £1,147 and the expense of maintaining the lights to £1,205.

PORTLAND 1716

Sir John Clayton had obtained a patent in 1669 for erecting a lighthouse on the south tip of Portland Bill, one light to be shown above another in the same tower, but his scheme lapsed, and not until some 40 years later did Trinity House come to consider that lights were desirable at this Point. In May 1716 it obtained a patent which described 'the passage by the island of Portland in dark nights being very dangerous and many ships . . . in a little space of time lost there'. In this application, the Brethren admitted that 'they co'd not demand and receive the Duties with't the King's licence'. These dues would be ¼d. per ton on English ships passing the light, and double on 'strangers'.

Subject to getting the patent, Trinity House, on 12th February 1716, gave a lease for 61 years at a rental of £100 to William Borrett, Francis Browne and others. It entitled

(a)   (b)

93 (a) and (b). The Portland lighthouses after re-building in 1788 (Whittock)

them to erect 'one or more convenient lighthouses on s'd island with good and visible lights to be kept continually there in the night season . . . so as Ships might the better come to their Ports with't peril'. Some such slight variation of the wording of Queen Elizabeth's Act of 1566 appeared in these patents. Charles Langridge or Langrishe, one of the patentees, erected the towers and kindled coal fires in glazed lanterns on 29th September 1716.

Though the lease stipulated clearly that on its expiry the patentees should 'peaceably and quietly leave, surrender and yield up' the lighthouse to Trinity House, the Corporation thought it well to seek legal opinion as to its rights and was advised in 1777 that when the day came it could take possession of the lighthouses, grounds and roads leading to them and that its first step should be to claim the dues collected for the patentees at the London Customs Office. Upon doing so the Corporation discovered that the patent did not give the right to collect dues in the Channel Islands where the ports were free: only an Act of Parliament could grant that authority.

In 1788–9 Trinity House rebuilt the two lighthouses at a cost of £2,000 and fitted *square* reflectors and argand lamps at the back tower and reflectors in conjunction with Rogers's lenses at the tall front tower.

About 1740 the annual net profits of the lights amounted to some £1,000 and from 1805 to 1815 they fluctuated between £1,076 and £3,100.

Skerries 1717

About 1658 a few shipmasters trading to Ireland called for lights in the Irish Sea, particularly for one on the Skerries, a cluster of Rocks 4 miles off Anglesey. But the undertaking was likely to be difficult and Trinity House both opposed and approved it on different occasions.

About 1705, after erection of the Eddystone lighthouse had demonstrated the feasibility of building towers on rocks, 140 sea-traders signed a petition drawn up by Captain John Davison asking for a light on the Skerries because 'many ships were cast away . . . chiefly for want of a light in the night on the Welsh Coast'. In 1711 Sir Edward Northey, the Attorney General, invited the views of Trinity House on a well-supported application for a patent which he had received in 1709 from Davison who 'hath taken partners' including Francis Browne, one of the Portland lessees. In reply, Trinity House claimed that Queen Elizabeth had given to it the right of erecting in England beacons, buoys and seamarks, 'yet sundry private persons had since procured letters-patent from the Crown and had thus diverted to themselves the profits from lights' which should rightfully go to the Trinity House charities. It claimed that all further lighthouse patents should be issued to it alone. The Corporation declared that there was no immediate necessity for a light on the Skerries but should the sea-traders to Ireland apply for a light and show readiness to pay a moderate duty, the Brethren would themselves erect one. Sir Edward advised the Crown that the Corporation had not an exclusive right to erect seamarks and suggested granting Davison's petition.

Probably some difficulty as to ownership of the site held up proceedings and the interest in a patent passed to William Trench on 13th July 1714. It gave him the right to dues of 1d. and 2d. per ton for 60 years at a rent of £5 to the Crown. In June 1713 he had obtained a 99 years' lease of the site on which the lighthouse should be built at a rent of £10 for the first year and £20 thereafter. The site was a small Rock that by mistake had been omitted from the deed of sale of farm land in the vicinity and so stayed with the previous owner.

In 1714 Trench loaded a ship with building materials and sent his son with six men to the Rock to commence operations, but she was wrecked and all lost their lives. He stated in 1723 that this calamity almost ruined his family and 'caused ye work to remain neglected until in ye year 1717' he completed his tower at a cost of over £3,000, 'about 150 foot higher than ye sea about it and on ye 4th of November a fire was kindled therein and ever since supported'.

When Trench died in 1729, heavily in debt, it appeared that over the previous 12 years his loss in maintaining the light exceeded £100 a year, which arose largely from inability to enforce payment of dues at Liverpool and possibly in Ireland. On production of figures showing these losses, his family had the good fortune to obtain an Act of Parliament which declared that as the cost had exceeded the dues collected and put Trench into debt, it was 'just and reasonable' that the lighthouse should be vested in his family 'for ever'. An amended patent extended to Ireland might have overcome any difficulty in collecting dues but no doubt it was considered that a grant in perpetuity required Parliamentary sanction. A Parliamentary Committee in 1834 regretted that such an exceptional and over-generous grant had been made.

For some time a man and his wife kept this isolated light at a salary of £15 a year. One night about 1739, while he fulfilled his duty of stirring the fire, his wife was terrified at the unexpected appearance of a negro entering their quarters, the survivor of a shipwreck that had just taken place on the Rock.

An account of 1777 gives the height of the tower as 36', tapering from 27' diameter at base to 21' at top, and brackets this fire with St. Bees as the worst lights in the kingdom. The grate burned 80 tons of coals a year and 100 tons during stormy winters. In 1801 the keeper stated the coal consumpt to be 150 tons but the previous figures are more likely. The chauffer measured 3' in diameter, 1' larger than St. Bees. On 20th February 1804 an oil light replaced the coal fire on the tower which had been raised by 22'.

On an average of the 7 years 1827 to 1833 the gross dues amounted to £14,479, the cost of collection to £1,604 and the expense of maintenance to £350, a profit of £12,525. This reversal of fortune since the death of Trench resulted from the development of Liverpool's trade with America.

St. Bees 1718

A lighthouse perched 300' above the sea on the cliffs of St. Bees Head greatly benefited small vessels trading between Wales and the Solway Firth. In 1718 Trinity House obtained a patent and granted a lease for 99 years to Thomas Lutwige at a rent of £20. As was usual in its leases, he would have the clear profit, keep the lighthouse in good repair and deliver it to the Corporation at the close of the term.

The coal fire burned in the open on a buttressed masonry tower. The grate used in 1801 measured 2' diameter at top, 1' 6" at base and 2' in depth. Such a small body of fire gave a variable illuminant which caused frequent complaints. The coal consumpt was said to be 130 tons but, as at the Skerries, this figure seems to have been an over-statement. It is unlikely to have exceeded half that amount, if one can judge from the complaints made about the fire. In 1814 Ayton, in a well-known description of the coast, mentions that he found the building 'of the meanest description and provided with a very bad light supplied by a coal fire. I imagine a light in this situation is admitted to be of very little use or such a one as this could not scarcely be submitted to or escape the vigilant observation of the Trinity House.'

Destruction of the building by fire in 1822 brought to an end this last coal fire lighthouse in Britain. Trinity House spent £2,322 on a new building with an argand and reflector light.

Cromer 1719

In an account of the Life family, owners of the land at Foulness near Cromer, it is said that Nathaniel Life, despite the fate of Clayton's unlighted tower, considered that the situation required a lighthouse and in 1717 built a tower on his land, hoping thus to be granted a patent for a light. It is more likely, however, and indeed is suggested by another source, that Life merely took steps for lighting the shell of Clayton's old tower. Assisted by Edward Bowell, a Younger Brother of Trinity House, he persuaded the Brethren to apply for a patent. They obtained it in 1719, the dues to be ¼d. per ton of general cargo and ½d. per chaldron of Newcastle coal. Life and Bowell jointly received a lease at a rental of £100, on Life's undertaking that the tower with one acre of ground should pass to Trinity House 'without it having been at a shilling of expense' when the patent expired in 61 years.

The patentees exhibited a coal fire enclosed in a lantern on 29th September 1719. In 1792 Trinity House, now in possession, fitted here its second flashing light, 5 reflectors and argand oil lamps on each of the 3 faces of a revolving frame. The frequent or rapid eclipse of the light annoyed some of the more conservative seamen, who described it as an *ignis fatuus* or will-o'-the-wisp.

CASQUETS 1724

About 1722, the owners of ships passing by 'certain dangerous Rocks called the Casketts' off Alderney in the Channel Islands, between England and France, applied to Thomas Le Cocq, the proprietor of the Rocks, as a proper person to manage a lighthouse upon them and offered to pay dues of ½d. per ton when their vessels passed the light. Le Cocq asked one of the Elder Brethren to put the proposal to the Corporation and they obtained the usual patent on 3rd June 1723 for lights to be continually burning in 'ye night season whereby seafaring men and mariners might take notice and avoid ye dangers'.

The prominent situation of the Rocks in mid-channel called for some special distinction as a contrast to the lighthouses on the opposite shores of England and France, and Trinity House decided that no less than three separate lights should be displayed in the form of a horizontal triangle. Accordingly, three towers containing *close fires*, i.e. coal fires burning in glazed lanterns, were erected and exhibited their lights on 30th October 1724. The towers were called St. Peter, St. Thomas and Dungeon.

The lease granted to Le Cocq by Trinity House lasted for 61 years at a rent of £50. He shared the profits with the Elder Brother who introduced him to the Corporation. This arrangement came to light on that individual's death and caused considerable displeasure among his fellow-Brethren; it led to a dispute that was brought to the Law Courts in 1741. His family held that he had been recompensed thus by Le Cocq for his services in designing the lighthouses as he was 'extraordinarily well-skilled in the manner of placing, building and constructing lighthouses and had frequently superintended such works and that such had in several instances been built and completed by his directions or plans as the architect or contriver thereof, and that he drew or corrected the plan for placing, building and constructing the lighthouses' erected by Le Cocq. The Brethren denied his technical pretensions and declared that he was 'an entire stranger to the nature thereof and utterly unqualified to give Thomas Le Cocq any assistance therein and that he had never had the direction of nor was concerned in any building of that nature or kind nor was ever in any lighthouse nor saw any lighthouse except in passing by the same at a distance at sea and that the lighthouses erected by Thomas Le Cocq were planned and designed and built and completed by the directions of William Norman who had before built sev'l structures of the like nature for several persons and was chiefly employed by the Corporation in building and repairing their lighthouses in several parts of the Kingdom'.

The London collector of the dues estimated in 1745 that they amounted to £650 per annum. Most years, since erection of the lights, had been 'years of peace and ye produce of ye dutys thereto not having been hurt by ye war with Spain only, to near so great a degree as they are likely to be hurt during ye p'sent war w'th France and Spain, they having more yn answer'd yt estimate on a medium of years to March 1743/4 w'n ye French war commenced, w'ch hath and is likely to hurt ye p'duce of ye s'd dutys, as ye posture of affairs is at p'sent, so as to fall under ye estimate'.

The three Casquets lights, having reverted to Trinity House, were converted to metal reflectors and argand lamps on 25th November 1790. Reflectors had been ordered by the Elder Brethren in 1779 but there is no record of their type or whether they were fitted. It is curious that Trinity House placed this order; the lease did not expire so soon.

NORE LIGHTSHIP 1731

Chiefly because of the obvious difficulties of keeping always on her station a vessel anchored out at sea and of finding men willing to endure the continuous hardship of such a situation, Trinity House condemned all the early proposals for establishing lightships. In poor visibility, too, the lights from such vessels would be ineffective, being merely a gleam from ship's horn-lanterns hoisted on cross-yards and containing candles or tiny oil lamps. Sir John Clayton had proposed one for the Nore in 1679 and the Brethren opposed it, perhaps automatically, as originating with their rival for patents. But many pilots and other seamen considered lightships to be not impracticable, such as Captain John Waggett of Yarmouth

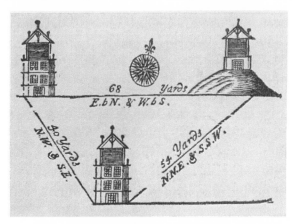

94. The 3 Casquets towers on a sea-chart of 1727

95. The Nore lightship, perhaps an
18th-century model (Barrett)

who stated in 1724 that only by using lightships would it be possible to reduce the ceaseless toll of vessels stranded on the numerous sandbanks off south-east England, but he could not convince persons in authority that his idea was sound.

It was by subterfuge that the first lightship came to be established. The affair originated with Robert Hamblin, a barber of Lynn who had married a shipmaster's daughter and thus became manager of a collier. After a varied and unsuccessful career, including adventures in smuggling, he found himself reduced to poverty about 1730 and fell in with David Avery, 'a gentleman of infinite projects, who rises every morning with 100 estates in his head, though most of them slip his pocket'.

Though not bred to the sea, Hamblin formed unusual opinions about navigation, one being that lightships should be moored at dangerous points on the coast. He saw that navigation suffered from the difficulty of distinguishing one lighthouse from another, despite the erection of two or three towers on the same headland or island, and considered that each lightship should show a different arrangement of lanterns.

Avery appreciated that profits might be gained from Hamblin's scheme for lightships but, anticipating the objections that would be raised by Trinity House, he decided that Hamblin should apply for a patent for distinguishing coastal lights from each other—'they moulded this project into the shape of a new invention, for which a patent for 14 years was to be obtained, as is usual and legal in cases of new inventions'.

So, in his petition to the King, Hamblin declared that the mistaking of one lighthouse for another 'hath often proved fatal both to men-of-war and merchant ships . . . that no method hath hitherto been made public sufficient to prevent these great and frequent disasters . . . the petitioner, having with great study, labour and expense, found out and invented a new method for distinguishing of lights whereby one light (erected for the guidance of shipping) may be perfectly known from another and consequently every ship's crew or single mariner be informed and know where they are or what coast they are off as well in the night as if it was day. . .'. On lodging an application incorporating this vague and apparently innocuous rigmarole he was granted a patent for 14 years from 4th July 1730, which disclosed that the lights should be 'composed of oil, tallow, wood, coals, pitch, tar or any other combustible, apart or mixed . . . and that the said lights be placed in such various forms, elevations, numbers and positions that one of them shall not resemble another in form. That as soon as the positions of the said distinguishing lights can be agreed upon and settled I, the said Robert Hamblin, will prepare and publish a new chart of all the sea-coasts of England showing all these lights.' None could guess from the terms of the patent that it concerned lightships and that he intended to moor them round the coast.

As soon as Hamblin received the patent, Avery took steps to carry out their project and in 1731 moored the first lightship close to the Nore buoy in the Thames estuary, and endeavoured to popularise the seamark by advertisement, by issuing charts of the area showing the channels through the sands and by publishing in the newspapers puffs as to the advantages of the lightship. These proved unnecessary, as coasters found her a great benefit and subscribed willingly to her upkeep. The lighting consisted of 2 ship's lanterns 12' apart, suspended on cross-arms from the single mast.

Hearing that Avery intended to moor another lightship off the Scilly Isles where it already exhibited a light and fearing that he would scatter others round the coasts and upset the lighthouse system, such as it was, and perhaps mislead navigation, Trinity House invited the Admiralty to join in objecting to the patent, chiefly on the technical plea that it disclosed no new invention, lightships having been proposed earlier. However, support was not forthcoming from the Admiralty, who approved of the scheme for lightships, so the Brethren were left alone to appeal to the Attorney General who explained that he had passed the patent in the belief that Hamblin intended to diversify lighthouses by using coloured lights. Ultimately, the King was advised to revoke the patent and he did so on 4th May 1732. Cancellation of a patent being unprecedented, the clerks had difficulty in drawing up the necessary document.

Avery then applied formally 'with much respect' to Trinity House for a lease of the Nore lightship, stating that he had spent £2,000 in fitting her out. As seafarers found her so useful the Brethren dared not remove her, so they obtained a patent in perpetuity, following the Skerries precedent, and granted Avery a lease for 61 years from 1733 at a rent of £100.

In 1736–7 they pressed a law-suit against a number of shipowners whose vessels passed the lightship and claimed that she had been 'exhibited at a very great charge' at 'the east end of the s'd Noreland'. They alleged that these persons had entered 'into a combination and confederacy' to defraud the Corporation of the duties, well knowing that the Brethren could not provide legal proof that the vessels had passed the light, or how often.

In defence, the shipowners relied on the general principle of the British Constitution that power to levy taxes lay entirely with Parliament. The lightship duties, they pointed out, had been authorised merely by Crown patent, so could not be exacted. The Court rejected this contention as being contrary to the practice with such patents and ordered that the dues should be paid. The Corporation's suit failed against British fishing-boats which, in the Court's opinion, 'have ever had an undoubted right and liberty to fish in the seas and rivers' without payment of tolls.

DUDGEON LIGHTSHIP 1736

A lightship at the Dudgeon or Wells sandbank some 26 miles from land and lying off the Wash, the large bay on the east coast of England, had been proposed by Captain Waggett in 1724. Avery, too, recognised that one would be of value to the colliers plying between Newcastle and London, so, when inviting their promise of contributions to the upkeep of the Nore lightship, he held out the additional inducement of another lightship at the Dudgeon. Accordingly, after he established the Nore, they pressed him for the promised second vessel at the Dudgeon where the exposure in the North Sea far exceeded that of the Nore which lay within the comparative shelter of the Thames estuary. Trinity House appreciated the difficulty of a ship holding her station at the Dudgeon but decided that if she broke adrift she would have plenty of sea-room for manœuvre so it applied for and obtained a patent in 1736.

To please the Corporation, Avery formed a small syndicate with two traders, whose names it had suggested, as partners, and its lease was made out to these three individuals for a term of 21 years. They established the lightship, a sloop as at the Nore, on 1st June 1736.

The Brethren disliked these lightships or *alarm vessels* and hoped to stave off proposals for others by charging a stiff rental for the Dudgeon, £200 for the first 2 years and £300 thereafter. In 1739 they received a proposal for another at the Cockle Gatt, a channel through sandbanks off Norfolk. This they turned down owing to the serious consequences of a lightship in that position breaking adrift, when the tides and winds would surely drive her on the adjacent sandbanks, an occurrence that 'might not only be fatal to those on board her but to others also, who might depend upon and miss her and whom such dependence might betray into ruin'.

FLATHOLM 1737

On pressure from sea-traders of Bristol, Trinity House agreed to the establishment of a lighthouse on Flatholm island in the Bristol Channel and obtained a patent on 2nd June 1737. Contrary to the usual practice the document specified that the lighthouse should show a *fire*, a restrictive term that had been used in the Forelands patent of 1636. One supposes that the local seamen still preferred coal fires to oil and candle lights. Considering the wrecks which took place frequently on the island, which blocked the direct track seawards from Bristol and the Severn ports, it is remarkable that a light was not set upon it earlier.

On 3rd September 1737 the Corporation granted a lease for 99 years to William Crispe, who erected a round stone tower to a height of 72' and lit it by an open coal fire on 1st December 1737. He paid a rent of £5 for the first 50 years and £10 thereafter.

Flatholm remained a coal fire until 7th September 1820 when an oil reflector light shone forth from the tower, raised to 90'.

LIZARD 1752

In 1748 Richard Farish, with the consent of Thomas Fonnereau the owner of the Lizard Point, proposed to Trinity House to erect the surprising number of four lighthouses there as a distinction from other lighthouses. The Corporation preferred only two towers, with less cost and smaller dues, and authorised Farish to invite seafarers to sign the usual petition. He obtained many signatures for 'good and sufficient' fire lights. Before his death in 1750 he assigned his *rights* as an applicant or first proposer to Fonnereau, with whom Trinity House made an agreement in 1751 by which it would apply at his expense for a patent and he would pay an annual rent of £80 for a lease for 61 years to commence from his 'kindling two convenient lighthouses'.

On 24th July 1751 two of the Elder Brethren, Captains Joseph Cartaret and Edward Smith, proceeded to the Lizard Point at Fonnereau's expense 'to mark out the most proper spot', and the lights were completed and exhibited on 23rd August 1752. Glass screens, if not closed lanterns, sheltered coal grates. The total cost of erection exceeded £3,000, which seems high.

The Trinity House solicitor prepared a lease in September 1753 which contained a provision that if, on Crown orders, the lights should be extinguished during war or on other occasions, the rent should be reduced in proportion to the time during which dues were lost. Despite this concession, Fonnereau received the document with fury and declared that several of the provisions had been 'artfully thrown into the articles to the secret interest' of Trinity House; he objected particularly to the Corporation's usual stipulation that on the expiry of the lease the lighthouse and the ground on which it stood should pass to the Brethren without compensation to him. The legality of this clause had never been tested in the Law Courts. He claimed too that the rent already agreed to by him should be reduced on the ground that he had been put to additional expense by their insistence on the towers being built to a height of 40′ exclusive of the lanterns, whereas he believed that a height of 20′ would suffice for towers set on the high cliffs of the Lizard. He took them to law and appealed against an adverse decision in 1765 but Trinity House succeeded finally in 1771.

A cottage was built between the two towers, in which an *overlooker* lay at night on a sort of couch, with a window on each side commanding a view of the lanterns. When the bellows-blowers relaxed their efforts, he would remind them of their duties by a blast from a cow horn. A similar method of attracting the keeper's attention when a light was not burning well was adopted at Lindesnes in Norway in 1782 when the Government took over the lights: a supervisor was appointed to live near and he warned the keeper by firing a gun.

SMALLS 1775–8

An account of the lighthouse built on these Rocks by Whiteside is contained in Section VIII.

AIR POINT 1777

The success of the reflector lights at Liverpool had the effect of spurring traders concerned in the neighbouring navigation of the river Dee to Chester (connected to the river Mersey by channels through the sandbanks) to establish seamarks, and the Chester Town Council applied to Parliament for an Act to set up landmarks and buoys in the river and lighthouses at either Air Point or Prestatyn. Their value would be entirely local so it is curious that Trinity House, which felt no concern with the Liverpool lights, petitioned against the proposed Act, putting forward the familiar claim that general powers to erect lighthouses in England had been conferred upon it and that the Act would interfere with its rights. The Brethren informed the Council that after discussing with the Admiralty a proposal to erect a light for the benefit of both Liverpool and Chester, they had decided that it would be useful and they offered to erect it. Eventually they gained in the Act recognition of their interest and leased the light to Chester Council for an annual contribution to their charities. The tower was placed at Air Point close to the river channel, having lights visible up and down stream which were lit on 30th September 1777.

On several occasions feeling ran high in Chester when Trinity House condemned the lighthouse as being badly kept. The Corporation took it over in 1816 and fitted reflectors and argand lamps. Under a Bill drafted in 1813 Liverpool had proposed to buy this lighthouse.

FARNES 1778

After Clayton built his unlighted tower on this cluster of rocks and islets, belonging to the Diocese of Durham and 2 miles off the Northumbrian coast, more than 100 years elapsed before seafarers agitated successfully for a lighthouse there. In the usual way Trinity House obtained a patent and gave a lease on 6th July 1776 to the predecessors of the Blackett family, occupiers of the islands, who showed lights, probably oil lamps, in 1778 from two lighthouses, one on the principal island and another on the Staples island, the latter a stone cottage with roof sloping up to a central glazed lantern. Robert Darling, grandfather of Grace Darling who assisted her father in saving the passengers and crew of the *Forfarshire*, which was wrecked on the Farnes in 1838, served here as a lightkeeper in 1795.

About 1800, on complaints as to the visibility of the lights which now were coal fires, Trinity House desired the Blacketts to fit reflectors and argands. When they demurred, the lease was examined and found never to have been executed, whereupon they hastened to accept the Corporation's proposals. To meet the cost, local shipowners agreed to pay increased tolls as authorised by a new patent of November 1810. For £8,500 Daniel Alexander, the Trinity House architect, built two new lighthouses on the Farne and the Longstone Rocks, both containing reflectors with argands, revolving every half-minute, and a third small tower with a fixed oil light. Trinity House desired that the Blacketts should not lose by the invalidity of the original lease and granted them a new lease but took over management of the lights and paid them annually the profits of the dues less the cost of upkeep. This generosity proved extremely expensive, for in November 1825 Trinity House was required to pay to the lessees £36,484 for the rights to the profits for the remaining 15 years (about £1,900 annually) and in addition it spent £6,063 in erecting a new lighthouse with other buildings on the Longstone.

In 1777 the Trustees of Lord Crewe had made elaborate arrangements to relieve shipwrecks along this coast. In thick fog a bell was rung from Bamburgh Castle and a *large swivel* gun fired every 15 minutes. During storms two men on horseback patrolled the shore from sunset to sunrise, one to give immediate assistance to ships and the other to summon help. Implements for raising stranded ships were kept ready for use, including a pair of chains 'for weighing vessels of even 1000 tons lost in deep water'. *Sailing Directions* between 1802 and 1820 conveyed the grim comfort: 'Dead bodies cast on shore are decently buried gratis'. Shipwrecked seamen were clothed and lodged for a week and a premium, doubled after midnight, was given to the first person reporting a wreck.

NEEDLES AND HURST *c.* 1786

The need for lights in the neighbourhood of the Isle of Wight was recognised some time before 1781 when, in accordance with the usual practice, shipmasters and merchants met to approve the terms of a formal petition to Trinity House (which obtained a patent in January 1782). It stated that 'ships and vessels have been lost . . . and the lives, ships and goods of his Majesty's subjects as well as the King's Royal Navy continue to be exposed to the like calamities more especially in the night time and in hard southerly gales'. The patent directed that lights should be 'kept burning in the night season whereby seafaring men and mariners might take notice of and avoid dangers . . . and ships and other vessels of war might safely cruize during the night season in the British Channel'.

Before receiving a patent Trinity House discussed several draft agreements with William Tatnall, merchant, of Ironmonger Lane, London, who projected the lights. In 1781 it was proposed that he should erect at his own expense lights, buildings and roads, and provide proper lightkeepers at the Needles, St. Catherine's Point and at two light-houses at Hurst, at sites to be chosen by Trinity House or its surveyor. The Corporation would receive the dues and would pay him £960 per annum for 21 years as compensation for the first cost and maintenance. If the first cost exceeded £2,000, the payment should be increased by 10 per cent. By an alternative draft Trinity House would erect lighthouses 'fit for the exhibiting therein of oil lights for the benefit of navigation' with 'houses or tene-ments proper for the dwellings of the lightkeepers' and pay £760 to Tatnall who would keep burning continually during the night season 'good, visible and suff't oil lights', but he would not be required to make good damage from fire, storm, tempest or 'firing of canon on Hurst Castle'.

In 1785 negotiations with Tatnall fell through and Trinity House erected to the designs of R. Jupp, three lighthouses at the Needles, St. Catherine's Point and Hurst. It lighted the Needles and Hurst towers on 29th September 1786. As shipping found the Hurst light to be masked from certain directions the Corporation constructed in 1812 an additional and higher light, as proposed originally, both to overcome the defect and to give a guiding line to vessels. After completing the tower for St. Catherine's, the Brethren abandoned it because mists and fogs would obscure the light, 750' above sea-level. They set the Needles light on the top of the cliff 474' above sea-level and for the same reason as at St. Catherine's replaced it in 1859 by the present tower at the end of the Point near sea-level.

OWERS LIGHTSHIP *c.* 1788

The Owers shoal trapped many ships making for Portsmouth from the east, but the idea of setting a lighthouse upon it seemed visionary, because the foundation would be under water and difficult to prepare. About 1785 the need for a seamark here became urgent, perhaps from the increasing use of Portsmouth by the Navy, and Trinity House decided that marking the shoal by a lightship would be the most feasible method and soonest done. A patent of 14th August 1788 authorised the imposition of dues and a lightship built at a cost of £4,500 was moored off the shoal soon after, with a lantern raised aloft, but she broke away so often, arriving once off St. Valery in France, that for some time it seemed doubtful if she could be held at her station.

As an alternative, a sunken rock at the east end of the shoal and 8 miles from land was thought to offer a foundation for an iron lighthouse, and the Corporation instructed John Smeaton to survey the rock and give his opinion. Setting out from the lightship in a 6-oared boat, he examined the area and found that the rock lay some 6′ below low water springs. He reported that by using a diving bell, a stone lighthouse might be constructed, but the expense would exceed £20,000. He would fit the lower stones upon the rock as he had done at the Eddystone but the underwater foundation work would be exceedingly difficult. Fortunately new moorings designed for the lightship held her successfully and obviated the building of a lighthouse.

WALNEY 1790

By an Act of Parliament of 1789, the merchants of Lancaster had authority to set a lighthouse on Walney island and collect dues. The Commissioners appointed to administer the Act raised a tower in 1790, engaged two lightkeepers and on 1st December showed a fixed light from ordinary oil lamps with parabolic reflectors.

According to their Minutes, Richard Walker, who had built quays at Lancaster, produced at their meeting of 7th October 1791 a model for the improvement of Walney light 'by making the Reflectors and their lamps revolve round an axis so that every point of the compass may in its turn receive the benefit. The light with model is approved and Mr. Walker is requested to go to Walney to make the necessary observations for carrying the same into execution.' This gave a welcome distinction from the lights of St. Bees and Liverpool. In May 1792 the Commissioners paid Walker's bill of £21. 11. 5½. No connection can be traced between Walker and Trinity House. It is likely that he knew of its new revolving apparatus at the Scilly Isles and of the reflectors at Liverpool, but made his own design which may have been executed by William King of Whitehaven.

Probably it is Walker's apparatus that Robert Stevenson described in 1801, 3 reflectors of 3′ diameter set back to back making a revolution in 15 minutes to give a long flash every 5 minutes. The reflectors were set upon a vertical axle fixed to a revolving drum of some 4′ diameter round which cords were wound. Weights drove the clockwork, checked by gearing placed near the lantern roof, and turned the drum. At that date a local farmer maintained the light very carelessly—his servants gave it attention when their usual duties permitted—and its visibility suffered.

NEWARP LIGHTSHIP AND HAPPISBURGH 1791

A terrible disaster in the Cockle Gatt or channel on 30th October 1789 caused an enquiry by Trinity House into the lighting of the Norfolk coast. Two fleets, the one consisting of ships with cargoes bound for London and the other of unladen vessels proceeding northwards from the Thames, ran foul of each other in a heavy gale. Over 23 ships sank, another 20 drove ashore and 600 lives were lost.

The Elder Brethren considered that the Caistor lights had contributed to the calamity and discontinued them as being misleading. Instead, they placed a lightship at the Newarp sand and erected two fine lighthouses with reflectors and argands at Happisburgh. In terms of a patent dated 30th October 1790 they were lit formally on 1st January 1791. The towers cost £5,500 and the lightship, which carried 2 horizontal lanterns, £4,500. There are variations of the name Happisburgh, such as Haisborough.

MUMBLES *c.* 1794

Empowered by Act of Parliament, Trinity House in March 1794 granted to Swansea Town Council a 99 years' lease at £5 rental of a light to be erected on the outer of 2 islets at the north end of Swansea Bay. An architect's design shows this lighthouse as a stone structure of probably 8 sides receding in steps as it rose to give the effect of 5 tiers. One coal fire in a brazier raised on legs appears on the top and another in front of the third tier, but it is likely that a lantern was set on top of this stepped tower 60′ high showing one oil lamp. Certainly in 1802 a glass lantern held reflectors with argands which numbered 13, according to a list of some years later. In September 1823 Trinity House offered unsuccessfully to buy back the remainder of the lease. About 1835 the Swansea harbour authorities took complete possession of the lighthouse. It had not been a lucrative investment: from 1793 to 1832 the gross dues amounted to £32,028 and after deducting the costs of maintenance, the profits over the 40 years totalled only £6,270.

GOODWIN LIGHTSHIP 1795

As stated already, no sandbank brought about the destruction of so many ships and seamen as the Goodwin sands, lying off the Kentish coast between England and France. In 1736 when two pilots suggested marking the sands by a lightship to carry 3 lights, Trinity House dismissed the proposal as *trifling*. About 1790, the increasing toll of wrecks forced further consideration of the problem but the extreme severity of exposure decided Trinity

96. A wreck off the Mumbles lighthouse *c.* 1870

97. A drawing about 1890 of the improbable story of the child lighting the Longships lamps when her father was kidnapped

House against using lightships—'a lightship would not ride, would break adrift and drown all the people'. A lesser objection was that a lightship might be invaluable to privateers and to smugglers who were said to have long used as a haven, a pool in the heart of the sands, near the proposed site of the mark.

In 1791 Trinity House received a definite proposition to set a lightship at the Sandheads, the north end of the Goodwins, and to move the North Foreland lighthouse nearer the Point. The petition had extensive and influential support. It described how on foggy nights, boatmen from Deal, Ramsgate and other Channel ports went out with their boats and ranged themselves along the outer edge of the Goodwins, which they knew intimately, 'in full expectation that some unfortunate ship will stumble on the sand when they seize them as their prey . . . nor do these men dread any thing so much as a light to prevent such calamities'. On one occasion the master of a vessel lying in the Downs had seen no less than 30 ships lost on the Goodwins. 'The bare interest of the property lost on the Goodwin sands in one year would maintain a floating light as long as this world endures.'

Impressed by the success of the Owers and Newarp lightships, the Brethren obtained a patent on 17th December 1793 and in August 1795 showed a light from a vessel that cost £5,000. Her establishment undoubtedly reduced the occurrence of wrecks, but despite the subsequent mooring of more lightships nearby, equipped with the best of lights and sound signals and radio beacons, these extensive sandbanks still remain a constant menace to navigation, and claim victims most years. The losses of the Goodwin lightships in December 1929 and November 1954 recall the doubts felt by the Brethren 160 years ago.

By the time the first Goodwin lightship was ready for service the Brethren were fired with undue optimism. The *Notice to Mariners* which they issued with a small chart in August 1795 intimated that in fog 'a large bell will be kept constantly ringing on board of Her, to warn Ships. . . . The situation of this Floating Light appears to be so well judged, that it will be impossible for any vessel to get upon the North Sand Head, or any part of the *Goodwin*, if the Master will but pay proper Attention to the three following Short and easy Directions. . . .'

LONGSHIPS 1795

Around the cliffs of Land's End, at the extreme south-west point of the British mainland, there is displayed during storms a wild panorama described by John Ruskin as an 'entire disorder of the surges . . . the whole surface of the sea becomes one dizzy whirl of rushing writhing tortured undirected rage, bounding and crashing and coiling in an anarchy of enormous power'. The headland is encircled by rocks on which countless ships have been lost in heavy seas or during poor visibility. Disasters occur infrequently at the present day because vessels navigating in the immediate vicinity have the aid of numerous seamarks equipped with the latest electronic devices: the Longships lighthouse 1 mile to the west, the lighted buoy on the Rundlestone 1 mile to the south, the Wolf Rock lighthouse 8 miles to the south and the Sevenstones lightship moored 16 miles off, midway to the Scilly Isles. Other more distant seamarks also assist vessels in this area.

In 1790 the area was completely devoid of such aids and the coast dwellers, many being active wreckers, gained an ample livelihood from plundering the ships driven on the rocks, of which each winter brought a full harvest.

146

It seemed impracticable before 1780 to erect and maintain useful lighthouses in this area. Coal fires would have been the most satisfactory type but they could not be recognised, one from another, unless erected in groups. That was impracticable on the small rocks that required marking and confusion might have resulted with the groups of two and three fires exhibited already at the Lizard and the Casquets. With formidable outlying dangers calling for seamarks, shipping had no alternative to recognising the Land's End area to be so dangerous to navigation that it should be avoided at night: seamen from the south and west who sighted the Scilly light must set their course accordingly.

98. The Longships lighthouse with the lantern stayed in the English style
(Daniell)

Ultimately the needs of navigators had to be met and seamarks planned in this dark region. From 1787 Trinity House took a closer interest in lighthouses and appreciated the possibilities of oil reflector lights. In June 1790, the Brethren employed John Smeaton to survey the islet of Roseveern in the Scillies for a lighthouse, as an alternative to one on the Wolf Rock. Eventually they decided that the site was too far distant from the actual dangers of the Wolf and Longships Rocks.

On 30th June 1791 they obtained a patent in the usual way after lodging a petition from seafarers, which seems to have envisaged a lighthouse on the Wolf. They avoided still the trouble to themselves of building any lighthouse difficult to construct, and gave a lease in October to Lieutenant Henry Smith, who afterwards came to the conclusion that the task was beyond him and it is doubtful whether he attempted any work on the Wolf under that lease. On 29th September 1795 he got another lease from the Corporation by which he would erect a lighthouse on the Longships and iron beacons on the Wolf and the Rundle-stone. The lease recorded that Smith got it 'as a reward for the suggestion'. It fixed the rental at £100 for Trinity House charities and the term as 50 years. As described in Section V the beacons which Smith fixed on the Wolf and Rundlestone Rocks were swept away immediately by the waves. Similar projects were attempted in 1835.

A lighthouse on Carn Bras, the largest of the Longships Rocks, which rose 40′ above high tides, seems to have been built in 1794–5 without undue trouble by Samuel Wyatt, architect to Trinity House. His circular granite tower had 3 storeys; the lowest contained water tanks and stores, the next formed a living room, and the lightkeepers used as a bedroom the top storey under the wood and copper lantern, elevated 79′ above the sea, which held 18 parabolic metal reflectors and argands, arranged in 2 tiers. None shone towards the land, thus saving expense in oil. Metal sheets blocked the windows in that direction.

99. North Foreland lighthouse in 1790

100. North Foreland lighthouse in 1792. The old tower had been raised to 64′ 7″ and Rogers's lenses set into the lantern panes, but Fenn, the artist, did not show them correctly

Soon after lighting the tower on 29th September 1795 Smith was declared 'incapable of managing the concern'. Trinity House took it over and remitted the profits to his family through the Court of Chancery. His address in 1806 was the Fleet Prison in London. As debtors lodged there, one might suppose his troubles to be financial. At an interview with Smith in that year Stevenson enquired as to what difficulties had been experienced in erecting the Longships tower and formed no high opinion of his capacity for sea-works.

The lightkeepers on the Longships led a primitive existence, cooking their meals in the lantern by the argand lamps. Four men stayed two and two on the Rock for one month at a stretch. They received £30 each per annum and free food at the lighthouse but when ashore they provided for themselves and had to take what additional employment they might find.

The tragedy surrounding the death about 1800 of the lightkeeper on the Smalls lighthouse, which apparently was a true occurrence, has not been overlooked among stories about lighthouses, but in 1876 a writer of repute went far in exaggeration and inaccuracy:

'Tales terrible, but true, of suicide and murder have long ago proved the inexpediency and dangers of smaller numbers than three lightkeepers living together at a tower.' In referring to the Longships in particular, he attempted to curdle his readers' blood by stating 'More than one untrained keeper has been driven insane from sheer terror'. The waves dashing into a cavern in the Rock and compressing the air within, formed the basis for his statement that 'one of the keepers of early days who was left alone there and had not been informed previously of the horrible noises caused by the pent-up air in the cavern below, became so terrified that his hair turned white in a single night'; but his story of a little girl left alone in the lighthouse, 'her father the keeper having been purposely kidnapped and confined by wreckers, and who was reluctantly obliged to stand on the Family Bible to light the lamps' cannot be substantiated. The incident is pictured in figure 97.

As at the Farnes, the generosity of Trinity House to Smith's family (apparently merely because he had first proposed the lighthouse) proved much more costly than intended. The free profit of the lighthouse rose to £3,017 in 1831 after meeting the maintenance cost of the light of £1,183. In 1836 the profit was £8,293 and with $9\frac{1}{2}$ years of the lease unexpired, the Corporation bought out the lessees for £40,676 inclusive of life-rents.

From the terrific seas which swept over the Rock during storms, the lantern was so often under water that the character of a fixed light could not be determined with certainty. This eclipse by the waves was the reason given for replacement of Wyatt's tower by Douglass's higher tower built 80 years later. The original building had served well: Trinity House retained it in service for 40 years after taking it over in 1836.

SUNK LIGHTSHIP *c.* 1798

The success of the lightship on the Goodwins led to further appeals for lightships elsewhere. The supreme importance to Britain of London as a trading port and the direct interest of Trinity House in marking the complicated navigable channels in the Thames estuary (the management of which, unlike that of other British navigations, lies in its hands), probably led to the choice of the Sunk sandbank as the site of the next lightship. This important position marked the entrance into the Thames channels from the north. Under a patent of 7th July 1796 a single ship's lantern was exhibited from a lightship costing £5,000 which was moored there about 1798.

LOCAL OR HARBOUR LIGHTS

An account of 18th-century lighthouses in England would be incomplete without a reference to the seamarks of Liverpool which, being required for that port alone, were apparently of no interest to Trinity House. Other harbours showed simple lights from candles or oil lamps, also without question by the Elder Brethren.

LIVERPOOL 1763–79

In 1959 Liverpool, second in importance after London as a British trading port, is entered by a channel, dredged ceaselessly, through a bar of sand stretching across the river Mersey. In the 18th century engineering was incapable of deep dredging, so ships had to proceed by devious and shallow shifting channels complicated by the river Dee, some

10 miles to the south, debouching into the same extensive sandbanks. By 1710 Liverpool glimpsed her destiny as a seaport and secured an Act of Parliament authorising construction of a dock. Seamarks were not overlooked. By 1683 some turning points in the channels through the banks had been marked by unlighted beacons or perches and by buoys. The first of two large unlighted beacons which in line would indicate a deep channel from the sea, was under construction at Formby in 1719.

In 1759 when trade across the Atlantic was increasing rapidly—141 vesssels sailed from Liverpool for America in the year 1764—it was proposed to moor a vessel with 2 lanterns

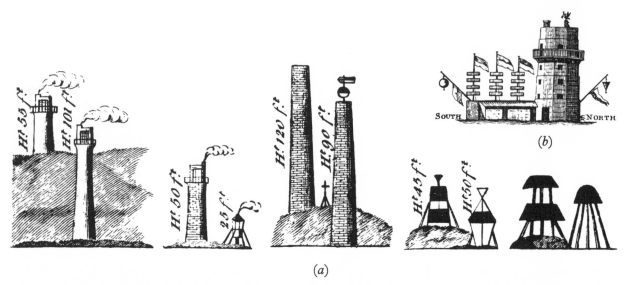

101 (*a*) and (*b*). Liverpool lighthouses and beacons on a sea-chart of 1771–7. (*a*): From the left, the pairs are the Sea Lights, the Lake Lights, and the Formby, Bootle and north-end beacons. (*b*): Above on the right is Bidston lighthouse in 1777 which served as a watch-tower, flags and shapes being hoisted on a long row of masts to warn each Liverpool merchant when his ship was sighted

off Hoylake at the entrance to one of the deeper channels. Her primary purpose may have been to assist pilotage but she would serve admirably to guide shipping. As the other sea-marks were unlighted, navigation through the sandbanks required to be conducted in day-light. The need to help vessels caught by darkness to cope with currents, calms or winds may have forced the provision of guiding lights. Such were authorised by Liverpool's second Navigation Act of 1762.

During 1763 and 1764 the town constructed four lighthouses, a pair of brick towers at Leasowe known locally as the Sea Lights, and another pair at Hoylake known as the Lake Lights which consisted of a tall rear brick tower and a low timber structure on the foreshore, which could be moved as the channel shifted. Each pair directed vessels through one of the navigation channels. After the front Lake Light was destroyed by sea erosion in 1771 a new rear light was erected on a 55′ high octagonal tower on Bidston Hill which gave the same guiding line in conjunction with the remaining Lake Light. It is likely that the lights consisted of flat-wick oil lamps. In addition to establishing lighthouses, the town erected at Bootle two timber leading beacons 51′ and 45′ high. The Formby beacons were now stone or brick towers 90′ and 120′ high. During 1764, 18 vessels had stranded, with a loss of 75 lives, in the approaches to the port. Soon, however, the four guiding lights reduced casualties materially. This complicated navigation had much need of all these lights, beacons and buoys; they provided vessels with a choice of 3 main channels over the bar and through the sands, by one of which they could enter the Dee estuary and pass through the banks after dropping some cargo to lighten their draft. A chart of 1771–6 shows that a boat was kept ready at Formby 'to save Lives from Vessels forced on Shore . . . *a Guinea*, or more, Reward is paid by the Corporation for every human Life that is saved by Means of *this Boat*'.

Parabolic facet reflectors were in use at the Liverpool lights from 1772. It is unlikely that they were installed earlier. The only contemporary references to the lights before 1772 are to *light fires* in 1764 and to *lamp lights* in 1767 which can describe oil lamps without reflectors.

From 1766 a scheme was worked out for a station in Anglesey where vessels making for Liverpool could pick up pilots. A deputation from the port examined several sites and chose one at Point Lynus. At first the pilots used a farm house on the Point as a look-out. After 1779 they exhibited in 2 directions oil lamps with Hutchinson's small metal reflectors.

Much trouble was taken with the navigation buoys at Liverpool. In 1794 Hutchinson mentioned that their chains 'for sake of lightness we make of a long eye bolt of 18″ and a short oval link of 6″ alternately'. He stated that 'as ships have been often lost by going on the wrong side of buoys, they may be much better distinguished from each other by the shape of their upper ends, than by different colours'. That view is accepted today. On the question of the best colour he wrote, 'as to distinguishing buoys by the colours of black and white; I think these colours difficult and very uncertain to be perceived, in the different states of our air; and white buoys are bad to be seen in broken waves. From many trials I have made of all the principal colours, red is the most striking and best to be seen on buoys, as well as landmarks'. Today most navigation buoys are painted black, red or green, or are striped or chequered.

X

SCOTTISH AND IRISH LIGHTHOUSES 1700 TO 1800

102. Cloch lighthouse established in 1797

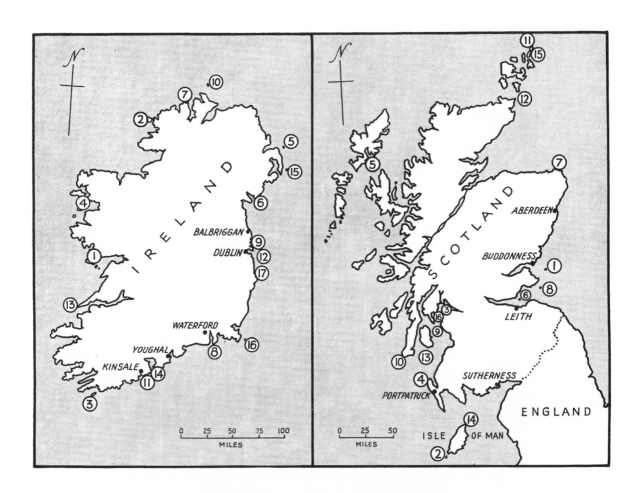

IRISH AND SCOTS LIGHTS IN 1819

The sites of the 17 Irish coastal lights and of the 16 Scots and Manx coastal lights are numbered and those of the weak or local lights mentioned in the text are named. The light of North Ronaldsay was extinguished in 1819 but was re-exhibited some years later

IRELAND		SCOTLAND AND ISLE OF MAN	
1. Aran island	10. Inishtrahull	1. Bell Rock	9. Little Cumbrae
2. Arranmore	11. Old Head of Kinsale	2. Calf of Man	10. Mull of Cantyre
3. Cape Clear	12. Kish lightship	3. Cloch	11. North Ronaldsay
4. Clare	13. Loop Head	4. Corsewall	12. Pentland Skerries
5. Copeland	14. Roches Point	5. Eilean Glas	13. Pladda
6. Cranfield	15. South Rock	6. Inchkeith	14. Point of Ayre
7. Fanad Head	16. Tuskar	7. Kinnaird Head	15. Start Point
8. Hook	17. Wicklow	8. Isle of May	16. Toward
9. Howth			

X. SCOTTISH AND IRISH LIGHTHOUSES 1700 TO 1800

Before 1780 the overseas trade of these countries was small and justified the establishment of only a few lighthouses; but after 1786 more were erected, some on the north and west coasts of both countries at sites involving unusual difficulties in transport and maintenance. All the new lighthouses were fitted with parabolic reflectors or lenses.

THE SCOTTISH LIGHTHOUSES 1700–1800

THE CLYDE LIGHTHOUSES

In 1656 Thomas Tucker, who had been commissioned by Oliver Cromwell to report on the condition of British trade, described that of Glasgow as 'chequered and kept under by the shallowness of her river . . . soe that noe vessels of any burden can come nearer up than fourteen miles, where they must unlade and send up theyr timber and Norway trade in rafts or floates; and all other comodityes by three or four tonnes of goods at a time'.

The gradual deepening of the river Clyde since 1750 was one of the chief causes of the transformation of Glasgow from a small market-town 22 miles distant from salt water, clustered round a medieval University and a Cathedral on the banks of a shallow stream meandering through green fields, into a smoky industrial city of nearly two million persons in 1930 on a navigable channel bearing up-stream vessels of 26′ draft and down-stream the world's largest-drafted ocean-liners and battleships. The river debouches into a considerable estuary and, 40 miles seawards from Glasgow, the two small Cumbrae islands block access to the Firth and split the sea-way into east and west navigable channels, the wide east channel between rocks and sandbanks, and the direct west channel, little more than a mile wide between rocks. In this area the old havens may have used small horn lanterns at their piers but not until 1755 were practical steps taken to set up a lighthouse.

No body with any interest in lighthouses existed then in Scotland, such as the Trinity House of London. Only the private coal light of the May island and the Dundee Trinity House's oil lights at Buddonness assisted navigation by night round the Scottish coasts.

Trade in the Clyde estuary was increasing, but ships dared not pass through the Cumbrae channels in the darkness; by anchoring until morning they sometimes missed a favourable wind and were delayed for a week before they could sail through.

In January 1755 the Town Council of Glasgow authorised promotion of an Act in the Union Parliament in London to establish a lighthouse on the summit of Little Cumbrae island, also to remove shoals and flats from the river Clyde and to set up 'beacons and marks for eviting such dangers' so that 'by makeing other necessary works the Navigation in the sd Firth and River of Clyde will be rendered more safe and commodious'. A Bill seems to have been presented to Parliament early in 1756. In March witnesses were heard in London, and in April the Act received the Royal Assent. This measure, obtained so speedily at a cost of some £200, was one of the chief practical steps taken to develop Glasgow for, in addition to authorising construction of Cumbrae lighthouse and other seamarks, it provided that any surplus from the dues of 1d. per ton on British vessels and 2d. on foreigners should be devoted to deepening fords in the river-bed. Most of the Trustees to operate the Act were nominees of Glasgow Town Council which transferred over many years so large a proportion of the Cumbrae lighthouse funds to meet the costs of deepening the upper reaches of the river, that the Glasgow shipowners and merchants ultimately took action and in 1880 persuaded Parliament to remove the lighthouses and the lower four miles of the dredged river-channel above Gourock from effective control by that Council and transfer them to a new independent body, the Clyde Lighthouses Trustees.

LITTLE CUMBRAE 1757

At the first meeting of the Cumbrae Lighthouse Trustees, which was delayed until 17th May 1757, it was agreed to build a circular stone tower for a coal fire on the top of the island, 404' above high-water level, which involved a stiff climb over rock and bracken from the nearest landing-place. The arduous carriage of coal to the tower was a strain on the lightkeeper that may not have been equalled at any other lighthouse. The Trustees believed that men would come forward so keen to take employment that they would offer surety for £100 for faithful attention to their service. But no one would accept that condition, and they had to appoint 2 men jointly at a wage of £15 per annum each. However, they decided 'to look out for a fitt person who will serve at a reasonable wage and live at the lighthouse' and soon found such a man willing to accept £25. 10. 0; but in 1761 they had to increase his wage to £30, at which figure it remained for 30 years. In 1769 they purchased a yawl for £6 so that he could sail to Great Cumbrae island for stores, and they gave him a leather coat and a cap for protection when stirring and blowing the fire. In 1792 he received an additional £5 for 'carrying fewel to the lighthouse'. It is difficult to imagine a family man content to exist on the tiny island on the conditions offered, yet the lightkeeper of 1761 remained many years at his post and was succeeded by his son and in 1804 by the latter's widow. The family gave good service to the crude coal fire but had not skill enough to understand reflectors and lamps. Though an agent visited the lighthouse occasionally to ensure that the job was done efficiently, an inspection in 1804 found the light to be kept so badly that most of the reflectors were out of alignment, several lamps missing, and oil running down the stair of the tower.

The lighthouse, 28' in height, and 18½' and 12½' in outside and inside diameters, had been built by James Ewing at the low charge of £140. 5. 8 and the fire was kindled upon it on 8th December 1757. Within a year the heat of the fire burned out the first grate costing £6. 18. 0. Grates were replaced from time to time, the price rising to £23. 6. 7½ in 1770. Around 1790 the annual cost of coals was about £170: transport by sea had added some 40 per cent. to the price for delivery on shore.

The Cumbrae Trustees took an extraordinarily wide view of their responsibilities. On assuming office, one of their first actions was to order a surveyor to furnish them with a chart of the whole Clyde area from the headlands or Mulls of Cantyre and Galloway up to Glasgow, a distance of some 100 miles, at a charge of £60. In November 1759 the movements of Thurot's squadron, which had been fitted out by the French to harass British shipping, caused alarm on the Clyde as at Liverpool; it had captured 34 ships in 2 years. In February 1760 rumour had it that after landing at Aros in Islay to collect provisions and then raiding Carrickfergus in Ireland with 1,000 men, Thurot had entered the Clyde. However, before the end of the month he was captured between the Mull of Galloway and the Isle of Man. At the height of the excitement the Trustees hired a wherry for £14. 7. 9 to enable a lieutenant to proceed to sea to search for the squadron and 'observe the enemy's motions', and 'on the apprehension of fear' they spent £100 in erecting Beauclark gun-battery at Greenock 'for security of ships in the river'. Eighteen years later they engaged in similar activities in response to the alarm caused by Paul Jones, the American naval hero, and paid for twelve 18 lb. iron cannons from the Carron Company, the Scottish armament firm whose name gave rise to the term *carronade*. All horses and carriages were removed from the shore to hamper his movements, but he came no nearer to Glasgow than the island of Ailsa Craig in the lower estuary. Again, when in March 1773 'a great number of saillers assembled and convened together in a mobbish and tumultuous manner' and for 10 days put a stop to all business at Greenock and Port Glasgow, the Cumbrae Trustees paid the expense of quelling the mob out of the 'excrescence' of the funds of Cumbrae lighthouse. The nerves of the community seem to have been easily set a-flutter: in 1796 £49. 10. 0 was spent by the Trust in putting the Greenock battery 'into a state of defence on appearance of a Dutch frigate'. It is right to add that about this time the Government also set up defences in the Firth in apprehension of a French invasion and of American privateers.

In 1785 seamen complained that the Cumbrae lighthouse, which attempted to serve 2 parallel channels from the top of the island, was too far distant from either and too high, being sometimes obscured by mists and rain. Others considered that an oil light would be better than coals. In 1786 the Trustees appointed a committee 'to convene with Mr. Travers an english gentleman now in town and who it is said understands the mode of lighting lighthouses'. The Minutes give no account of the meeting, so a veil remains over Travers and the extent of his information about sea-lights.

In 1792 the Trustees held a meeting with shipmasters who, in discussing their complaints about the lighthouse, declared that 'the light in Pladda is the best light they knew of anywhere'. This statement induced the Trustees to apply to Thomas Smith and he offered to set a 'fireproof lantern' on the existing Cumbrae tower and reported on the alternatives of erecting one or two lighthouses at lower levels. In January 1793 the Trustees decided as an experiment to erect one lighthouse with a lantern at a lower level overlooking the west channel, while retaining meantime the coal fire on the summit of the island. Robert Stevenson supervised the construction of this new lighthouse for his step-father Thomas Smith. The builder, Anderson, received £289 and other contractors £73. Smith exhibited his reflector light on 1st October 1793 and its immediate success induced the Trustees to discontinue the coal fire on 31st December.

CLOCH POINT 1797

Navigators now called for a similar light nearer Glasgow, and in 1794 the Trustees chose a site near Cloch Point. James Clarkson is mentioned as its architect and measurer. Smith supplied a lantern and reflectors and put the light into operation on 11th August 1797. The cost of this lighthouse was a severe burden on the Trustees because they had already exhausted their funds on improvement of the river, chiefly by deepening. In their need for economy, they authorised a committee to reduce the number of lamps at Cloch or to suspend its lighting altogether for a period, and called on the Government to refund £529. 9. 7½, the cost of the Greenock battery as well as £50 spent on a bomb-proof magazine. They announced that they could no longer, with propriety, apply more of their lighthouse funds for such purposes. However, in 1799 they paid £116. 10. 0 towards the expenses of raising a volunteer corps of artillery at Greenock and they did not suspend their somewhat costly visits of inspection to the two lighthouses. In August 1799 a committee of the Glasgow magistrates spent £39. 13. 5 on such an expedition, including 10 guineas for wines; in 1801 the charge on a similar occasion increased to £47. 3. 7. It was of course proper for the Trustees, who were not paid for their services, to examine the Trust's properties at a moderate cost and check the doings of their officials.

When the Trustees appointed a lightkeeper at Cloch in 1796 on a salary not to exceed 30 guineas, they stipulated that 'he shall not in his dwelling house or in his lighthouse sell spirituous or any other kind of liquers'. His small pay induced him to look for additional work. Complaints from local pilots that in his spare time he competed against them by piloting ships evoked from the Trustees the unsympathetic response that so long as he did not neglect his duty as keeper of the light, they felt unconcerned.

THE NORTHERN LIGHTHOUSES

The first detailed charting of the Orkney islands and the west coast of Scotland, carried out by Murdoch Mackenzie in 1750–57, did not succeed in assuring shipowners that their vessels could navigate in security through the Irish Channel, the Minch and the Pentland Firth: navigators required the additional help of lighthouses at salient points of the Scottish coasts.

The example of the Trust, authorised by Parliament to manage lighthouses on the Clyde, pointed the way to a similar system for lighthouses on the Scottish coasts. Several public-spirited Scotsmen obtained an Act of Parliament in 1786 to establish four light-houses, at Kinnaird Head, Mull of Cantyre, Glass island (Eilean Glas) and North Ronaldsay. It appointed as Trustees, to erect and maintain them, the two Law Officers of the Crown, the magistrates of certain towns and the sheriffs or local judges of maritime counties. This composition of the Board remains unchanged to this day. The Act authorised the levy of inclusive dues of 1d. per ton on British vessels passing any or all of the lighthouses and 2d. on 'strangers', and permitted the Trustees to obtain loans up to £1,200. This low limit of borrowing and the usual stipulation that the dues should not be levied until all the 4 lights should be exhibited eventually made the Act unworkable.

The moment to set up lighthouses could not have been timed better: excellent and reliable reflector lights might now be provided. But an organisation to operate them in Scotland would face difficulties, as most of the sites could be serviced only from the sea, being on distant rocky islands often inaccessible because of weather and tidal conditions. To visit the 4 proposed lighthouses by sea would involve a circular voyage of 800 miles, apart from the return through the sheltered Forth and Clyde canal, and it would be subject to delays from adverse winds. The delivery of stores posed a different problem at each site.

The newly-appointed Trustees had no knowledge of maritime affairs, and probably none had visited a lighthouse, but before their first meeting on 1st August 1786 they collected information about several lighthouses in Britain, including details of the coal lights at the May and Cumbrae and of the 4 reflector lights at Liverpool, and they obtained a copy of William Hutchinson's book. Thomas Smith, a manufacturer of lamps in Edinburgh, submitted observations on lamps and parabolic reflectors along with a small model, and he urged the adoption of that lighting system. The Trustees appointed a committee to study all this information.

At a committee meeting on 1st September, one of the Trustees referred to Ezekiel Walker's light at Hunstanton which had been mentioned in letters from Liverpool, and they invited Walker to undertake erection of the four lighthouses. In reply, he offered 'to come here and erect one of the Lighthouses himself and give directions for the other three, and for fifty guineas would instruct any person the trustees thought proper to send, in the whole of his principles and improvements'. They now came to terms with Smith as their engineer, and recorded on 22nd January that having considered Walker's letters 'and also that Thomas Smith, whiteironsmith in Edinburgh, has made proposals for constructing the lighthouses by lamps and reflectors and has made several experiments for that purpose and laid models before the Trustees, which on account of his want of experience have not hitherto been agreed to, therefore and in order that no assistance may be wanted for having those lighthouses constructed in the most complete manner', they resolved that Smith should go to Lynn and gain whatever information Walker had to impart. This instruction to Smith comprised Walker's short but helpful connection with the Scottish lighthouses.

On Smith's return from Lynn, the Trustees appointed an architect named McKay to make drawings for the lighthouse buildings (apart from Kinnaird Head) to Walker's and Smith's directions, and instructed Smith to procure lanterns of iron covered with copper and to buy sheets of mirror-glass in Glasgow for the reflectors which, with the lamps, he would make in Edinburgh. They noted that he was then at work on a mould for the reflectors. He was directed to get the work carried out at Kinnaird Head and to choose the sites for the other 3 towers. Advertisement failed to produce contractors willing to build lighthouses, so George Shiell, a foreman-mason, was sent with workmen to Eilean Glas and Cantyre and later to Pladda to erect the buildings. Smith arranged for the purchase and transport of building-materials and chose lightkeepers.

The resemblance between Smith's early reflectors and a reflector which Walker constructed in 1795 is very close but it is impossible to say whether Smith departed greatly from Walker's original design. But he certainly improved the lamps, so that they could be withdrawn from the reflectors, and he introduced metal pipes which separated each wick from the others and obtained small smokeless flames. All the 4 Northern lighthouses showed fixed lights. That they were good for their purpose is proved by the immediate demand by seamen and shipowners for the erection of others of the same type.

The drafters of the Act had based its financial provisions on absurdly low estimates of costs. Before 2 of the lighthouses were completed it was apparent that the dues were too low and the borrowing powers insufficient. So in 1788 a second Act raised the dues to $1\frac{1}{2}$d. and 3d., half to be levied at once and the full rates on completion of the fourth lighthouse, and increased the sum that could be borrowed to £4,200.

The Clyde shipowners now applied for a light on Pladda island, south of Arran, and as it seemed likely that lighthouses would be demanded elsewhere, the Trustees obtained a third Act in 1789 which permitted them to erect lighthouses anywhere on the Scottish coasts and islands, according as the receipts from the dues already granted might allow.

One payment of dues by a vessel would include all the lighthouses, except those on the Clyde and on the Isle of May. This arrangement differed from the complicated and expensive English system by which a vessel was charged different dues for each lighthouse that she passed. The dues collected in Scotland in 1789, including part of 1788, amounted to only £290. 14. 6: loans from helpful Scottish bankers on generous terms and on the uncertain security of estimates of tonnage kept the Trust in operation.

By careful planning and strict economy the Trust established the 5 lighthouses by 1791 for £10,000, erecting simple and partly-temporary buildings. In that year the Trustees put the management of their lighthouses on a business footing with regulations governing the purchase of supplies and the appointment of lightkeepers, and they instructed the engineer to visit each lighthouse annually, to arrange for repairs, to report on the service given by the keepers, and to charter each summer a ship of about 100 tons to carry stores to them.

In 1793 a demand came for lighthouses on the Pentland Skerries and the Bell Rock. The income from dues had now risen to some £3,000 annually, all loans had been paid off and the Trust had £2,000 in hand. This enabled the Pentland Skerries project to be undertaken, but during the next 10 years the Trustees limited their other capital expenditure to improving their earliest lighthouses, including provision of landing-places and roads, while accumulating funds towards the construction of the Bell Rock lighthouse.

A fourth Act of 1798 incorporated the Trustees as 'the Commissioners of the Northern Lighthouses', the title under which they still function as a Lighthouse Board.

The Commissioners enjoyed a great practical advantage over other Lighthouse Authorities in being able to start an entirely new service, so the following account of their first 6 lighthouses lacks many of the features which complicated erection of the English lighthouses and which arose from interplay of many interests and prejudices.

KINNAIRD HEAD 1787

This first work of the Trustees consisted in setting a lantern on one corner of an old castle at a height of 120′ above the sea. In April 1787 Smith carried a letter of introduction from the Trustees' Clerk to Lord Saltoun, the proprietor, as 'the person employed by them

103. Facet reflectors at Kinnaird Head lantern 1787

104. Eilean Glas lighthouse on Scalpay island, a refuge of Prince Charles Edward in 1746

for constructing the lighthouses'. The Scots newspapers advertised the light to be shown 'from the going away of daylight in the evening till the return of daylight in the morning', commencing on 1st December 1787.

The lantern contained 17 reflectors arranged in 3 horizontal tiers to show over some 180° and staggered so as to light the darker sectors that would occur between adjoining reflectors. Smith took a risk in arranging the reflectors in this way which carried out Hutchinson's apparently untried idea of using a *parcel of lamps*.

Smith's written instructions to the lightkeeper included a warning that when he visited the lightroom to attend to the lamps, 'you must take care not to stand before the light any longer than is necessary' or he would hide it from the mariners.

MULL OF CANTYRE 1788

This lighthouse was erected on a precipitous cliff 240′ above the sea and inaccessible from it, but the rocky and desolate interior of Cantyre peninsula made the lighthouse site scarcely more accessible by land. Materials and stores had to be landed by boat 6 miles away and taken by horseback over the mountain with 1 cwt. as the limiting load. A single journey from landing-place to lighthouse represented one day's work. After two working seasons, the light was shown in October 1788.

EILEAN GLAS 1789

This lighthouse also took two seasons to build, 70′ above the sea on the island of Scalpay in Harris. Fortunately, materials could be landed in a cove close to the site. The light was exhibited on 10th October 1789.

NORTH RONALDSAY 1789

Erection of this tower on one of the Orkney islands offered no difficulty, except that transport of workmen and materials by ship from Leith slowed down the work. It was lighted on 10th October 1789.

PLADDA 1790

A tower erected on this small island in the Clyde estuary was lighted on 1st October 1790 whereupon it was considered advisable to make it distinct from the other fixed lights in the area, namely, those at Cumbrae, Mull of Cantyre and Copeland in Ireland. Therefore a small lantern was built as a projection from the tower in 1791 to show a second fixed light from 9 reflectors, 20′ below the principal light. As an even better distinction, a second lighted tower subsequently replaced this subsidiary light.

PENTLAND SKERRIES 1794

Enquiries as to the choice of a site for a lighthouse in the Pentland Firth, notorious for strong cross-currents and sunken rocks, drew a difference of opinion among seafarers, but on the recommendation of the shipowners of the Clyde ports and Liverpool, the Trustees decided that the site should be on the Pentland Skerries, a cluster of rocks between Orkney and the Scottish mainland. Here Smith set up 2 towers 60' apart as a distinction, one 80' high and the other 60'. He lighted them on 1st October 1794. This site proved to be the most inaccessible of all the 6 in Scotland on which lighthouses had been erected: only in particular directions of wind or with a calm sea could a landing be made with any degree of safety. Even with carefully-designed landing-places, difficulty remains to this day. After completing the 2 lighthouses Smith left the Skerries in the sloop *Elizabeth* which had attended the operations. On her voyage south she was becalmed off Kinnaird Head and he continued his journey by land. A violent gale drove the ship back to the Orkneys where she was wrecked and all on board perished.

In 1799 Stevenson proposed to substitute a revolving light requiring only 10 reflectors and lamps in one tower for the 66 reflectors in the two towers, but before carrying out this economical project he decided to inspect the English lighthouses to see the latest improvements in revolving lights.

LIGHTHOUSE MAINTENANCE

For the first few years after the erection of these Scottish coastal lighthouses, Smith delivered stores to each by hiring a small vessel for a few months every summer. As time passed, repairs at the lighthouses became necessary, which he effected by carrying on board artificers who did the work as they came to each lighthouse: when it was completed, the ship passed on.

Many troubles beset the lighthouse voyages. In May 1798 the stores for all the lighthouses had been collected at Leith and put aboard the *Thomas* of Stromness, a hired vessel. When she was about to sail, the pressgang seized her sailors, and three weeks elapsed before they could be freed. This check was unexpected, for the men as well as the ship were by law immune from such seizure, as they belonged to Orkney, the Scottish county that had the exclusive privilege against impress warrants. Later on in the same voyage, when the ship lay off Kinnaird Head, a privateer approached within a mile but made off when a British warship came into sight.

In 1799 no vessel could be hired, owing to the demand for ships brought about by the increase in overseas trade. So in that year Smith bought a sloop nearing completion on the stocks at Elie in Fife, fitted her out and named her the *Pharos* of Leith. This purchase solved the transport problem for a few years to come, and it offered much advantage over the previous system of hiring a different vessel each year with a crew who were not acquainted with the intimate navigation of the coasts and were strangers to the circumstances of landing on the rocks at particular lighthouses. This lack of experience had added considerably to the difficulties of servicing the lighthouses.

In August 1799 the *Pharos* was held up at Campbeltown by an embargo. Stevenson informed the Commissioners that 'he feared to push the matter too far in case they bring us to with a couple of 18-pounders and strip our sails'. Such an action had been taken against another ship. However, after lying 3 days in harbour, 'at twelve at night the windlass was muffled, the vessel having been previously hove short. We weighed anchor and in the quietest manner got clear of the harbour and the wind being S.W. and blowing hard, we put in to Lamlash to wait a fair wind where we were at liberty to sail, being out of reach of the Harbour Officer and his people.'

HARBOUR AND PRIVATE LIGHTS

BUDDONNESS

From 1700 to 1720 the front light consumed 1 barrel of oil annually and the rear light used 8 stones of candles. In 1714 both lights consumed candles amounting to 40 stones: perhaps oil was considered too expensive at 6s. 8d. per pint. After 1720 both lights burned oil in 16 common iron lamps or *cruisies*. Before 1740 the lights burned only in winter. In 1789 Smith fitted 6 reflectors and oil lamps in the larger tower and 3 in the smaller.

LEITH

The Burgh records of Edinburgh show that the remuneration of the keeper of a 'lanthorn' at Leith pier before 1721 was 30s. per annum. In 1758 the erection of one new lighthouse was recommended to replace two lighthouses then in use. In 1788 the small stone lighthouse was repaired and Smith supplied a new lantern with reflectors and oil lamps.

PORTPATRICK

From about 1750 to 1850 this harbour, which was subsidised for military and postal purposes, was much used for Packet sailings to Ireland despite its dangerous situation in a cleft between cliffs. In 1789 after a spark from an oil lamp destroyed its lantern and reflector, the tower on the pierhead was raised by 10′ and fitted with 'a globe lamp which did not serve'. A coal fire burning in the open air took its place but proved unsuitable because 'in a stormy night the Packets are in danger of being set on fire by the sparks flying from the light'. Smith fitted 5 facet reflectors and flat-wick lamps, probably in the same year, and these remained in use until 1834.

ISLE OF MAY

The increasing interest in lighthouses in Scotland which had led to the establishment of the Northern Lighthouse Board in 1786 induced the Chamber of Commerce in Edinburgh in the same year to send a committee to the Isle of May to investigate complaints about its light. Attempts to improve it had included enclosing the grate by some sort of lantern, but it was removed 'as it smoked the glass so much as to render the light useless'.

105. Buddonness lights in 1819

106. Portpatrick harbour light in 1819 (Daniell)

The committee described the lighthouse as a square building 39′ 4″ high and 24′ square with a parapet all round the top. A circular grate at the centre, 21″ deep, 33½″ broad at top, and 28″ at bottom, rested on a stone platform and consumed 200 tons of coal annually.

The lightkeeper, George Anderson, with his wife and children lived alone on the island. He received £7 a year and 5 bolls, or 30 bushels, of meal and was obliged frequently to go out to fish for the maintenance of his family. His absence at night resulted in no light being shown. The quality of the coals was often bad. They had no cover, being tipped

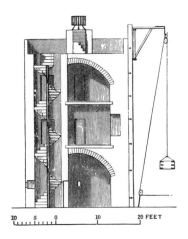

107. Isle of May coal beacon
c. 1800

out of boats and left near low-water mark. Thence Anderson carried them to the tower on his back. The committee recommended to Miss Scott, the patentee, that good coals be got from West Wemyss in Fife, as supplied for Heligoland lighthouse, that they should be landed in summer in vessels not larger than 20 tons which, being smaller than those in use, could come in closer to the rocks and land them dry, that they be covered there and that a crane be provided on the tower parapet. Two chimneys which obscured the light should be lowered, the grate should be enlarged and the mode of carrying coals improved. A kind of umbrella should be built as a roof over the grate which should be raised on legs. As a result of the recommendations a second keeper was appointed, the grate was enlarged and raised, a horse was provided to haul the coals and better coals were obtained but the other suggestions were not carried out.

In January 1791 fumes entered a window from cinders which had piled up against the walls of the house and suffocated Anderson, his wife and 5 of his 8 children. Miss Scott undertook the custody of an infant lifted from the breast of its dead mother.

In 1796 the Chamber of Commerce desired a change to a reflector and oil light and got an offer from Thomas Smith who estimated the cost of a lantern, without building work, and 36 lamps and reflectors at £276. 11. 0, and the annual maintenance at £50. Miss Scott's agents appointed a third keeper but declined to fit an oil light.

Accounts for the year ending May 1799 show that the collection of dues produced £1,600 whereas the expenditure amounted to £549. 14. 7. It included payments of £180 to the collectors, £226. 1. 0 for 366 tons of coal (including £83. 10. 0 representing freight to the island); £69. 4. 0 wages for 3 keepers; £28. 10. 0 for discharging coals, pilotage and carrying provisions; £33. 19. 3 for hay and beans for the horse, ropes, blocks, mason's, slater's and sadler's accounts, and £11. 19. 7 for Anderson's child. English vessels paying dues were still treated as foreigners at 3d. per ton as against 1½d. on Scots ships.

THE IRISH LIGHTHOUSES 1700–1800

LIGHTHOUSES 1700–90

On 22nd November 1704 Reading's patent was surrendered to the Crown and the Government put the lighthouses into the control of Commissioners. It may be that this change was made in consequence of disapproval of Reading's management of the lights. In November 1703 the burgesses of Kinsale had complained to the Irish Parliament that

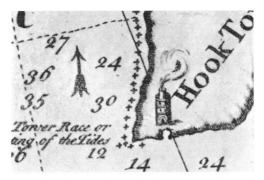

108. Hook tower in Ireland on a sea-chart of
1737

the light on the Old Head had been discontinued for the past 20 years 'to the hazard of several ships'. In the same year Howth lighthouse was declared unsatisfactory, and it was proposed that it should be 'built higher, the light larger, and be better kept'. Eventually it was re-built on the top of Howth peninsula, as a coal fire.

In September 1717 the aldermen and merchants of Limerick petitioned the Irish Parliament for a light on Loop Head, complaining that many ships had been lost for want of a light there. A Parliamentary Committee reported that a light would be of extraordinary use to the public and the Lord Lieutenant, who represented the King, declared that he would be 'pleased to give all proper encouragement to the proposal' for a light. Ultimately the coal fire was re-established in its former position and was in operation in 1796. Hook tower was shown as a lighthouse on a sea-chart of 1737. The *Compleat Irish Coaster* of 1749, which described the coast for seamen, mentions lighthouses only at Howth, Hook and Kinsale and a lightship at Dublin: the surveyor gives so much detail that it is unlikely that he omitted to mention any lights that were in operation.

In 1767 an Act of the Irish Parliament transferred the management of the lighthouses to the Commissioners for Barracks. In 1774 Hutchinson was preparing reflectors to be fitted at Wicklow.

DUBLIN SEAMARKS 1740–82

In 1740 the Dublin lightship, with red and black buoys called *water-marks*, all managed by James Palmer, a patentee, was moored close to a long line of piles that marked the south edge of the entrance channel and vessels passed between her and a white buoy laid to the north. In 1756 her two lanterns, set out at opposite sides of the mast, were lighted only around high-water. 'In the day her ensign is displayed from half-flood till half-ebb. In the night her lantherns are light from half-flood till half-ebb.' By 1782 Dublin showed a light at each side of the port entrance, probably in place of the lightship which it must have been difficult to keep moored in shallow water without injury to the piling or the ship.

LIGHTHOUSES 1790–8

The Commissioners for Barracks made no noteworthy changes in the lighthouses until 1790 when Thomas Rogers, who was a partner or employee of George Robinson the supplier of reflectors and lamps to Trinity House, fitted on the Howth tower a 12′ diameter lantern

(*a*) (*b*)

109. Dublin harbour lights, (*a*) on the south wall and (*b*) on the north wall

with 8 of his catadioptric lights, each consisting of a lens, an oil lamp and a spherical reflector. This apparatus superseded the existing coal fire. In 1791 he fitted a similar lantern with 12 lights at Hook. In 1792 he severed his connection with Robinson and settled in Ireland.

From 1793 to 1797 he was occupied in building a lighthouse on the sea-washed South Rock. Attention to this difficult work did not prevent him in 1796 from setting a 6′ diameter lantern to hold 6 of his lights on one of the angles of the old 40′ high square tower with circular top on the small island of Copeland or Mew, 27 miles distant, which previously had borne a coal fire consuming up to 1½ tons of coal on a windy night.

Another Act of the Irish Parliament of 1796 transferred the lighthouses from the Barracks Board to the Revenue or Customs Board and provided for the construction of more lighthouses. It stated that 'the coasts of Ireland are notoriously deficient in so much that there is not a single light round the north and western coasts from the Copeland islands off the county of Down to Loop Head at the mouth of the Shannon. . . . The price of insurance of ships and cargoes is greatly enhanced from the said deficiency of lights.' After declaring also that shipping was 'subject to frequent losses from the want of a light off the coast of Wexford which is low and full of shoals', the Act authorised the construction of 2 lighthouses on the coasts of Mayo and Galway and another off Wexford, but apparently the Government was so inappreciative of the difficulties experienced in building the lighthouse on the South Rock and of the expenses that were being incurred in that work that an expenditure of only £5,000 was authorised by the Act to cover the erection of the 3 intended lighthouses.   When the last of the 3 had been established in 1815, their total cost exceeded £45,000.   Rogers constructed the first of them in 1798 on Arranmore or Aran island off the coast of Donegal.   The choice of this island, lying 50 miles north-east of Mayo, certainly fulfilled the spirit of the Act by providing a light on that coast, though the site was established beyond the area stipulated.   At Arranmore Rogers set 10 of his lights in a 12′ diameter lantern upon a granite tower.

SOUTH ROCK 1793–7

This seamark, sometimes called the Kilwarlin lighthouse, was designed and constructed by Thomas Rogers on a Rock with one side above high-water, some 3 miles off Newcastle in County Down.   Though not exposed to the full force of the ocean, it could claim fairly to be listed as an isolated sea-swept tower.   It exists still, though its use as a lighthouse ceased in 1877.

Belfast merchants petitioned the Irish Parliament in 1767 for a lighthouse on this Rock and a committee reported it to be 'highly necessary. . . . A sufficient lighthouse might be erected according to a plan laid before them by Major Charles Vellancy' for £5,173.   As nothing was done to implement the report, they petitioned again in 1783: Colonel Vellancy's plan would now cost £6,991. 7. 6.   Eventually another committee recommended a grant of £1,400 towards the project which was promoted by Lord Kilwarlin with others.   Details of the Vellancy plan are not known.

The tower which Rogers erected had a conical outline with considerable batter: its diameter narrowed from 30′ at base to 18′ at a height of some 55′.   Its ventilator rose 67′ from the foundation.   The tower was solid for 20′ and was crowned by a lantern of 8′ diameter with glazing 6′ tall.   The tower contained 4 compartments, the lowest to store coals and water, the next for oil cisterns, the third for a kitchen and the fourth for a living room.   Holes 2′ square cut in the floors allowed passage within, and a wooden ladder could be lowered to give access from the rock below.   Vertical iron rods 4″ square, 8 arranged in a ring through the walls and one in the centre, bound the courses together.   At every 8th course they were attached to cast-iron plates 2′ 9″ × 2″ thick.   Accounts of their exact positions horizontally are contradictory.

The tower was constructed of granite blocks, the courses being arranged in outer rings with a cross inside.   The stones 4′ to 5′ long that formed the rings had vertical joggles so that each had a grip on its neighbour by projection or indentation.   After the cross stones were laid on their beds, holes were bored in them for cramping or binding with iron bands. The four triangular spaces between the stones were filled in with a concrete or rubble mixture 'well-tramped on the building with the feet of the labourers'.

At first, blocks of stone were cut from lumps of granite exposed in the fields near Wexford, but transport by sea to Newcastle, a distance of 180 miles, proved precarious and dilatory.   The risk entailed drew such high insurance rates that the hire of shipping was precluded.   Of two sloops of 60 and 90 tons bought to carry the stones, one was wrecked on her first trip and the other was driven to Penzance with Rogers and his cargo.   Fortunately, he discovered a small quarry near Newry from which boats in the ordinary course of trading could bring stones to Newcastle through the Newry canal, a distance of 40 miles. Masons from the lighthouse works went occasionally to the quarry to assist 5 quarriers who were sent there by Rogers.

167

Operations began in September 1793 and at Newcastle during the summer of 1794 a masonry platform 30′ in diameter was prepared for assembly of the stones when dressed. Upon it, two courses were set at a time, paper templates of these being kept for use with the next course. A short quay with loading-sheers was constructed as a harbour. Daily, in a 6-ton wherry and a rowing boat, a foreman, 3 masons and 18 labourers set out from Newcastle to cut out the circular foundation to half-tide level on the Rock and they completed it in the autumn.

110. The South Rock lighthouse built by Rogers in 1797, with the levels of high and low waters

111. Photograph of South Rock tower in June 1958 showing its excellent external condition despite its disuse as a lighthouse for 81 years

In March 1795 the workmen arriving at the Rock to resume operations were amazed to find that the foundation which they had cut so exactly to a level was even more irregular than it was before they started work in the previous spring: during the winter the soft strata in some places had been eroded by the sea to a further depth of 5′. By June the site had been levelled again, and building of the tower began. To save boating, a schooner-rigged ship on which the men might live, was bought for £400 and was moored in August close to the Rock, with a 5′ square stone as anchor. But owing to her sharp bow and being a *fine sailer*, she rode so hard that the men were seasick. After 8 unhappy days, they slipped her cable in a gale and decided to resume their former laborious practice of rowing out to the Rock daily. By October, when work was suspended, 4 masons working with the labourers had raised the tower to 14′.

They resumed work early in 1796, but in laying the first course of the new season (it was the 15th course) the men omitted to set the closing stone before leaving one evening and that night the sea washed away the whole course. Robert Stevenson visited the works in April and found the men grappling for the stones. From May, building the tower continued until the light was exhibited on 25th March 1797. Altogether 20 masons, 18 labourers, 2 smiths and 2 foremen had been employed with two sloops, a wherry and a row-boat.

A gully running into the Rock had enabled a boat to bring the stones close alongside the site. At first the materials were thrown overboard from her on to the Rock, then they were landed more carefully at low-water. Eventually a gangway was run out to low-water neaps, a distance of 38', to serve as a wharf. This consisted of fir planks raised on iron supports. It enabled stones to be lifted from the boat directly to a trolley which was wheeled to the base of the tower. The walls of the tower were built first, the floors being omitted until the walls were completed. Then the cross stones were wheeled into the void and built upwards.

The chief difficulties in carrying out the work had lain in obtaining speedy delivery and transport of stones from the quarries and in landing them on the Rock. After the tower was finished, disintegration of the foundation, which consisted of alternate layers of clay and slate, caused much trouble and expense.

The light consisted of a revolving frame giving a white flash from ten 15" silvered reflectors. The lamps had 2" diameter wicks. In 1812 the curve of the reflectors was uncertain: five were set on each side of the frame. Greenside Callum of Edinburgh renewed the entire apparatus and also fitted bells to be rung by machinery in fog. Previously the keeper hit a bell repeatedly for half-an-hour and then rested. Early in 1812 one of Stevenson's foremen had inspected the lighthouse and was appalled at its condition; he wrote that unless the place was cleaned up it would only be throwing money away to fit new machinery and reflectors. He reported that the lightkeeper lived in the tower with 3 children in squalid circumstances, their food then being a few potatoes. Shortly afterwards, Halpin succeeded Rogers and conditions were bettered and 4 lightkeepers were appointed, 3 to be always on the Rock and their families living ashore.

In 1801 alarm for the safety of the tower was occasioned by the sea undermining its foundation so that a section of the outer wall for about one-fifth of the circumference hung unsupported, several feet above the rock. This was remedied by packing the cavity with granite blocks bound together by an iron chain.

Stevenson visited the lighthouse several times with a view to solving his problems at the Bell Rock. Rennie saw it in September 1805 when he had occasion to be in the district and condemned the materials and design—'constructed with but little judgment . . . unless some speedy and effectual steps are taken, I apprehend its duration will scarcely exceed the Life of the Architect . . . the Commissioners of Customs are much dissatisfied with Mr. Rogers about this business'. But despite Rennie's considerable catalogue of defects his prediction of disaster has still not been fulfilled. He stated that the lighthouse had cost £22,270 and estimated that repairs to the paving of the Rock would require £7,000, a total of £29,270 against an original estimate by Rogers of £9,535. 'The north and west sides have been paved with granite blocks laid on edge and fixed together with transverse wooden pins, many of which have given way.' Rogers in 1802 told Stevenson that the cost had been £16,372 and estimated that a landing-pier which was required would add £2,253. He had spent on the tower £391 on iron work and £113 on lead, run into joints and joggles.

The light was discontinued in 1877 because it was too far distant from the sunken Rock that formed the real point of danger. The vicinity was better marked by the lightship which then took its place.

T. S. Sloane, a former engineer to the Irish Lights Commissioners, wrote in 1873 that though the South Rock tower 'is seldom heard of, the Eddystone and the Bell Rock, deservedly popular as they may be, sink into insignificance when the exposure they are subject to is compared with that of South Rock'. But a glance at charts of the locality is sufficient to disprove his assessment of the relative exposures.

In June 1958, A. D. H. Martin the engineer of the Irish Lights Commissioners visited the tower and found its exterior generally in excellent condition after withstanding the sea for 160 years, thus vindicating Rogers as an able designer and builder of an extremely difficult work.

XI

NORTH AMERICAN LIGHTHOUSES BEFORE 1800

Sambro Light-house, south-east distant 1 Mile.

112. Sambro lighthouse in Nova Scotia in 1781

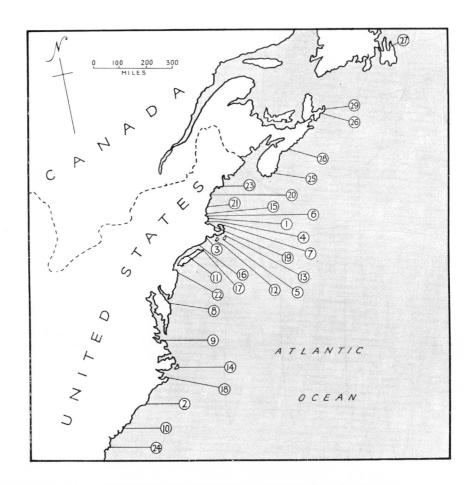

LIGHTS IN NORTH AMERICA IN 1800

The sites of the navigation lights are numbered

XI. NORTH AMERICAN LIGHTHOUSES BEFORE 1800

The lighthouse erected in 1716 on Little Brewster island off Boston is considered to have been the first established in North America, and a tower built by the French at Louisburg about 1740 was probably the first established in Canada. Before 1800, 24 lighthouses were erected in the United States, their chief purpose being to direct vessels to the entrances of harbours. Oil lamps without reflectors provided the illumination of all the lights. About 1798 an eclipser apparatus was tried at Cape Cod.

UNITED STATES OF AMERICA

BOSTON 1716

Nearly two-score islands are encompassed within the great bay of Boston, Massachusetts, and in their midst, facing the full Atlantic swell, lies the island of Little Brewster with a lighthouse which first gave forth its beam to the world on the night of 14th September 1716. From the south of the bay a long spur of land juts northwards to Point Allerton where before 1673 a beacon bore an iron basket in which 'fier bales of pitch and ocum' flamed to the skies, not to guide sailors, but to give warning of possibly hostile craft. The beacon was set ablaze when more than three ships appeared to be approaching.

No doubt before the Boston merchants planned the Brewster tower they assisted navigation by setting up unlighted beacons among the islands. In 1680–1 there is a reference to one of the Brewster islands being reserved for a *General Sea Marke* and in 1701 the *New England Almanac* pointed out the need for a lighthouse on Point Allerton.

In 1713, under the Colonial Government of Queen Anne, the General Court of Massachusetts appointed a committee, including experienced shipmasters, to meet the merchants who proposed 'the Erecting of a Light Hous & Lanthorn'. A survey of the islands resulted in agreement that 'the Projection will be of general publick Benefit & Service & is worthy to be encouraged' but questions of finance and management delayed a decision. The town of Boston, sensing a profitable transaction, sought to obtain 'the preference in the charge of erecting and maintaining the lighthouse' and thereafter to being 'intituled to the Profitts and Incomes thereof'. In 1715, after the accession of George I, the General Court 'with the approval of Gov'r Dudley' authorised erection of the lighthouse at the State's expense in an Act which stated in the preamble that the want of such a seamark 'hath been a great discouragement to navigation by the loss of the lives and Estates of Several of His Majesties Subjects'.

The cost of the lighthouse with a house for the keeper came to £2,385. 17. 8½d. For its maintenance, ships using the port (with some exceptions) had to pay one penny per ton inwards and the same rate outwards. The Act provided that the lightkeeper 'upon Conviction of Neglect of his Duty according to the Degree and Circumstances of his Offense' should be liable to a fine of £100, two-thirds going to the Government and one-third to the informer, a penalty which would be difficult of exaction from a man whose salary amounted to just half that amount, it having been resolved that 'fifty pounds be allowed & paid out of the publick Treasury for the Hire of a Person to take care of the Light House for the first Year, to begin when the lights are set & kept up'.

In November 1718 the loss by drowning of George Worthylake, the first lightkeeper, along with members of his family, a friend and a negro slave while returning to the island after receiving his pay at Boston, disclosed the dangers attending residence at the lighthouse and Benjamin Franklin, then a boy of 13, commemorated the event in verse. He states in his autobiography that his brother, a printer, 'engaged me to write two ballads. One,

113. Boston lighthouse on Little Brewster island, 'with a great Gun to answer Ships in a Fogg' 1729 (Burgis)

called *The Lighthouse Tragedy*, contained an account of the shipwreck of Captain Worthilake and his two daughters; the other was a sailor's song on the capture of the noted pirate called *Teach* or *Blackbeard*. They were wretched verses in point of style, mere blindmen's ditties. When printed, he despatched me about the town to sell them. The first had a prodigious run, because the event was recent, and had made a great noise.' It has been suggested recently that Worthylake was drowned in different circumstances, but the events seemed to be clear to Franklin and the suggestion may arise from the coincidence that the man appointed immediately as a temporary keeper soon met the same fate as Worthylake.

In 1720 a fire caused extensive damage put at £200 and for several weeks the Court advertised the light as extinguished, the lightkeeper's salary being withheld until he satisfied it that he did not cause the fire. He explained 'that it being the Memorialist's manner to go to bed early in ye evening & rise about nine o'clock at night, about eight o'clock he was waked out of his sleep by his wife, who told him she suspected ye Light House was afire, that he immediately ran up with two pails of water but ye fire was too violent to be subdued, that however he saved many things belonging to the Light House. That he suposes ye fire was occasioned by ye Lamps dropping on ye wooden Benches & a snuff falling off & setting fire & that ye said fire was not occasioned by ye least neglect of ye Memorialist.'

An inspection in 1723 attributed cracks in the tower not, as some had supposed, to a great storm of that year, but rather to the fire of 1720. Repairs followed in 1726. A mezzo-tint picture by William Burgis dated 1729 shows a tower of attractive design about 60′

114. Boston lighthouse in 1789

high with a glazed lantern and a balcony to facilitate cleaning of the glass panes. An outside balcony had not been incorporated in the original tower but in 1719 the lightkeeper asked for one so that during winter he could clear ice and snow from the lantern on the seaward side. The tower depicted in Burgis's view can challenge comparison with European lighthouses of its day in suitability as a seamark and for its pleasant aspect. But the stone-work continued to give trouble and in 1734 orders were issued that 'Seams and Cracks be well filled with mortar or putty' and the outside encased with oak planks 2½″ thick and en-circled with iron hoops every 4′ upwards. In 1751 another fire occurred and a ship's lantern served as a temporary light. On rebuilding the tower a metal lantern replaced the former one of wood. In winter, because of the extreme cold, the lightkeeper had to keep up a fire in the lantern 'for preventing ye Oyle from congealing'.

A treasured possession of the Marine Society of Boston is a seal made in silver in 1754 representing 'a ship arriving at the light House from a storm and the Sun breaking out of the Clouds'.

During the revolt of the Colonies against the British Government from 1775 to 1783, several exciting episodes centred round the Boston lighthouse. In 1775, during its occupa-tion by the British, American troops carried off the lamps and oil and fired the tower. By another raid they interrupted its repair. The British fleet sailed from Boston in 1776 leaving a train of gunpowder which blew up the tower an hour later. For some seven years after, no light was shown on the island, but an unlighted beacon took its place in 1780.

A new stone tower completed in 1783 at a cost of £1,450 is shown in an engraving published in 1789. It is described as 75' high including an octagonal lantern 8' wide. The conical outline tapered upwards from a diameter of 24' at the base with walls 7½' thick. Strangely enough, a balcony for cleaning the outside of the lantern panes had no place in the new design though its advantage must have been well proved in the original structure. This second tower had to be strengthened by iron hoops in 1809, and raised 20' and lined with brick in 1859. It endures to the present day.

Though lightning frequently damaged the 1783 tower, it stood without the protection of a conductor until about 1788—this measure being opposed, as apparently at Genoa, by several of the Bible-searching men of those days who declared it to be vanity and irreligion 'for the arm of the flesh to presume to avert the stroke of Heaven'.

NEW ORLEANS 1721

A French engineer constructed an unlighted beacon 62' high at Fort Boulaye in the Mississippi delta in 1721, and it is possible that the French used lights for navigation in New Orleans soon after.

TYBEE 1740

There is uncertainty as to the second lighthouse to be established in the United States. A claim for Tybee rests on an attestation of 10th November 1740 which applied to 'the island of Tybee with the lighthouse which has been of the greatest Use to all Ships falling in with this part of America'. It was described as a brick tower built before 1755 by the Colony of Georgia and apparently designed as an unlighted beacon. It may be that a lighthouse established before 1740 lapsed for a period.

BRANT POINT 1746

Subject to doubt about Tybee, the lighthouse erected at Brant Point, Massachusetts, in 1746 at the cost of £200 is accepted as the second to be established in the States. The town of Sherburn, now Nantucket, provided the tower in the expectation, which proved misplaced, that shipping would pay voluntarily for its maintenance.

Fire destroyed this wooden structure after 12 years' service and in 1774 a great gale blew down its successor, also a timber affair. The Colony then recognised the usefulness of the light and the cost it entailed on the town, and agreed to a tax on shipping. In 1786 fire destroyed the third tower. A fourth timber structure, consisting of a wooden lantern with glass windows hoisted between two spars proved unsatisfactory and gave place to a fifth tower, a timber trellis structure, which was blown down in 1788. Contemporary lists of navigation lights omit mention of this light until 1825 when it is included again. Looking to the danger of entering the harbour in the dark it seems unlikely that none was in use between 1788 and 1825. The succession of eight or nine different buildings set up near the same spot for a lighthouse is surely a world record.

BEAVERTAIL 1749

The Colony of Rhode Island authorised the building of a lighthouse at Beavertail in 1738 but the outbreak of war with Spain caused postponement of the undertaking. On the establishment of peace in 1748 the Colonial Assembly decided that 'there appears as great a necessity of a Lighthouse as ever, several misfortunes having very lately happened for want thereof'. So the lighthouse was erected and benefited particularly the town of Newport which carried on a highly profitable trade at that time, by outward ships taking rum to Africa and returning with slaves, either to the southern States or to the West Indies, thence molasses to Newport for the rum factories.

115. Boston lighthouse in 1754 as engraved by Hurd on the seal of the Marine Society of Boston

116. A ticket for the lottery to provide funds to build New London lighthouse in 1761

Des Barres' chart of 1776 shows the lighthouse and a buoy marking a sandbank and such curious local features as a rope-walk for twisting ships' cables and a pest-house for persons afflicted by the plague or 'divers fevers'.

NEW LONDON 1761

The Colony of Connecticut decided in 1760 to erect a navigation light at the rocky entrance to New London and appointed managers to fix a site, build a tower at a cost of £500, and choose a keeper who should procure oil for lamps. It authorised raising the money by lottery, 12 per cent. being deducted from the sale of tickets to defray the cost and recompense the managers for their trouble. They took up office with an oath to discharge their duties faithfully and they erected a handsome masonry tower faced with dressed blocks, of a height of 64', with diameter of 24' and the thickness of the walls tapering from 4' to 2'.

The dues proving insufficient, the Colonial Assembly increased the tax on shipping and reimbursed the surviving manager in 1774 to the extent of £20, which he had spent from his own pocket to maintain the light.

In 1791, after the lighthouse had been handed over to the Federal Government, President Washington signed a contract under which a New London merchant would furnish a year's supply of oil, cotton wicks, candles and soap. The light, consisting then of 'three Lamps of three Spouts each' required annually '800 Galls strained Sperm Ceti Oil at 42 cents per gallon Dolls 333·00'.

In 1799 the tower showed a 10′ crack extending from the top, and the wooden lantern, which required frequent renewal, had decayed to an extent beyond further repair, so a new masonry tower designed for endurance took its place in 1801 at a cost of $16,500 including oil lamps. As seamen had difficulty in picking out the light from those of adjacent houses, an *eclipser* was proposed, to give an occulting aspect to the new light.

SANDY HOOK 1764

In May 1761 the New York Colonial Assembly passed an Act to raise £3,000 by not more than three lotteries, for purchasing land at Sandy Hook in New Jersey and erecting a lighthouse there. The estimated cost proved insufficient, so in December 1762, during the European war in which Britain was engaged, it passed another Act authorising two additional lotteries to raise £3,000 more. This stated that 'from the many Various and unusual Expenses this Colony has been obliged to be and still is at in this Just and Necessary War it is become expedient to devise such Methods of raising Money . . . as will not increase or add to the Load of Taxes this Colony already Labours under'. The second lottery would consist of 10,000 tickets of 40s. each, whereof 1,684 would be 'fortunate'. Half the proceeds would go to building the lighthouse.

By 1764 a newspaper described the newly-lighted tower as octagonal in shape, 103′ high, 20′ diameter at base and 15′ at top, containing nine stories. The iron lanthorn, of 7′ height and 33′ circumference, had a copper top; 48 oil *blazes* or wicks gave the illumination. The reporter added that no expense had been spared to make the lighthouse the best on the continent.

117. Cape Henlopen lighthouse equipped for hoisting signal flags *c.* 1790

118. Sandy Hook lighthouse in 1790 showing ventilators on the dome and stays to assist in cleaning the lantern panes (Anderson)

Though slightly damaged in 1776 during naval operations against the British, the original tower is used still as a lighthouse, thanks to its substantial stone walls 7′ thick which had been lined with brick.

Cape Henlopen 1765

In 1761 the Assembly of Pennsylvania had recourse to a lottery to raise £3,000 for a lighthouse on Cape Henlopen. As the balance of subscriptions after deduction of prizes fell considerably short of that sum, a supplementary Act provided for the issue of 6 per cent. Bonds to make up the amount. Until completion of a permanent stone tower in 1767 a temporary structure housed the light.

Military operations damaged the lighthouse during the Revolution and put it out of action between 1777 and 1784, when it was repaired and relighted. Though from time to time moving sand menaced the foundations, the tower carried a light until 1924. In 1926 the sea completed its destruction.

Charleston 1767

A lighthouse at Charleston in South Carolina seems to have been the first established in the southern States. By an Act of 1750 the Colonial Government provided for erecting a beacon and placing buoys at the harbour of Charleston and a proposal was made to set a light on a church tower. But no description exists of the seamarks actually established. An Act of 1765 authorised erection of a stone lighthouse and local 'worthies' laid its foundations with much ceremony.

A second lighthouse built in 1802 received so much damage during the Civil War that about 1863 another had to be provided.

Plymouth 1768

When the Governor's Council of Massachusetts decided on the erection of the Gurnet lighthouse at Plymouth in 1768 it adopted a novel plan as a distinction from other American lighthouses. This consisted of double lights set horizontally in the same structure. A timber house built at a cost of £660, 30′ long and 20′ high, had a *lanthorn* at each end to contain two four-wick lamps.

In 1802 fire destroyed the house but the merchants of the town promptly subscribed to replace it by temporary lights, as the Government had no immediate funds at its disposal. An Act of Congress of 1802 allotted $2,500 for building another set of twin lights and reimbursing the merchants for their expenditure.

Though the idea of twin lights at Plymouth seemed an excellent distinction from a single navigation light shown at Barnstable harbour in the vicinity, they proved not entirely advantageous and a sea-captain blamed them for causing his shipwreck. He had seen the light from only one tower and identified it with confidence as the Barnstable light: apparently, from a particular direction one tower hid the other. But local prejudice in favour of retaining the twin lights as a distinction prevailed until 1924 when, at last, opposition ceased to the recommendation which the Lighthouse Board expressed frequently that a single light would be preferable. Even 100 years earlier one light would have been more satisfactory as a seamark than the pair, because of variation in the intensity of each.

A Fuller Account of Certain Lighthouses

PORTSMOUTH 1771

In 1771 the Colonial Assembly of New Hampshire directed that a light should be established at Fort William and Mary at the mouth of the harbour of Portsmouth, New-castle, and be maintained for 3 years only, by a charge on shipping. At once a large lantern was purchased and hoisted every night on a mast that supported a flagstaff. A few years later a lighthouse took its place. An Act of 1784 authorised its repair and the appointment of a lightkeeper. All ships anchoring in the harbour paid dues for its maintenance, whether or not they did business at the port.

In May 1791 the keeper who held the contract for oil and other stores received official intimation of the transfer of the lighthouse to the United States and directions to attend to it as previously, including the following instructions: 'You will see that the Glass of the Lanthorn is kept clean at all times, that the pan containing the oil is duly supplied therewith . . . you will pay particular attention to the Snuffing of the Wicks & see that no wick is used but such as is of a proper Size to afford the best light.' In 1792 the lightkeeper's contract stipulated that he would 'keep on hand at all times a Quantity not less than One Hundred Gallons of Oyl, for the use of the said Light which shall be Oyl of the Fish called Hake'.

Another wooden lighthouse 78' high, erected in 1804, continued in use until 1877.

CAPE ANN 1771

Before 1771 all the lighthouses that had been erected on what is now the territory of the United States were established on sites where they indicated the whereabouts of important harbours and to some extent assisted coastal navigation; but in that year two lighthouse towers primarily to assist general coastal traffic were erected at Cape Ann, Massachusetts. As with the twin lights of Plymouth and with many others in Europe, the adoption of two towers offered seamen a fair distinction from other coastal lights; but though this method of distinction had long been outmoded by 1861 with a large variety of lights to choose from, local conservatism caused a pair of granite towers to be built in that year at Cape Ann to replace the original pair. Opposition to discontinuance of one of the lights (which the lighthouse authorities characterised as entirely sentimental) did not cease until 1932. Similar opposition is met in many parts of the world to changes proposed in lighthouses and lightships: seamen are naturally conservative in their profession.

GREAT POINT 1784

In 1784 the Massachusetts General Court caused a light-tower with a small dwelling house to be erected at Great Point at the northern end of Nantucket island at a cost of £3,389. 15. 5. Much of the building seems to have been of wood: fire is noted to have destroyed it in 1816.

NEWBURYPORT 1788

In 1786 the Massachusetts Assembly authorised the building of two beacons on Plumb island at the entrance to Newburyport and they carried lighted lanterns occasionally. Ships keeping *the two lights in one or in line*, would pass safely over the Newbury bar. This is the first recorded use of guiding lights in America. At least one of these lights was designed so that it could be moved easily as the bar shifted.

FEDERAL LIGHTHOUSES 1789–1800

By an Act of the first United States Congress of 7th August 1789 the new Federal Government undertook the upkeep of all seamarks ceded to it by the several States, formerly the British Colonies, and vested their management in a Lighthouse Service which began its operations with the twelve lighthouses described already. The Service erected another twelve before the century expired. These were:

1791	Cape Henry Va.	1798	Bakers island Mass.
1791	Portland Head Maine	1798	Cape Cod Mass.
1791	Tybee Ga.	1798	Hatteras N.C.
1795	Seguin Maine	1798	Ocracoke N.C.
1796	Bald Head N.C.	1799	Gay Head Mass.
1797	Montauk N.Y.	1799	Eatons Neck N.Y.

All these American lighthouses were sited on the Atlantic coast, the shores of the Pacific Ocean being still *terra incognita*, unsettled and uncharted.

CAPE HENRY 1791

The new Service put up its first lighthouse at Cape Henry, Virginia, where before 1789 stones chosen for the purpose had been deposited on the beach by the Colonial Government. The octagonal tower, composed of hammer-dressed sandstone, remains in good preservation to this day. It stood 72′ tall and was to have a foundation diameter of $27\frac{1}{2}$′ and a top diameter of $16\frac{1}{2}$′ with wall thickness tapering upwards from 6′ to 3′. From fear of faulty earthing, two lightning conductors were fitted.

The contract dated March 1791 included a detailed specification which shows that 8 wrought-iron bars 3″ square supported the roof of the iron and copper lantern 10′ high and 10′ in diameter. It had an outer platform 6′ wide and held 28 panes of glass 14″ × 12″. The specification required the lantern to be 'covered with a net work of strong brass wire so as to preserve the Glass in the lantern from injuries by Hail or flights of Birds in the Night' and directed that 'the rafters of the Lantern shall be well fastened to an Iron hoop over which shall be a Copper funnel through which the smoke may pass into a large Copper ventilator . . . turned by a large Vane'. Eight lamps each containing 8 quarts of oil would hang in two tiers transversely in the lantern. At a convenient distance, in a vault with a strong door, the oil would be stored in 8 cedar-wood cisterns holding 200 gallons apiece.

The contract stipulated that the stonework should be founded in the sands at a depth of 13′ below the *Water Table*—presumably the level of high-water. But when digging began in the sand, it appeared that the foundation must be sunk 7′ lower and the diameter enlarged to 33′ with the wall 11′ thick. This increased the contract price of $15,000 by some $2,500. In December 1792 the contractor and the Government agreed that recompense to him for the extra cost should be decided by three disinterested persons as arbiters.

A later tower is now used as a lighthouse.

MATERIALS FOR TOWERS

As might be expected in a country where timber was the chief building material—obtainable near the site, plentiful and quickly worked—wood was used for most of the early lighthouse structures. Stones brought from England formed the material for certainly one tower. They are said to have been imported as ship's ballast and probably had been picked with a definite view to building. To build a tower satisfactorily from the odd stones usually taken at random from an English beach to ballast sailing-vessels would scarcely be possible.

ILLUMINANTS

Except at Tybee, where candles gave the illumination in 1791, simple oil lamps (now considered extremely crude) lighted the early lighthouses. The lamps had no glass chimneys, and mirrors and lenses are not recorded as being used.

119. Louisburg lighthouse, Nova Scotia,
from a drawing by Ince during the siege
of Louisburg in 1758

It is curious that no attempt was made to burn open wood fires on masonry towers—wood being so plentiful. The reason lay probably in the proximity of timber dwellings which a flying spark would ignite. An open fire on a high masonry tower was proposed for Florida before 1780.

The light from one lighthouse differed from that of another only by the exhibition of one light or two, except at the Highland lighthouse at Cape Cod, where some kind of *eclipser* arrangement was fitted in 1798, its purpose being to give a difference from the Boston light. It seems to have consisted of one metal screen revolved by clockwork round a central oil lamp or a cluster of lamps. It merely occulted and disclosed the light gradually every 8 minutes without magnification. The arrangement was not satisfactory as full light was shown for only a few seconds within that period: seamen disliked the long eclipse.

LIGHTKEEPERS

Usually only one keeper was appointed at each lighthouse. He led a hard and lonely life and had to produce much of his food from the soil by his own labour. His small pay pressed him to undertake any other work that offered. A lightkeeper at Ocracoke, blessed with neighbours, had the idea of keeping a tavern at the lighthouse, but in 1797 the Government forbade this use of the premises, as also the retailing of spirits.

With frequent shipwrecks and consequent heavy loss of life, the Lighthouse Service took a severe view of keepers' defaults. President Jefferson, appreciating that lighthouses must be reliable, put on record his opinion that 'the keepers of lighthouses should be dismissed for small degrees of remissness, because of the calamities which even these produce'.

CANADA

The first lighthouse to be established in Canada was probably the tower erected about 1740 at the French stronghold of Louisburg on Cape Breton island, Nova Scotia. As designed in 1733, this round tower 22' in diameter had the lantern ventilator 75' above the base. The illuminant was by oil lamp, 15 or 16 burners bunched compactly in the centre, an unusual arrangement which should give an excellent light showing all round the horizon. In having a double-lined roof and a ventilator to prevent back-draught, the lantern was much in advance of the times. An engraving published in 1762 depicts the lighthouse according to a drawing made during the British siege of Louisburg in 1758.

Lighthouses were established also on Nova Scotia at Sambro island (1758) and Cape Roseway (1788), and another on Cape Breton island (before 1777), probably at Scatari. St. John's, Newfoundland, had a harbour light in 1791.

XII

FRENCH LIGHTHOUSES IN NORMANDY AND AT CORDOUAN
1739 TO 1797

120. The lighthouses at La Hève, from a painting by Turner

FRENCH LIGHTS

The sites of the 17 coastal lights existing in 1819 are numbered and those of the local or reputed ancient lights mentioned in the text are named.   The Casquets lights were English

1. L'Ailly	5. Cette	10. Groix	14. Port-Vendres
2. Baleines	6. Calais	11. La Hève	15. St. Mathieu
3. Barfleur	7. Chassiron	12. Penmarc'h	16. Ushant (Stiff)
(Gatteville)	8. Cordouan	13. Planier	17. Villefranche
4. Bouc	9. Fréhel		

XII. FRENCH LIGHTHOUSES IN NORMANDY AND AT CORDOUAN
1739 TO 1797

In 1775 the Rouen Chamber of Commerce established 3 lighthouses in Normandy and after extensive enquiries, tests and advice from scientific persons, lighted them by coal fires in open lanterns. So much coal was consumed that smaller grates were fitted but the results did not satisfy seamen who complained of inferior illumination and remained dissatisfied after successive changes to coal fires in glazed lanterns and to spherical reflectors. Similar complaints were evoked at Cordouan in 1782 when a coal fire was replaced by spherical reflectors and in 1790 by revolving parabolic reflectors which should have produced the finest light of the period.

After the Middle Ages, the English Channel gradually became of consequence to the trade of north-west Europe and by 1600 could claim to be the most important sea-route of the world, reckoned both by numbers of ships using it and by considerations of sea power.

Yet it is remarkable how slowly its western approaches came to be lighted. In France, as in many other countries, the reason lay largely in a general doubt as to the effectiveness of lighthouses: often their feeble gleam could not penetrate beyond outlying dangers except during good visibility, and their varying illumination could mislead vessels. England had a particular reason for discouraging the establishment of lighthouses on her shores as well as for hesitating to chart her coasts: she feared these developments would assist enemies to penetrate her defensive insularity, a consideration that mainly prevented the continuance of the Lizard light after 1620.

Consequently, up to 1680, complete darkness shrouded the western approaches of the Channel: a ship approaching from the south or the west got no guidance at night until she had sailed for 350 miles between the rocky coasts of France and England, which were bedevilled by out-lying rocks and sandbanks, and had sighted the English private lighthouse at Dungeness. While on this passage she was exposed to great risk of shipwreck during low visibility or darkness and, if disaster occurred despite the utmost skill in seamanship, to plunder of her cargo and possibly to slaughter of any survivors at the hands of wreckers on both coasts. For instance, after the wreck of the *Association* in the Scilly Isles in 1707, Admiral Sir Cloudesley Shovel escaped drowning and gained the Cornish shore, only to be murdered by a woman covetous of the rings on his fingers.

By 1700 four lighthouses had been set up in the area, two in France at Ushant and Cap Fréhel near St. Malo, and two in England at St. Agnes in the Scilly Isles and on the Eddystone Rocks. Ushant and St. Agnes bore coal fires burning in the open, the Eddystone tower showed candles sheltered in a lantern and Cap Fréhel displayed blazing torches under a roof with open sides. Of these four, Cap Fréhel scarcely served general navigation owing to its embayed position, far off the usual shipping track. Until 1777 Ushant was lighted only from October to March.

In 1723 the Channel navigation benefited enormously from the establishment on the

Casquets Rocks in the Channel Islands, right in the centre of the area, of a unique lighthouse, distinct from all others, consisting of 3 towers each with a coal fire.

Between 1700 and 1780 new Channel lights were established on the English coast at Portland (1716) and Lizard (1751), each consisting of two towers with open coal fires, and on the French coast in 1775 in Normandy at Gatteville near Barfleur, La Hève near Havre, and Cap l'Ailly near Dieppe—all open coal fires under roofs. Two towers were erected at La Hève, single towers at the other places. In 1715 a small coal fire to burn some 34 tons of coal annually, replaced the torches at Cap Fréhel.

Seamen uttered no serious complaints about the English and Channel Islands lighthouses, so the four private individuals and Trinity House who maintained them met little trouble in their tasks. Nor were serious complaints recorded about the French lights of Ushant and Cap Fréhel. But the Normandy lighthouses of 1775 brought endless difficulties to the Rouen Chamber of Commerce which erected them: not until 36 years had elapsed could one of these lights be made satisfactory to seamen. Yet the Chamber and other Authorities concerned took the greatest trouble to discover the best means of illumination and all the practical steps they took were eminently reasonable and proper; experiments were made, alterations carried out, experts in navigation and lighting consulted, information obtained from abroad and even English lighthouses visited.

Similar troubles arose with the lighting of Cordouan, culminating in the surprising failure of a new revolving oil light installed by Teulère in 1790.

THE NORMANDY LIGHTHOUSES

PROPOSAL OF 1739

In 1739 the French Admiralty, which managed the coal light at Ushant and continued to do so after 1830, became concerned as to the almost unlighted coasts of France. In 1740, at the entrance to the naval base at Brest, it erected St. Mathieu lighthouse with oil lamps in a glazed lantern, despite experience at Baleines and Chassiron where oil lamps, having proved ineffective, had been replaced by open fires of coal and wood respectively. Chassiron showed two superimposed wood fires. At the same time, the Admiralty approached the Chamber of Commerce at Rouen as to the need for a lighthouse to reduce the frequency of wrecks near Barfleur and informed the Chamber that one of two methods of illuminating it should be adopted: either by a fire of wood or coal burning in the open air and blown up by bellows when the wind was insufficient to make a blaze, set in a tower 12′ high with ventilator funnels opening from its sides to force a draught to the grates, with a coal-store and a keeper's dwelling; or by candles or oil lamps shown from a tower 20′ high, having 3 floors—the lower for stores, the middle as a dwelling, and the upper with a roof and 3 glazed windows facing seawards, each window showing a candle or a three-wick lamp. The Admiralty considered that a wood or coal fire would be preferred by seamen and added that attending to it would occupy a keeper so much throughout the night that he must sleep during the day. Alternatively, it pointed out, a candle or oil light would require attention once only during the night: so the keeper could sleep most of the night and, being free to accept other employment during the day, he would be content with lower wages. The light could be discontinued during the summer.

After consulting neighbouring seaports, the Chamber decided that one lighthouse at

Barfleur and two at La Hève (for distinction from other lighthouses as well as to guide vessels to the entrance to Havre) would be useful, though it believed that a multiplicity of light-houses might confuse the mariner. Its members preferred coal fires without bellows, and

121. A design *c.* 1740 for a lantern at Barfleur

122. Wreckers on the Brittany coast

lights to be shown all the year round. A store would be unnecessary, as they considered that coals would improve when exposed to air and rain. All the seaports agreed that the cost should be borne by the National Treasury, but as soon as the Government indicated that the public purse would not be opened for this purpose, the project dropped.

PROPOSAL OF 1765

The frequency of wrecks around Havre, as many as 40 having occurred in three months, forced reconsideration of the lighthouse question in 1765 and the Chamber worked out costs on the basis of annual consumpts of 40 tons of coal at Barfleur and 70 tons at each of the La Hève towers. Three *chaloupes* which had been armed, lest they should encounter hostile craft, put to sea to observe a 40′ flag-pole on the headland at La Hève and endeavoured thus to determine the proper heights for towers. Stakes set in the ground marked the chosen positions. After lengthy discussions to settle the details, the Chamber applied to the King for a patent to authorise the building of four towers (1 at Gatteville Point, 2 at La Hève and 1 at Cap l'Ailly) and the levying of dues on shipping for their upkeep. In the course of the negotiations the Chamber resisted successfully an Admiralty claim to appoint the light-keepers, a claim which was put forward on the ground that only seamen could know how to manage a sea-light properly. At last the Chamber satisfied the Treasury as to the estimates of cost, and in December 1773 the King granted a patent authorising dues of 1 to 5 sols per ton on various classes of French vessels and 6 sols on foreigners.

At the same time, the Government stated that it did not approve of the Chamber's endeavour to save expense by building simple towers devoid of ornamentation, and declared that as such works would serve posterity they should reflect the genius of the period and accord better with the dignity of the monarch who authorised their erection, thus continuing the national propensity to decoration that had been demonstrated at Cordouan.

In February 1774 the Chamber accepted tenders for the building of four towers of more ornamental designs, and although it favoured open coal fires it delayed a decision on the method of illumination as the Minister of Marine had drawn attention to the advantages of reflector or mirror lights as being economical and giving a constant bright light and as having proved successful at English lighthouses. He had the Liverpool reflectors in mind. At the same time he counselled them against accepting novelties without experiment.

Tests of Fires and Reflectors 1774

In 1766 a gold medal had been awarded to A. L. Lavoisier, a French chemist of international repute, for combining tiny mirrors with oil lamps to light the streets of Paris, in substitution for candles. He had rejected the parabolic curve as concentrating the light-rays from a lamp too much in one direction, and recommended a spherical mirror of small focal distance which, with an oil lamp with relatively wide wick, would give a considerable spread of light. The adoption of his proposals greatly improved street-lighting and brought considerable profit to the maker, Tourtille Sangrain, a Paris optician. Lavoisier was less fortunate: he went to the guillotine as a Royalist in 1794, the Tribunal having sentenced him with these words: 'The Republic has no use for scientists.'

Sangrain got the notion that the mirrors would be acceptable for sea-lights and in 1773 he constructed a model lighthouse lantern glazed with 24 square panes of good quality glass and containing 16 spherical reflectors, each with its own lamp, arranged in a circle facing outwards to show light all round the horizon. In January 1774, after tests at Montmartre in Paris which satisfied the Minister of Marine that the arrangement might serve for a lighthouse, Sangrain made a full-sized apparatus at the cost of the Treasury and offered it to the Rouen Chamber for trial. The offer was accepted and at the same time the Chamber ordered from Liverpool one of Hutchinson's parabolic facet reflectors, and managed to obtain its delivery along with his plans and other helpful information, despite the prohibition of English imports. At Rouen in the summer, various observers, including the Curé of Freneuse, tested these two types of reflectors against an open coal fire. Opinion favoured the coal fire as it lit equally the whole of the horizon—whereas Hutchinson's single reflector lit only a narrow sector. Sangrain, whose light was rejected, considered that his reflectors had not appeared at their best and after the test wrote to say that he had improved them, but the Chamber adhered to its decision to adopt coal fires under a roof. From the apparatus and information put before it, its decision seems to have been right. It had not overlooked simple oil lights burning in a lantern as at Genoa and Leghorn but did not give them a trial, believing that the reflectors and coal fire would be brighter. It also made a series of tests with coals from France, Spain and Britain. Of these, coals from Bo'ness in Scotland gave the best blaze.

Coal Fires adopted 1775

So the four towers of dressed granite were surmounted by unglazed lanterns to shelter the iron grates measuring 3' in diameter at the top and tapering to an 18" diameter grille 3' below, in accordance with information got from England. But from the first night of exhibition on 1st November 1775, seamen declared the fires to be unsatisfactory, though a few individuals were grateful for sea-lights of any variety. Their illumination was sometimes imperceptible: on windy nights the flames were beaten down and rose only 4″ against 5′ when calm. The actual consumpts of coals at l'Ailly and La Hève exceeded expectations. At the latter, the cause was supposed to be the position of the towers on the high cliff, much

123. One of the La Hève lighthouses in 1776 with unglazed
lantern

exposed to the winds. At Gatteville the consumpt of coal during the first fortnight reached nearly 9 tons against an estimate of 2½ tons. According to British practice a grate of such large dimensions might consume up to 15 tons in that period. The Isle of May lighthouse at one period burned some 25 tons in a winter's fortnight. The heavy cost of shipping coals from Scotland to France, which was augmented by import duties, coupled with the adverse reports of seamen, induced an immediate review of the lighting of the towers.

DEFECTS OF COAL FIRES

The grates were examined first: new designs were prepared, models were made in wood, and a grate was imported from London which was understood to be identical with those used at some English lighthouses. After more trials, the Chamber issued smaller grates to the four towers. At l'Ailly the new grate proved unsatisfactory at once, so the original one was replaced and stacked with less coal.

Meantime, further enquiry was made regarding the English coal fire lighthouses. In France, the top of the grates had been set flush with the top of the masonry so that only the flames rising above the grate were visible seawards, whereas in England the grates were raised above the masonry so that seamen had the advantage of beholding the whole body of fire within the bars. In England too, the keepers renewed the coals every four hours and stirred them frequently: the regulations required one of the two keepers to remain constantly on duty and, to ensure observance of this rule, only one small bed was provided between them. This saving of expense in providing furniture was declared to be worth while.

But nothing that the Chamber could do allayed the seamen's discontent, and its own annoyance at the bad lights was aggravated by the discovery that at La Hève a blacksmith operated his forge at the Chamber's expense, the rascal's daughter carrying away from the towers baskets containing coal covered by burnt-out cinders. Trouble arose unexpectedly from lighted cinders, blown from the fires by the wind, setting alight the heaps of coal held in reserve and even farm buildings some distance off.

The small space round the grates at the top of the towers made it difficult for the lightkeepers to attend to the fires without being scorched in clothing and person and their living conditions were unbearable. Smoke sometimes drove them from their apartments; one keeper and his wife were found insensible from carbon monoxide fumes. On the other hand some of their complaints appear trivial when the conditions at some other contemporary lighthouses are considered. They objected to the labour of carrying coal to the top of the tower some 50′ above the base to which it had been brought by horse and cart; this objection was met by fitting an ingenious arrangement for raising coal in a basket by pulley so that the basket could not be upset in high winds. What would they have said of the tremendous task of the single keeper at Cumbrae who from sea-level carried a larger quantity for a long distance to a height of over 400′?

Glazed Lanterns fitted 1777

One of the architects suggested that glazing the lantern should reduce the coal consumpt, prevent cinders from being blown from the fire, and stop rain and melted snow from pouring down the staircase in the tower and flooding the keepers' apartments. In October 1776 therefore, the Chamber instructed a certain Jacques Clement to proceed to the Casquets lighthouse to get first-hand information as to the English practice of surrounding coal fires with glazed lanterns, and on his return with plans and other information it applied to the Treasury in Paris for approval of the expenditure necessary to adopt that system.

With the Government's sanction, the Chamber ordered four lanterns of wood and glass containing smaller grates in May 1777 and erected them in October at Gatteville and l'Ailly and in November at La Hève. The result was a marked reduction in the coal consumpt. But little light was emitted seawards and in certain directions the thick lantern pillars and ornaments obscured the smaller fires entirely. Seamen declared now that the lights at La Hève had been reduced as much as from a torch to a candle, and the Admiral at Havre passed adverse comments to the Chamber and to the Minister of Marine. Alterations to the glazing failed to effect a remedy and in February 1778 the Government drew the Chamber's attention again to Sangrain's spherical reflectors now in use at the Ministry of Marine's light of St. Mathieu, where 60 little mirrors measuring 200 mm. overall, each with an oil lamp and arranged on the four sides of a fixed metal frame, cost much less to maintain than did the coal fire at Ushant.

In March 1778 a storm damaged the lantern of the south tower at La Hève, and the Admiral, angered at the still less effective lighting which resulted from enclosing the fires, ordered the removal of the glazing from both towers so that coal would burn in the open air as it had done originally. He held the principal keeper, Turbot, to be responsible for the accident to the south lantern and sentenced him to a month's imprisonment and suspension from duty for another month. This treatment shocked the Chamber, but the Admiral justified his action by referring to the unceasing complaints of navigators about the bad lighting which, they alleged, was caused by unsuitable lanterns. The Chamber obtained a Court Order to reglaze the La Hève lanterns and, to avoid irritating seamen further by suspending the lights even for a night, arranged to carry out the work in one day between

124. St. Mathieu lighthouse near Brest, where spherical reflectors were installed about 1778 (Perrot)

sunrise and sunset. Bohemian glass was used, presumably for transparency and strength. On completion of the alterations at all the lights, observations at night from the sea brought reports that Gatteville light could be seen at 5 leagues, l'Ailly 6 to 7 and La Hève at 7, even in somewhat unfavourable weather. These encouraging results were due chiefly to more frequent cleaning of the glass panes, probably on the English plan of sponging them every half-hour. In making every effort to placate the Admiral, the Chamber contracted with a glazier to clean the lantern at La Hève frequently for 200 livres per annum, thus taking the duty from the lightkeepers and freeing them from possible blame in that respect.

SPHERICAL REFLECTORS ADOPTED 1779

In May 1778 Necker, the famous Finance Minister, after examining the lighthouse accounts, drew attention somewhat curtly to the expense of the coal fires and the considerable economy of reflector lights. His remarks spurred the Chamber to get in touch again with Sangrain who invited its members to test his latest spherical mirrors under practical conditions and sent by carriage from Paris to Havre a reflector which he had just completed for Chassiron lighthouse. When he had fitted it, in pristine condition with lamps in perfect order, at the north tower at La Hève, they desired the Minister of Marine to nominate an impartial person to observe it and report whether he found the reflector or the coal fire to be the more suitable for navigation. This Commissioner's report, and perhaps the half-hearted views of several mariners, favoured the reflector, so, in the hope of avoiding more trouble and keen to reduce expense, the Chamber instructed Sangrain to instal his mirrors at the two La Hève towers. He undertook to improve the lanterns and announced that he had discovered a method, which he would introduce in October, of increasing the brilliancy of his lights even further. Formal approval by the Ministry and a new Royal patent, which was required, were not forthcoming immediately and not until November 1779 could the new reflectors be exhibited and the stocks of coal sold at the lighthouses.

In September 1780 Sangrain fitted his reflectors at Gatteville and in November at l'Ailly. From these lighthouses, unlike those at La Hève, light had to be distributed equally

125. Cordouan lantern in 1727 with Bitry's plane reflectors placed above a coal fire

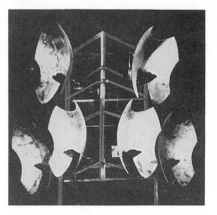

126. Sangrain's spherical reflectors with flat-wick burners *c.* 1780, set up for exhibition on two sides of a triangular stand. (A photograph)

over a wide horizon. An iron frame, square in plan, held 16 spherical reflectors, arranged four-a-side and in two tiers. Each of the 8 lower lamps had 3 flat wicks and each of the upper lamps 2 wicks. But, as explained in Section XVI, despite brilliant polish, the spherically-curved mirrors were incapable of even doubling the illumination from the lamps. Soot soon obscured their slight reflecting qualities and their effect was to screen from the mariner the direct light from some of the lamps. On the whole, the seaman would have received more light had the 16 lamps been arranged alone without reflectors.

The most suitable oil for the lamps was chosen after trials of several varieties and at last seamen accepted the lights as being the best that the Chamber could produce, though they never ceased to complain about them and to regret the removal, because of the cost of maintenance, of the original open coal fires which, when burning sufficient coal and stirred frequently, gave most satisfaction to them and to the French Navy.

LIGHTING 1783–1835

Recognising the inadequate lighting of the lighthouses, the Chamber attempted some improvements about 1783. These had no good result and it could do no more than keep the reflectors well-polished and send to Paris from time to time any that required re-silvering. The next alterations to the lighting apparatus of these lighthouses were made in 1811–18 at La Hève, in 1820 at l'Ailly, and in 1835 at Gatteville.

It has been stated wrongly that Sangrain's mirrors were revolved at l'Ailly lighthouse about 1781 to give a flashing light.   The fact is that no French or English lights, apart from lights tested at Dieppe, were revolved before 1790 and that if Sangrain's mirrors had been revolved, their spherical curve and the 2 and 3 broad wicks of the lamps would have failed to produce an effective flash.   This failure would have been emphasised by the speedy destruction of their polish, the distortion of the thin metal of which they were composed and the confusion with the relatively strong light emanating from the lamps fixed on the adjacent faces of the frame.   Certainly, one contemporary account of l'Ailly light by a layman in 1795 suggested that it consisted of 6 reflectors and was revolved but, clearly, he supposed that the lever arrangement provided to jack-up the frame of reflectors for cleaning purposes would rotate it.   Presumably, too, his note of the number of reflectors as 6 was printed in mistake for 16.   An official description of the French lighthouses of 1800 and other contemporary accounts make no mention of l'Ailly as a revolving light.

CORDOUAN LIGHTHOUSE

The French Ministry of Marine and the other Government Departments in Paris, La Rochelle and Bordeaux which were concerned in the management of the lighthouse of Cordouan, faced troubles no less vexatious than those that had fallen upon the Chamber of Commerce of Rouen.

FIRE GRATE LOWERED 1717

The stonework of the open lantern sheltering the grate had become so much damaged by the nightly burning of the oak fire during many decades that in 1717 the upper part of the tower had to be demolished.   The consequent display of the fire 22′ lower reduced its geographical range by over a mile, which affected navigators.   Larger quantities of wood were consumed to make a better fire and this brought complaints from the lightkeepers who had to give it more attention and from the boatmen who laboured to bring the bulky cargoes of wood from the mainland.   Substitution of coal for wood as the fuel was suggested and in September 1724 Boucher, the supervisor at Bordeaux, wrote to the British Admiralty asking it to send him a plan of the grates fitted at English lighthouses and particulars of the coals they burned.   It was then decided in France that a change to coal would meet the complaints best and that the fire need not be reinstated at its former height.

OPEN LANTERN FITTED 1727

So, in 1727, Bitry, the fortress engineer at Bordeaux, set a lantern with metal pillars like an iron cage on the top of Cordouan, to contain a coal grate with an inverted cone of polished flat metal plates which he hoped would reflect the brightness of the flames below and increase the glow.   The wood fire had required replenishing every 3 hours: now, he expected, the fire in the new grate containing 225 pounds of coal, would last all night. Though soot covered the plates and made them useless as reflectors, seamen seem to have approved of the new fire, but it is disconcerting to learn that when they wanted a greater blaze they had to discharge a gun as a signal to the keepers to stir it.   By 1780 the cost of importing foreign coals had increased so greatly and the difficulty of transporting and landing fuel in the islet and carrying it over the sands and rocks to the lighthouse and up the awkward stairs of the tower had been found so burdensome that consideration of alternative methods of lighting again became necessary.

SPHERICAL REFLECTORS ADOPTED 1782

The reported success of Sangrain's spherical reflectors at other French lighthouses led to his visit to Cordouan by invitation in June 1781 so that he could state a price for an oil light, and in May 1782 the Minister of Marine accepted his tender to supply a lantern with spherical reflectors. Of these he supplied no less than 80, arranged in 5 tiers. Each measured 217 mm. overall, and it backed a single 18 mm. flat-wick lamp. The new lantern had 12 sides, an iron roof overlaid by copper sheets, and 4 ventilators opening to all winds to carry off smoke. The ventilator on the top of the dome rose 150 French feet above the rock base.

On 12th November 1782 Sangrain exhibited his light, and at once navigators declared it to be greatly inferior to the former coal fire: at a distance of $1\frac{1}{2}$ leagues it appeared as a feeble star and at 4 or 5 leagues the light seemed to vanish. The supervisor supposed the lightkeepers to be negligent and ordered them to scrub the soot from reflectors several times during the night, which gradually injured their polish. Sangrain brushed aside criticism of his apparatus with the remark that every new light he installed was at first greeted by complaints from prejudiced pilots but that soon their murmurs ceased. He claimed to have produced at Cordouan a solid ball of fire 6′ 6″ in diameter and 6′ 9″ in height which should delight seamen.

Seafarers continued to complain and the lightkeepers reported that they were choked by the smoke which obscured the lantern glass and could not attend properly to so many lamps. Sangrain declared that a conspiracy had been formed against his light and challenged qualified persons to find it faulty. He requested that a Commission should observe it as had been done at Havre in 1778. The Minister of Marine consented and appointed 6 experienced sea-captains who observed it between the 15th and 17th of May 1783 at various distances. They declared without hesitation that the light was much inferior to a coal fire, one of which, as a comparison, was exhibited from the tower at the same time.

The Minister then ordered Teulère, a well-known master-mason and engineer, to examine the apparatus. He reported that it had been assembled by a workman without understanding, who had set the reflectors at a wrong inclination and the wicks too low. After much argument Sangrain removed his 80 reflectors and replaced them with fewer and larger spherical reflectors, but it is not recorded whether they were spare reflectors from Chassiron and Baleines or new models made one-third larger. The alteration which he carried out failed to appease seamen and the Minister decided on a thorough enquiry into sea-lighting in general.

This developed into practical investigations and tests in which clockmakers, philosophers and scientists took part. The knowledge that parabolic reflectors had been revolved in 1781 at the Carlsten lighthouse in Sweden led to experiments at Dieppe, commencing in 1783 with eclipsing and revolving lights. References to these experiments are contradictory. The most definite mentions that trials would be made there in the winter of 1787-8 with 3 silvered parabolic mirrors revolved in conjunction with Argand's or Quinquet's oil lamps. Teulère's name is associated with these trials so, probably from experience thus gained, he designed a new light for Cordouan.

TOWER RE-BUILT 1788–90

Teulère's inspections at Cordouan around 1782 showed the need for extensive repairs to the tower which he described as 'la tour qui menaçoit ruine', and he noted that the low elevation of the light made it invisible to small vessels sailing along the fringes of the outer surrounding sandbanks. Commencing in April 1788 he removed the upper part of the building and replaced it by a higher and less ornate column of stone, which exists now. The alteration of the tower raised the light 60′ higher than Sangrain's lantern. Teulère supervised the alteration and shared with Borda and Jallier the credit for evolving a design which skilfully reduced to a minimum the external contrast between the old and the new work and preserved the elaborate vaulted halls which were outstanding features of de Foix's design. While the work proceeded, a coal fire was shown from the outside of the tower.

PARABOLIC REFLECTORS REVOLVED 1790

On top of the tower Teulère set a new lantern of 10′ diameter with 12 sides and glazed for the unusual height of 15′. Its exceptionally large size and the incorporation of many ventilators seemed to provide amply for carrying off smoke from the lamps. The lantern contained the revolving light consisting of a triangular frame rotated by clockwork and carrying on each face 4 parabolic reflectors 32″ in diameter set in vertical rows. They were made by Lenoir of Paris. At the focus each had an oil lamp made by Quinquet. This new revolving light shone forth on 29th August 1790, mariners having been warned that they would see one flash every minute, and that this flashing character would afford distinction from the stars and the lights of ships, and from the neighbouring spherical reflector lights of Baleines and Chassiron.

With the excellent glazed lantern, parabolic reflectors and lamps with double current of air, the result should have been a wonderful light with a range of some 20 miles on a clear night. But seamen condemned it immediately.

COMPLAINTS REGARDING THE LIGHT

It was said that the Chevalier Borda, a philosopher charged to supervise construction of the apparatus, had not tested it fully before despatching it to Teulère who installed it as he received it. On the day after first lighting it, he noticed that the lamps were out of focus. Adjustments produced approximately 5 seconds' duration of bright light. This duration, corresponding to an arc of 10°, would now be considered too long, but up to about 1852 the French Lighthouse Commission believed that seamen preferred long flashes. Teulère, who held the same view, at once asked Borda to agree to an increase of the diameter of the circular wicks from 33·8 mm. or 1·3″ to 54·0 mm. or 2·1″, as he desired originally. Borda agreed to this alteration and to any other improvement that Teulère might suggest. The broader wicks, by increasing the horizontal divergence, extended the flash to 30 seconds' duration but they eliminated any actual eclipse or period of darkness between flashes, an unwelcome result which Teulère supposed was due to defects of the mirrors. At 5 leagues he considered the light to be as brilliant as Sangrain's had been at 3 leagues. He lost it to view at 6⅔ leagues. It should be explained that the flash from these 4 large parabolic reflectors with argand-type lamps should have been overwhelmingly better than the light

197

from Sangrain's spherical reflectors and flat-wick lamps, and that its excellence as a sea-light should have been obvious to all who beheld it.

Complaints from navigators and pilots continued to pour in to the Ministry of Marine: they begged for a return to a coal fire. In February 1793 Teulère came to the conclusion that an increase of the diameter of the wicks to 67·5 mm. or 2·6″ would benefit the light,

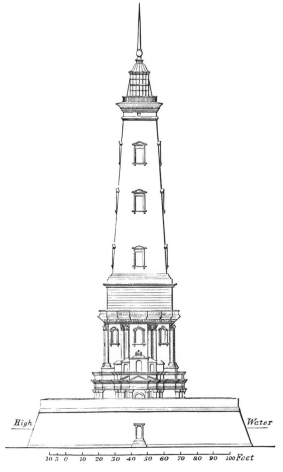

127. A drawing of Cordouan in 1834 showing Teulère's reconstruction of the tower in 1790

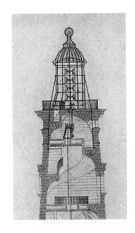

128. Cordouan lantern in 1822 showing 2 of the 3 vertical rows of Teulère's parabolic reflectors

and in May the Minister informed his representative in Bordeaux that Borda and Teulère had convinced him that the apparatus which they had fitted should give satisfaction and he remarked that the new system of parabolic reflectors served well in England and Spain. He was reluctant to return to coal as the fuel, in view of its expense and the trouble in bringing it to the island. He wrote direct to Teulère agreeing to the cost of supplying new lamps with broader wicks and called on him to improve the light in any other way, so that complaints should cease.

Teulère tested the reflectors with the broader wick lamp and noticed that the light was nearly eclipsed at $4\frac{1}{3}$ leagues and invisible at $5\frac{1}{2}$ leagues. When he carried out these observations on a warm night without a breath of wind, the smoke from the chimney-less lamps filled the lantern so that the keepers could not remain within it without choking.

In July 1793 Teulère reported to the Minister that he had fitted the new lamps with 2·6″ wicks and asked that, after he had received glass chimneys to suit them, another independent Commission should be appointed to compare his improved light with a coal fire. He added that his object in enlarging the wicks was to increase the duration of the flash (surely, increased enough already) and pointed out rightly that chimneys would give a more intense flame and reduce the production of smoke.

COMMISSION OF ENQUIRY 1793

The new Commission, consisting of two sea-captains, Tabois and Delurnis, arrived at Cordouan on 22nd August 1793, although Teulère had not received the chimneys he wanted. They examined the apparatus and found the mechanism excellent, but all the reflectors lacked silver, due to corrosion from smoke in the absence of chimneys. With a coal fire also displayed, they proceeded out to sea and observed one vertical row of 4 reflectors to give a better light than the coal fire but the other two rows 'très inferieures'. On return to Cordouan they immediately took on board their vessel two more sea-captains and two pilots. These men confirmed the conclusions and noted the inside of the lantern panes to be coated with soot and oil. The Commission reported that the arrangement of mirrors and the mechanism which rotated them could not be bettered but, for 'plus grand utilité', this system of marine lighting should be replaced by a coal fire whenever hostilities with Britain should cease and coals be procurable. Teulère, who attended the test, declined to sign the report condemning his light but the Minister accepted the verdict. Some time later, Captain Tabois, disappointed at the retention of Teulère's apparatus in the tower, took up his pen on behalf of the seamen who preferred coal fires, and published a *mémoire* declaring that by intrigue certain individuals had obtained the right to maintain oil lights at all the French lighthouses for 9 years and that a return to coal fires was thus prejudiced. Sangrain had a share in this contract system which continued after 1835, but it seems not to have included maintenance of Cordouan lighthouse. In 1797 he failed to obtain a contract for maintaining it: its management remained with Teulère.

CAUSES OF COMPLAINT

As Teulère had studied reflectors since 1783 his views as to the failure of his apparatus should have careful consideration. In 1803 he recounted its history and described the absence of glass chimneys and effective double-air-current lamps as the chief reason for his troubles, another being defective mirrors. The lack of chimneys arose from the difficulty of making them large enough to surround the unnecessarily large circular wicks which he fitted. Their absence caused smoky flames which required the wicks to be turned lower, thus producing a smaller height of flame and less vertical divergence of the light. The effect of this was to focus the light too much on the horizon and therefore the beam of light proceeding from the lantern high above the sea was not seen by vessels when sailing near the tower although the broad wicks gave a large horizontal divergence, resulting in a long flash of low intensity.

Investigations of Lenoir's reflectors about 1814 disclosed that the wicks at Cordouan had been increased to 80 mm. or over 3″ in diameter: tests showed that a diameter of 13·5 mm. gave the best light and reduced the consumption of oil. Two further objections applied to the reflectors at Cordouan: their vertical arrangement caused soot from those below to settle on those above, and their type of manufacture, cast-steel covered by three or four thin leaves of silver, laid them open to rapid corrosion. Their thickness gave them an advantage over Sangrain's thin mirrors which became much distorted, but their weight strained the machine which could only drive them by jerks.

Spare mirrors supplied by Lenoir for Cordouan were sent in 1794 to St. Malo, Dunkirk and elsewhere. One wonders why Teulère did not use them in replacement of the mirrors at Cordouan, corroded after 3 years' use, before the visit of the Commission in 1783. It is likely that the lightkeepers could neither carry out the exchange nor service properly the 4 reflectors fixed in almost inaccessible positions at the tops of the 3 vertical rows.

However, irrespective of technical explanations, it is obvious that, with flames of the lamps kept low to reduce smoke, reflectors which had lost their polish, and lantern panes obscured with smoke and oil, the Commission had ample reason for condemning Teulère's apparatus. With a slightly better arrangement and more skilful execution of the various parts, it would have been a splendid light.

Teulère's apparatus remained at Cordouan until 1823 when it gave place to Fresnel's first revolving dioptric apparatus, constructed with lenses and prisms. Fresnel chose Cordouan to receive his new light because the complaints from navigators had never ceased. In 1822 he expressed surprise at the low intensity of the light emitted from Lenoir's mirrors and assumed that the poor result followed their having been set in slightly different directions deliberately so as to lengthen the flash or, rather, the considerable duration of light.

XIII

THE BELL ROCK LIGHTHOUSE 1806 TO 1811

129. The Bell Rock lighthouse painted by Turner

130. The refuge beacon erected in 1807 (Lorimer)

XIII. THE BELL ROCK LIGHTHOUSE 1806 TO 1811

Probably no site proposed for a lighthouse has had so many diverse designs put forward to mark it as the Bell Rock. Eventually it was decided to construct a stone tower of the type of Smeaton's Eddystone. The building operations were remarkable for the low level of the foundation relative to tidal levels and for the methods devised to speed the work. This sea-tower was the last to be built in the days of sail.

The Bell Rock or Inchcape Rock, which lies directly in the track of shipping along the east coast of Scotland, is a sunken reef in the North Sea about 11 miles off Arbroath. From time immemorial, as instanced by the tradition of the Abbot of Arbroath's bell and by its description on an early sea-chart as 'a great hidden Rock called the Inchcape', the Rock formed a frightful and much-dreaded hazard for vessels. Only during daylight, if visibility were good, and about the time of low-water of spring tides did breaking waves disclose its whereabouts. At high-water its highest peak was submerged about 11′.

The reef rose steeply from the sea-bed on three sides and sloped away for about half-a-mile to the south. No sandbanks encircled it as at Cordouan from which ships, if trapped, might hope to escape on the rise of tide. In storms it offered an indirect danger to vessels because, being without warning as to when they neared it, they often elected to give its vicinity a wide berth and stand out to face the turbulence of the open sea rather than risk striking it while seeking the shelter of the Firths of Forth or Tay.

After 1750 the frequency of wrecks upon it increased markedly corresponding to the growth of sea-trading. By 1790 all concerned in navigation round Scotland agreed that the Rock must be crowned by a seamark; the publication in 1791 of Smeaton's *Narrative* of building the Eddystone towers may have evoked dreams of a similar venture. But though the Northern Lighthouse Board had obtained authority from Parliament in 1789 to erect lighthouses anywhere on the Scottish coasts, it had been financed parsimoniously and before 1800 it had not accumulated funds sufficient to build an expensive lighthouse in the sea. Smeaton's Eddystone tower of 1759 had cost some £20,000 and Rogers's South Rock lighthouse, a roughly-constructed tower of inconsiderable exposure, had been erected in 1797 for about £22,000, with its rock platform yet to be consolidated, as against a total estimate of £9,000: it was supposed that £100,000 might be required for a tower on the Bell Rock.

In December 1799, a great storm brought the perils of the reef prominently to public notice. In a gale lasting three days vessels from as far south as the Kentish Downs, the popular anchorage off the Forelands, were blown northwards and fully 70 ships, helpless as butterflies in a breeze, were wrecked on the Scottish shores. At least two struck the Bell Rock; others drove ashore in their anxiety to avoid it. Several stranded in the Orkney islands, including a vessel on passage from London to Gibraltar which, after reaching Ushant in France, had been forced to the Downs by contrary winds and was driven thence into the North Sea. A collier proceeding light from London to Newcastle was carried completely round the north and west coasts of the British Isles, the first land she identified after Flamborough Head in Yorkshire being the Land's End of Cornwall. More and better lighthouses would have helped some of these unfortunate ships to determine their positions and make for safety.

PROPOSALS FOR ERECTING A LIGHTHOUSE

Many traders in Scotland clamoured for the establishment of a lighthouse on the Rock. Some towns urged their Members of Parliament to take action. Leith merchants declared the reef to be a 'frightful bar to navigation' and Leith Trinity House advertised for suggestions for marking it. Private individuals of humane purpose erected on it first one simple timber beacon and then another. In July 1803 a public subscription made it possible to erect a third beacon of more substantial construction with 4 main struts 40′ long. In turn each of the three was speedily destroyed by the waves or by travelling boulders.

The Northern Lighthouse Board had not been inactive and in 1800 it instructed Robert Stevenson to report on the problem. Foreseeing that one day he would be called on to deal with it, he had been studying the scanty information available about comparable sea-works but found little of use beyond Smeaton's *Narrative*. He had visited the South Rock lighthouse during its construction and had made detailed models of different structures that might be suitable for the Bell Rock. But as soon as he set foot upon the reef, he concluded that only a lighthouse of stone on the lines of Smeaton's Eddystone would have any chance of enduring. In 1800 he prepared plans accordingly and estimated the cost of a tower at £42,630 which included erection of a temporary beacon of wood as a refuge for the workmen during the construction. In 1803 the Board applied for an Act of Parliament authorising it to erect a lighthouse, to levy dues on shipping, and to borrow £30,000 which with its surplus funds, swelled considerably owing to increased sea-trade, would finance the undertaking. But its application to Parliament, which the eminent engineer Thomas Telford undertook to support by evidence before a Parliamentary Committee—he had already inspected the Rock with one of the Commissioners—had to be withdrawn, as the Corporation of London insisted on a reduction of the area from which dues would be collected and the consequently smaller collection would be inadequate to maintain the lighthouse. In 1806 one of the Commissioners published an account of the steps taken by the Board and referred to the stone tower which Stevenson proposed.

Cheaper forms of structure were advocated by various persons and probably no lighthouse site has had so many different structures proposed to mark it. One ingenious inventor suggested that a stone tower should be set upon hollow metal pillars into which the sea-water could enter: although the quantity of metal required would be small, he hoped the thin water-filled pillars would resist the force of the waves. Another design showed a tower on stone pillars. Yet another idea was to build upon a timber frame in Montrose bay the 20′ high base of a stone tower and float it into position on the reef.

Faced with such conflicting ideas, the Commissioners laid Stevenson's plans for a stone structure before John Rennie, probably the leading British engineer of the day, though he too had no experience of sea-towers. After visiting the Rock Rennie approved of a stone tower and in 1806, before another Parliamentary Committee enquiring into the Commissioners' new application for an Act, corroborated Stevenson's evidence and confirmed within £630 his estimate of cost. Some opposition was raised to the proposed expenditure, on account of the depletion of the British Exchequer by the cost of the continental war then raging, but the evidence presented to the Committee convinced it of the urgent need to prevent wrecks along this coast and it recommended that the lighthouse should be erected without delay and that the Government should lend £25,000. The offer of this amount satisfied the Lighthouse Board, which had accumulated £28,000, that it could undertake the work and Parliament passed the Act in July 1806. It provided for the levy on shipping of one-half of the authorised dues 'as soon as in the Course of building the said Light House, a proper beacon or distinguishing Mark or Object' should be erected on the Rock, and for the imposition of the full duties whenever a ship carrying a light as a seamark should be moored near it.

John Rennie was appointed by the Commissioners to be chief engineer or consulting engineer for the lighthouse, but in fact he did not assume that office in the modern sense. Stevenson prepared all the plans (which were not even submitted for Rennie's approval) and arranged for and carried out the construction of the tower (which Rennie could not do from his London home). The Commissioners and Stevenson had the benefit of Rennie's opinions and advice, particularly in December 1806 before the plans were made. Thereafter in the autumn of each of the next three years Rennie visited the work-yard at Arbroath and, though he seems never to have set foot in the tower, he landed on the Rock or sailed round it and on each occasion informed the Commissioners that the operations were proceeding excellently. During the years of construction Stevenson had the advantage of friendly correspondence with Rennie who never took a decision or issued directions or instructions but occasionally offered suggestions which Stevenson was free to adopt or reject as he pleased. This relationship led to a claim by Sir John Rennie in 1849 that his father designed and constructed the lighthouse; various facts bearing on this point are dealt with in the Appendix at the end of this book.

OPERATIONS IN 1807

Early in this year Stevenson began his working drawings, engaged foremen and assembled 30 artificers, chiefly masons, at the little harbour of Arbroath to prepare a yard with working sheds, a lime-kiln and a circular masonry platform of 44′ diameter upon which each course of the lighthouse would be placed for exact fitting of the stones after dressing. In these times it was often impossible to procure materials at short notice, so large quantities of stores and tools likely to be required were collected before work started.

For a temporary lightship, as provided by the Act, a pilot recommended by the Trinity House of London advised the purchase of a Prussian fishing-dogger 67′ long and of $82\frac{29}{94}$ tons register, which with the help of Leith shipmasters was re-rigged with 3 masts.

In building on this sunken Rock covered by the sea so deeply on every tide, problems would be faced which could be solved only as the work proceeded. It was obvious, however, that no opportunity should be missed of working upon it on all the limited days of the summer season when the fortnightly low spring tides coincided with good weather. This would necessitate a large company of artificers being kept at hand ready to start work on the Rock immediately each tide fell and continuing to work until driven off by its rising: so they must reside in a ship kept close to the Rock. The unusual conditions might attract a few adventurous men, but it would be difficult to persuade a sufficiently large number of skilled men to endure confinement in a heaving vessel anchored in the ocean and the labour of rowing one or two miles before and after each tide's work.

As the Lighthouse yacht, a cutter of 81 tons which carried stores regularly to the scattered Scottish lighthouses, could not be devoted entirely to the Bell Rock works, a sloop of 40 tons, named the *Smeaton*, was built to serve as a tender for the lightship and to bring to Arbroath undressed blocks of stone, stores and implements from Aberdeen, Dundee and Leith.   She could accommodate 24 men at a pinch while the more roomy lightship, named the *Pharos*, was fitted with berths for 30 men in addition to her crew.

The Pharos Floating light

131. The temporary lightship *Pharos*

Smeaton

132. The Bell Rock tender *Smeaton*

1807 JULY

It was notorious among seamen that peril would attend the movements of shipping around the dreaded reef, so it was hardly surprising that as the lightship was about to sail from Leith for Arbroath at the end of this month, two sailors took alarm and ran off when they learned of her destination.   But soon their places were filled and, escorted by the Lighthouse yacht, she set sail and, after testing the sea-bottom for holding-ground, anchored in 17 fathoms one mile E.S.E. from the Rock.   A formal *Notice to Mariners* announced that she would be lighted as a seamark on 15th September.

1807 AUGUST

On the 7th August the *Smeaton* laid permanent moorings ¼-mile off the Rock for the use of attending vessels, while Stevenson marked out sites for the tower and the temporary beacon and selected two landing-places that were accessible to row-boats entering from east or west through gullies screened by low shelves from the opposite winds.   A party of 6 masons, chosen as being accustomed to life at sea, cleared seaweed from these areas. When they returned to Arbroath, and described their novel experiences, many of the other men at the yard supposed that work on the Rock would be a welcome relief from their usual occupations and applied to be transferred to it.   But Stevenson required the men he engaged to undertake to remain afloat with him for at least 4 weeks without going ashore. He explained that they would be sea-sick and weary of ship-life and would wish to return to land, thus causing inconvenience to the operations from frequent changes of workers, whereas continuing for a month afloat should render them sufficiently sea-hardy to remain with little discomfort until the close of the season. Twenty-four artificers accepted his conditions and took up their quarters in the *Smeaton* while a party of Aberdeen masons engaged themselves for a year at '20s. per week summer and winter, wet and dry, with free quarters ashore and likewise our victuals when we are at the Rock. As for Sunday's work and premiums we leave that to the honour of our employers.'

To avoid accidents in the vicinity of the reef, instruction in boating had first priority and every man was allotted a particular place in one of the *Smeaton's* two boats each holding 12 persons. The landing-master steered one and Stevenson, always the last to leave the Rock, steered the other. A sharp watch on the weather and on the level of the rising tide ensured that the party should always leave it before conditions for withdrawal became dangerous.

As far as tidal levels and daylight permitted, a landing on the Rock was attempted on both tides of each day, though every fortnight for 5 days or so neap tides prevented landings as the sea did not ebb sufficiently and the working areas remained under water.

The larger extent of rock exposed at low-water offered some constructional advantages over the Eddystone, one being that there was ample space upon it for setting up a smith's portable forge; thus there could be avoided the loss of time, deplored by Smeaton, in carrying ashore all tools to be sharpened. But the bellows, tinder box, fuel and embers of the previous fire had to be carried to and fro on every trip, a great inconvenience in the boats. The demand on the forge kept the smiths employed continuously, for the sea-hardened sandstone quickly blunted the tools: whenever the rising tide extinguished the forge or endangered the bellows, the masons' work came to a standstill.

On the 18th August the artificers made their first landing at 5 a.m. shortly after the reef emerged from the water. During the next 6 days landings took place on 7 tides and good progress was made in boring into the rock dovetailed-holes 20″ deep and 2″ in diameter to hold the 12 iron stanchions to which the legs of the beacon would be attached.

On the 22nd the *Smeaton* sailed to Arbroath for provisions, and the artificers exchanged her limited accommodation, which would have been unbearable in bad weather with hatches closed to keep out seawater, for that of the lightship with the attractions of a relatively spacious sleeping-space and less cramped row-boats. But the smallest wave set that flat-bottomed vessel in motion when at anchor and it was said that in bad weather she would 'roll out her masts' and 'even turn a halfpenny if laid upon her deck'. Her behaviour destroyed at once any illusion on the part of the artificers or Stevenson that they had become sea-hardy persons, and the men found it more awkward to clamber between lightship and row-boats and disliked having to pull 4 times daily at the oars over twice the former distance. Gradually troubles disappeared: most of the men ceased to be affected by sea-sickness which at first made them very miserable and thankful to leave the ship for the Rock, and boating became a favourite amusement, prizes being given in team races.

1807 SEPTEMBER

The method to be adopted for bringing stones to their ultimate position in the tower remained undetermined. Alternatives included dropping the stones over the site at high-water or floating out stones attached to corks or air-tanks, or sinking barges or cylinders containing them. An experimental stone-carrying barge or praam had been built already, which it was intended should be filled with stones, anchored close to the Rock and, when the tide fell, towed through one of the gullies to a landing face. Trial of this procedure on the 1st September gave satisfaction but a suitable method of hauling the heavy stones thence over the jagged rock surface to the site of the tower was not apparent. No risk could be taken of losing even one of the carefully-prepared stones—replacing it might interrupt the operations for a week—nor must their fine edges be exposed to damage.

On the 2nd there occurred an incident that might have resulted in tragedy and which emphasised the need to complete the beacon as a refuge. The artificers who had landed from the *Pharos* in 2 boats had been joined by 8 men in a boat from the *Smeaton* which lay close to the Rock. After they arrived, the sea-motion increased and 2 sailors took it upon themselves to return in their boat to the *Smeaton* to help their mates to handle her moorings; but she broke away and drifted with her boat for 3 miles to leeward. By the time the crew were aware of her drift, a considerable gale had arisen which prevented her boat from returning to the Rock before it overflowed with the rising tide. There would not normally have been sufficient room in the *Pharos's* 2 boats for all the men then on the Rock. Providentially at the moment when the party prepared to leave it, the unexpected arrival of a pilot-boat averted the danger that would be faced by 2 overladen boats in a rough sea, and she carried the 8 surplus men to the *Smeaton*.

By the 5th 12 masons, working sometimes knee-deep in water, had almost completed the holes for the beacon legs, while others had begun to excavate the foundation of the tower. On the evening tide, low-water occurred too late for a landing: a violent storm arose suddenly and during the night the *Pharos* with a full complement of artificers broke adrift, her cable being severed by floating wreckage from an unknown vessel. When the storm passed, another position was chosen for her moorings 2 miles from the Rock so that she would be less likely to drift upon it if her cable should snap again.

On the 15th when the tides again favoured landings, the chief smith fell into the sea on leaping from the boat and as his wet tinder did not strike fire the forge could not be lighted and the masons had to abandon their work. The yacht arrived on the scene after her annual delivery of stores to the Scottish lighthouses and the artificers transferred to her more agreeable accommodation.

On the 19th the *Smeaton* brought in tow the 6 principal beams 50′ long and 18″ square which would form the legs of the beacon; 40 artificers and seamen landed and erected a 30′ derrick with guy-ropes and bolted a winch to work the purchase-tackle. The men had been divided into squads to perform different duties. On Sunday the 20th the row-boats towed the raft formed by 4 of the beams lashed together and anchored it at high-water over the site of the beacon where it grounded as the tide ebbed. All hands, numbering 52, then landed and began working in water up to their waists. One squad raised one beam to become the prop of the tackle for raising the second beam. Thus 4 of the 6 legs were set up as a pyramid of 33′ base, secured at the top temporarily by ropes. Another squad inserted the 5′ iron stanchions into the rock and lashed the beams to them. These stanchions had been kneed to suit the angle of the beams and they fitted perpendicularly into the holes bored in the rock, there to be secured by wedges, first of soft timber, then of oak and finally of iron, driven in successively—a method which gave more security than pouring molten lead into the gaps. This tide was blessed with a calm sea which permitted as much as 7 hours' work. Four artificers who previously had objected to Sunday employment turned out with the keenest workers and they never afterwards rejected it. Sunday labour transgressed the religious upbringing of the Scots artificers and they were never pressed to undertake it. They did so with the conviction that the lighthouse would prevent shipwrecks. If they had not been willing to seize the opportunities of working on suitable tides on Sundays, the duration of the operations would have been extended by a year at least.

On the 21st the favourable weather continued; again 52 men landed and set up the remaining two legs. Difficulty of transporting and victualling so many persons then made it necessary to reduce their numbers, so the less expert men were carried in the *Smeaton* to Arbroath to work in the yard.

Sir Joseph Banks

133. The Bell Rock tender *Sir Joseph Banks*

134. The method of attaching the beacon legs to the rock

On the 22nd 30 men landed from the yacht and connected up 4 of the 20′ struts joining the legs, and on the 23rd they fixed bracing chains to connect the last 2 struts. The *Smeaton* returned with provisions but heavy seas prevented her from delivering them to the yacht which a gale forced to take refuge in St Andrews bay under the lee of Fife Ness. On the 24th and the 25th the yacht returned to the Rock but on each occasion landings proved impracticable and strong winds drove her back to the bay each evening. The beacon, though still insecure, appeared to be standing undamaged. It was fortunate that good weather had prevailed during the tricky operation of erecting it.

On the 26th, 30 men landed and worked for $8\frac{1}{2}$ hours. Two events made this day memorable and eased transport: the parts of the forge could be lashed to a temporary platform on the beacon when the men left the Rock, so freeing the boats of this encumbrance, and instead of the artificers eating at irregular times their dinner was cooked on the yacht and brought out to the Rock daily at their normal hour.

On the 27th, 10 of the men returned to the yard, leaving 20 carpenters and smiths to complete the beacon to which, at high-water in a calm, they could now step directly from a boat; so, throughout neap tides, work upon it continued daily although its foundation remained covered by water. Its height of 48′ made it a conspicuous and most welcome mark to shipping.

1807 OCTOBER

After 3 days of bad weather 20 artificers spent 5 days in excavating the rock for the foundation of the tower and strengthening the beacon on which as much as $16\frac{3}{4}$ hours' continuous work was obtained on one day. In a trial for the next summer, night-working by torches proved feasible, though after their extinction the contrasting darkness added to the awkwardness of withdrawing the boats through the gullies.

Before the season's operations on the Rock were terminated the lower parts of the beacon were treated for preservation: brushwood was piled round its legs and lighted and the charred timbers were covered by coats of pitch to the height of 12'. For the relief of shipwrecked persons, cases containing 56 lb. of biscuits and 4 dozen bottles of water were fixed to the top.

The progress made in this short season gave assurance of success and fulfilled Stevenson's hopes. His chief concern arose now from the delay in receiving granite from the quarries. At one time 3 men travelled round the quarries in north-east Scotland seeking large blocks for the tower. Yet at the end of October 10 blocks were lacking of the 123 required for the 1st complete course, 30 lacking for the 2nd and 20 lacking for the 3rd, and unless more blocks were obtained soon, there would not be enough material at Arbroath to employ the 44 artificers throughout the winter and it might not be possible to lay 3 courses on the tower next season, which was the aim.

OPERATIONS DURING WINTER 1807–8

The cessation of the operations on the Rock gave Stevenson the opportunity to put in hand preparations for the next working season.

The accommodation for the men in the ships had to be improved and their labours in boating eased: this could be effected by providing a more commodious tender devoted entirely to attendance on them—to manoeuvre according to wind and current and drop and pick up the boats and so reduce rowing. Therefore a schooner, named *Sir Joseph Banks* after the Arctic explorer, was built to accommodate 15 sailors and their officers, and 50 artificers and their foremen. On deck and over the stern, she carried three 8-oared boats 20' long; each could seat 18 to 30 persons according to weather conditions. At the suggestion of Henry Greathead the South Shields boatbuilder, who had incorporated the ideas of Lionel Lukin a coachbuilder and William Wouldhave a painter in producing excellent lifeboats, Stevenson increased the buoyancy of the boats by lining them with cork; this reduced the danger at the critical moments when the men transferred between the schooner and the boats, and when they passed through the gullies in the reef with the tide not sufficiently low for the rocky shelves to give shelter from the waves—already, several had been upset and damaged and oars lost.

To speed the transport of the building-stones, 3 more praams 28' 6" × 8' 6" were built. They were lined with casks for buoyancy and had a central hawse-hole to suit a new method of slipping moorings quickly.

It was decided to transport the stones over the sharp irregular rock surface between the landing-places and the tower, an extreme distance of 300', by a level cast-iron railway to skirt the tower foundation and extend to the landing-places. The rails would be carried on frames with side supports varying in height from 6" to 5' according to the irregularities of the rock surface. The stones could be wheeled on iron trolleys jointed to suit both the curved and the straight rails.

Standard cranes and winches could be obtained for raising shipments at the landing-places, but visits to crane works disclosed no appliances capable of lifting stones from

135. The cast-iron railway which carried materials from the boats to the lighthouse site

the trolleys and laying them in position perpendicularly. Lifting-sheers as used at the Eddystone, by which Smeaton transferred stones directly from boat to tower, would be slow and inadequate in reach; so a new type of crane was designed, of which 2 were provided with 21′ shafts for the tower and one with a 28′ shaft for the masonry platform at Arbroath.

136. Templates for shaping stones

During the winter the Lighthouse yacht attended to the lightship and carried artificers to the Rock occasionally to examine the beacon. The sailors shifted stones at Arbroath and took turns of duty in the lightship where life was so uncomfortable and dreary that but for the dreaded activities of the pressgang, seamen might not have been obtained to man her. In the 5 ships occupied ultimately in the Bell Rock works, in addition to the yacht, 35 sailors received an Admiralty certificate of protection which was effective only so long as each man remained on board the vessel which it specified. In 1810 the pressgang seized one of the young protected seamen while he was visiting friends near Arbroath: he passed 5 months in prison before the Law Courts in Edinburgh heard an appeal by the Lighthouse Board on his behalf, when he was released.

As in all subsequent British sea-towers, Smeaton's plan of dovetailing stones was adopted by Stevenson, also his precaution of using trenails, wedges and joggles to keep them in position while the cement hardened and until they were weighed down by the completed course above. At Arbroath up to 60 masons, smiths, and carpenters cut and stored the blocks brought in the *Smeaton* from the granite quarries of Aberdeen and Peterhead and the sandstone quarry at Mylnefield near Dundee. Several courses were prepared at the same time, according to the dimensions of the blocks received. Movement of the great mass of masonry required careful planning so as to reduce to a minimum the handling of stones which weighed up to 3 tons. From the full-sized outlines of portions of each course drawn on a polished platform measuring 70' by 25', a wooden mould or pattern with positions marked for joggle, trenail and wedge was cut for each shape of stone and its edges were stiffened by iron plates. These moulds were stored so that any damaged stone could be replaced promptly.

OPERATIONS IN 1808

In March 1808 Stevenson visited the Rock and found the beacon unaffected by the winter's gales. He decided therefore to try out his original intention of enclosing its upper part as a cabin in which the men could live in the summer months and thus not only avoid the labour and delay of sea-transport often 4 times daily, but be ready to descend to the Rock as soon as the tide receded. If this plan should succeed, many additional hours of work on the Rock would be obtained. This radical alteration of the beacon would be put in hand in the coming season but meantime, as every precaution was taken to avoid accidents which would discourage the men to the great disadvantage of the enterprise, the beacon would be strengthened by iron ties. An open platform would be fitted upon it 20' above the rock, to accommodate 2 forges clear of the sea and provide a space for mixing mortar: its 2" floor planks would fit loosely so that a mounting wave might displace them without damaging the structure.

Subject to interruption by adverse weather conditions, the operations in the season of 1808 followed a regular programme: during each fortnight of spring tides the tender *Sir Joseph Banks* lay at anchor off the Rock, landings being attempted at about three-quarters' ebb and work perhaps continuing into the evening by torch-light—gaining one hour's work on a tide was worth all the trouble of double transport—while during each fortnight of neap tides all the men returned to Arbroath to assist the masons preparing stones.

1808 MAY

On the 26th May the tender *Sir Joseph Banks*, after laying moorings, took out from Arbroath the first party of the season, consisting of 18 artificers who again had to be instructed in boating. Several men suffered from seasickness as before and disliked living on a ship, but the extra pay and the unusual circumstances never ceased to attract volunteers from the yard.

At the end of the month 22 workmen and 6 sailors strengthened the beacon, deepened the foundation pit when the tides fell sufficiently, and set up frames for the railways.

1808 JUNE

On the 7th June, with 25 men occupied on the excavations, Stevenson's diary described the scene: 'The Bell Rock this morning presented by far the most busy and active appearance it had exhibited since the erection of the Beacon. The surface of the Rock was crowded with men, the two forges flaming, the one above the other, upon the Beacon, while the anvils thundered with the rebounding noise of their wooden supports and formed a curious contrast with the occasional clamour of the surges. . . . In the course of the forenoon the Beacon exhibited a still more extraordinary appearance than the Rock had done in the morning. The sea being smooth, it seemed to be afloat upon the water, with a number of men supporting themselves in all the variety of attitude and position, while,

137. Pumping the foundations before setting stones (Scott)

from the upper part of this wooden house, the volumes of smoke which ascended from the forges gave the whole a very curious and fanciful appearance.'

The master of the lightship, lying at anchor 2 miles away, referred to the men at work on the Rock in the evenings by torch-lights at sea-level as 'resembling the fiends in the lower regions'. Strangers sometimes supposed the columns of smoke rising from the sea to proceed from a ship on fire.

In a gale during the night of the 9th June, the tender 'rolled and pitched in such a manner that the hawser by which she was made fast to the buoy snapped and she went adrift. In the act of swinging round to the wind she shipped a very heavy sea which greatly alarmed the artificers who imagined that we had got upon the Rock.' Hampered by nearly 60 persons on board and with 2 boats lashed on deck, she ran for shelter to the Firth of Forth.

In the intervals between carrying stone from the quarries to Arbroath the *Smeaton* brought out artificers to the Rock and stood by, so that on the 20th as many as 62 men landed to work. The number was limited by the sleeping accommodation on the tender, the seating of the row-boats and the working space on the Rock. Eighteen sailors in addition to managing the boats carried tools between the masons and the smiths, stowed and wedged in clefts and gullies as many of the heavier implements as could be left on the Rock, and carried the stone chips from the excavations to the *Smeaton* to ballast her after discharging her cargoes.

By the 23rd the submerged parts of the foundation had been encircled completely with low concrete walls designed to exclude the wash of the waves and by the end of the month, despite the loss of time in baling water from the pit, its excavation was nearly completed. The railway was being extended gradually from the east landing-place and a third forge was set up on the reef temporarily during each visit to expedite the incessant sharpening of tools.

At Arbroath on the 14th June the 1st entire course was ready for shipment after a year's work. The hope of obtaining enough granite stones of 18″ depth to complete the course had been disappointed and stones of 12″ depth had to be used instead: little extra labour would have been required in handling and transporting the larger stones.

1808 JULY

By the 7th July all cracked and doubtful rock had been cleared from the foundation pit and it was seen that 18 holes of various shapes and sizes must be filled to bring up the rock to a level seat of 42′ diameter for the 1st entire course. A light row-boat carrying a dimensioned mould of the largest hole set out immediately for Arbroath where masons in relays worked for two nights and one day to prepare a stone to fit it. On the 9th a praam brought this stone over the site of the tower and with a quiet sea at high-water dropped it gently on the rock. On Sunday the 10th a derrick and guys moved this mass of 20 cubic feet to fill its shaped cavity. During the neap tides from the 14th to the 23rd the sea-level did not fall low enough to expose the rock, but when it did so on the 26th the other 17 stones of special shape were inserted in their holes.

The way was open now to lay the 1st complete course. Trial of the process of transporting stones from the yard, transferring them to the praams and leading these barges through the gullies had been satisfactory, but as the railways had not been advanced far enough to carry the stones from the landing-places to the tower base it was decided to drop the stones upon the site at high-water as had been done with the foundation stone. So it proved fortunate that the 1st course had been reduced in thickness, as the smaller stones could be dropped through the water and then moved more easily.

1808 AUGUST

On the 4th August one of the cranes was raised beside the foundation. This enabled the first 4 stones of the 1st course to be deposited: they were trenailed or spiked to the rock through 2 holes bored into each stone at Arbroath. On the 12th the laying of the 1st entire course of 123 stones was completed. It contained 508 cubic feet of granite and 76 of sandstone, a total weight of 104 tons; 4,519 square feet had been dressed and 798 cut and bored for wedges and trenails.

As the railway from the east landing-place had been extended to the tower and the second crane raised at its other side, every stone of the 2nd course of 18″ depth could be lifted from a railway trolley and deposited in its final position in the tower base by one or other of the two cranes. By this means the 2nd course of 136 stones weighing 152 tons was completed by the 27th, raising the base to 2′ 6″. As it overtopped the rock all round, pumping was discontinued and much inconvenience and delay avoided.

1808 SEPTEMBER

On the 9th September, after 10 stones of the 3rd course had been laid, gales prevented landings. When they were resumed it was found that the waves had raised some of the stones above their beds with the trenails acting as stilts. On the 18th, 31 stones were laid in 6¼ hours and on the 21st, completion of the 3rd course brought the base to a height of 4′.

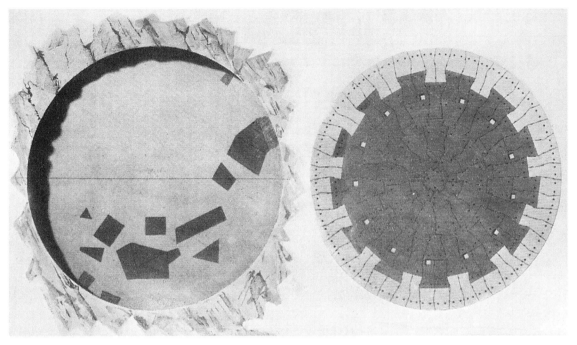

138. The 18 shaped stones which were set below the 1st entire course   139. The arrangement of stones in the 1st entire course

But the occasion was saddened by the loss of a young seaman who, in attending to one of the moorings, was swept away by the current when a boat capsized.

As heavy swells prevented the use of the east landing-place and as the railway to the west landing-place was not completed, Stevenson decided to suspend the operations for the season and did not cut joggle-holes in the stones of the 3rd course lest they might give a grip to the winter's waves. When informed of the excellent progress, Rennie wrote twice to urge him to buy a large quantity of lead to spread on top of the course to anchor it down, but he decided rightly that this precaution was unnecessary.

During this season the extent of working on the Rock was 265 hours, only 80 hours being spent in building the tower. Four hundred stones had been laid weighing 388 tons: they had been cut with such accuracy that there was no delay in placing each in position.

OPERATIONS IN 1809

Throughout the winter, as before, a few men from Arbroath visited the Rock occasionally to carry out small repairs to the beacon and the railways and thus ensure that no obstacle should impede the start of the next season's operations, when Stevenson hoped to set the remaining 22 courses to complete the solid base of the tower.

215

The search continued for large blocks of granite, which were desirable both for durability and as weighting 18 per cent. more than sandstone, and new faces were opened at quarries near Aberdeen in the effort to obtain enough blocks to sheathe the exterior of the tower to the top of the solid base 30′ high.

During the winter Mylnefield quarry ceased to produce sandstone blocks, as they would crack if cut and worked during frost. But a small supply of stones that had been cut there in the autumn could still be had. In February, when the *Smeaton* sailed up the Tay river

140. A view of the work in September 1808 (Slight)

to the quarry above Dundee to fetch them, all hands laboured to save her from damage by floating ice: on the return journey when she crossed the Tay bar in a snowstorm to enter the North Sea the entire crew except the helmsman were forced to take to the rigging for safety and no succour could be given to another sloop which foundered close-by. This incident emphasised the possibility of an accident to the Lighthouse ships. As an insurance against the suspension of operations at the Rock in such an event and also to expedite the transport of stone, the *Patriot* of Kirkcaldy, a sloop of 40 tons burden, was purchased; another sloop, the *Alexander*, was hired; and 2 more praams were built at Arbroath.

1809 APRIL

The season's operations began on the 30th April when the tender brought to the Rock 15 artificers with the immediate tasks of extending the railways, cutting joggle-holes in the exposed surface of the 3rd course and fitting the beacon for residence. The cabin would be divided into 3 habitable rooms at levels of 28′, 35′ and 42′ above the rock, with the tip of the roof ventilator at 61′.

1809 MAY

At the beginning of this month 36 workmen and sailors made frequent landings in rough seas and bitterly cold weather. On the 24th the *Sir Joseph Banks* brought out the first stones of the 4th course. The weather became worse and work on the Rock proceeded in wintry conditions which culminated on the 31st with snow lying 3″ deep on the deck of the tender and the landing-master having difficulty in guiding the boats through snow-showers.

1809 JUNE

On the morning of the 1st of June the weather took a sudden turn for the better and at mid-day 11 artificers remained on the beacon on the rise of the tide, according to routine. Suddenly a stiff gale rose which prevented the use of the row-boats and forced the *Smeaton* to slip her moorings and make for shelter in the Firth of Forth; but the tender stood by the men on the Rock and rode out the gale. In the beacon cabin which was not yet ready for residence, with old sails for protection from the wind and rain, the men made shift for

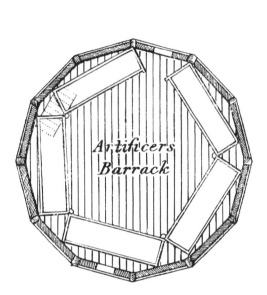

141. A tier of sleeping bunks in the beacon-house

142. The kitchen on the beacon, with a boat for emergencies

30 hours until the storm abated sufficiently to allow a boat to approach. Undeterred by their experience 33 artificers joined their comrades to work on the next tide. The waves had raised 3 stones of the partially-laid 4th course but, as before, they held by their trenails. The crane at the east landing was broken. The low platform of the beacon had been torn up and the casks of lime and cement left upon it had been washed away.

On the 11th, 16 hours' continuous work extending over the two tides was devoted to building the tower and to fixing a rope-bridge to connect the base to the beacon so that the men could pass between them without waiting for the tide to ebb. On the 17th a rough sea again prevented withdrawal of the same 11 artificers, but they spent the night under better conditions than before, with the cabin more complete and provided with bedding and an emergency supply of food. Stevenson had now to restrain the keenness of the men who landed at daybreak whenever tide and weather suited. On Sunday 25th, 57 persons landed at 3 a.m. Working over the two tides they completed the 7th course and raised the base to 10' above the foundation. At Arbroath the masons were cutting granite for the 16th course and sandstone for the 21st.

1809 JULY

On 2nd July the 9th course was completed to a height of 12′. Several disadvantages followed the attainment of this level. First, the operation of raising the moveable crane to each higher course increased in difficulty and its guy-tackles, from their angle, became almost unmanageable: a balance-crane on a new principle was therefore designed and constructed. Secondly, it was seldom possible to work on the tower during darkness, as torches could rarely be kept burning, being more exposed to the winds. Thirdly, the waves, no longer broken up by the shelving rock, struck directly at the upper parts of the tower and freely washed out the mortar from between the stones, which had often to be re-laid. Until the base was raised a few feet above high-tides, this loss of mortar brought about a heavier demand for the mixers' services.

143. Landing stones at the Rock (Scott)

On the 6th the joiners working at the beacon were allowed to take up their quarters in it during spring tides to avoid 'the continual plague of boating', a transfer welcomed by all as leaving the boats less crowded. The outside of the beacon had been coated with tar and tarpaulin and the interior packed with moss to make it wind-tight and warm. A brick hearth had been built-in but the men were warned of the dangers of fire, when a rescue might be impossible. One of the joiners fitting the berths and bedding took up continuous residence in it with a small black dog for company: he suffered greatly from sea-sickness and had a fear of boating and an aversion to climbing the makeshift ladder.

The speed of laying stones on the tower now exceeded that of their delivery at the Rock, so night-shifts were arranged to expedite the moving of stones at Arbroath, namely, the delivery of blocks from the quarries and the shipment of finished stones to the Rock. On the 8th when the base was raised to 13′ rejoicing ensued when it was noticed that the high-water of the neap tide did not overtop it.

On the 15th the artificers landed at 6.45 a.m. and as the water again did not overflow the tower they continued to lay stones until midnight, setting no fewer than 52. This day's work brought the 12th course to completion and raised the tower to 15′. As the joiners had lodged without mishap on the beacon, 23 artificers and a cook petitioned to follow their example and were allowed to do so.

On the 22nd an embargo interrupted the proceedings by confining all British ships to port, in consequence of the projected military expedition to Walcheren in Holland. An application for exemption for the Lighthouse vessels was despatched immediately to London and, though it was granted without undue delay, 10 days of weather good for transport had been lost. However, the artificers who were isolated on the Rock had not been idle and in addition to extending the west railway had raised the lower crane on a temporary masonry stool so that it could lift the stones directly from the trolleys and free the upper crane for depositing them on the tower.

1809 AUGUST

On the 1st August 46 men were working on the Rock and because of the increased numbers now lodging in the cabin the beacon's legs were strengthened further. But its considerable tremors in a gale frightened the artificers and several applied to return to the

144. A view of the works in August 1809, the solid portion nearly completed (Slight)

tender. Fifteen remained in residence, joined by Stevenson who was glad to be relieved from making the sea-passage daily between the tender and the Rock in an open boat.

During fog on the 19th, one of the boats lost her way back to the tender after leaving the Rock on the evening's flood-tide. The first land she sighted was Fife Ness 14 miles distant. In the morning the occupants, who had been without food, reached the tender, exhausted after rowing for 16 hours.

On the 20th August the entire 23rd course containing 51 stones was laid in one day; being a Sunday a religious meeting was held at noon when 30 men crowded into the upper room of the beacon, two of them joining hands to support the Bible which was read by Stevenson. On the 25th the solid portion of the lighthouse was finished; this was the 25th entire course and the last containing granite. Building the tower halted, as the solid base would best resist winter's storms and the need for another crane on the tower was urgent, the guy-ropes of the one in use being then of the unmanageable length of 80'.

1809 SEPTEMBER

The furnishings of the tower were put in hand including the construction of a lantern to contain a revolving coloured light from reflectors and argands on 4 sides of a rotating frame, 2 opposite sides each with 3 reflectors covered with sheets of red glass and the other two opposite sides each with 7 reflectors without coloured glass. This arrangement achieved with this size of lantern the maximum possible power and range for the white flash and distinction from other near lighthouses by the red flash when close to.

1809 OCTOBER-NOVEMBER

The artificers to the number of 24 lived in the beacon until November, strengthening its supports and extending the railways. The cranes and other implements likely to break loose during the winter were dismantled and taken ashore or stacked on top of the tower or the beacon.

Already some 1,400 tons of stone had been built into the tower, but 700 tons of sandstone were still needed. Severe frost had split many fine stones completed at the yard at Arbroath, despite careful covering, and interrupted work at Mylnefield quarry so much that it was unlikely that it could produce enough blocks in time to complete the tower in the next season, which Stevenson considered to be possible, so he decided to obtain an additional supply of stones from Craigleith quarry, near Edinburgh, which yielded an excellent sandstone that was not damaged by being cut during frost. Its use for the top courses of the balcony, would enable the lantern under construction in Edinburgh to be fitted temporarily upon them and so would reduce much trouble and time in erection on the exposed Bell Rock tower. So a yard was rented in Edinburgh to which masons were transferred from Arbroath.

OPERATIONS IN 1810-11

Much work had to be done to complete the tower. The 66 courses above the solid base would be of less diameter than the lower courses and so contained fewer stones, but they required more careful fitting as they were shaped to suit the compartments, the stair and the furnishings. Most of the stones had still to be brought from the quarries and dressed to shape. All had to be transported to the Rock (57 courses from Arbroath and 9 from Edinburgh), raised and set in place. The operations involved had been improved in details either to ease labour and hasten the work or to reduce the risk of accidents. After the masonry work was done the structure had to be made habitable by fitting much woodwork throughout, and crowned by the lantern and the light. Further, 4 stone houses for the lightkeepers had to be built at Arbroath.

Stevenson introduced an important improvement on the system adopted by Smeaton at the Eddystone lighthouse and by Sir Christopher Wren below the dome of St Paul's Cathedral in London of tying the circular walls together by chains built-in to form horizontal rings. He used a ring of Swedish iron instead and designed the floors of each compartment with the stones grooved laterally so that they became as one; thus the pressure acted perpendicularly on the walls instead of thrusting outwards as with an arch. The walls were bound together by projections and grooves cut in the horizontal surfaces of the stones.

1810 APRIL

Having laid moorings off the Rock, the tender *Sir Joseph Banks* opened the season's campaign by carrying out 17 artificers on the 18th April; in view of the uncertain weather of spring they lived in the ship instead of in the beacon and as formerly rowed to and from the Rock every tide. In 10 days they repaired the railways, which had been damaged by loose boulders weighing up to 10 cwts which the winter waves had lifted up from the sea-bed and rolled over the reef, and replaced the swaying rope-bridge between the tower and the beacon by a rigid timber gangway 44' long and 6' wide which was floated out in sections. It would facilitate passage to the tower and, through a hatch in its floor, materials could be raised more easily from the trolleys.

1810 MAY

The artificers who sailed for the Rock on 7th May when neap tides had passed were warned that as the works would be pressed to a conclusion before the winter, 3 or 4 months might elapse before they returned to Arbroath. As the weather continued boisterous—spray was flying 20' over the tower and 50' above the Rock—they remained in the ship until the 10th, when a landing could be made. They brought the beacon cabin into condition as a dwelling and, to get more living space, shifted one of the forges to the top of the tower where they fixed the base of the new balance-crane. On the 11th, 18 men who were anxious to avoid boating took up residence in the beacon. On the same day the *Smeaton* was loaded with 38 stones at Arbroath but she failed to land them on the Rock as the weather worsened and she was driven by a gale to seek shelter in Leith Roads. For several days at high-water the men in the beacon had the unpleasant experience of the sea 'breaking over the top of the building in great sprays and rangeing with much agitation among the beams of the beacon' but when, 'tired beyond measure for want of employment', they crossed by the gangway to the tower at about three-quarters' ebb of each day-tide when the wind abated, they bored the joggle-holes in the 25th course and got the balance-crane into working order. It traversed in a 'collar-chamber filled with cast-iron friction balls', an early use of ball-bearings.

On the 18th the wind fell away and the first cargo of stones of the season, 23 in all, was landed from the *Smeaton*. They were raised quickly through the gangway hatch and laid on the tower. For the next 10 weeks up to 31 persons including Stevenson lodged in the beacon and some 15 sailors rowed to the Rock most days to shift the building materials.

On the 21st the last cargo of sandstone from Mylnefield for the tower was delivered at Arbroath by the *Patriot*.

As the tower rose, the space on the open top became much cramped from its shrinking diameter and the situation of the men at work was precarious. Lest anyone should slip when the Rock was covered by the sea, a boat was suspended from the beacon and a seaman, ready to loose a life-line of 200 fathoms, kept watch for accidents. When the Rock was dry the men working below were in danger from falling tools.

1810 JUNE

As the continuance of stormy weather interrupted delivery of stones at the Rock and caused anxiety that the tower might not be completed before the winter, every effort was made to hasten the work. For instance, as soon as the *Patriot* entered Arbroath harbour at 11 p.m. on Saturday 2nd June the engineer's clerk called out the men at the yard. They began loading her with dressed stones at midnight: she sailed with a full consignment at 4 a.m. and within an hour reached the Rock when the 18 stones were at once taken off.

On the 17th June the west railway and its landing-place were completed by torch-light to the full length of 290', but the east railway being only 90' long was preferred whenever wind and sea permitted its use. Ropes attached to additional iron rings fixed into the rocks gave more security in the passage of boats through the entrance gullies.

On the 21st an attempt to reduce the handling of stones by landing them at high-water directly from a praam manoeuvred below the gangway hatch failed, as the lift of the sea caused a jerk and strain on gangway and beacon which tended to loosen their joints. But by bringing into service both landing-places and railways, the speed in handling the stones exceeded so much the rate of building the tower that either the *Patriot* or the *Smeaton* might have been dispensed with or the hire of the *Alexander* terminated were it not that an accident to one of the ships would have disrupted the whole operation. It was also possible that one of these vessels might be required to replace the lightship. Having been at sea continuously for three years her condition gave cause for concern; though so far as could be seen from a partial careening at her station, woodworm had not affected her hull excessively.

On completion of the railways the company residing in the beacon was reduced to 22, but it was increased when two more smiths were brought to the Rock to keep in good order the many appliances that expedited the work.

1810 JULY

Danger still remained for the men on the beacon. On the 4th July during a strong gale and a heavy swell, the sea broke up its low platform and caused alarm. The waves dashing over the gangway prevented passage to the tower which, with 68 courses laid, now rose 80' above the Rock. Several men had been anxious to take refuge in the substantial tower rather than remain in the beacon: had they done so their plight would have been worse. Morning disclosed that the waves had overtopped the open walls and windows and water had poured down the stairs and out at the entrance doorway. When the storm abated two days were devoted to repairing the beacon and the gangway and replacing mortar between the stones of the upper courses.

On the 6th the last course to be dressed at Arbroath was completed and ready for shipment, leaving only the 23 steps of the stair to be cut. The *Smeaton* carried to Leith the carter James Craw with his horse Bassey and the Woolwich sling-cart which had shifted all the blocks and stones at the yard and harbour at Arbroath. They would bring to the ship at Leith the stones for the parapet and the parts of the lantern which were being fitted together in Edinburgh. On arrival there Stevenson had the pleasure of meeting Mrs Dixon, one of Smeaton's daughters, who had intended to visit the Bell Rock but from its inaccessibility had to be content with inspecting the upper courses and lantern.

145. James Craw and his horse Bassey moving a stone by the sling-cart. The skeleton of this horse was exhibited for many years in the museum of the Royal College of Surgeons in Edinburgh

On the 9th the last cargo of stones dressed at Arbroath was delivered at the Rock and on the 12th the *Smeaton* brought from Leith the first cargo of Craigleith stones. Accompanied by the *Patriot* she returned there to fetch more stones, the lantern and the lighting apparatus.

After completion of the 68th course the raising of a stone from the trolleys involved coiling over 45′ of the chain of the balance-crane. This took much time so the continuous lift was split into two, by fixing another winch and a beam to project from one of the tower windows. The stones of the parapet were small and were handled quickly but the slabs for the lightroom floor, each $7\frac{1}{2}'$ long and weighing over 1 ton, were covered with matting and raised with difficulty to the height of 95′. On the 30th July the last stone of the tower was laid, to close the 91st course. In case completion of the operations in 1810 should be prevented, the lower parts of the beacon were again treated for preservation.

1810 AUGUST

On the 4th the building work was finished so all the masons returned to Arbroath to build the 4 houses for the lightkeepers, using the stones of the masonry platform and sandstone from Mylnefield quarry. The lease of the yard was surrendered, only 4 of its 7 years' period having expired. The accuracy of the position of the Bell Rock reef on current sea-charts being doubtful, Stevenson set out a long base-line along the shore at Barry and corrected the position by angles.

On the 14th the *Smeaton* carried to the Rock 17 craftsmen to complete the woodwork. During that night a storm arose which increased in violence until it surpassed in severity the worst that had been experienced by any of the men when residing in the beacon. The ship broke adrift and as usual made for the shelter of the Firth of Forth. The tops of the

146. The Bell Rock lantern and fog bells. In 1843 the complete lighting apparatus (reflectors, lamps and revolving machinery) was shipped
to Newfoundland and illuminated Bonavista lighthouse until after 1872

waves struck the beacon directly and alarmed the occupants greatly but the damage done to it was slight. Not until the 18th could a boat put out from the lightship to help them. On the 20th materials for repairing the beacon were brought out to the Rock with parts of the lantern. After raising these to the top of the tower the balance-crane was unscrewed and lowered 'in mournful silence' in token of its efficient service. It was taken ashore and preserved for the building of another lighthouse.

The Bell Rock Lighthouse 1806 to 1811

1810 SEPTEMBER–1811 FEBRUARY

On Sunday 2nd September the heavier furnishings were brought to the Rock and the gangway was cut away and replaced by the former rope-bridge. A rope-ladder gave direct access to the tower from the rock. Eventually brass rungs to form an external ladder were inserted into the stones of the tower though Rennie expressed the mistaken opinion that they would offer a grip to the sea and weaken the tower. On 25th October after 36 hours' work by daylight and by torches, plumbers and glaziers inserted the lantern-panes and put the finishing touches to the lantern and connected the machinery to toll in fog the two 5-cwt bells which cost £60 each. The Lighthouse yacht now took over the duties of the lightship as a tender and the *Smeaton* and the *Patriot* resumed their former occupation of carrying to Arbroath for the houses cargoes of sandstone blocks from Mylnefield.

Lack of red-tinted glass delayed exhibition of the light. No sheets as large as 25″ square, which was the size required, had been made hitherto in Britain. Eventually James Oaky, a glass worker of London, 'a very ingenious artist . . . rather an irregular correspondent', contracted to supply them; but frequent letters and calls on Oaky failed to obtain delivery, so a foreman travelled by the coach from Edinburgh to London with instructions to remain in attendance at Oaky's premises until he produced the glass sheets. When he did so, the customary *Notice to Mariners* was issued to announce completion of the lighthouse and the intended exhibition from the 1st February 1811 of the light and the tolling of a bell during fog and poor visibility.

On the evening of the 1st February the crew of the lightship raised her 3 lights as usual and extinguished them at the moment when the permanent light shone forth from the top of the Bell Rock tower. On the conclusion of this vessel's uncomfortable vigil of $3\frac{1}{2}$ years, many of her crew married Arbroath girls and remained in the Lighthouse Service as lightkeepers or as seamen in the attending vessels. Four lightkeepers were appointed to serve in the lighthouse, one remaining ashore for a fortnight. From a signal-tower erected at Arbroath communication with the lighthouse by heliograph and flags was arranged, and a pigeon-post was maintained for several years.

COST OF THE WORKS

Including the purchase and hire of shipping and the erection of the dwellings at Arbroath the lighthouse works cost £61,331. The tower contained 28,530 cubic feet of stone weighing 2,076 tons. The light, measured from the centre of the reflectors, had been elevated 88′ above high-water of spring tides or about 104′ above the foundation.

EMPLOYMENT OF THE MEN

An outstanding feature of the Bell Rock works was the enthusiasm of the men to complete an undertaking that fired their imagination despite the hardship and danger to which they were exposed continuously. By sharing their discomforts afloat and on the beacon and clearly doing all that was possible for their welfare, Stevenson won their adherence to the enterprise. It is certain that his requiring them initially to engage themselves for one month was a critical point in its early completion. The men formed a splendid team in which the key posts were filled by able and reliable persons such as the masters of the vessels and the chief mason. The engineer's clerk at Arbroath had a great responsibility in providing a continuous supply of materials and supplies for the large company in the ships and on shore.

The men received remuneration that was high for the times. They got payment for overtime and the issue daily of rations which included ½ lb. beef, 1 lb. bread, 2 oz. butter, oatmeal, barley, vegetables and 3 quarts of beer. The current price of whisky was 11s. per

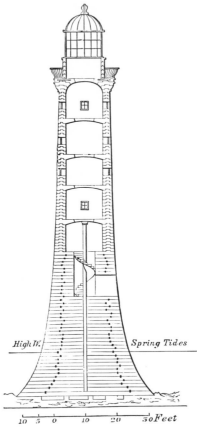

147. A sectional elevation of the tower

gallon. Every effort was made to recompense them for confinement afloat by caring for their welfare and keeping them occupied and cheerful. Men lodging on shore received schooling at night and those who might benefit had instruction in architectural drawing. Every Sunday a religious service was held aboard ship or on the Rock and sittings were reserved in an Arbroath church. Each man received a glass of rum after working in wet weather, when beginning particularly early in the day or ending late, and in celebration of all unusual incidents. Postal rates being heavy, their correspondence was sent free of cost.

CONTROL OF WORKS

The full advantage taken of the peculiar features of the reef, the decision to employ so many men and vessels, and the immediate devising of new contrivances as the work proceeded makes the building of this tower outstanding in the history of lighthouses. Much delay was avoided by Stevenson's control of the operations, the members of the Lighthouse Board accepting his recommendations with little question when he brought before them even such expensive items as the purchase of ships. No more detailed description of the construction of any lighthouse has been published than his *Account* of the erection of this tower, a narrative begun by him at the request of the Lighthouse Board in 1811 and issued as a book in 1824.

THE LIGHTHOUSE SINCE 1840

In 1842 there was installed in the lantern a new reflecting apparatus by which the revolving light beams were fully equalised and the original apparatus was sent to Newfoundland for fitting in a lighthouse under construction. In 1902 a new lantern, perhaps unnecessarily large, was set upon the Bell Rock tower to continue the emission of red and white beams

148 (*a*). A view of the kitchen in the tower (Evans)

of light from one of the finest lenticular optical apparatuses then made; it had equiangular prisms and a focal distance of 1,330 mm. In December 1955 a helicopter dropping newspapers on the reef without the permission of the Lighthouse Board lurched against the lantern and was destroyed with its crew. It damaged the lantern slightly and the light was extinguished for a week.

The Bell Rock tower remains firm on the reef, undamaged by the violence of the North Sea during the 146 winters that have passed since its completion. In storms the waves still bring up from the sea-bed the travelling boulders which have failed to erode its granite sheath or the hard sandstone rock at its base. To relieve the lightkeepers each fortnight when the weather allows, larger boats pass up the gullies to tie up at cast-iron railways of the original design but not extending so far out from the tower.

SIR WALTER SCOTT'S VERSE

In 1814 Sir Walter Scott accompanied several of the Northern Lighthouse Commissioners and Stevenson on a 6 weeks' tour of the Scottish lighthouses in their yacht *Regent*. Early on 30th July the party landed on the Bell Rock where they had breakfast in the tower.

On being invited to inscribe his name in the visitors' album, Scott sat down, paused for a few minutes, then wrote the following verse:

Pharos loquitur

Far in the bosom of the deep
O'er these wild shelves my watch I keep
A ruddy gem of changeful light
Bound on the dusky brow of Night
The Seaman bids my lustre hail
And scorns to strike his timorous sail

148 (*b*). Transferring a cargo of stones from the *Smeaton* to a praam-barge

XIV

LIGHTHOUSES 1800 TO 1819 IN THE BRITISH ISLES, FRANCE,

SWEDEN, N.W. RUSSIA AND THE UNITED STATES

149. Turner's impression of Calais lighthouse. To
provide a lighthouse urgently in 1818, a lantern was
set on the belfry of an existing building

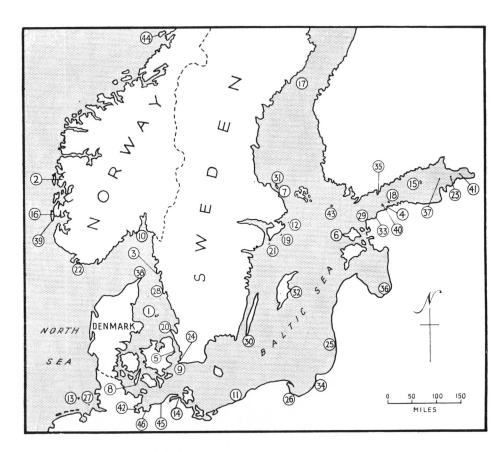

LIGHTS IN NORTHERN EUROPE

The sites of the navigation lights mentioned in the text are numbered

1. Anholt	13. Heligoland	25. Memel	36. Riga
2. Bergen	14. Hiddensoe	26. Neufahrwasser	37. Seskär
3. Carlsten	15. Hogland	27. Neuwerk	38. Skagen (Scaw)
4. Catherendal	16. Hoyvaden	28. Nidingen	39. Skudenaes
5. Copenhagen	17. Holmögadd	29. Odensholm	40. Surop
6. Dagerort	18. Kokskär	30. Olands Sòdra Udde	41. Tolbuhin
7. Djursten	19. Korsò	31. Örskàr	42. Travemünde
8. Fakkebjerg	20. Kullen	32. Östergarn	43. Utò
9. Falsterbo	21. Landsort	33. Pakerort	44. Villa
10. Ferder	22. Lindesnes (Naze)	34. Pillau	45. Warnemünde
11. Gollenberg	23. London Chest	35. Porkkala	46. Wismar
12. Grönskär	24. Malmò		

XIV. LIGHTHOUSES 1800 TO 1819 IN THE BRITISH ISLES, FRANCE, SWEDEN, N.W. RUSSIA AND THE UNITED STATES

Though wars afflicted Europe and North America in 1800–15, the number of the world's lighthouses rose considerably in these 19 years. Few were established on the continent of Europe but in the British Isles the increase was 50 per cent. and the number in the United States was doubled. The adoption of parabolic reflectors with argand lamps, the best lighting of the period, was most noticeable in the British Isles and the Gulf of Finland: few Lighthouse Authorities had knowledge of the apparatus fitted in lighthouses of other countries.

ENGLAND

Lighthouses and Lightships in 1800

In 1800 the English coasts were lighted by 30 lighthouses and 6 lightships, excluding lights intended to serve ports and harbours only. Of these 36, Trinity House managed 8 lighthouses and the 6 lightships. Of the 22 private lights, Air, Hunstanton and Mumbles might be considered as mainly of local value and Harwich (coal and candles), Wintertonness (candles) and St Bees (coal) were inferior lights of low power. Deducting these 6, the number of coastal lighthouses and lightships can be put at 30.

The typical Trinity House lantern as constructed about 1800 cost £1,000 and had a floor of stone and a roof of iron ribs covered with copper sheets. Its panes of $\frac{1}{2}''$ plate glass measured $21'' \times 18''$. The oil lamps were argands and the parabolic reflectors were made of silvered copper. The lanterns and lighting apparatus were manufactured in London by George Robinson assisted by Robert Wilkins. Parabolic reflectors and argands seem to have been fitted already at 6 Trinity House lighthouses—Portland (1789), Scilly and Casquets (1790), Happisburgh (1791), Cromer (1792) and Lowestoft (1796); and at 5 private lighthouses—Winterton (1791), Dungeness (1792), South Foreland and Orfordness (1793) and Longships (1795).

Improved Lighting 1800–19

Between 1800 and 1815 Trinity House was much occupied with naval shipping and buoyage work arising from the continental war, but the Brethren were not unmindful of their lighthouse interests. In 1806 they spent £5,000 on a new lantern and revolving apparatus at their lighthouse on the Scilly Isles, 10 parabolic reflectors being arranged on each of three faces. As leases fell in, other lights were converted to parabolic reflectors and argands, such as Harwich in 1818 where the lower light was changed to red in 1819, and Spurn in 1819. £3,000 was spent at the Eddystone in 1810 on a new light from 24 reflectors and argands, thus displacing Smeaton's candelabrum; and £5,000 on 2 new lighthouses at the Lizard in 1812. The Brethren pressed the owners and patentees of all the private lights to change over to reflector lights and at the cost of £8,500 to the patentees they built three new towers on the Farne islands, two as a pair and a third at a different position, to the design of Daniel Alexander who succeeded Wyatt as their architect; they fitted revolving reflectors and argands at the pair of towers.

NEW LIGHTHOUSES 1800–19

In this period the Corporation built two entirely new lighthouses—at Flamborough, lit on 1st December 1806, and at the South Stack, lit on 9th February 1809, at costs of £8,000 and £12,000. The former, designed by Wyatt, was set on a cliff 200′ above the sea,

150. Flamborough lighthouse built by Samuel Wyatt in 1806 (Daniell)

151. South Stack lighthouse built in 1809. The sheers supporting the bridge appear in the centre of the picture, *c.* 1830

close to Sir John Clayton's old tower which had remained *without fire* for about 130 years. Someone suggested that an aerial sound signal should be set up too, but the Brethren decided that bells were useless at a lighthouse on land though suitable on lightships to

152. Tynemouth lighthouse, the first English coastal lighthouse, ceased to be a private light in 1836

153. A shipwreck off North Shields lighthouses which were re-built in 1805–8 (Carmichael)

which ships would pass close. The lighthouse on the South Stack, an island off Anglesey which greatly endangered navigation, was designed by Alexander and it also was set 200′ above sea-level. Captain Cotton, one of the Elder Brethren, claimed in 1818 that this light, unlike the light at Howth in Ireland, was 'never obscured by clouds'; but this rash assertion was soon disproved and some years later recourse was had to a curious railway by which, when fog shrouded the light, a lantern with a subsidiary light was lowered down the cliff to sea-level.

At the South Stack the chasm 90' wide through which the sea 'boiled with great force and impetuosity' was crossed by a hempen cable 70' above sea-level, along which a sliding basket was drawn carrying a passenger or stores which on the mainland side had been carried down a flight of 400 steps cut in the rock. In 1828 this system of conveyance was replaced by an iron suspension bridge 5' wide.

In 1815 Trinity House obtained the usual type of patent for lighthouses at Burnham in the Bristol Channel but, strangely and in accordance with its old practice, it leased to an individual its authority to erect them and to retain the dues. In 1819 the Corporation began to build a pair of lights on Lundy island at the entrance to the Bristol Channel.

DESCRIPTION OF LIGHTSHIPS 1809

Allison Davie, who had been appointed buoy-keeper at Yarmouth by Trinity House in June 1786, gave particulars in 1809 of the lightships at Happisburgh and Dudgeon to which he attended. The Happisburgh vessel of 112 tons was anchored in 11 fathoms, 1 mile from the north end of the Newarp sand by 120 fathoms of 12" cable and a 16-cwt mushroom anchor. Her chain of 2" iron had links 11" overall and was made at the King's Yard. It was renewed most years and a complete set of moorings was held ready in case of accident. The chains were examined 'at every good opportunity, now and then, to observe the effect the salts may have in corroding the iron' and the ship was taken to harbour every third year to repair her hawse-pipes and clean her bottom. She had a crew of 6 seamen always on board, holding protections from the pressgang, and a master and a mate. She was relieved monthly so that each man served two months at sea and one month ashore at Yarmouth 8 miles distant, where supervision was given to 22 buoys moored in the vicinity by 7 to 15 fathoms of chain, 'according to depth and dangerous situation'. Their longest chains weighed 11 cwts and the buoys were anchored with 13-cwt square stones 18" thick with a hole in the centre. A duplicate of each buoy was kept ashore ready for service. A tender of 60 tons attended to the lightship and the buoys, and a 20-ton cutter continually made surveys of the channels through the sandbanks so that the buoys could be moved to mark the deepest water.

The Dudgeon lightvessel was of 131 tons and had similar moorings. Her chains were supplied by Huddart & Co. of Limehouse, a business owned by the well-known hydrographer who was an Elder Brother of Trinity House. A peculiarity in this ship was the use of the best butt leather for protecting the cable from friction at the hawse-hole and at her bows and bottom, and care was taken to avoid strain at the windlass. The ship was stationed in 8 fathoms, 7 leagues distant from her base at Wells. Like the Happisburgh lightvessel she was attended by a 60-ton tender and had a similar crew. This lightship had been adrift twice in 20 years: on the last occasion in January 1798 by stress of weather, and she had been run into several times. No sails were used to steady her. She exhibited 2 lanterns on yard-arms from her mast. The best sperm oil was provided for the lamps, each being made 'in the form of a compass and balanced in the same manner, with 5 flat tubes on the top surface for the wicks'. A set of lamps was kept as spares for these crude lights.

The Happisburgh and Dudgeon lightships were also called Newarp and Wells.

NEW LIGHTSHIPS 1800–19

Trinity House established one new lightship in this period, at Stanford about 1802, for navigation through the sandbanks off Lowestoft. To assist the Navy in the continental war, the Brethren designed 3 lightships which were built at the national expense at a cost of some £5,000 apiece and were moored at sites believed to be unnecessary for commercial shipping. These were the Galloper (1803) at the north entrance to the Thames estuary, the Gull (1809) off the Goodwins, and Bembridge (1812) to the east of the Isle of Wight. Each carried two lights. Eventually they were considered essential for commercial navigation and Trinity House took over the Galloper in 1816 and the others after 1820.

154. Dungeness lighthouse in 1819 (Daniell). Only the base and dwellings remain

155. The old low lighthouse at Harwich in 1815

Apart from a lightship moored as a temporary mark off Plymouth during the construction of its great breakwater, Liverpool was the next port after Dublin to establish a lightship: in December 1813 the N.W. buoy on the Mersey bar was replaced by a vessel of 78 tons called the *Good Intent*, showing a red light that was hoisted in a small lantern. She was prone to break adrift and seems to have been re-fitted and re-laid in October 1814 with 3 masts each carrying a white light which, according to a description of 1817, traversed upon frames. This lightship was coppered and wall-sided. She was criticised as carrying too much rigging.

LIGHTHOUSES AND LIGHTSHIPS IN 1819

In 1819 at least 26 English lighthouses had silvered parabolic reflectors and argand lamps.
Eight of the English lights were revolving: Scilly (1790, renewed in 1806); Cromer and Walney (1792); Tynemouth (1802); Flamborough, red and white (1806); South Stack (1809); Farnes, a pair (*c.* 1811) and Casquets, a trio (1818). Walney, Tynemouth and Farnes were not Trinity House lights.
Excluding the three somewhat local lighthouses as previously, also Wintertonness and St. Bees lights which remained inferior, the coastal lighthouses in England and Wales numbered 28 in 1819 with 9 lightships in addition. Trinity House had 14 lighthouses and

8 lightships. The 16 coastal lights held by other interests included the two Admiralty lightships. The lightships at Stanford and the Mersey and another marking the breakwater under construction at Plymouth were mainly of local value.

For the British Government Trinity House of London arranged in 1811 for the erection of a new lighthouse at Heligoland which had long shown a coal fire. The buildings were designed by Alexander and the light from 24 parabolic reflectors and argands came from Robinson.

SCOTLAND

LIGHTHOUSES IN 1800

Nine coastal lighthouses were established in Scotland in 1800, 6 operated by the Northern Lighthouse Commissioners, Little Cumbrae and Cloch by the Cumbrae Lighthouse Trustees, and the May still a private light. The pair of lighthouses at Buddonness, while excellent in structures and lights, served chiefly one port.

The lanterns supplied before 1800 cost £600 and had wood frames for the roofs covered with iron plates within and copper sheets without. The panes measured only 12″ × 8″ and the glass was of poor quality. But the lights were satisfactory. Facet parabolic reflectors and piped lamps gave an illumination that could have been excelled only by metal reflectors and argand-type lamps.

COMPARISON OF ENGLISH AND SCOTTISH LIGHTHOUSES 1801

Thomas Smith held the position of engineer to the Northern Lighthouses until 1804 when he was succeeded by his assistant Robert Stevenson who had already taken over the greater part of his work. In 1800, before building more lighthouses in Scotland, Stevenson decided to examine lighthouses erected elsewhere—previously he had visited the South Rock lighthouse in Ireland twice during its construction by Rogers. So in 1801, with the approval of his Commissioners and the concurrence of Trinity House, he journeyed round the English lighthouses for two months, mainly by coach and on horseback, from Maryport in Cumberland by way of Wales and the Isle of Man to Cromer in Norfolk. The tour took in the Smalls, Longships and Portland lighthouses, but bad weather prevented a visit to the Eddystone. Observations from sea of the Scilly and Cromer lights convinced him of the advantages of revolving lights and he found the English lighthouses were built more substantially than those in Scotland. On his return the Commissioners accepted his recommendations to construct their future buildings to a higher standard than before and to fit silver-plated reflectors and argands at new lighthouses. He made further tours of the English lighthouses in 1813 and 1818: the published accounts form a unique contemporary record of these seamarks. The Commissioners gave him scope to adopt whatever improvements he noticed at lighthouses in other countries and to introduce his own ideas. In consequence he improved the Scottish lighthouses beyond recognition between 1800 and 1819.

NEW NORTHERN LIGHTHOUSES 1800–19

The first Scottish lighthouse built after 1800 was erected on Inchkeith island off Leith. It was fitted with a metal-framed lantern with plate-glass panes 29″ × 18″, containing reflectors about 21″ in diameter obtained from three different makers, Robinson, Howard and Smith, which seem to have been intended for a comparative trial. This light was exhibited in September 1804 having cost in all £5,000, whereas one of the Scots 18th-century lights would have cost £1,500.

The first revolving apparatus in Scotland was set on a tower at Start Point in Orkney which had been completed in 1802 as an unlighted beacon, though designed for a future lighthouse. The exhibition of this light in January 1806 was considered to render redundant the near-by light of North Ronaldsay, so the latter was extinguished in 1809; but it had to be re-built later. For Start Point Stevenson designed parabolic reflectors of 25″ diameter and of a new type which simplified servicing while ensuring that the lamps after cleaning were

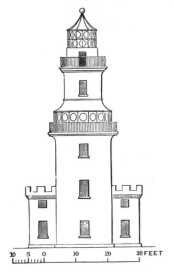

156. Design by Robert Stevenson in 1810 for a double light on the Isle of May (not carried out)

157. Stevenson's original design for the Carr Rock beacon enclosing a tidal machine to strike a fog-bell

158. The 2 lighthouses of 1818 on the Calf of Man with synchronised revolving beams

returned strictly to the focus as designed. Henceforth in Scotland parabolic reflectors were supplied of 25″ diameter for revolving lights and of 21″ diameter for fixed lights. With identical lamps the smaller reflectors gave greater horizontal divergence or spread of light, which suited fixed lights.

The construction of the Bell Rock lighthouse took up most of Stevenson's attention from 1806 to 1811. A lightship was moored temporarily off the Rock while the work proceeded.

From about 1780 traders had voiced complaints about the coal fire on the May island, although it had a grate capacity about double that of any other coal fire and its blaze should have been excellent. In December 1810 two naval frigates, the *Nymphen* and the *Pallas*, with 600 men aboard were wrecked near Dunbar, 12 miles distant, in consequence of mistaking a lime-kiln in that neighbourhood for the blazing fire of the May. Nine men perished and the vessels valued at £100,000 became total wrecks. After long negotiations with the patentee, the Northern Lighthouse Board agreed to purchase for £60,000 the island and the rights to the dues. An Act of Parliament of 1814 enabled the bargain to be carried out by authorising a loan of £30,000 from the Government. A fixed light from argands and reflectors replaced the coal fire in February 1816 and to avoid confusion from having two fixed lights in the same area, the light at Inchkeith was on the same date altered to revolving, to give white beams.

In 1815 a revolving light with red and white beams was erected at Corsewall.

In the same year, at the request of Liverpool and Manx traders, the jurisdiction of the Northern Lighthouse Board was extended by Act of Parliament to include the Isle of Man, which benefited already from several harbour lights with parabolic mirrors. The Commissioners stationed an experienced shipmaster on Calf island, at the south end of Man, to observe weather conditions over a period and, upon considering his report, decided to build two lighthouses on that island which by their line would indicate the direction of the submerged outlying Chickens Rock. They were lighted in 1818 by synchronised revolving white lights. On the same date a revolving light giving red and white beams was shown from another new lighthouse at the Point of Ayre at the north end of Man.

The principal founder of the Northern Lighthouses Trust, George Dempster, declared in 1809, in reference to the Scottish highlanders, that it had 'illumin'd by night their seas, and coast, and bays with all the splendour of a noontide blaze'.

OTHER NEW LIGHTHOUSES 1800–19

The Nith Commissioners about 1810 erected a reflector light of local value at Sutherness Point in the Solway Firth, and in 1812 the Cumbrae Lighthouse Trustees erected a white revolving light at Toward Point which might be termed a coastal light as it served several ports.

THE CARR ROCK BEACON 1813–21

The frequency of wrecks around the headland of Fife Ness induced the Northern Lighthouse Board to undertake erection of a stone beacon upon the Rock, as a buoy was not sufficiently conspicuous. A hollow stone pillar was designed to carry a bell, 5′ across the lips, to be tolled automatically by clockwork fitted within the beacon and operated by the rise and fall of the tide, as had been demonstrated successfully by a model. Operations began in June 1813 and in August Stevenson visited the Wolf Rock off south-west England, from which Smith's beacon had been swept away, and so he could assess to some extent the difficulties which had not been overcome in 1795 in endeavouring to fix a few iron bars on that exposed Rock.

The top of the Carr Rock lay below the low-water of spring tides and the maximum diameter of rock available for a foundation was 18′. These two features, coupled with strong currents and exceptional exposure, made the proposition extremely difficult. Much unsound rock had first to be removed by a cofferdam, an inconvenient appliance which had to be lifted from the sea-bed whenever work was interrupted. On only two or three tides each fortnight did the sea recede to a level that allowed work to proceed. Its quick susceptibility round Fife Ness to the slightest adverse change of weather prolonged the work far beyond the expectation of Stevenson and his small gang of men who had gained experience of tidal work at the Bell Rock. The expense of this tedious enterprise would not have been justified but for the construction simultaneously of a lighthouse on the May island $8\frac{1}{2}$ miles away, where work was available whenever a rough sea prevented operations on the Carr Rock. On completion of the May lighthouse, expeditions were made to the Carr Rock when other lighthouse work permitted.

The operations proceeded reasonably well during the first two seasons 1813–14, considering that only one-sixth of the hours worked in two years at the Bell Rock 17 miles distant were obtained. The foundation was prepared and 10 dovetailed stones laid. At the end of 1815 the sea carried away the 3rd complete course of 9 blocks before the cement had time to harden. During the summer of 1816 a sudden gale forced the men to leave the work before securing the 7th course, and several of its stones were washed away. At the end of that season 16 courses to a height of 20′ were completed and anchored for the winter by a weighty cover of 4 tons of lead. The year 1817 saw the beacon raised to within a few feet of its intended height when a storm removed its top above the 5th course. The design was then changed so that this base would be surmounted by six cast-iron columns carrying a ball about 10′ lower. This superstructure was completed in 1821, £5,000 having been spent during the 9 years of intermittent work.

This experience showed that at such an exposed site more weight was required to resist the sea action, that is, a higher tower and a broader base were necessary. In 1887 a manned lightship was established in the vicinity.

LIGHTHOUSES IN 1819

By 1819 the coastal lighthouses in Scotland and Man had been increased to 15, of which 12 were operated by the Northern Lighthouse Commissioners and 3 by the Cumbrae Lighthouse Trustees. Sutherness and Buddonness are excluded as being too local. Four gave white revolving beams: Start (1806); Toward (1812); Inchkeith (1816) and Calf of Man, a pair (1818); and three revolving red and white beams: Bell Rock (1811); Corsewall (1816) and Point of Ayre (1818). All had metal parabolic reflectors and argands except Cumbrae, Cloch, Sutherness, Buddonness and the 2 towers on the Pentland Skerries where in 1818 Stevenson stated that the 66 facet reflectors gave good service: not until 1834 were they displaced.

IRELAND

LIGHTHOUSES IN 1800

Eight coastal lighthouses seem to have been managed by the Customs Board in 1800—Howth, Copeland, Old Head of Kinsale, Loop Head, Hook, Wicklow, South Rock and Arranmore. All showed fixed lights except South Rock which had a revolving light from Rogers's small patent 2″ diameter oil lamps with reflectors. The lighthouses at Kinsale and Loop were coal fires, the Wicklow towers (a group of two as a distinction from the single towers at Howth and Hook) had candles and one reflector apiece, and the other 5 had Rogers's apparatus with 6 to 12 of his lamps. The harbour lights of Balbriggan and Kinsale (Charles Fort) had candles and that of Waterford (Duncannon Fort) had probably an oil lamp. Lenses were fitted at from 6 to 10 lights including Balbriggan and Duncannon Fort.

LIGHTHOUSES 1800–10

New lighthouses were established at Cranfield and Clare island in 1802 and 1806. Both were fixed lights from oil lamps. Cranfield lighthouse at the entrance to Carlingford Lough was a granite tower built by Rogers, 130′ high with a 12′ diameter lantern containing

11 of his lights. From the tower the state of the tide was indicated at night by a small subsidiary lantern containing 3 lamps and during the day by a ball hoisted on a mast. A bell was tolled in fog. Clare lighthouse was erected by the Marquis of Sligo: its lamps had wicks of 1″ diameter. Rogers built a new tower of limestone at Loop Head in 1802 containing 12 of his lights as at Howth, and fitted 3 at each of the harbour lights of Waterford and Kinsale when the Revenue Board took them over in 1803–4.

Between 1800 and 1806 four Acts of Parliament were passed for the management of the Irish lights. They gave power to the Revenue Board to purchase land for lighthouse buildings and to levy dues of 2d. per ton on all vessels trading to Ireland: three more Acts passed between 1810 and 1812 changed the control of the lighthouses and altered the light-dues.

CONTROL PASSES TO BALLAST BOARD 1810

For some years before 1810 the British Government had been receiving complaints as to the inefficiency of the Irish lights. Being satisfied of their justification, it approached the Revenue Board which operated the Customs Service and had little interest in lighthouses. The Board agreed that the Ballast Board of Dublin, which for over 30 years had managed Dublin harbour and its entrance light of Poolbeg, was a more suitable body to control them and accordingly in 1810 an Act transferred 10 lighthouses and 3 harbour lights, the change taking place in the summer of 1810, probably in July. In September and October of that year the Ballast Board appointed 3 inspectors to visit the lighthouses without the knowledge of Rogers and they reported that they were 'in a very bad state, every one of them, and most wretchedly supplied in all respects, some without reflectors, and those that were in use as bad as could be'.

The inspectors offered no adverse comments on Rogers's oil lamps which were fitted with glass cylinders and can be accepted as serving their purpose excellently. But they found most of the lenses broken or shattered: according to one keeper, those under his care had been in that state throughout his service of 16 years. South Rock's 10 lamps and reflectors showed a flash every 90 seconds. Old Head had 12 lamps without reflectors; the two Wicklow towers had 2 'large looking glass reflectors and many lantern panes were bull's eyes'; Howth had 8 lamps, reflectors and lenses; Copeland had 6 lamps in a lantern of only 5′ 7″ diameter; Hook had 13 lamps and reflectors and the 13 lantern windows were filled with 10 large lenses and 3 panes of plate glass; and Cranfield had 12 lamps and reflectors and 11 lenses. The harbour lights were lit at Balbriggan according to the weather by from 2 to 7 candles set in an iron frame suspended by a cord, at Charles Fort by 3 lamps and reflectors and at Duncannon Fort by 3 lamps, reflectors and lenses 'broken in such a manner that it is surprising they remain together as the rain beats through them'. At Hook 2 new lenses awaited the arrival of a person to fit them in the lantern. Rogers had shown exceptional ability in designing sea-lights and in building the South Rock lighthouse but his notable invention of catoptric lighting (plano-convex lenses with spherical reflectors) in 1788–9 had resolved into merely setting lenses into lantern panes: so producing sectors of variable illumination unsuitable for fixed lights.

The Revenue Board had managed the lighthouses by contract, as in France. In 1810 Rogers contracted to manage 10 while the Marquis of Sligo, a clergyman named Hamilton and George Darby (under a supervisor named Dudgeon who received a salary of 30 guineas) contracted for the lights of Clare island, Balbriggan and Wicklow respectively. This system of management was changed gradually by the Ballast Board. It limited Rogers's successive contracts to periods of 6 months and bound him to supply cotton wicks and oil not inferior in quality to samples which he submitted and which were locked in a safe. First Howth and then Cranfield lighthouses were taken over from him and in March 1812 he was informed that when his current contract for maintaining 8 lights expired on 1st July it would not be renewed. He complained to the Lord Lieutenant in Dublin that he had been induced to come to Ireland in 1788, that his employment was being terminated without any reason being given, and that he had to support a wife and 10 children 'many of whom yet required some years of paternal care'. He claimed to be considered the permanent *Contractor and Inspector of Lights and Builder of Lighthouses*, but though in practice he filled these posts, no documents had been signed which supported his claim. When his last contract terminated he received no compensation. No doubt the Revenue Board had been lax in control but his own methods had not produced satisfactory lights. He seems to have attempted to manage the lighthouses with little or no assistance and to make an excessive profit. According to the foreman connected with the Northern Lighthouse Board who visited the South Rock lighthouse in 1812, Rogers appointed unsuitable men as lightkeepers and gave them too little training. He paid them an average of £15 per annum and allowed them to keep the unburned candle-ends and to carry on trades, and even to use their dwellings as taverns. At Hook the lightkeeper was in business as a herb-doctor. Rogers's contract price for maintaining 9 lights was £5,899 in 1810 when he maintained only one lightkeeper at each lighthouse, whereas the cost of maintaining the same lighthouses in 1832 was £3,363 which covered the services of several keepers at larger salaries; these totalled £209 at South Rock.

After receiving the confidential report on the lighthouses in 1810 the Ballast Board lost no time in planning improvements. It appointed George Halpin senior as engineer and inspector of lighthouses and as quickly as possible removed most of Rogers's lanterns and all his lighting apparatus from the 9 or 10 coastal or harbour lights where he had installed them. Evidently a deputation of the Board visited South Stack lighthouse in Anglesey and saw George Robinson's revolving reflector light which was superior to Rogers's. At once lamps and reflectors were ordered from Robinson for a fixed light at Cranfield and installed there in 1811, and in the next 7 years he received orders for lighting apparatus for all the other Irish lighthouses except South Rock at which the Greenside Callum Company of Edinburgh fitted a lantern and revolving apparatus of 10 argands and reflectors in 1813 at a cost of £1,447. 6. 8. Robinson's charge for a lantern and 21 similar lights was £2,850: eventually his prices were considered too high and for that reason he lost the Irish lighthouse contracts to Swan of Edinburgh and other firms.

LIGHTHOUSE WORKS 1811–19

The works carried out by the Ballast Board in these years were numerous and very necessary, although the Parliamentary Committee which investigated the three British Lighthouse Services in 1834 considered the Irish capital expenditure had been too large. From 1811 to 1819 it exceeded £150,000 and from 1820 to 1834 £183,270 was spent or authorised. The fact that many of the lighthouses were built on out-of-the-way islands as in Scotland added materially to their cost. The Committee complained that the Board sometimes started to build lighthouses without an estimate of the ultimate cost and that it succumbed to local pressure to provide lights that should be paid for locally. It is likely however that, as in Scotland, the dues received at many harbours and piers would have been insufficient to provide lights. The Committee elicited the curious fact that the Ballast Board, like some other administrative bodies, had the right to punish for trespass and damage to its property, without recourse to a Court of Law: it was empowered to sentence individuals to whipping and to imprisonment with hard labour for 6 months.

159. Dublin entrance light on the south wall about 1810, known as Poolbeg light

160. Howth lighthouse as re-built in 1814 (Creswick)

Between 1811 and 1819 the Ballast Board re-built the towers at the Old Head of Kinsale in 1814, Copeland and Clare in 1816, and Wicklow in 1818. Several excellent lights were established at harbours and others were improved. A lightship was moored at the Kish bank in November 1811 and new lighthouses were lighted at Inishtrahull in March 1813, Howth in March 1814, Tuskar in June 1815, Fanad Head (Lough Swilly) in March 1817, Roches Point (Cork) in June 1817, and Cape Clear and Aran island (Galway) in May 1818.

Fire had destroyed the lighthouse on Clare island in 1816, a result of the custom of throwing into a cask in the lantern the snuffings of the wicks, and the tower was re-built immediately at the cost of £9,297. The new lighthouse at Howth was built at the cost of £15,497 at a low level to replace the old lighthouse near the top of Howth hill which was often obscured by fog. The Kish bank lightvessel, being some distance off Dublin harbour entrance, was of value for general navigation. She carried 3 lights arranged as a triangle. During fog her crew beat a gong and fired an 18-pound gun when the Packet from Holyhead was due. About 1840 it was decided to replace her by a screw-piled beacon, but after the expenditure of £4,432 the piles were destroyed in a gale in November 1842: the project was abandoned and the lightship was retained. By the inroads of the sea Cranfield lighthouse had become unsafe in 1819 so, to replace it, work was begun on the Haulbowline tower, 'a single pillar standing in the sea'; but though lighted in September 1824 it was not completed until 1826 at a cost of £28,424.

A Fuller Account of Certain Lighthouses

TUSKAR LIGHTHOUSE 1811–15

The Ballast Board followed up the provisions of the 1796 Act for setting a lighthouse among the shoals that girt the Wexford coast and chose for its site the Tuskar Rock, an islet 6 miles off the shore, which was highly perilous to shipping. This important lighthouse was the first work by George Halpin who, after completing the plans, began to build in 1811 a granite tower rising 101′ from rock to vane: he lighted it in June 1815. As the Rock was elevated well above the highest tides, it was not believed necessary to limit operations to the good weather of summer. But at 3 a.m. on the 19th October 1812, after a prolonged storm when the Smalls lighthouse was damaged, the sea rose to an unexpected height and a huge wave swept away a wooden building in which 24 of the workmen were lodged. Some were drowned immediately. Others clung by their fingers to the irregularities of the rock surface. Ten survived the ordeal of exposure to the weather for two nights without food or shelter. A letter from the Secretary of the Ballast Board to Stevenson describes the incident. 'The sea raged with great violence, going clean over the Rock. Many men would not quit the wooden house until the sea began to tear it to pieces. When they did, all was confusion in the dark. . . . If these men had presence of mind to have passed a rope across the top of the Rock to the many ring-bolts they might, every soul, have been saved. The wooden houses were fastened to the Rock by timbers bolted and run-in with lead and chained to the rings for the purpose, by passing the chain round each shed and over the roof. In fact, all who saw the preparations thought the precautions quite unnecessary. . . . The Tuskar is about 25′ or 30′ above H.W. ordinary tides.' To commemorate their escape from the giant wave the surviving workmen composed a song beginning 'We are the boys, just thirty-three . . .'. The disaster did not deter them from remaining in the employment of the Board: on completion of the Tuskar tower they proceeded cheerfully to build lighthouses elsewhere in Ireland. Pensions were granted to those who were maimed or otherwise injured in the disaster and to the dependants of those who lost their lives.

LIGHTHOUSES IN 1819

By the enterprise of the Ballast Board and the excellent efforts of Halpin the number of coastal lights was increased to 17 by 1819, including 1 lightship. Many of the local lights that were improved or newly-established were also of service to coastal shipping. One of the features of several was the adoption of white lights with red sectors, an early use of colour.

All the important lights were fitted with metal reflectors and argand-type lamps. South Rock, Tuskar and Cape Clear had revolving white lights. Inishtrahull and Aran gave revolving red and white beams. South Rock apparatus had five 25″ reflectors set on each side of the rotating frame. The others had 3 sides each with seven $20\frac{1}{2}$″ reflectors. The fixed lights were at Howth, Kinsale, Loop, Hook, Wicklow, Copeland, Arranmore, Cranfield, Clare, Kish, Fanad and Roches Point.

FRANCE

LIGHTHOUSES IN 1800

A list prepared in 1800 by the Minister of Marine in Paris named 20 lighthouses and harbour lights then in operation in France—Dunkirk, Calais, Boulogne, Dieppe (revolving), l'Ailly, La Hève, Barfleur, Fréhel, St. Mathieu, Ushant, Pen-marc'h, Groix, Baleines,

242

Chassiron and Cordouan (revolving) in the Channel and the Atlantic; and Port-Vendres, Cette, Bouc, Planier and Villefranche in the Mediterranean. The first four were described as lights without towers: like the light at Ramsgate in England they were intended to mark harbour entrances. The Mediterranean lights also marked harbours but they might be looked on as coastal lighthouses because they had as good lights and were as useful marks as most of the contemporary lighthouses in the Mediterranean and in the United States of America. So the number of coastal lighthouses in France in 1800 might be put at 16.

The Cordouan and Dieppe lights had argand-type lamps and parabolic reflectors. All the other lights had flat-wick oil lamps, mostly with Sangrain's spherical reflectors. The Minister's list included a tower at Lorient which carried a clock and a fog bell but no light, and the lighthouse at Ostend. Calais light was tidal and had a parabolic reflector. Dunkirk had a reflector but its curve was not described.

LIGHTHOUSES 1800–19

About 1801 the wooden beacon at Dieppe was destroyed by fire and its small light, with revolving reflectors or screens, was not replaced. In 1805 two local towers were erected at La Canche, south of Boulogne, each lighted by 6 of Sangrain's spherical reflectors.

In 1808 a complicated method of eclipsing reflectors had been proposed for Baleines. If tried, it proved unsuccessful.

In November 1809 Bordier-Marcet's first two *pharillons* or *fanaux sidéraux* of 15″ diameter were introduced at Honfleur and gave much satisfaction. Because of the well-known rapid deterioration of the surfaces of silver-plated reflectors of marine lights from salt spray combined with smoke from the common lamps, a spare set of reflectors had been provided for this light; but the use of the smokeless argand lamp rendered them unnecessary for several years.

Dunkirk had no sea-light in 1814 but received in that year a *fanal sidéral* of only 11″ diameter which fitted into a small lantern set near sea-level and designed to offer little obstruction to the waves which rose to its level in storms. A duplicate was supplied to Boulogne. It seems that originally one of the French Ministers ordered *fanaux sidéraux* for these two ports 'qui en avaient le plus urgent besoin' at a cost of 50,000 francs. The price included lanterns of 10′ diameter and 8′ high, consisting of cast-iron frames covered with copper and holding 100 glass panes. The apparatus was rejected, to the loss of Bordier-Marcet. He informed Stevenson that this was done 'par un injustice sans égale et sur un pitoyable et méchant rapport fait par la Commission des Phares' but he did not state the reasons. A *fanal sidéral* of 32″ diameter was ordered for the port of Quilleboeuf in 1815 and was installed in July 1817. During trials, small reflecting wings were added to utilise light escaping from its sides. Its lamp had 5 *becs*, presumably flat-wicks, with a chimney.

In 1808 Bordier-Marcet's *fanaux à double effet* were tested at the south tower at La Hève and fitted there permanently in May 1811 to the number of 6. In August 1812, 6 were ordered for the north tower and fitted in 1814. In 1818, 4 more were set in each tower with argand lamps with 0·83″ diameter wicks. In the same year the Commission had a demonstration of these reflectors in the Champs Elysées in Paris where their beam lit up distant trees: 9 reflectors arranged in an experimental lantern on each of two frames or faces combined to form two huge reflecting surfaces of 49 square feet which were revolved by clockwork designed by Wagner, a Paris clockmaker. Bordier-Marcet calculated that each beam gave the equivalent of 40,000 candles, but the large oil consumpt of the 36 lamps precluded the use of the apparatus at a lighthouse.

A request by the British Government in 1817–18 for better lighthouses on the French coasts led to improvements of the Channel lights, the first being a new light set up hurriedly in December 1818 on a belfry at Calais. A ready-made lantern was purchased from Bordier-Marcet and in it six 32″ reflectors from Lenoir were arranged on a revolving frame with two opposite faces, 3 on each side, to give a beam of light from 16 square feet of reflecting surface every 90 seconds. Many mariners considered the flash too short. According to Bordier-Marcet its duration was 4 seconds.

Tests of that optical apparatus in Paris and subsequent reports from La Hève and Calais assured the Commission that it could now supply good lights and in 1819 it decided to instal parabolic reflector lights at other lighthouses. Lenoir's reflectors were ordered for a revolving light at l'Ailly, and Bordier-Marcet's *fanaux à double effet* for a fixed light at Ushant and for revolving lights at Cap Fréhel, Baleines and a new lighthouse at Four. All these apparatuses were put into service in 1820–2.

LIGHTHOUSES IN 1819

The light at Calais, which seems to have been the only addition to the French coast lights since 1800, brought their number to 17. Cordouan and Calais were revolving with Lenoir reflectors, and were by far the finest lights in France. La Hève too was a good fixed light. The benefit of argands was accepted at these 3 lighthouses. The other 14 lighthouses had flat-wick burners, mostly with Sangrain's spherical reflectors. For one reason or another it was not until 1835 at Barfleur in the Atlantic, and in 1843 at Cette in the Mediterranean, that the last of his unscientific reflectors, after 70 years' use, were replaced by parabolic apparatus. One cannot doubt that the lamps at Cordouan had been fitted with chimneys before 1819.

A searching review of the lighting of the French coasts was undertaken in 1825 by Rossel, an honorary Admiral and a member of the Lighthouse Commission. He proposed to establish many new lighthouses and harbour lights at which he would instal the lenticular or dioptric lights evolved in 1823 by Fresnel. He planned three grades of lighthouses of varying importance and smaller lights for ports, using four different sizes or *orders* of Fresnel's apparatus. He proposed for the Channel and the Atlantic twenty 1st-order, five 2nd-order, and thirteen 3rd-order apparatuses and twenty-nine port lights, and for the Mediterranean seven 1st-order, and four 3rd-order apparatuses and six port lights. The interior diameters of these orders were specified as 2, 1·40 and 0·50 and of the port lights 0·30 metres. These figures were double the focal distances. Though the lights along the French Mediterranean coast were not inferior to most in that Sea, he stated that the lighting of that coast and of its harbours had been neglected and pointed out that the light at Cette was particularly poor and that no light or beacon fire had ever been provided to assist naval vessels to enter their principal base at Toulon.

The lack of development of the French lighthouses by 1819 was due to unsettlement which began in 1789 with the Revolution and continued until the Napoleonic wars ended in 1815; also the failure of the revolving mirror light of Cordouan had sapped confidence in the lighting apparatus. Where was a satisfactory light to be had when the best light that engineers and scientists had evolved had already been set up on that tower and still drew the condemnation of seamen? Another cause was the system of management by contract which was continued after 1835, by which a contractor offering the lowest price for specified articles maintained the lights and even appointed the lightkeepers. This arrangement cut off from personal contact with the lighthouses the officials sitting in Paris who took decisions and controlled expenditure. Bordier-Marcet pointed out that the English did not hesitate to spend money on improving their lighthouses, whereas in the 20 years from 1800 the French expenditure on lighthouses was but a minute fraction of what was being spent in the British Isles.

Though in numbers and quality the French lighthouses were of less service to navigation in 1819 than were those of the British Isles, it was in France that valuable investigations into lighthouse optics were commenced at this time under the Lighthouse Commission. After 4 years' work, Fresnel raised the curtain on a new era in lighthouse illumination on 25th July 1823 when he crowned the lighthouse of Cordouan with the first revolving dioptric light conjoined with an oil-pumping-lamp of concentric-wicks which gave an intensity of flame transcending previous achievement with lamps. His lens and lamp were of great importance in the history of illumination and they opened the door to advances in the design of lighthouse optics which lighthouse engineers have been presenting to seamen continuously step by step from 1819 to the present day.

SWEDEN

LIGHTHOUSES 1800–19

In 1800, 11 coastal lighthouses were in operation within the present territory of Sweden. Seven were coal fires on towers—Falsterbo (*c.* 1202); Kullen (*c.* 1560); Nidingen, a pair, (1624); Landsort (*c.* 1669); Djursten (1767); Grönskär (1774) and Ölands Södra Udde (1785). Holmögadd (1763) had a vippefyr. The lighthouses of Örskär (1687) and Korsö (1750) showed oscillating mirrors and Carlsten (1781) showed revolving mirrors.

In 1817 the coal fire at Kullen was enclosed in a glass lantern as was also a coal fire set on a new tower at Östergarn in 1818.

So, in this period, the number of Swedish lighthouses of coastal value increased from 11 to 12.

COAL FIRES IN SWEDEN

It is remarkable that though Sweden introduced to the world the means of obtaining beams of powerful light by parabolic reflectors and had established by 1781 three lights, two oscillating and one revolving, which utilised these reflectors, she did not establish another such moving light until 1837. Her first fixed reflector light was set up at Malmö in 1822. The number of her coal fire lighthouses was increased from 7 in 1781 to 11 in 1838, the last being replaced by reflectors in 1854.

The reason for this preference for coal fires is not clear: the Swedish Government was well aware that other countries were increasing the numbers and intensities of both reflector and lens lights, and it is hardly likely that even with the universal conservatism of seamen the Swedish navigators preferred coal fires to the excellent foreign revolving reflector lights. It has been suggested as an explanation that Sweden had suffered so much from protracted warfare that the expense of the conversion to reflector lights could not be faced and that the amount of her sea-trade did not justify it. But she did in fact indulge in considerable expense after 1816 in setting glazed lanterns on her lighthouses to enclose coal fires and in altering the towers to lead air to the grates to improve combustion. So it seems likely that climatic, rather than economic, conditions influenced the preference for coal fires.

Writing in 1819, Robert Stevenson observed that the use of coal at great expense at the Baltic lighthouses was due perhaps to 'the difficulty of maintaining the combustion of oil in a cold climate' and only in Sweden is it noted that oil lamps were covered with skins, obviously to retain heat and prevent the oil from congealing: these were the argand lamps supplied to Carlsten lighthouse in 1823.

In all countries liable to atmospheric temperatures falling to several degrees of frost, difficulties were met in winter where oil lamps burned even refined sperm oil. Scotland, the United States and Denmark record that light-rooms required to be heated. In Scotland, where a frozen sea is never seen from a lighthouse as in Sweden, a *frost-lamp* was lighted under each argand lamp oil reservoir in cold weather from about 1810. In the U.S.A. congealing oil was a frequent trouble in the winter. A report of 1846 on Dutch lighthouses refers to the 'difficulty in keeping the oil in a proper state for burning during cold weather' and mentions that because reflectors and argands could not be 'confined in a smaller space than the lantern, and the flames small, it frequently happens that to a stove must be added a *frost-lamp* for each of the reflectors'. Fine salt was used regularly at night for rubbing the lantern panes to remove ice and snow. At that period, the Danish lightships were removed in the autumn and replaced 'at as early a day in the spring as the ice will permit'. The Swedish climate is not warmer than the Danish: winter trade to certain Swedish ports is restricted to ships strengthened to resist ice. From the experience of these other countries one would expect even greater troubles to arise with oil lamps in the colder Swedish climate.

It may be that in cold weather trouble with oil lamps in Sweden arose from lack of ventilation, as in England. In 1843 Trinity House consulted its scientific adviser Michael Faraday on the difficulty in ventilating the lanterns of its exposed lighthouses. He pointed out that at some English lighthouses the lamps consumed 20 pints of oil in one winter's night, which produced more than 20 pints of water. 'The ice on the glass within, derived from this source, has been found in some instances an eighth or even a sixth of an inch in thickness and required to be scraped off with knives.' He recommended that the products of combustion should be carried from each lamp by a funnel to a large ventilator at the top of the lantern as in the Russian reflector lights, which probably had the additional advantage of heating by stoves.

Whatever the reasons, the continuance and even the increase in the numbers of coal fires in Sweden, and in Norway also after 1823, when they had been abolished in other countries, is remarkable.

THE GULF OF FINLAND AND THE WESTERN BALTIC

By 1801 navigation in the Gulfs of Finland and Riga benefited from numerous light-houses. Along the south shore of the Gulf of Finland and on its islands for a stretch of 250 miles the Russians had lighthouses at Dagerort, Odensholm, Pakerort, Surop, Hogland,

Seskär, Kokskär and Tolbuhin (of which the last 3 were timber trellis-structures with lights from oil lamps); while on the north of the Gulf the Finns showed lights at Utö and Porkkala.

Utö lighthouse had many changes of illumination in this period. Its tower of 1753 was destroyed during the war of 1808–9 and in 1814 a square tower of stone 70' high took its place, surmounted by an octagonal lantern 22' high which held a great parabolic frame of wood of 10' diameter covered with small pieces of mirror glass. At intervals this reflector was moved by hand towards a different direction; but in a few years clockwork was

162. Seskär
lighthouse
in 1801

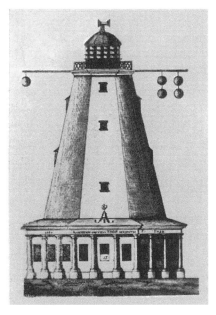

161. Riga lighthouse built in 1819.
The crowned initial honours the
Czar Alexander I. From a sea-
chart of 1820 showing tide signals

163. Hogland lighthouse in
1820

fitted which stopped the reflector for 5 minutes in each direction, then moved it on. At first 7 candles and later 10 candles were bunched together round the focus, 936 lb. of candles being consumed annually. In 1818 the tower received a new lantern holding 7 silver-plated copper reflectors which were oscillated through 45° every 4 minutes, and lamps burning hemp oil or turnip oil. In 1820–2, 7 new reflectors and lamps were fitted to show a light every 10 minutes. In 1826, 2 reflectors were added and the lighthouse showed a fixed light.

Porkkala lighthouse was established in 1800 and lighted by 10 parabolic facet reflectors with gas-jets. This gas was produced from wood distilled on the spot in the Russian manner and it was claimed that the sale of the by-products, charcoal and tar, covered the cost of maintaining the light. In the war of 1808–9 the tower was destroyed and a wood fire burning on the Rocks near the ruins of the lighthouse guided shipping. The next tower of 1814 was a square structure of grey stone 46' high and lit by candles until machinery was completed to rotate a frame carrying 10 facet reflectors. Each lamp had 2 flat-wicks and consumed half a pint of oil per hour. In 1823 the tower was doubled in height by the addition of a brick top and the customary lighting of the Russian lighthouses was introduced: 17 parabolic reflectors of brass over 20″ in diameter with argand-type lamps were arranged in 2 circular rows to show a fixed light.

By 1813 Captain Leonty Spafarieff had improved the Russian lighthouses greatly by re-building many of the structures in stone, including Seskär and Tolbuhin. He seems to have tried out parabolic reflectors first at Catherendal light at Reval in 1806 with 3 or 5 reflectors set close together to give a narrow beam of light over a sector of 6° to mark a passage through low-lying Rocks. By 1819 all the lights in the Gulfs of Finland and Riga had masonry towers but none of the lights was revolving. At this time Spafarieff issued charts on which he showed both revolving and fixed lights. Several of these lights were proposals only and were not carried out as early as he hoped. He is credited with introducing a 'perfect' lighting system which one can infer comprised parabolic reflectors probably of brass with argand-type lamps. He indicated effectively on charts the ranges of fixed lights by arcs, adding arcs of continuous dotted loops for revolving lights.

A light at Memel which was purchased in England, probably from Robinson who exported reflector lights before 1818, consisted in 1796 of 5 large and 4 small concave reflectors, combined with large candles and a double patent lamp. These details of illuminants set ex-focally suggest an inefficient apparatus, but as the resulting light gave satisfaction these particulars may be erroneous. According to a pilotage book, when a vessel was 4 miles distant the light 'appears like a coal fire, at 3 miles like the rising full moon, but when 2 miles distant the separate light of each reflector may be clearly distinguished'.

After being 5 years in construction, a tower at Pillau in East Prussia was lighted in 1811 with 11 parabolic reflectors and argands. About 1812 the London Chest shoal was marked by a lightship.

A feature of the marking of these Baltic waters at that time was the use of spars as buoys, moored in deep water and carrying horizontal barrels or brushwood, or showing flags coloured red or white.

The names of the Finnish and Russian lighthouses mentioned in this Section are as given in early British hydrographical books.

UNITED STATES OF AMERICA

LIGHTHOUSES CONSTRUCTED IN 1800–12

In 1800 the United States maintained 24 lighthouses, listed in Section XI, all of which had value for coastal navigation though several were set at harbour entrances. From 1800 to 1812 the following 21 new lighthouses were erected:

1801	Annisquam Mass.	1808	West Quoddy Head Me.
1801	Georgetown S.C.	1808	Wood island Me.
1802	Cape Poge Mass.	1808	Chatham Mass.
1802	Falkner island Conn.	1809	Sands Point N.Y.
1802	Old Point Comfort Va.	1809	Black Rock Conn.
1803	Saybrook Conn.	1810	Point Judith R.I.
1804	New Point Comfort Va.	1811	St. Simon Ga.
1806	Little Gull island N.Y.	1811	Bayou St. John La.
1807	Whitehead Me.	1812	Boon island Me.
1807	Franklin island Me.	1812	Cape Lookout N.C.
1807	Watch Hill R.I.		

Lighthouses 1800 to 1819

Great difficulties were overcome in founding structures on the low-lying Boon island—a wooden beacon in 1800, which was destroyed by the sea in 1804, and a stone beacon in 1805.

Despite the destruction by fire of several lighthouses, including one at Gurnet near Plymouth in 1801, a few of the new towers were still built of wood, such as those at Chatham and Cape Lookout. The tower at St. Simon was built of blocks of oyster shells and lime.

ILLUMINATION 1800–12

Up to 1810 oil lamps made locally, including 'the spider lamp burned in the lantern as it might have been in the window of a house', and possibly candles, illuminated the United States lighthouses, without reflectors. Oils of various sorts fed the lamps. There is a record of correspondence in 1807 between the American Treasury and the owners of the ship *Coromandel* at Rangoon, who had offered for sale 5,000 gallons of *earth oil* which they commended as being the 'best article known for burning in lighthouses, making a very strong, clear and bright flame, emitting at the same time a great volume of smoak': this claim to produce much smoke was an ample assurance of its unsuitability.

Attempts made over several years before 1810 to improve the Boston light failed to satisfy seamen who complained that the American lights lagged much behind the standard of those in west Europe. One of the complainers was Winslow Lewis, a sea-captain who picked up information about lighthouses when voyaging in Europe. After carrying out simple trials of reflectors and lamps Lewis fitted a revolving light at Boston lighthouse in May 1811: an advertisement announced that it would appear *brilliant* for 40 seconds and *obscure* for 20. It seems to have consisted of two faces each of 7 reflectors with oil lamps supposed to be like argands, set on a revolving frame. The light was described as brilliant merely as being visible and not in the sense of having great intensity. He claimed that this installation saved oil 'equal to 100 per cent', which meant that the consumpt was halved; and this tremendous reduction in its expense of maintenance won universal approval.

Lewis then fitted his apparatus at Cape Cod and Cape Ann and their new lights were reported to be visible at greater distances than had been their previous lights—doubtless in the direction of the axis, when the apparatus was new.

LIGHTHOUSES CONSTRUCTED IN 1812–19

The years 1812–16 covered the war with Britain, which was largely a struggle at sea around the Atlantic coast and in the Great Lakes, the States hoping to seize Canada: a project that failed owing to incompetent military leadership which allowed the British and Canadians to occupy Washington. For several years lights were extinguished.

When peace came, the construction of lighthouses was resumed at an increasing rate, 36 new ones being established by 1825 including the following 7:

1816	Race Point Mass.		1818	West Chap Mass.
1817	Petit Manan Me.		1819	Bird island Mass.
1818	Tarpaulin Cove Mass.		1819	Presque Isle Pa.
1818	Buffalo N.Y.			

Therefore, at the end of 1819, 52 lighthouses were established. This number might be reduced by say 2 if judging these lights on the same basis as the European lights, according to an arbitrary definition of coastal rather than of local value for shipping.

ILLUMINATION 1812–19

In March 1812 the United States Congress approved a contract with Lewis by which he would fit his lens and reflector apparatus at the lighthouses then in operation. When he fulfilled it at the end of 1815, another contract was entered into by which he would supply the best quality of sperm oil for 7 years, visit each lighthouse personally every year and report on its condition. He would receive as remuneration one-half of the previous annual cost of the oil at each lighthouse. He found this contract so remunerative that on its expiry he was content to accept a reduction of his share of the savings to one-third, in return for its extension by 5 years.

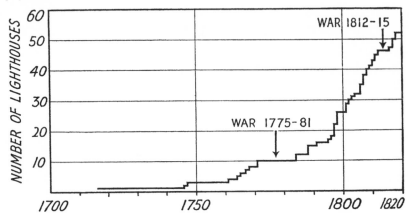

164. The curve shows the increasing number of lighthouses in the United States up to 1820. Some had periods of discontinuance

For his fixed lights Lewis arranged 6 to 8 reflectors in a lantern, presumably each with a lens in front. They were revolved at Charleston and perhaps at 4 other lighthouses.

Between 1789 and 1820 there were 5 periods when the management of the Federal lighthouses was held successively by Officers of the Treasury and of the Revenue Departments, but the establishment after 1800 of so many lighthouses along the extensive American coast showed that the Officers had appreciation of navigators' requirements. Their staffs, changing frequently, were unlikely to have the time or the inclination to make the long voyages necessary for inspection of the lights at night and they were not qualified to assess the usefulness of optical apparatus: as these Washington Offices had no direct contact with seamen, Lewis could install his lights without check. At first, navigators would consider that any light, however inferior, was better than none.

Statements that have appeared recently in American books, praising Lewis's lights and even declaring that he introduced argand lamps into the States and studied under Fresnel in France, are not true: contemporary accounts and official documents published in America contradict such assertions completely. Lewis's lights were definitely very bad, worse than Sangrain's which at least did not include a defective lens to obstruct the flame of the lamps from showing directly seawards and to block a large proportion of the rays from the reflector. Lewis was stated to be ignorant of optics and to have said that lighthouse lighting was not subject to optical laws. The *bull's eyes* which were the worst feature of his arrangement were removed gradually from all lighthouses after about 1830, to the benefit of the lighting. The last was taken from the lighthouse of Falkner island in 1840.

XV

AUTHORITY TO ESTABLISH ENGLISH LIGHTHOUSES

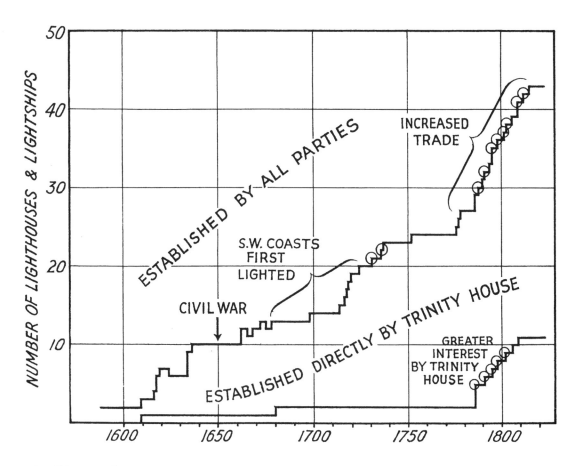

165. Diagram showing the numbers of coastal lighthouses established in England and Wales by Act or patent up to 1820. Lightships are marked by circles. Only entirely new lights are included; replacements such as Happisburgh for Caistor and Winterton for Corton are therefore excluded. Air, Mumbles, Wintertonness, St. Bees and Stanford lightship are included. The diagram shows that of 43 coastal lighthouses established before 1820, 11 had been established by Trinity House and 32 by other Authorities or private persons

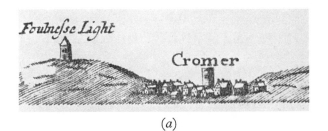

(a)

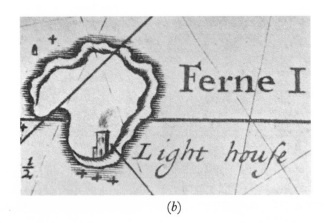

(b)

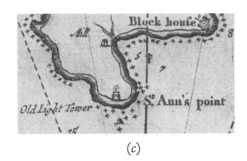

(c)

(d)

166 (a)–(d). Forsaken lighthouses in England. Three lighthouses erected about 1670 by Sir John Clayton were never lighted, on Flamborough Head, Foulness (a), and the Farnes (b).   A lighthouse (c) established on St. Ann's Head near Milford Haven was discontinued about 1668 by desire of Parliament. Flamborough lighthouse (d) was depicted by Gold in 1805.   The others appear on sea-charts c. 1690

XV. AUTHORITY TO ESTABLISH ENGLISH LIGHTHOUSES

In England before 1836 the levy of dues on shipping to pay for the construction and maintenance of a lighthouse required authority in each instance by a Crown patent or an Act of Parliament. Usually the business of establishing a lighthouse was arranged between its proposer, several hundreds of local seafarers who approved of the proposal and undertook to pay specified dues, the Elder Brethren as navigation experts, and Government officials who issued the patent. When other interests were concerned much complication ensued. From 1690 only Trinity House received patents: it permitted the proposer to erect the lighthouse at his own expense and, on payment of a small rent for a term of years, it allowed him to collect the dues and retain the balance after maintaining the lighthouse.

SEAMEN'S ASSOCIATIONS

From the earliest times, at all ports and harbours, however small, agreement has been necessary among seafarers as to mooring and handling boats. Often this developed into recognisable associations which accumulated funds to help old seamen, widows and orphans.

By the 16th century in Britain, several of these associations or guilds had grown to considerable importance and at various dates had adopted the title of Trinity House—in England at Hull, Newcastle-on-Tyne, Dover, Scarborough and Deptford Strond, an ancient haven on the Thames, and in Scotland at Leith and Dundee. These bodies took over the control of pilots in their districts and expressed the views of their members on navigation questions such as the desirability of seamarks at particular positions. Some, by authority of Crown or Parliament, levied dues for maintenance of beacons, buoys and even lighthouses. The Newcastle guild existed in 1492, when it purchased the site of its present House, and Hull claims establishment about the same date. The Newcastle Trinity House still maintains a handful of unlighted buoys. The Dundee Trinity House was dissolved a century ago.

Early in the 19th century, a Trinity House, also with navigational duties, was in being at Quebec in Canada.

TRINITY HOUSE, LONDON

The Trinity House of Deptford Strond became the most influential and wealthy of these associations and, in connection with seamarks, is now referred to generally as Trinity House. Henry VIII, who later reformed the English Church, in 1515 established the House by Charter, as a permanent Corporation with the title of *Guild or Fraternity of the most glorious and undividable Trinity of Saint Clement*. It received authority to make rules for the benefit of English shipping and to penalise transgressors thereof. The grant empowered it to hold property—which it may have done already without the protection of legal status —and required the members to say Masses not only for the souls of former members but also for the King, his Consort Catherine and his 'progenitors deceased'. The governing board consisted of a Master—the first being the Comptroller of the Navy, Sir Thomas Spert, who died in 1541—four Wardens and eight Assistants, who might admit *Brethren* and *Sisters* as ordinary members. But as the Corporation's connection with the sea increased, so the entry of women lapsed. At the present time Trinity House consists of some 300 seamen known as Younger Brethren, who elect a dozen of their number as Elder Brethren, by whom the affairs of the Corporation are conducted. In addition there is a handful of honorary Elder Brethren consisting of members of the Royal Family and prominent politicians.

In 1566 an Act of Parliament forged the first link connecting Trinity House with seamarks. It described the Corporation as 'a company of the chiefist and most expert masters and governors of ships' and authorised them 'at their costs' to erect 'beacons, marks, and signs for the sea, in such place or places of the sea shores, and uplands near the sea coasts, or forelands of the sea, only for seamarks, as to them shall seem most meet, needful, and requisite, whereby the dangers may be avoided and escaped and ships the better come into their ports without peril'. The Act explained that Trinity House received this authority because of the destruction and removal of 'certain steeples, woods and other marks' being 'beacons and marks of ancient times accustomed for seafaring men'. By lack of such marks, 'divers ships with their goods and merchandises' sailing from foreign ports, and especially in the Thames estuary, had been 'miscarried, perished and lost in the sea, to the great detriment and hurt of the commonweal, and the perishing of no small number of people'

Doubts that had arisen as to whether this Act empowered the Corporation to place buoys in channels and off the shore, were dispelled by a grant by Queen Elizabeth in 1594 which widened the scope of its authority to include such seamarks.

Though there is no mention of lights or *phari* in any of these three documents—the term *pharos* had not yet been displaced by *lighthouse*—Trinity House persisted until about 1750 in claiming that *beacons* and *seamarks* were intended to include lighthouses and in consequence that these documents gave it the sole right to erect coastal lighthouses in England and Wales. But this claim never succeeded, as the Law Officers, backed by the Law Courts, took the view that both the Crown and Parliament also retained that power, and both acted accordingly. In any case, none of the three documents gave authority to charge dues on shipping to pay for the erection and maintenance of lighthouses. When each lighthouse was erected specific authority to collect dues for its maintenance had to be obtained from the Crown or Parliament.

Trinity House never sought to erect and maintain lighthouses, beacons and buoys for marking pier-heads and entrances to ports: that service has always been provided by individual local Authorities. The Point of Air lighthouse was a partial exception.

AUTHORITY TO ESTABLISH LIGHTHOUSES

In Britain, permission to erect lighthouses and charge dues on shipping was granted usually by the Crown, as also in France, by a document called *Letters Patent*, referred to simply as a patent, or infrequently by Act of Parliament. The practical effects were similar.

By these patents, the Crown, acting through the Crown Law Officers, allowed the erection of a lighthouse, subject to agreement with a landowner, and empowered the patentee to collect dues for a term of years from every vessel passing that lighthouse: these were paid when she touched at a British port. The Crown or the Government received a rent annually from the patentee. The patentee might be Trinity House or any individual, generally without any connection with the sea but with a local interest such as in ownership of the land where the lighthouse would be erected. The term *private light* was frequently used to denote a lighthouse not managed by Trinity House, even including those on lease from the Corporation.

A different class of Crown patent allowed an individual to exploit an invention for 14 years. In 1731 by using intentionally vague terms, David Avery obtained a patent of this type which he hoped would allow him to collect money from establishing a lightship at the Nore. But this type of patent was inappropriate for that purpose and when, by mooring his vessel, he disclosed his scheme, Trinity House, which he had circumvented, prevailed on the Law Officers to cancel the patent.

Parliament by its Acts granted the right to erect lighthouses and collect dues in special circumstances—for rebuilding the Eddystone and for erecting or maintaining Tynemouth, Skerries, Smalls and Spurn lighthouses. In each of these cases there had been a previous lease or patent and probably only an Act could clear up a complicated situation.

Though from the financial angle an English patent, grant or lease seems to have been considered a desirable possession, the profit was hardly excessive until the unforeseen growth of over-seas trade after 1750. Most of the patentees solved the practical difficulty of collecting the dues by making an arrangement with the Trinity House agent at the London Custom House who employed collectors at some 100 ports and havens and paid them a percentage commission. Frequently this agent and the Clerk or Secretary to Trinity House became persons of great influence in its affairs.

PETITIONS FOR PATENTS

According to the standard procedure for obtaining a patent adopted ultimately in England, Trinity House or some individual submitted a petition to the Crown accompanied by a statement signed extensively by shipmasters and merchants, explaining the need for a lighthouse at a particular place and declaring their willingness to pay dues of a certain amount. None of the monarchs concerned issued a patent directly—each application went to the Privy Council who obtained the expert opinion of Trinity House and often made enquiries in other quarters and then advised the King. To ensure proper management of the lighthouses, care was taken to grant patents only to persons of some substance and education, who lived near the sites or would employ a local agent to control the lightkeepers and provide fuel and stores.

Trinity House was seldom the first to propose lighthouses, perhaps only one—a light at Winterton—between 1620 and 1785, and it objected to many. In 1791 the Brethren declared that their policy was not to propose lighthouses until shipping interests demanded them, but this statement is hardly to be reconciled with their frequent answer when objecting to a proposal, namely, that if a light were necessary, Trinity House would have provided it. Between 1681 and 1780 Trinity House gave to individuals leases of all rights which it received under lighthouse patents and it was understood generally that the first proposer or projector of a lighthouse became its lessee. This was confirmed in the Longships lease of 1795 and the 'understanding' brought about the issue in 1796 of a rare pamphlet by Henry

Taylor, a pilot of North Shields, who claimed to have been the first to propose the Happis-burgh lighthouses and the Newarp lightship. He reproduced letters and other documents with some 400 signatures in support of his claims, and in 1792 he petitioned for a lease of the projected Goodwins lightship, as a reward for having proposed the lights. But Trinity House denied his priority and apparently declared that it would issue no more leases to individuals or reward projectors. However, its subsequent grants of the leases of the Longships lighthouse in 1795 and of Burnham lights in 1815 contradict these assertions.

COURT INFLUENCE

The 17th-century diarists mention instances when individuals desirous of obtaining a lighthouse patent approached courtiers who might influence members of the Council or even the King to accede to their desires, perhaps promising a share of the dues to be collected. In 1661 Captain Murford offered Samuel Pepys one-eighth of the profits, for advancing his application for a lighthouse patent. In another instance a definite sum was stated—'£100 per annum if you can bring it about'. The rewards seem to have been offered for getting the proposal to the Council, not for influencing its decision. It was customary at that time to make a gift in return for a favour. Even wealthy noblemen received a present of gold pieces in such an affair—'as a token of your kindness'.

Between 1662 and 1678 Andrew Marvell, the English poet and the representative in Parliament of the burgesses of Hull, took much trouble to further the interests of Hull Trinity House regarding proposed patents for the Spurn lights. He contacted persons of influence in London, prospective patentees, builders, lawyers, and Court officials, and approached the London Trinity House circumspectly, as its interests did not coincide with those of his clients. The 'endless worries and wearisome delays' and other complications surrounding his negotiations are shown by his letter written to Hull in 1662: 'There are strange reasons and junctures at Court in all businesses that must be catched or waived.' In that year he sent them an account for disbursements amounting to £79. 16. 8, including small sums to porters and servants but chiefly legal charges that were obviously necessary for examining leases and patents and drafting petitions. Several payments were made to Mr. Scroggs, evidently an attorney who attended the Privy Council. 'Spent on Mr. Scroggs at dinner 18/4.'

An impression has long been current that the Stuart monarchs were induced by their friends to give lighthouse patents indiscriminately and were rapacious in fixing rents. The suggestions are quite untrue. Many proposals for lighthouses were put forward, but there was no lavish issue of patents in the Tudor or Stuart reigns nor did the Crown grant any that the needs of navigation did not justify fully.

For 2 or possibly 3 lighthouses James I and Charles II issued patents to their friends and stated openly that the reason for their choice was that they had rendered services, but it is not unlikely that these persons were best fitted to carry out the duties involved and they did so satisfactorily. If the monarchs are to be censured for issuing patents to these persons, the proceedings of Trinity House cannot be overlooked. In 1665 it was instru-mental in obtaining the Harwich patent for Sir William Batten, its former Master, a transaction criticised by Pepys. From 1690 to 1837 it obtained from the Crown all patents for new lighthouses except Skerries and Smalls, which were special cases, and between 1690 and 1815 it passed on to its own nominees the rights to erect some 13 of these lighthouses and collect the dues and retain any profits after paying small rents and maintenance costs.

Henry VIII issued the patent or grant for Tynemouth (*c.* 1550). Edward VI, Mary and Elizabeth issued no patents for lighthouses. James I (1603–25) issued two patents to individuals (Dungeness, and Winterton with Wintertonness); Charles I (1625–49) issued two to individuals (North and South Forelands, and Orfordness); Charles II (1660–85) issued three to individuals (Harwich, Hunstanton and Spurn) and two to Trinity House (Winterton and Scilly). James II issued none and William and Mary granted one for the Eddystone to Trinity House in 1694. The patent issued by the Lord High Admiral (for the Lizard) in 1619 and apparently confirmed by Charles I in 1623, and that issued by Charles II to Sir John Clayton (for Corton, Flamborough, Farne and Cromer) were abandoned by the persons who obtained them, as they permitted merely the collection of dues paid voluntarily, which proved insufficient for maintenance. All these sites were eminently suitable for lighthouses. The lighthouses specified in the Minchin and Sunderland grants of 1667 and 1669 were merely incidental to the harbours and entirely local in purpose.

In a letter dated 1st December 1673 from Charles II to the 'Deane and Chapter of our Cath'all Church of Duresme [Durham]', stating that he had granted a patent to Clayton and Blake to erect lighthouses on the coast, including one on the Farne islands, it was recommended that when the Chapter should give a new lease of the islands the missive should reserve one acre of land 'for the erecting of a Lighthouse, together w'th a highway to it'. The missive should also specify ground on which to store coals and provide for a safe landing-place for boats and lodging for the lightkeeper, and permit him to use a spring of fresh water.

Patents for other lighthouses may have been issued and annulled, such as two issued by Charles II, the one to Sir Robert Reading for Irish lighthouses which was cancelled before 1671, and the other issued in 1662 to several individuals for St. Ann's Head light at Milford Haven, cancelled in 1668. The King apparently accepted without demur, and acted immediately upon, Parliament's petition for these cancellations.

The Reading patent seems to have been re-issued. The other 6 patents that were granted by James I and Charles II or were supported by them but which had lapsed or had been withdrawn were for lighthouses at the Lizard and St. Ann's, and Sir John Clayton's 4. Subsequently Trinity House declared these lighthouses essential for navigation and it received new patents for all.

After 1679, all the patents for new lighthouses were granted to Trinity House except one for Skerries which was replaced by an Act of Parliament, as also was the Crown lease for Smalls, and the monarch seems henceforth to have ceased to give personal consideration to lighthouse patents.

RENEWALS OF PATENTS

A patentee usually applied for renewal of his patent several years before it expired, that is, when he considered conditions for obtaining it were favourable. After 1822 it was laid down that a renewal could not be applied for until 5 years before expiry.

On each renewal the Crown made a charge in the form of a fine. This amounted to £3,000 for the Foreland lights about 1715. Such a large sum was fixed when the lighthouse accounts disclosed that for 10 years ending Lady Day 1713 the dues collected amounted to £15,061 and repairs and expenses to £4,081, leaving a clear profit of £10,980—nearly £1,100 per annum.

No less than five patents in succession were granted for Hunstanton. The first patent of 1665 was due to expire in 1726. About 1709, with 18 years to run, the condition of the rear lighthouse called for considerable repairs so the patentee petitioned for a renewal to ensure return of any capital expenditure. At that time, after payments including £16 for coals for the one light and £3 for candles for the other, the net profits were merely £43. On this occasion Trinity House claimed that the patent should be given to the Brethren under Queen Elizabeth's Charter, but the Attorney General advised the Crown against 'their pretensions', as he did in the case of the Skerries lighthouse, and a new patent for Hunstanton to terminate in 1760 was granted to the holders in February 1710 at a fine or duty of £15. For family reasons the holder applied for a third patent in October 1751 and received it, for a fine of £100. It would terminate in 1801. Similarly a fourth patent was obtained in 1785 to terminate in 1837, at a fine of £150. In accordance with the regulation of 1822, not until 1832 could another be sought. In that year this fifth patent was granted in anticipation, in the different form of a lease for 11 years from 1837 at a rent of £1 to the Crown along with 4/15ths of the profits, then totalling £458. The new lease required the surrender of the lighthouse—a wooden erection of little value—to the Government on the termination of the lease.

CHANGES IN PROCEDURE—1550–1837

The Crown issued the same sort of patent over this long period, in that it authorised the erection and maintenance of a lighthouse and the levy of dues on shipping, subject to an annual rent. Considerable changes took place in points of detail, particularly in the attitude of Trinity House towards the establishment of lighthouses. The changes fall broadly into five periods of years. Approximate dates of establishment are stated.

1. PROCEDURE BEFORE 1610

For the first English coastal lighthouse, at Tynemouth about 1550, the simplest kind of authorisation sufficed, that is, a Crown patent was issued to the individual who possessed the site at Tynemouth Castle.

Trinity House had no connection with lighthouses until the lights of Caistor and Lowestoft were established after 1600. Being considered at first as chiefly of value to local navigation, they were financed from the ample local buoyage dues which Trinity House controlled: thus patents to authorise the levy of additional dues were unnecessary. Presumably the Brethren had not yet had the idea of supporting their charities from lighthouse dues.

In 1610 the managers of lighthouses established in this period were as follows:

TRINITY HOUSE	OTHER HOLDERS
Caistor, a pair of lighthouses, 1600	Tynemouth, *c.* 1550
Lowestoft, pair, 1609	

2. PROCEDURE 1610–75

In this period Trinity House established no lighthouses. Individuals erected 11 with a Crown patent and 1 with a patent from the Lord High Admiral, the only instance of one not from the Crown. The patentees who erected lighthouses at the Lizard (1619 to 1625) and Corton (1675 to 1678) discontinued them soon after erection because of the insufficiency of the voluntary dues collected. A lighthouse erected at St. Ann's Head, Milford Haven, was discontinued in 1668 after Parliament objected to dues being levied on the demand of the patentees. The patent seems to have been granted in 1662 and to have permitted the acceptance of dues paid voluntarily.

The refusal of Trinity House to erect a lighthouse at Dungeness (1616), when invited to do so by the Privy Council, may have influenced the Council against it when it proposed to erect lighthouses later. During the 17th century the Brethren opposed most of the petitions by individuals for a lighthouse patent, sometimes not for navigational objections only, as in the case of the Lizard about 1620.

The erection of lighthouses at sites which Trinity House had objected to previously may point to a failure to anticipate the needs of navigation. In the case of the Spurn lighthouses in 1672 it continued opposition to the lighthouses when other bodies interested in navigation objected no longer. It was suggested, however, that the acquiescence of the Trinity Houses of Hull and Newcastle in the proposal was gained by offers from the prospective patentees of annual contributions of £40 or so to their charities rather than by convincing arguments.

In 1675 the managers of new lights established in this period were as follows:

TRINITY HOUSE	OTHER HOLDERS	TRINITY HOUSE	OTHER HOLDERS
None	Dungeness, 1616	None	Orfordness, pair, 1636
	Winterton, 1617		Harwich, pair, 1665
	Wintertonness, pair, 1617		Hunstanton, pair, 1666
	North Foreland, 1634		Spurn, pair, 1672–8
	South Foreland, pair, 1634		Corton, 1675

3. PROCEDURE 1676–80

A change in the usual negative attitude of Trinity House towards establishing new lighthouses was brought about principally by the success of Sir John Clayton in obtaining a patent in 1669 for as many as four lighthouses for all of which he erected the towers. Only his Corton lighthouse had been lighted by 1675. Trinity House destroyed Sir John's expectation that voluntary dues would meet the expense of its maintenance when in 1676 it replaced one of its Lowestoft towers by a new tower and a stronger light for which it charged no dues. The Brethren let it be known that they did this out of their own funds: 'what we are doing at Lostoffe, we do without any expectation of profit'.

Soon after, navigation required a second light at Winterton and the Brethren proposed to make the customary petition to the Crown for a patent authorising the levy of dues. Samuel Pepys, Master of Trinity House and Secretary at the Admiralty, reminded them that in the use of their funds for such a purpose lay the only advantage they had over Clayton and others who sought to obtain patents for lighthouses and hoped to make a profit thereby. He counselled them to erect lighthouses at their own expense and trust that the Crown or

Parliament would recognise their generous action by subsequently granting dues for maintenance. He deplored that the Brethren had not 'timeily apply'd themselves to the providing of those lights which, through our failure, have been done by private men and found as useful as those which Trinity House has been the founders of'. His advice seems to have been followed: they established the new Winterton tower in 1677 and the patent is dated 1678.

Perhaps spurred to action by proposals by prospective patentees for a light at the Scilly Isles, Trinity House erected a light there itself and got a patent in 1780. This patent and that for Winterton permitted surplus dues, after payment of expenses of maintenance, to be devoted to its charities. The Scillies patent differs from others in stating that the dues should be reasonable—it fixed no rates.

In 1683, supported by a petition from shipmasters alleging neglect of the Tynemouth light, the Elder Brethren endeavoured to persuade the Crown to transfer it to themselves, but failed to get this or the Spurn lights.

In 1680 the managers of new lights established in this period were as follows:

TRINITY HOUSE	OTHER HOLDERS
Winterton, 1677	None
Scilly, 1680	

4. PROCEDURE 1681–1784

Petitioners for lighthouse patents expected that they would need to make every effort to circumvent the opposition of Trinity House, but when Whitfield made his proposal to build a lighthouse on the Eddystone he applied direct to the Brethren for their assistance. This created a new situation, as their keenness to further his humanitarian scheme balanced their aversion to undertaking the difficult work themselves or to financing it. But they applied for and obtained a patent with the usual authority to levy dues, and made a bargain with Whitfield that was novel in English lighthouse affairs, namely, that he should build the tower at his expense and divide any profits with them. They made a somewhat similar arrangement with Winstanley when he took Whitfield's place. After the destruction of Winstanley's lighthouse in 1703, they obtained an Act of Parliament to entitle them to rebuild it and leased their rights to the dues to Colonel Lovett for 99 years for a rent of £100. The temporary establishment of a lightship marking the Eddystone Rock from 1756 to 1759 should be mentioned here because the Elder Brethren held that under the terms of the patent granted for this temporary light, it must be continued on its station in 1758 although Smeaton offered to show a light from his uncompleted tower which would have allowed its withdrawal.

They objected to a proposal by Captain Davison for a light on the Skerries on the grounds that it was unnecessary. Their usual claim that they alone were entitled to erect lighthouses was turned down by the Law Officers about 1709. Davison and his supporters did not establish a light: their proposal seems to have lapsed. In 1714 the Crown granted a patent for this lighthouse on a rental of £5 directly to William Trench. In 1730 an Act of Parliament with extraordinary generosity gave his family the right to the dues for ever.

The arrangement made at the Eddystone whereby Trinity House obtained the patent or grant and then leased its rights for a fixed rent, appealed greatly to the Corporation and it made similar arrangements for other lights until 1786. An exception was the Smalls where it did not oppose an application by John Phillips for a lease from the Crown, believing that he would not succeed in building a lighthouse. But when he did so, and required money for repairs, Trinity House obtained an Act of Parliament and leased its rights to him for 99 years at a rent of £5. This lease replaced the former Crown lease. Another modification in the usual arrangement was made at the Point of Air lighthouse in the Dee estuary.

The rents received by Trinity House from its leases of lighthouses varied from £5 for Flatholm to £300 for the Dudgeon lightship.

Several reasons can be suggested for the practice, adopted by Trinity House in this period, of following the precedent of the Eddystone by not erecting and maintaining lighthouses between 1680 and 1780, but passing on its rights to individuals. One was the trouble in erection and management, a type of work that was foreign to the shipmasters with long sea experience who became Elder Brethren. Local agents had to be appointed to manage their four lighthouses. One supervised the early group of Caistor-Lowestoft-Winterton lights and another managed the Scillies light of 1680. Another likely reason was that the capital cost of erection would reduce their charitable funds and there was a risk that the dues from a new lighthouse might prove insufficient to cover its maintenance. The attention of the Elder Brethren was taken up continuously by pilotage in the Thames, coastal buoyage, and management of their charities.

Before 1785 the unreliability and other disadvantages of contemporary lighthouses tended to obscure a view of their possible ultimate value. Their unreliability was certainly appreciated by the Corporation who may have been disinclined to maintain them and thus were apt to incur the frequent complaints of mariners. Whatever the reasons, Trinity House was obviously glad not to undertake the tasks of erecting and maintaining lighthouses and was satisfied to accept small fixed rents from its lessees instead of larger but uncertain sums brought in directly by the dues.

It is curious that not until 1714 was the first lighthouse established permanently on the west coast of England, a delay certainly not due to a lack of shipping in that quarter. Around 1670 Trinity House expressed approval of lights there, yet in 1709 it declared that if a light were required at the Skerries, the Brethren would have established it. Did they not feel any obligation to assist seamen in that area, or to spur others to do so? Is it possible that they had little personal experience of navigating there? The facts are contradictory and one must suppose that they felt the duty lay with others. Navigation to and from London was their paramount consideration. Undoubtedly, seamen owed much to the individuals who undertook to establish the private lights.

In 1780 the managers of new lights erected in this period were as follows:

TRINITY HOUSE	OTHER HOLDERS	TRINITY HOUSE	OTHER HOLDERS
None	Eddystone, 1698	None	Nore lightship, 1731
	Milford, pair, 1714		Dudgeon lightship, 1736
	Portland, pair, 1716		Flatholm, 1737
	Skerries, 1717		Lizard, pair, 1752
	St. Bees, 1718		Smalls, 1776
	Cromer, 1719		Point of Air, 1777
	Casquets, three, 1724		Farnes, two, 1778

5. PROCEDURE AFTER 1785

In accordance with the usual procedure of 1680–1781, Trinity House obtained a patent in 1782 for three lighthouses at Needles, Hurst and St. Catherine's, in the Isle of Wight, but the negotiations for a lease which began in 1781 broke down in 1785 because of the onerous terms which their projector proposed. Accordingly, the Brethren undertook their erection themselves, these being the first lighthouses to be built by them since the Scillies in 1680.

In 1785 the Corporation had a new outlook on lighthouses. Several leases were about to expire and the lighthouses falling thus into its possession would require management. By undertaking this, its charities would be benefited enormously from receipts of the entire dues. Brighter and more reliable lights were available from parabolic reflectors and argand lamps manufactured in London. The increase of trade called for more and better lighthouses. Perhaps the example of the Scots in coming to London to obtain Acts of Parliament to establish public Trusts to erect and manage lighthouses on the Clyde, and generally round their coasts, impressed it. The total effect of such influences encouraged the Brethren to erect new lighthouses themselves and undertake the management of those in existence as the leases expired.

Their experience with various types of reflectors since about 1779, though clearly not successful enough, inspired them to improve lighting, and what they saw on their visit to Dieppe in 1787–8 showed the type of reflector and lamp that should be adopted. So they experimented at Blackheath and Portland and, commencing in 1788–9, fitted reflectors, lenses and argand lamps at some of their lighthouses and pressed their lessees and the patentees of private lighthouses to improve them similarly.

Between 1785 and 1800 Trinity House erected several new lights in England under the usual patents. In two cases it gave leases as before, for Longships and Mumbles. Building a lighthouse on the Longships Rock (originally intended to be on the Wolf Rock) may have seemed so difficult and expensive that the Brethren may have looked on the certain rent of £100 as sufficient benefit to their funds. Later, they took over its management from the patentee. The Mumbles was far from London and though its situation offered less difficulty and risk than the Longships, a local agent would have been required to arrange maintenance. This consideration may have induced them to treat it similarly.

In 1800 the managers of new lights erected since 1784 were as follows:

TRINITY HOUSE	OTHER HOLDERS
Needles, 1786	Walney, 1790
Hurst, pair, 1786	Mumbles, 1794
Owers lightship, 1788	Longships, 1795
Happisburgh, pair, 1791	
Newarp lightship, 1791	
Goodwins lightship, 1795	
Sunk lightship, 1798	

After 1800 Trinity House continued to obtain patents for new lights, but passed on only one on a lease, for a pair of towers at Burnham, to the Reverend D. Davies in 1815.

During the wars which ceased in 1815, the British Admiralty moored lightships to assist the Navy, at Galloper, Gull and Bembridge. Trinity House took over the Galloper in 1816 and the Gull in 1826 but charged no dues, so patents were unnecessary.

In 1819 the managers of new lights erected since 1800 were as follows:

TRINITY HOUSE	OTHER HOLDERS
Galloper lightship, 1803	Gull lightship, 1809
Flamborough, 1806	Bembridge lightship, 1812
South Stack, 1809	Burnham, pair, 1815
Stanford lightship, 1815	

PROFITS FROM LIGHTHOUSES AFTER 1800

Owing to the development of trade, the dues received from shipping increased greatly for most lighthouses, and by 1800 the public, frowning at the large profits, forgot the moderate profits and even the losses of the original patentees or lessees. Some of the rates permitted by the patents had been reduced, but for the 11 years 1805-15 the free profits after expenses which Trinity House received from lighthouses totalled £358,000, against which new seamarks cost £50,000. The difference of £308,000 was diverted to Trinity House charities. In 1818 these benefited 7,024 pensioners and the inmates of 165 almshouses which the Corporation maintained. The annual sum which it spent in charity increased from about £20,000 in 1805 to £27,000 in 1815.

The British Government appeared to accept as permanent the system of lighthouse patents: in 1808 Parliament passed an Act authorising the Treasury to grant leases of lighthouses for 31 years.

About 1815, when challenged, Trinity House defended the system of taking profits from the lighthouse dues, disclosed freely the sums spent to help seamen and their dependants, and proved that the need for this charity was glaring. But shipowners and traders contended that funds for charity should be provided from some source other than dues raised from shipping for the stated purpose of providing seamarks. This view was emphasised when Manx and Liverpool traders applied to Trinity House for the erection of lighthouses in the Isle of Man. It proposed such high dues—which the Brethren explained included a contribution to their charities—that the traders insisted that the proposed sea lights of the island should be placed under the jurisdiction of the Northern Lighthouse Board whose lower dues were devoid of sums for charity. An Act of 1815 authorised this arrangement which holds to the present day.

When the Admiralty lightship at the Galloper sandbank was transferred to Trinity House in 1816 the Brethren did not apply for a patent but maintained it out of their other lightship dues. Similarly, Greenwich Hospital, which had become owner of the Forelands lighthouses, maintained the Gull lightship out of its dues.

PURCHASE OF PATENTS AND GRANTS AFTER 1822

By an Act of Parliament of 1822 Trinity House was enabled to purchase private interests in lighthouses and proceeded to do so, when the patentees asked for sums that appeared to be moderate after an actuarial investigation had been made into the varying receipts from dues and the different periods for which leases had still to run. It bought Flatholm in 1823 for £16,057; the Farnes in 1824 for £36,446 and Burnham in 1829 for

£16,057. In 1832 the Government authorised purchase of the North and South Forelands for £8,400.

In 1834 Trinity House received £117. 5. 0 in rents from lighthouses and buoys, including Longships £100, Smalls £10, Mumbles £5 and Hunstanton £1.

PARLIAMENTARY INQUIRY OF 1834

The profits from lighthouses continued to increase to such an extent that mounting dissatisfaction resulted in the appointment in 1834 of a Parliamentary Committee which made a thorough investigation of British and Irish lighthouse affairs in all departments and demanded and published the accounts of each lighthouse, general and local, for the year 1832. From the six lighthouses still held by individuals under patents direct from the Crown (Harwich, Dungeness, Winterton, Wintertonness, Orfordness and Hunstanton), the total free profits were shared as to £9,224 by the patentees and £10,425 by the Crown. The three lighthouses (Tynemouth, Spurn and Skerries) which had been granted to individuals in perpetuity by Acts of Parliament yielded them £24,176; and the three lighthouses (Smalls, Longships and Mumbles) which were held by individuals under lease from Trinity House brought £17,196 to the patentees. The ports, too, profited considerably from their lighthouses: Liverpool gained £8,422 clear of expenses from six lighthouses and one lightship.

The Committee described the leases by Trinity House of Smalls and Longships as 'examples of improvidence and mismanagement exceeded only' by the three grants in perpetuity given by Parliament itself. But Trinity House could defend its actions by pointing to the conditions when the lighthouses were built. Like the Eddystone, they were very real adventures. Should Trinity House have furthered these projects to the extent of reducing the funds much needed for its own charities? If Phillips and Winstanley decided to attempt what all experienced men considered impracticable, should not they use their own funds and be allowed to reap reward if successful?

As a Parliamentary Committee in 1822 had directed that no more extensions of lighthouse patents should be made, the 1834 Committee found Government Departments at fault in granting extensions of patents for Winterton and Orfordness in 1826 and for Hunstanton in 1832.

The Committee considered that the surplus dues from only Scilly and Winterton, the latter discontinued in 1791, should have been diverted to Trinity House charities, these being the only patents that mentioned that destination. The action of Trinity House in passing on to individuals by leases the privileges granted to it by patents was referred to, and it seems not improbable that had this action been challenged in the Law Courts, objection might have been upheld.

ABOLITION OF PATENTS AND GRANTS

Following the Committee's investigations, an Act was passed in 1836 authorising the purchase by Trinity House of the patents of the coastal lighthouses still remaining in private hands. £302,419 in all was paid for Harwich, Hunstanton, Dungeness and the five lighthouses at Winterton, Wintertonness and Orfordness which were held under patents;

£211,164 for the Smalls and Longships which were still leased by Trinity House; and £879,193 for Skerries, Spurn and Tynemouth. Trinity House and the Government had failed to agree with the owners of the Spurn and Skerries lights as to the purchase prices and had recourse to arbitration by local juries which awarded sums of £309,531 and £444,984 to the respective owners. The purchase price for Hunstanton included recompense for cancellation of the lease granted 5 years in advance of expiry of the existing lease. The Mumbles lighthouse which gave little profit was taken over as part of Swansea port about 1835.

The last patent to be granted for a lighthouse was issued in 1837: it enabled Trinity House to erect a lighthouse at Start Point.

The Act of 1836 placed Trinity House on the same basis in England as the Northern Lighthouse Board has been put in Scotland by the Act of 1789. From 1837 Trinity House could erect a lighthouse in England without a patent or an Act, and instead of dues being levied separately for each lighthouse a uniform rate was charged irrespective of whether vessels passed one or more lighthouses in one voyage.

After the Act of 1836 came into force, all profit to individuals or to Trinity House from coastal lighthouses ceased, and the dues collected were devoted entirely to lighthouse purposes. By 1841 the transfer of private coastal lighthouses from individuals to Trinity House had been completed.

PATENTS AND GRANTS IN SCOTLAND AND IRELAND

In Scotland and Ireland the position was never complicated by a Corporation like Trinity House. In only one instance did individuals obtain a patent for a lighthouse in Scotland—for the Isle of May in 1636. The Scots Parliament and the Convention of Royal Burghs of Scotland confirmed this grant of a patent through the Scots Privy Council.

The Scots Parliament was merged with the English Parliament in 1707 and with the Irish Parliament in 1801, but for some years later, the patent rolls of the three countries were kept independently. The Scots or the British Parliaments authorised the establishment of all Scottish lights, also the purchase by the Commissioners of Northern Lighthouses for £30,000 in 1814 of the Isle of May and the dues for its light. This formed a precedent for similar action in England.

For Ireland, a patent of 1665 authorised an individual to erect and levy dues for 6 lighthouses, but in 1704 Parliament placed under a Public Board those that had been established and subsequently transferred them on several occasions to somewhat similar Boards.

PART THREE

ILLUMINATION OF
EARLY
LIGHTHOUSES

XVI

ILLUMINANTS AND OPTICAL APPARATUS

167. West Kapelle fixed light. This parabolic
reflector light, the first in Holland, was established
in 1818 on a church tower. This view of the
lantern which had unusual roof ventilators shows
13 of the 15 reflectors and argand lamps burning
rape oil (Valk)

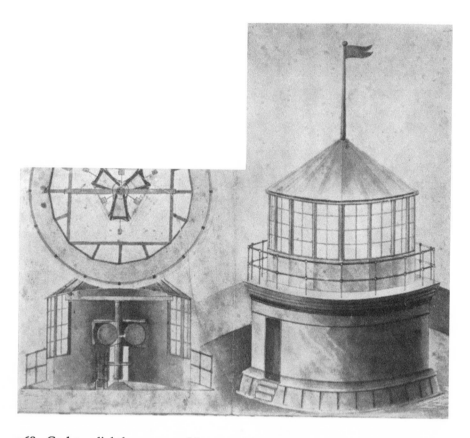

168. Carlsten lighthouse near Marstrand in Sweden. This drawing *c.* 1820 shows the first revolving light in the world, established by Norberg in 1781. The top left plan shows 3 large lamps each serving 2 reflectors, and smaller lamps and reflectors added between the pairs of vertical frames. The lower left elevation was intended to represent 2 of the large reflectors with their lamp but the reflectors were cut vertically. The apparatus turned on a pivot raised from the floor

XVI. ILLUMINANTS AND OPTICAL APPARATUS

This Section explains details of the illumination of early lighthouses from which their value to navigation can be appreciated.

A. ILLUMINANTS

WOOD FIRES

The principal lighthouses of Antiquity carried wood fires burning in the open air, perhaps under a roof; but after the Dark Ages, as soon as glass panes could be made without great expense, candles and oil lamps in glazed lanterns replaced them in the Mediterranean and, along with coal fires, in north-west Europe.

The last well-known lighthouses to exhibit wood fires were Cordouan and Chassiron in France in 1727 and 1782 respectively, probably Anholt in Denmark about 1800 and Utö in Finland temporarily during the wars of 1807–14. It is possible that small navigation lights burned wood later in the Baltic where forests skirted the sea. Three wood fires which served as navigation lights on the wild shores of Kamchatka are listed as having been replaced by oil lights about 1855.

The chief objection to wood fires lay in their quick burning, which called for transport of large quantities of bulky fuel. The disappearance of a forest from the island of Anholt was said to be due to the insatiable demand for fuel for its lighthouse fire.

TORCHES AND PITCH FIRES

Though used extensively in Europe for ordinary

169. An English coastal beacon to give warning of sea-raiders, from a sea-chart c. 1690

outside lighting before 1820, torches seldom served for seamarks: such small bodies of fire fluctuated too wildly in light value. After several years' use, they were discontinued at Fréhel in France in 1710 as a roof failed to protect them from extinction by rain. So great was the volume of smoke which torches produced that their use within closed lanterns or glass screens was impracticable: soot sullied the inside of the panes and soon blocked the emission of light-rays.

Maps and charts about 1600 depict a score of gibbet-type beacons on the south and east shores of England. These did not benefit navigation but stood ready to broadcast a warning of attack by sea-raiders more surely and quickly than messengers could carry it. Their flare came from cressets or iron baskets holding crude torches made up of coiled rope smeared with pitch. Somewhat similar beacons served for minor navigation signals on the Baltic shores. During the construction of the towers at the Eddystone and Bell Rocks, torches or flambeaux were necessary for evening work but did not serve as navigation signals.

CANDLES

Provided the wicks of candles, those made from tallow in particular, were trimmed frequently to stop guttering and the consequent incomplete combustion which produced smoke and soot, they gave a comparatively steady flame and so afforded the cleanest form of illuminant for sea-lights before the invention of the smokeless argand lamp in 1782. They were not the *snuffless* candles formed by plaiting the wick dipped in chemicals: that excellent variety was invented after 1820, when candles were no longer used at lighthouses of importance.

At English lighthouses the sizes of candles varied from 3 to the pound at Caistor in 1628, to 1 pound each at Harwich in 1676. In 1777 Hutchinson mentioned candles of 2 pounds each. Large candles, of which 60 lighted the Eddystone in 1713, gave longer burning but the illumination emitted by all sizes did not exceed 3 standard candles per candle, the standard being a spermaceti candle of 6 to the pound burning 120 grains per hour. When short of victuals, lightkeepers turned

170. Harwich low light in 1712 with candles burning in a hanging lantern

to tallow and beeswax candles for cooking and even for eating. Candle-ends were among the highly-prized perquisites of lightkeepers, as they were of most persons in service, including those of high rank who waited on Royalty—a year's accumulation of candle-ends had a high monetary value.

Accounts of the North Shields harbour lighthouses in 1541 detail purchases of candles, such as expenditures of *xviii pence* (1s. 6d.) for a dozen pounds and *iiiis, iiid.* (4s. 3d.) for 33 pounds. At Workington harbour in 1801 small horn-lanterns containing candles were warped to a pole outwith the pierhead and at Harwich between 1712 and 1813 the lantern at the low lighthouse contained candles. At the Eddystone lighthouse in 1810 oil lamps and reflectors took the place of candles weighing about half-a-pound apiece which, to the number of 24 and 12″ in length, were arranged in the two circular tiers of a candelabrum. Each candle might be reckoned as giving light equal to that from 2·8 standard candles, a total of 67 candlepower. If the keepers did not raise the candelabrum completely, after lowering it for snuffing, light from the lower tier became hidden from the seamen as the candles burned low in their sockets: the reduced illumination drew complaints from shipping. One of

the Wintertonness lights was the last British coastal lighthouse to show candles. It was discontinued after 1828 when its low candlepower made it useless for navigation.

Ezekiel Walker asserted in 1802–3 that the illumination obtained from candles was proportional to the material consumed. By setting a candle at an angle of 30° to the perpendicular he avoided snuffing and increased the light.

Many lighthouses and port lights on the continent of Europe were served by candles. At Dieppe in the winter months around 1785 one candle marked the harbour entrance. It was complained of as being indistinguishable from the lights of dwelling-houses and as being often extinguished.

The lanterns provided at navigation lights to shelter candles were generally one foot to two feet in diameter and had translucent or glass panes let into the sides. It was desirable that while they should have good ventilation they should also be free from draughts that might play variably on the flames, but it was none too easy to fulfil both conditions. Candles seem to have had an

171. The candelabrum of Smeaton's Eddystone lighthouse *c.* 1800

advantage over oil lamps in offering greater convenience in transport and storage of supplies, but candle lights were more expensive in maintenance.

COAL FIRES

Introduction of coal fire beacons

The increasing use of coal in Europe after 1500 extended to lighthouses where it met with favour as being a more compact fuel or illuminant than wood, as burning longer especially in rainy weather, and as requiring less attention by the keepers. The proximity of coal mines in north-west Europe induced the establishment of coal fires in that region, but not in the Mediterranean as the transport by sea from Britain made their cost prohibitive: fortunately, candles and oil lamps sufficed for the average clearer atmosphere.

As Tynemouth, the earliest British lighthouse of value

to coastal shipping, was sited close to an extensive coal-field it was convenient to provide a coal fire when it was established about 1550. Mining in Britain developed so rapidly that by 1600 the amount of coal produced exceeded 5 times the total raised on the continent of Europe and this ready supply encouraged its use for Dungeness and the Lizard, the next lighthouses, solely to serve coastal navigation, that were set up in England.

The proximity of coal-fields to the first Scots light-house, on the Isle of May in 1636, also influenced the choice of coal for its illumination. British coal, parti-cularly from Scotland, proved to be more suitable than coal from other countries in giving the intense light desired for fire beacons, and was exported before 1810 to many European lighthouses ranging from France to the Baltic.

Preference for coal fires

Before 1770 seamen preferred a coal fire for a seamark: they could readily pick out its flaming aspect from afar and identify it as a lighthouse but they could not distinguish a single coal fire lighthouse from another. In full blaze it transcended all other navigation lighting, the flames of candles and oil lamps appearing as mere

172. The typical open coal fire at Dungeness before conversion to oil and reflectors in 1792

glimmering tapers. After 1780 the preference for coal fires waned, as the advantage of parabolic reflectors conjoined with oil lamps became understood. It is easy now for many reasons to condemn coal fires but when it is remembered that not until 1858 was the last coal fire lighthouse discontinued in Europe, one is forced to wonder whether such fire beacons were not relatively more efficient than is generally supposed and what were the circumstances in which shipping preferred them.

Coal fire versus parabolic light

The only recorded comparative test of a coal fire and a reflector light was made at Rouen in 1774, as described in Section XII. It resulted in the preference of a coal fire to an oil lamp with a parabolic reflector supplied by Hutchinson. The problem to be solved then was how best to light an extensive angle of the horizon. The decision was right: one parabolic reflector was inadequate for the purpose. The idea of arranging a number of reflectors in a circle was not put forward at that time.

The number of coal fires

The number of coal beacons compared with other forms of navigation lights in England and Scotland increased from 1 out of 1 before 1600, to 12 out of 15 in 1700, and to 21 out of 26 in 1760, exclusive of the Eddystone lighthouse and the two English lightships which necessarily were lit by candles or oil lamps. To give distinction, or to guide ships through channels by setting up pairs of towers in line, 10 of these 21

lighthouses of 1760 had additional accompanying lights, 5 being coal fires and 5 oil or candle lights. At the Casquets 3 coal fires formed a single cluster simply to give distinction. In Britain about 1780 oil reflector lights gradually superseded coal fires, St. Bees, the last, being extinguished in 1823.

The French Atlantic coast had 5 main lighthouses in 1700, of which 1 burned wood and 1 coal; and in 1760 out of 6, 4 burned coal and 1 wood or coal. Coal fires for lighthouses ceased in France in 1782 but in 1793 the French Government promised navigators to revert to a coal fire at Cordouan whenever the cessation of hostilities should allow the import of coal from Britain, a promise never kept because reflector lights showed their superiority in France before 1815, when peace had been established.

In Sweden 4 lights out of 5 burned coal in 1700 and 4 out of 6 in 1760 and the number of coal fires increased to 11 in 1838, but all were discontinued by 1854.

The last coal fire in Europe, at Villa in Norway, ceased in 1858.

Hutchinson's assessment of coal fires

Writing in 1777, William Hutchinson gives an account of the defects of coal fires, which is valuable because as a seafarer he had long experience of them: 'It is well known from reason as well as experience, that open coal fire light, exposed to all winds and weathers, cannot be made to burn and show a constant steady blaze to be seen at a sufficient distance with any certainty, for in storms of wind, when lights are most wanted, these open fires are made to burn furiously, and very soon away, so as to melt the very iron work about the grate, and in cold weather, when it snows, hails or rains hard, the keepers of the lights do not care to expose themselves to the bad weather, [so] are apt to neglect them till the fire is too low, then throw on a large quantity of coals at a time, which darkens the light for a time till the fire burns up again, and in some weathers it must be difficult to make them burn with any brightness. And when they are inclosed in a glassed close light-house, they are apt to smoke the windows greatly, nor afford so much constant blaze (that gives the most light) as oil lamps, or tallow candles of two pounds each, but these last require often snuffing to prevent their light from becoming dull, so that after trial of these different sorts of lights, we have fixed upon lamp lights, with proper reflectors behind them to answer best here at Liverpool.'

Hutchinson's conclusion was limited to Liverpool where the problem of showing a narrow sector of light along a navigable channel was solved by erecting one large parabolic reflector with an oil lamp.

Varieties of coal fires

Like wood fires, coal fires at first were burned unprotected in the open air: at lights of major importance, in fixed grates on towers; and at lesser lights, in an iron basket of less capacity hoisted on a pole or at the side of a building. Occasionally, as at Tynemouth, a roof alone or a vertical screen protected the open fire on a tower, but such partial shelter seldom gave satisfaction. About

173. A typical lever light burning coals
c. 1800

1625 Pedersen Groves in Denmark invented the *vippefyr* or lever light in which an iron basket containing burning coals was raised very simply some 14′ to 30′ above ground-level or above the top of a tower.

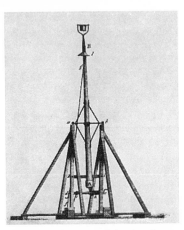

174. Smeaton's temporary lever
light at Spurn Point in 1785

Smeaton visited Spurn Point in 1767 and approved of the principle of the lever light established there and designed an improved form, specifying such details as a small umbrella to protect the rope from falling cinders. He found that with a well-balanced beam the operation of filling the bucket with a shovelful of coals and hoisting

it could be carried out in a few minutes and eased the keepers' work. The umbrella *l* appears in figure 174.

Some coal fires were enclosed completely in glazed lanterns and gave a smaller yet steadier glow: these made less demand on the attention of the lightkeepers and consumed less coal than open fires and thus alleviated somewhat the problem of transport of large quantities of fuel, always an important consideration, particularly when it had to be carried across the sea to remote and isolated sites like the Scilly Isles, the Casquets and the Skerries.

The total number of coal fires enclosed completely in glazed lanterns was small and they were found notably

175. Harwich high light before 1815—an
enclosed coal fire with a brass reflector

in England before 1780 and in Denmark, Sweden, Norway and Holland after 1800. Of the coal fires at 21 sites in Britain in 1760, the grates at 9 were enclosed in accordance with the preference of Trinity House. Enclosing the fire at Kullen in Sweden in 1817 was so successful that the Swedes were encouraged to enclose 6 more, the last at Holmögadd in 1838. Enclosing coal fires did not always gain approval. With the concurrence of the Trinity Houses of London and Dover, the Forelands coal fires were enclosed in 1719 but complaints from seamen forced a return to open fires in 1730. Perhaps the lanterns had been designed badly or the grates were too small or, maybe, sailors remembered the maximum blaze of the open fires as being more conspicuous than the steadier but lesser blaze from the enclosed grates.

Mirrors and bellows to increase blaze

Mirrors proved of little value with coal fires. A brass plate placed behind the small enclosed coal fire at Harwich high lighthouse between at least 1790 and 1809 and metal plates which Bitry set above the open coal fire at Cordouan in 1727 may have increased the glow slightly, but the deposit of soot soon destroyed any reflection from them.

The use of bellows increased the brightness of coal fires and was resorted to at many lighthouses.

Funnels to increase blaze

Funnels built in towers to lead draughts up to the grates had a beneficial effect in improving combustion and increasing the blaze of coal fires. This method was adopted by John Smeaton at the Spurn in 1776 and it was used at Danish, Swedish and Norwegian lighthouses

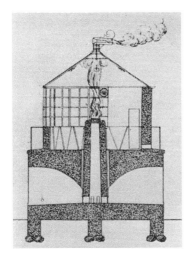

176. The enclosed coal fire at Fakkebjerg in Denmark in 1804 with a draught led to the grate from below

after 1800. These were all enclosed lighthouses. The funnel system was also fitted by Polheimer at an open fire at Kullen in 1792 and proposed in France about 1740.

Smeaton took considerable trouble in designing the enclosed coal fire for the high light at Spurn Point. The arrangement is shown in figure 177. Coals were hoisted to the lantern in a basket by rope and windlass through the tube S R. Ashes from the grate in the centre fell into the *receptacle* L and heated the air-stream entering the tube M by any of 8 inlet-pipes such as K, built into the tower so that each could be opened according to the direction of the wind. In the calmest weather the heated air passing up the tube M N caused a draught through the grill and blew up the fire to a steady glow. The ashes, raked out of the floor of the *receptacle*, were tipped into a vertical chute with opening V which carried them to ground level. The smoke from the fire passed through a copper roof tube O, the draught in the lantern to drive it out being varied by adjusting numerous air inlets y y fitted round the lantern base. The grate measured 15″ in diameter and 4″ in depth and had the remarkably small capacity of 0·35 cubic feet. The

induced draught coming from below blew up the coals into a glowing mass of an intensity far greater than achieved at any other coal fires. Unfortunately the

177. Smeaton's enclosed coal fire at the rear Spurn tower of 1776 (Record)

small body of fire was consumed so quickly that unceasing vigilance by the lightkeeper was required in stoking it. The lantern had a *decagon conical roof* composed of 10 flagstones.

178. A typical Swedish coal grate as at Kullen in 1791 (Polheimer)

The Kullen grate before 1791 was drum-shaped with a diameter of 1′ 10″ and depth of 18″. The grate which Polheimer fitted in 1792 rested on a pipe K as shown in figure 179 and consisted of a circular grill g g of triangular iron bars, some 22″ in diameter sunk 18″ below the top. The pipe K brought air from 6 apertures in the lower part of the tower which, according to the direction of the wind, could be opened or closed at will to regulate the draught through the grill. The reduction in the coal consumpt which Polheimer obtained was only proportional to the reduction in size of the grate, but he achieved a more glowing fire.

179. Polheimer's coal fire of 1792 with a draught led to the grate from below

Capacities of grates

The grates or braziers of coal fires consisted of vertical and horizontal bars of cast-iron or wrought-iron. The shape of fixed grates was cylindrical or the sides tapered inwards to the grill at the base which was either set close to an iron or stone hearth or raised clear on legs up to 12″ in length. There was no standard design of grate: each was made locally and details were altered often in the effort to reduce the wastage of fire-bars from the heat or according as it was desired to burn more coal or less.

The grate which is preserved at the Scilly Isles has diameters at base of 2′ 9″, tapering to 2′ 0″ and spreading to 2′ 11½″ at top. The heights of the lower and upper portions are 3′ 6″ and 1′ 0″. The cast iron is 1″ thick. There is an aperture in the side for raking out the ashes.

180. The coal grate preserved at the Scilly lighthouse

Grates had capacities in cubic feet somewhat as follows:

Unprotected	Isle of May (1799) 19·5	St. Bees 4·7
	Skerries 11·8	Kullen (1791) 3·3
	Isle of May (1780) 9·0	Kullen (1793) 1·8
	Nidingen 7·9	"Danish vippefyr 6·1"
	Lindesnes 5·1	"Spurn lever (1776) 3·1"

Roofed	Normandy (1775) 11·5	Ostend (c. 1790) 10·0
Enclosed	Scilly 7·3	Spurn (1776) 0·35
	Tynemouth (1800) 5·0	

Consumpts of coals

The consumpt of coals varied primarily according to whether the fires were open or enclosed and to the number of hours' burning annually; and from time to time, according to the prevalence of winds, the rainfall and, not least, the skill of the keeper in stoking his fire economically while satisfying seamen as well as his master.

Annual consumpts of coals were noted approximately in tons:

Isle of May (1799) 350–400	Scilly 107
Isle of May (1786) 200	Forelands (1698) 100 each
Cumbrae (after 1761) 180	Kullen (1793) 61
Cumbrae (before 1761) 160	Lowestoft 40
Kullen (1791) 112	Fréhel 31

These figures include coals used by the lightkeepers for cooking and heating, which might amount to 10 tons at any lighthouse.

Measurements of coal consumed nightly at Kullen during the seasons August 1791 to April 1792 and August

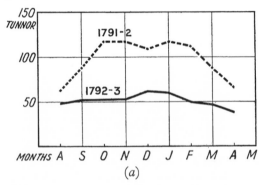

(a)

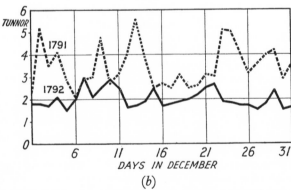

(b)

181. Curves showing the coal consumpts at Kullen before and after Polheimer installed his new coal fire with a draught led to the grate. (a) shows the monthly fluctuation and (b) shows the nightly fluctuation in December due to weather conditions

1792 to April 1793 show that Polheimer's new grate reduced the consumpt from 856·75 tunnor or barrels in the first period to 460·42 in the second period, or from 112 to 61 tons. They show also the effect of wind and weather on the burning of coals during December 1791 and December 1792: the nightly consumpt of the old grate varied violently from 2·2 to 5·56 tunnor and that of the new grate from 1·46 to 3·0 tunnor. One tunna of coals equals 5·9 cubic feet or 2·6 cwts.

The keepers at St. Bees and Skerries lighthouses informed Robert Stevenson in 1801 that they consumed annually 130 and 150 tons of coals respectively. He regarded these figures as being too high and they cannot be accepted as correct since seamen complained more about the unsatisfactory keeping of these two fires and of the two candle lighthouses at Wintertonness than of any others in England.

The open grate supplied for the Isle of May after 1786 burned up to 400 tons per annum, which seems to have been a maximum for coal fires. 366 tons were brought to the island in 1799. During a stormy night 3 tons were burned, requiring the unceasing attention of all 3 keepers. On the basis of 45 cubic feet to 1 ton, in December 1800 they had to set 4 cwts of coals in the grate every hour. The grate had a diameter of 3′ 6″ and a depth of 2′. It was raised on legs on top of the tower and burned without roof or screen every night of the year. This grate may be taken as a standard for a comparison with others.

The number of carts delivering coal to gabbards for shipment to Cumbrae lighthouse was noted from 1757 to 1793. The following figures show that on the basis of 9 cwts to a cart, the consumpt of coal at this fire beacon started at about 160 tons and soon increased to 180 tons. The variation of the annual quantities is partly due to irregular deliveries, so averages must be struck.

Coals shipped annually to Cumbrae lighthouse:

| Period | Numbers of Carts | | Weight in tons |
	Actual	average	
1757–60	270 to 350	310	160
1761–71	348 to 505	400	180
1782–93	372 to 430	400	180

Maintenance of coal fires

Where open coal fires were exhibited from towers, the keepers led a hard life. In addition to the usual duties of carrying fuel and watching the fires, they exposed themselves to great danger from the flames in approaching and stirring the coals and feeding the fire in all conditions of wind and weather, to asphyxiation with their families in the neighbouring houses (from the fumes arising from incomplete combustion of the cinders), and to never-ceasing dust and dirt. The quantities of cinders dispersed round coal fire towers, perhaps concealed now under a grassy surface, remain as a proof that this type of illumination had been used.

The transport of coals to lighthouses was troublesome and laborious, not only overland along the rude tracks of the times but on the open sea, especially to the Casquets with three fires to be fed. Cumbrae was another lighthouse difficult to maintain, for at the end of the sea-journey the coals had to be dumped below a cliff and carried thence by the lightkeepers over bog and boulders to the top of the island where the open tower was perched 404′ above sea-level. In comparison, the labour of raising coals to the top of a 100′ tower as at Ostend was trifling.

OIL LAMPS

No comprehensive account is possible of the varieties of oil lamps that illuminated lighthouses from ancient times. There was no standard type even in one country: local craftsmen devised their own patterns and in producing a lamp to need the minimum of attention usually gave it a considerable oil reservoir and a small wick which reduced smoke. A lamp of one candle-power was maintained more easily and cheaply than a candle. Before Argand produced a smokeless lamp about 1782, lamp wicks were flat, or round and solid. Skill in design and maintenance might produce from such a lamp say 5 candles' worth of light, but smoke and soot would be emitted unless it were examined and adjusted every few hours.

Smeaton chose oil lamps for the candelabrum at the Eddystone lighthouse in 1759 and was disappointed to find that their smoke, though imperceptible, obscured the lantern panes to such an extent that he had to substitute candles.

Among the many arrangements tried out to overcome the smoke from oil lamps of early design, one at Boston in America about 1790 consisted of 4 lamps each with 4 wicks. Each lamp had a metal tray to hold oil, in the form of one-quarter of a circle of 3′ diameter, the inner point being cut off so that air could ascend through a central square opening (supposed wrongly to be following the principle of the argand lamp) and so 'the smoake receives a proper direction to escape' at the top of the lantern. In one night's burning, the 16 wicks set round the circumference of the trays lowered the level of the oil by 2″. About 1796 an inspector found the arrangement to be ineffective as 'the lantern became in a short time full of smoak' and so suffocating that it was painful for a person to remain within it for any considerable time. A stove consuming charcoal or 30 bushels of coal in a winter, instead of wood as formerly, had to be provided in the lantern 'to prevent the oyl from chilling'.

Crude or refined oils of vegetable and animal origin such as were obtained from crushing olive and rape seeds and from herrings and other fish were burned in oil lamps in various countries according to the readiness of supply. In England about 1800 spermaceti oil was

182. The flame of an argand lamp showing glass chimney and spreader (photograph *c.* 1860)

taking the place of Greenland whale oil, costing 3s. per gallon, which was known before 1550 as train-oil—*traen* in Dutch.

As stated on pages 61 and 62, Argand's oil lamp revolutionised illumination in all spheres and in particular ushered in a new era for lighthouses. Gradually manufacturers produced this type of lamp for domestic use: it gave a strong steady light and required no attention in operation apart from occasionally removing carbon from the top of the wick, trimming it to get an even top and adjusting its height. Features of the argand lamp that

might be varied to suit lighthouse reflectors were the oil reservoir and the wick tube and, unless the lamp was fixed to the reflector, the method of withdrawing the lamp for cleaning.

Argand's lamp with one wick of $\frac{3}{4}''$ to $1''$ diameter which gave an illumination equalling 7 candles was the best illuminant that was produced before 1823. He made lamps with 2 and 3 concentric wicks in 1802 and obtained a brilliant light, but the excessive heat destroyed the metal burner-tips which held the wicks and boiled the oil. Other experimenters took up development of his lamp and eventually about 1822 Fresnel and Arago evolved two, three or four concentric-wick lamps with a chimney, which they claimed gave light equal to 50, 100 or 200 candles. Their four-wick lamp, 90 mm. in wick-diameter, gave about 3 times the intensity of Argand's one-wick lamp in the important quality of candlepower per unit of vertical area of flame.

In 1794 Sir Benjamin Thomson, an American who had received the Papal title of Count Rumford, announced that he had obtained from an argand lamp 12 times as much light as from a candle. But 7 times was a normal amount in experiments.

Other accounts of the argand lamp give credit to Argand for utilising the double current of air, to Meunier for the glass chimney, and to Lange for reducing its diameter to form a shoulder.

An idea current about 1800 that reflectors were not required for navigation lights and that by using a number of oil lamps alone a powerful light could be produced was scotched by trials at Havre in 1807: they proved conclusively that it would be impossible in practice to provide enough lamps to produce as powerful a light-beam as was emitted by one lamp at the focus of a good parabolic reflector. They would fail in giving sufficient intensity of light, and the consumpt of oil and its expense would be enormous.

GAS

Gas from the distillation of wood lighted a tower at Porkkala in Finland between 1800 and 1809. The gas, of small light-value, illuminated 10 lamps, probably bunched together round the focus of a facet parabolic reflector. The sale of charcoal and tar, produced as by-products during the manufacture of this gas, covered the entire cost of maintaining the lighthouse.

After the Trinity House experiments around 1800 showed coal gas to be unsuitable, it seems to have had a further trial in England in 1805 with reflectors. But its first use at a lighthouse was at Salvore near Trieste in 1818. Accounts of this novel lighting were broadcast with much flourish but it was soon discontinued. In 1819 a small gas-plant was set up at Neufahrwasser lighthouse in Germany to supply two parabolic reflectors of 530 mm. opening and 229 mm. depth, having three gas-jets at the focus of each. About a year earlier, gas was used at a harbour light at Washington in the United States.

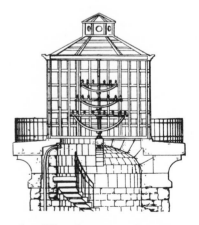

183. The lantern of Salvore lighthouse with 3 tiers of coal gas flames (Aldini)

278

Hopes were high before 1820 that coal gas might prove suitable for lighthouse illumination: the gas had constituents valuable for light-giving that are removed at 20th-century gasworks. But except in Ireland for a period from 1870 to 1900 these hopes were disappointed.

The chief objection to coal-gas lighting was that it involved transport to a lighthouse of much coal and provision of gas-making plant and skilled operators. In more recent times, illuminants of greater intensity were provided more easily.

B. POWERFUL AND DISTINCTIVE LIGHTS

Advantages of powerful lights

Rain, snow-showers, fog and mist limit the visibility and reduce the range of even the most powerful sea-lights.

In good visibility a light of low candlepower has a long range and may be as useful to ships as one of high candlepower, but in poor visibility it is obscured and its range may be reduced so much that it loses most of its value to a navigator: a great increase in candlepower is then necessary to increase the range. For instance, in approximate figures, when a light of 10,000 candles becomes invisible in a mist of uniform intensity at 3 miles' distance, one of 100,000 candles would be invisible at 4 miles and one of 1,500,000 candles at 5 miles.

The average visibility at sea varies in different parts of the world and according to the season of the year. It is clearer on the Mediterranean shores than on the Atlantic, and in summer than in winter. Fog may be ten times as prevalent near one lighthouse as at another. At Seguin lighthouse in Maine in the United States, fog or poor visibility has been known to occur for the large amount of 2,734 hours in one year, that is, during one hour out of three.

In 1959, when fog obscures lights and other seamarks by night or by day, a navigator expects help from aerial sound signals, radio, radar and other electronic devices, but for technical reasons such aids to navigation cannot yet take the place of light signals direct to his eyes; this is demonstrated by the ever-increasing number of navigation lights in all parts of the world. So a lighthouse engineer must select a light of a particular power in accordance with the prevalence of poor visibility at the site chosen for such a seamark and with the importance of the passing traffic. He can now provide a light of 20 million candles at large capital and maintenance costs but not unlikely his choice will be tempered by the financial resources at his disposal. In 1819 he had little choice, 20,000 candles being the maximum power of light installed at a lighthouse. That figure is now rarely considered powerful enough for any coastal light.

Inadequacy of illuminants alone

For sea-lights the value of an illuminant alone is small, whether it be a coal fire, candle or lamp, because a navigator receives only the few rays of light proceeding directly to his eye from the actual flame. From the argand lamp, the best illuminant of 1819, he would receive experimentally a light of 7 candles, or 6 candles in actual practice.

The rays that shoot out from the flame towards the horizon all round are useful to navigators in other directions but the overwhelming remainder of the rays escape upwards into the sky or downwards into the sea: the waste of light is enormous. The direct rays reaching him could certainly be added to by burning more fires, candles or lamps; but as only the same trifling fraction of light, to the extent of say 7 candles, would reach him from each, the additional capital and maintenance costs consequent on multiplying the illuminants would be unjustified; nearly 3,000 argand lamps would be required to provide 20,000 candlepower. The same argument applies to modern illuminants of larger candlepower than argands.

Concentration of rays

The rays that escape behind an illuminant can be reflected by a mirror and those that escape in front can be refracted by a lens and prisms. Proper shapes of mirrors, lenses and prisms can collect a large proportion of these rays and concentrate them into a powerful beam of light and direct it towards the horizon to reach the seaman many miles away in clear weather, or at a greater distance in poor visibility than could be attained by unconcentrated light from an illuminant.

By 1757 Norberg made a practical test of concentration with a parabolic reflector of 8″ opening. In good visibility from a distance of 14 miles he could see light from one candle placed exactly at the focus; whereas without a mirror the candle flame would have been visible for only a short distance.

At 9 to 10 miles' distance Hutchinson's small reflector light was visible to the naked eye, whereas a common oil lamp alone could be seen only with a spy-glass.

A silver-plated mirror of 21″ diameter of the best manufacture of 1819 gave a concentrated beam of light 350 times the candlepower of the illuminant. That was a parabolic reflector of 4″ focal distance combined with an illuminant of $1\frac{1}{4}$ square inches of vertical area. With an argand lamp of 7 candles at the focus it gave a beam or flash equal to 2,450 candles.

The mirror system is called reflecting or *catoptric* and the lens and prism system refracting or *dioptric*. When the systems are used together in a single apparatus, it is described as *catadioptric*.

Divergence

An essential point to be considered in every illuminating system for lighthouses is the shape, height and breadth of the illuminant. If the illuminant placed at the focus of a parabolic reflector or of a suitable lens were merely a pinpoint in size the optical system would be too perfect: the light from the reflector would be focused exactly and so would travel seawards in the form of a narrow cylindrical beam of the exact diameter of the reflector or lens and resembling an over-concentrated searchlight, and there would be little chance of the beam catching the eye of any seaman. Therefore in practice the illuminant, though placed at the focus, must have height and breadth to give ex-focal light over a sufficient angle. Its rays then travel forth to the horizon in a conical beam ever expanding outwards and certain to catch the eye of the seaman. See figure 184.

184. Engraving illustrating the conical beam emitted from a lighthouse, spread by divergence

This spread of light is called *divergence*. Without sufficient vertical divergence a navigator would not see any light emitted from a high lighthouse on a headland, as the beam would pass above his vessel. Insufficient vertical divergence below the horizon (the mistake of either the designer of the light or the person who placed it in the lantern) has caused wrecks. Halving the height of an illuminant or doubling the focal distance of the optical apparatus halves the vertical divergence. If the illuminant is narrow the horizontal divergence will be small and the flash from the light may be too short in duration. In 1819 21″ and 25″ parabolic reflectors with an argand lamp flame of about 1½″ in height and 1″ in diameter gave vertical and horizontal divergences sufficient for the needs of navigation, except from particularly elevated lighthouses. A possibility of insufficient divergence is inherent today in the use of small electric filament lamps with large dioptric apparatus.

Diagram 185e is important as showing the divergence caused by the rays of light from the sides of an illuminant striking the same point P on the reflector surface and producing a conical beam of light APB. Greater concentration of light comes from the rim of a reflector or lens than from its centre, as the greater distance of the illuminant reduces the angle of divergence.

Owing to divergence the intensity of the light from a reflector faded off gradually at each side of the axis, the concentration with a Scots 21″ reflector decreasing from 350 times along the axis to say 35 times at 8°. When such reflectors were set in a circle in a lantern to give a fixed light, it was considered reasonable to supply about 7 reflectors for each 90° of azimuth or horizon to be lighted. Though this arrangement of reflectors did not produce a light that was of equal power in all directions yet in practice it proved satisfactory. The light from one reflector was reinforced by the light diverging from the sides of its neighbours and direct from their lamps, so that with the 21″ reflectors, the light transmitted in various directions would vary from perhaps 1,100 to 2,450 candles. According to Drummond, Trinity House experiments of 1829–30 showed that the number of Robinson's 20⅝″ reflectors and lamps for an all-round light should be at least 21: at the Eddystone 24 gave satisfaction.

To use the flame of the standard argand lamp to most advantage, the focal distance of the 21″ and 25″ reflectors did not exceed 5″. With a smaller flame or a longer focal distance the divergence would be too small.

Advantage of quick identification

Navigators have always desired quick identification of a lighthouse from others in the same area, by day and by night. Before 1780–90, when all lights were white, *i.e.* without coloured shades, they also desired every light to be fixed in character and of the same intensity from all directions. However, if all lighthouses exhibited fixed white lights they could not be distinguished from each other, so these two desires were irreconcilable except to the extent that two or more fixed lights might be shown from the same lighthouse or from adjacent towers. A fixed light assisted a navigator to take a bearing and so learn the position of his ship at sea, whereas ready identification of a lighthouse from others lessened the risk of shipwreck. The navigator of a vessel approaching a coast in darkness or fog after an ocean voyage often knew that she might be in great peril: since his last sight of land the ship had been so buffeted by winds and beset by storms for several weeks that he did not know her position within say fifty miles. So he required all assistance in quickly identifying the coast he saw first and any lighthouses, and avoiding out-lying dangers while laying off his next course. One of many instances of wrecks occasioned by failure to identify a lighthouse occurred in 1802 when an East Indiaman mistook the Hook tower at Waterford in south Ireland for the Eddystone off south England.

Gradually after 1790 navigators appreciated the advantage of revolving lights as an alternative to fixed lights in giving distinction, but at first they demanded a long flash or duration of the light-beams for 5 seconds or more. It was not until about 1880 that most seamen and Lighthouse Authorities had freed their minds from the belief that a long flash was essential for navigation: some Authorities had concurred too readily in the conservatism of seamen. Today navigators are content with flashes lasting half a second and they no longer call for a fixed light for taking bearings. Many varieties of flashing lights are now available to afford unmistakable distinctions. Fixed lights are provided rarely except at harbours because, although with a fixed light showing equally round the horizon from an illuminant of 1,000 candles concentration of vertical light produces a light of say 10,000 candles, the opportunity is missed of producing a revolving light of say 200,000 candles by concentrating the horizontal light as well.

C. CHARACTERS OF LIGHTS

Before 1820 very few characters were available for navigation lights and the difficulties experienced by seamen in distinguishing lighthouses at night cannot be appreciated fully by those with knowledge of lighthouses at the present time unless it is explained that the quick-flashing light was not introduced until after 1819 and the group-flashing system not until 1874.

In 1819 about 85 per cent. of the world's lighthouses showed fixed lights, the remainder showed revolving, oscillating or occulting lights.

Single fixed lights

Before 1780 the best fixed light (sometimes termed a *lunar light* because it gave a steady glow like the moon) was got from a coal fire, or from a cluster of candles or oil lamps placed sufficiently apart so that the vertical bars or astragals of the lantern did not obscure it entirely from some directions. Such lights gave a power of under 100 candles. By its aspect a seaman could usually distinguish a wood or coal fire burning in the open from a light in a lantern, but it varied so much in intensity that its light value was not dependable. A disadvantage of the fixed light was the possibility of confusing it with other navigation lights, shore lights, ships' lights and even the stars. In 1736 the artist Allan Ramsay was a passenger in a ship approaching the Italian coast when the steersman mistook two stars for the lights of Leghorn and might have wrecked the vessel.

In 1819 the most powerful fixed light was got from parabolic reflectors and argands set in a circle in a lantern. The power varied in different directions.

Multiple fixed lights

The earliest sure means of distinguishing a lighthouse from others showing fixed lights was by erecting two lighthouses close together, as at Wintertonness before 1618. In a few cases 2 lighthouses were built in line to indicate either a deep-water channel as at North Shields about 1540, or the direction of a sunken rock as at the Calf of Man in 1818. At Chassiron in 1733 2 separate fires were set in the same tower at different levels. The unique distinction of a group of 3 lighthouses was chosen in 1724 for the Casquets where a prompt identification was important. In 1800 a lantern was placed on each side of Anholt tower as a distinction from neighbouring lighthouses which were as tall.

Apart from the expense of maintaining two or three lighthouses in place of one, multiple lights had the disadvantage that rarely did the pair or trio exhibit their lights with identical intensity: one might have a longer range and so, from a distance or in poor visibility, the intended distinction was absent. Though the introduction of revolving lights of different periods and of grouping flashes and colours had rendered multiple lights unnecessary by 1890, it was difficult to persuade a community to discontinue them, if they had been long established. At Plymouth in the United States popular prejudice caused retention until 1924 of two lighted towers which the Lighthouse Department had long desired to replace by one lighted tower.

Around 1819 most lightships showed either two or three fixed lights from candles or oil lamps in lanterns, as the best distinction from the lights of other vessels, all under 5 candlepower.

Oscillating lights

It was apparently in Finland and Sweden that the first attempts were made to break away from the universal objective of fixed lights of uniform intensity. The system of moving a screen at Utö in 1753 so that the light indicated one of two channels alternately led to Jonas Norberg's oscillating lights at Korsö in 1757 and Örskär in 1769: at both lighthouses the reflectors were turned to and fro horizontally.

Revolving lights

Norberg brought his successive developments of oscillating lights to a climax in 1781 when he produced at Carlsten in Sweden the world's first revolving light, but because of its low power it seems to have made no impression on seamen as being an improvement. France and England followed in establishing revolving lights in 1790. By 1819 the most powerful revolving light in use gave a beam of some 20,000 candles.

In revolving lights the illuminants are not extinguished: the seaman sees the light or flash when the reflectors or lenses face his direction. He gets the same effect now from a fixed dioptric or lens light by the lighting and extinguishing of the illuminant automatically.

When Sir Walter Scott visited the coal fire on the May island in 1814 he was informed that in a strong wind the flames were visible from only one side of the island. This prompted his question: 'might not the grate revolve?' But his idea was impracticable.

Synchronised revolving lights

Another distinction introduced before 1820 was the synchronisation of two white revolving lights on separate towers at the Calf of Man in 1818.

Occulting lights

At Cape Cod in the United States in 1798 a screen revolving round oil lamps obscured their light at intervals, a simple means of distinction that gave a candlepower of under 20.

Coloured lights

So long as navigation lights were of low candlepower, without parabolic reflectors, distinction by colour was useless as coloured glass dulled them and reduced their range too much, absorbing say 80 per cent. of the light when red and 85 per cent. when green. The proposal to show a green light at the Smalls about 1775 seems to have been the earliest for a coloured light in England. Flamborough had a revolving red and white light in 1806.

Before 1820 an uncoloured light was described as *white*, *bright* or *clear*. These adjectives signified the natural colour of the illuminant without coloured glass such as red or green. Both blue and green glasses give what are observed and described as green lights. It might be noted here that with oil-wick lamps as the illuminant, navigation lights had a yellow or orange tint which was very noticeable when compared with the cold-white or bluish tint that came after 1890 from lights using an incandescent oil lamp or an electric lamp even with a carbon filament.

Flashing lights

The first attempt to introduce a *quick-flashing* light, if indeed that was its aim, was made at the lighthouse built at Lundy island in England in 1819 which was lighted in 1820 and was furnished with two lanterns 30' apart. One showed a fixed light and the other a light which revolved so quickly that no period of darkness was detectable between the flashes. The effect was what Teulère hoped to achieve with the reflecting apparatus which he had in mind about 1783, namely, a fluctuating fixed light. The Lundy lanterns were elevated 538' and 508' above sea-level and at 5 miles distance the two lights merged into one. From their great height they were often hidden by fog, although the island itself could be seen. The impression given of a fixed light led to confusion, as in November 1828 when the ship *La Jeune Emma* of 500 tons on passage from Martinique to Cherbourg arrived in Carmarthen bay in thick fog and mistook the Lundy lights for the fixed reflector light of Ushant and was wrecked. Of 19 persons on board 13 were lost, including a young niece of the Empress Josephine.

The first lights deserving of the description *quick-flashing* were established in Scotland in 1825 at the Rhinns of Islay with a flash every 12 seconds and in 1827 at Buchanness with a flash every 5 seconds.

Up to about 1920 a *revolving* and a *flashing* light were considered as having different characteristics: now both varieties are termed *flashing*. When parabolic reflectors were revolved at lighthouses before 1820, a light appeared out of the darkness, gradually it increased in intensity to a maximum and then it faded into the darkness. The observed duration of light, called a *flash* for lack of a better English term, extended over say 15 seconds in good visibility, or 5 seconds in poor visibility when the mist absorbed the ends of the flash. Now the flash of light from a lighthouse extends for perhaps half a second: it stabs the darkness so that no increase or diminution of light is apparent. The slowly-revolving light is a thing of the past.

The *group-flashing* system—in which from 2 to 6 flashes appear in quick succession to form a group of flashes—was introduced in England in 1874 by John Hopkinson: this radical invention was one of the most valuable advances in lighthouse engineering.

D. REFLECTORS AND LENSES

When considering the optical apparatus of these early lights it should be kept in mind that manufacturers did not adhere rigidly to particular dimensions for their reflectors and lenses: so mention of slightly different dimensions for the same type of apparatus is understandable.

Reflection

Two simple rules that govern reflection are illustrated in diagram 185a, namely, (1) the incident ray of light from a source or focus o which falls on a reflecting surface and the reflected ray which leaves it are always in one plane, which is perpendicular to the reflecting surface at the exact point of reflection P; and (2) the angle which the reflected ray makes with the reflecting surface is always equal to the angle which the incident ray makes with it, that is, the angle of reflection α is equal to the angle of incidence β. Those two rules apply to every shape and variety of reflector or mirror.

From all mirrors, irrespective of the shape or curve, there is considerable loss of light on reflection varying with the type of surface and condition, but the concentration of rays achieved by a spherical or parabolic mirror is greater than that loss.

Curves of reflectors

The various curves that have been used for the reflecting surfaces of lighthouse mirrors are (i) parabolic or paraboloidal, (ii) spherical, (iii) flat or plane, (iv) conical and (v) elliptical.

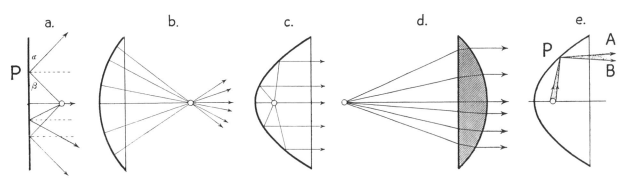

185. Diagrams illustrating reflection from various shapes of mirrors, refraction from a lens, and divergence:
(a) a plane mirror, (b) a spherical reflector, (c) and (e) a parabolic reflector and (d) a plano-convex lens.
Diagram (e) shows the angle of divergence APB caused by rays from each side of the illuminant at o

(i) The parabolic is the most valuable curve for light-house reflectors as it is the only one that concentrates the light from an illuminant into a horizontal beam. As shown in diagram 185c a parabolic mirror with an illuminant at the focus o reflects all light-rays from the illuminant that fall upon its surface in a direction parallel to the focal plane.

The concentrative property of the parabolic curve was known to the ancients. The 1658 edition of Porta's 16th-century *Natural Magic* contains a section headed 'merry sports with plain looking-glasses' and explains that a parabolic mirror will reflect heat, cold and the sound of a voice. Among shrewd observations is the statement that for the illuminant at the focus, 'candles are naught because they alter the places of reflection' as they burn down, so the flame of a lamp is to be preferred as it does not consume itself to a lower level.

One of the earliest proposals for the practical use of the parabola was put forward in 1763 by an artist named Le Fevre who intended to light cross-roads, 'where it would be dangerous for strangers to travel', by 4 paraboloids set 90° apart, the whole contained in a glass drumhead as shown in diagram 186. The smoke from each lamp would be carried by a tube H to a common chimney M. A recess G in the base of each reflector would hold the oil and the wick.

(ii) A spherical mirror, like Sangrain's, reflects back to the focus as shown in diagram 185b all rays of light from the illuminant that fall upon its inner surface. Thus it reinforces the rays that originally proceed forwards and are dispersed mostly skywards and downwards. In practice a spherical mirror might add $\frac{1}{3}$ to $\frac{1}{7}$ to the value of a diaphanous or transparent illuminant such as the flame of a candle or of an oil lamp, and to that slight extent the horizontal strip close to the focal plane is of use for a fixed sea-light.

(iii) A large flat or plane mirror disperses so widely the rays that it reflects that it is practically useless for a sea-light but, as with a spherical mirror, a small horizontal strip of a flat mirror set immediately behind the illuminant increases its value.

A parabolic facet reflector can be built up from a large number of small pieces of flat mirror glass as in figure 194. The central point of each piece reflects correctly to the horizon the ray from the focus, as also by divergence does the small area round it.

186. Le Fevre's design for parabolic reflectors set 90° apart

(iv) A cone, as used at the Scilly Isles in 1790, reflects directly merely narrow rings of light in the direction required but disperses the remainder too widely to be useful.

(v) An elliptical curve has a reflective action intermediate between the parabolic and the spherical, but, for lighthouses, it disperses the light too much.

Varieties of curves

Before 1820, Argand and Bordier-Marcet were lone venturers in experimenting with reflectors beyond the single parabolic and spherical. Argand's idea of a bi-catroptric reflector, one half being a parabola and the other half an ellipse, was given a practical test as a sea-light by Bordier-Marcet. The reflector failed because it spread the rays too widely or thinly in some directions, but the test led him into designing his *fanal à double effet* shown in figure 192 in which two parabolic reflectors of different sizes each with an illuminant at its focus are set on the same axis. The arrangement dispersed the light from the two reflectors over a slightly wider sector than each would do alone and so reduced the intensity of light that would be given by two separate parabolic reflectors set in the same direction. Figure 191 shows Bordier-Marcet's second invention of the *fanal sidéral* which also made use of the parabolic curve. It produced a fixed light of equal intensity all round the horizon by concentrating the vertical rays from the flame of one lamp. In practice it increased its candlepower five-fold to ten-fold, that is, with an argand in the focus a power of 35 to 70 candles was emitted.

Construction of reflectors

Before 1820 lighthouse reflectors were formed of single pieces of metal or built up of facets of mirror glass. When made of metal the material was polished steel, copper or brass, or silver-plated steel or copper. A mirror of 11″ diameter and 4″ focus of a special alloy, *Mudge's telescope metal*, was used at Point Lynus by Hutchinson before 1790. The cheapest mirrors were made of brass. The great differences in the manufacture of reflectors and in the standards of their maintenance at various lighthouses render pointless any assessment of the reflective values of the different materials forming their polished surfaces, but it can be accepted that silver-plating and mirror-glass gave the best reflection. In Denmark the reflectors were mostly brass and concave in shape (not necessarily parabolic); silver-plating was considered too expensive and gilding too perishable. Cleaning and polishing aggravated the corrosive effect of smoke and oil in destroying gradually the polished surfaces of reflectors. The Scottish reflectors were plated so thickly that they could afford the loss of silver by cleaning and so they gave long service: metallic silver was recovered from them by collecting and burning the cleaning cloths.

Silver-plating was carried out about 1750 by fusing in a furnace plates of copper and silver with a flux of borax and nitre. The product was rolled and hammered on a mould to the shape desired. The Scottish reflectors were formed by rolling together two plates each 9″ square—one of 6 ounces of pure silver and the other of 1 pound of pure copper—to form a thin plate 28″ square, which was hammered to shape, as shown in figure 187. In 1846 Wilkins, who succeeded Robinson, offered for sale in America at £32 apiece parabolic reflectors of that composition which he stated he could supply with Stevenson's lamp arrangement in figure 197. Alternatively he would supply reflectors of an average quality of 4 ounces of silver to 1 pound of copper at £25 or of a thinner quality as specified by Halpin in Ireland of 2½ ounces of silver to 1 pound of copper at £21. These proportions contrast with the mixture of half an ounce of silver to 1 pound of copper that was used for domestic silver-plated table-ware about 1812. In France where the proportion of silver on steel or

copper reflectors was small, the Lighthouse Commission contracted every year for re-shaping and re-silvering one-fifth of the reflectors at each lighthouse.

Stevenson noted in 1819 the method of making reflectors adopted by Boulton and Watt at their Soho workshop. 'Take and cut 8-ply of silver leaf to the size wanted. Then put the reflector on a clear charcoal fire.

187. Shaping a Scots parabolic reflector
c. 1840

Heat it slowly until it comes to a faint red, then put the silver on with a pair of nippers, pressing it on with a burnisher and so on until finished.' Afterwards it was hammered to shape.

The few silvered-glass spherical reflectors made by Rogers about 1790 were probably too fragile for use at a lighthouse.

Parabolic reflectors of cheap tinware were supplied for some lights but they soon deteriorated. Tests were made of reflectors of white porcelain or earthenware at Monaco about 1800 by Count Rumford and in Italy and England before 1819, when they were given a surface of silver lustre. But the reflection was not good enough and the lustre was removed in the cleaning.

Efficiency of reflectors

The value of a reflector for a sea-light, though dependent initially on its shape, size and focal distance and on the quality of its reflecting surface, might be reduced or lost entirely by shortcomings in setting it in the lantern in relation to the illuminant and to the horizon, or by lack of careful maintenance including polishing. When the metal base was too thin, distortion by hand-pressure occurred during cleaning and faults in alignment arose from frequent removal from the supporting frames. Aware of this, Robinson warned light-keepers against disconnecting lamps and reflectors from their frames for cleaning. Fortunately the small focal distance of the reflectors combined with the relatively large size of the lamp wicks gave a divergence large enough to overcome the usual defects. Another cause of inefficiency was the obstruction of a useful portion of the reflecting surface by too large lamps and too thick lantern bars. Diagonal bars were not introduced until after 1830.

Lightkeepers could not be expected to adjust mirrors or detect defects, the effects of which were sometimes cumulative. Checking the setting of optical apparatus is always extremely difficult to carry out at a lighthouse even to engineers with experience of that work, and in 1819 Lighthouse Services did not employ such persons on their staffs or arrange for frequent inspection of their lights. An exception—perhaps the only one—was the Northern Lighthouse Board which, partly because its lighthouses were established on distant islands, arranged almost from its inception for its engineer to make a voyage to inspect them at least once every year.

The glass facet reflector as adopted by Hutchinson, the two Walkers and Smith could not claim to reflect light as perfectly as the best polished metal reflector but, because of the properties of glass in resistance to distortion and immunity to surface corrosion with a consequent loss of reflecting quality, its value before 1820 was higher than might be supposed. The non-corrosion of the glass surfaces made it the only type that could be used confidently with an oil lamp without chimneys which was liable to deposit soot on the reflecting surfaces: the glass surfaces of the facets were cleaned easily. But eventually moisture working through the plaster between the facets destroyed their metallic backing: Smith credited his reflectors with an effective life of 10 years. The facet reflector lost more light vertically then the metal reflector but its greater spread horizontally was advantageous for an all-round fixed light, a fact recognised by Ezekiel Walker and Smith in arranging their shaped facets: the maximum candlepower of a reflector was not the criterion of its suitability. A serious defect of the facet reflectors made by Hutchinson and those at Walney was that the plaster was set on a wooden frame which became distorted by oil and condensation. The reflectors found at Trinity House and those made by Smith were free from this trouble, the plaster being set on metal.

In 1801 Stevenson estimated that 2 of Robinson's 20½″ metal reflectors equalled 3 of Smith's facet reflectors. Though he adopted metal reflectors for new lighthouses after that date he considered it unnecessary to replace facet reflectors at the existing Scottish lighthouses: their inferiority was not obvious to seamen. Ezekiel Walker's replacement in 1795 of facet reflectors which he fitted at Hunstanton about 1776, although he knew that metal reflectors were used at other English lighthouses, confirms that they gave an excellent beam.

Light values of reflectors

Before 1820, reflectors of identical shape, size and focal distance differed in manufacture and setting in a lantern; lamps differed in design, wicks and type of oil; and lanterns differed in design and ventilation: all apparatus differed in so many respects that the candlepower of a light might only be one-tenth of that produced by an apparently similar apparatus at another lighthouse. The following figures now put forward apply only to well-kept apparatus of the best manufacture.

The basis of calculation of candlepower is scarcely controversial: namely, that the argand lamp of 1819 with one circular wick and a glass chimney gave a light of 7 *bougies* or candles according to Bordier-Marcet and other experimenters, and that in use with a reflector at a lighthouse a figure of 6 candles could be counted on.

The Scots 25″ and 21″ diameter parabolic reflectors of silvered copper concentrated the argand light 450 and 350 times to 3,150 and 2,450 candles, giving intensities of 6·4 and 7·0 candles per square inch of reflecting surface. A similar French reflector of 19·7″ diameter in 1840 concentrated its lamp light 270 times to 1,890 candles, giving an intensity of 6·2 candles. These figures indicate that a new parabolic reflector with an argand lamp in 1819 should produce a light intensity of 6 candles per square inch of reflecting surface, in which case its total candlepower would vary according to its diameter thus: 18″ 1,530, 21″ 2,076, 25″ 2,940 and 31½″ 4,680. Such were the maximum amounts reflected along the axis of each reflector.

The 1840 French reflector with argand lamp was stated to give a concentration of 270 along the axis and, owing to divergence, concentrations of 160, 74, 44, 18, and 2 at successive angles of 2° up to 10° at each side, *i.e.* candlepowers from 1,620 to 12. The average concentration over the 10° sector was declared to be 86·4 or 520 candles but these figures were of no value to a navigator because, as with a ship which is concerned only with the minimum or *ruling* depth in a navigable channel, he is assisted, not by the average of light spread over certain angles, but only by the beam sent in his direction. The diagram 188 shows the light received by a seaman when these French reflectors were spaced equally round a circle in a lantern. Curve A shows the distribution of light from 12 reflectors 30° apart (1,620 candlepower to nil), curve B from 24 reflectors 15° apart (1,620 to 264), and curve C from 48 reflectors 7½° apart (1,884 to 966). In addition the seaman would always receive direct light in all directions from the lamps contained within 90°; in the 3 arrangements this additional light amounted to 18, 36 or 72 candles respectively.

As the divergences varied greatly, the amount of light emitted in directions several degrees from the axis has to be calculated in each case, but it is likely that the light emitted from between the reflectors of a fixed light varied in practice from one-quarter to one-half of the maximum light emitted along the axis. The *fanal à double effet* and the reflector with horizontal facets had advantages for fixed lights.

Bordier-Marcet experimented with reflectors and found that his *fanal à double effet* of 80 cm. diameter gave 4,776 *bougies* and that of 66 cm. gave 3,822, while Robinson's 20½″ reflector gave only 1,284. Their intensities per square inch were 6·1, 7·2 and 3·9 respectively but Robinson's apparatus was more efficient as it was fitted with only one lamp against two at the *fanal* and so gave a more powerful beam for the same consumpt of oil. The figure observed for his reflector seems

on emerging from it. If the lens be designed suitably, each ray will emerge in a direction parallel to the focal plane, while the deflections vary with the refractive index of the glass, which for lighthouse purposes is usually about 1·51.

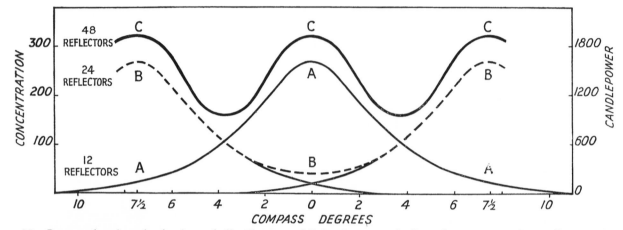

188. Curves showing the horizontal distribution of light from parabolic reflectors spaced equally round a lantern—curve A from 12 reflectors, curve B from 24 and curve C from 48. The zero of the compass degrees is the axis of any reflector. 6 reflectors covering 90° emitted light varying from 264 to 1,620 candles

too small; Bordier-Marcet records that when his assistant pointed out that the lamp did not seem to be set correctly at the focus, he replied that Robinson had surely set his apparatus correctly.

Hutchinson's parabolic facet reflector of 13½′ diameter with its huge crude wick giving fluctuating light emitted a maximum beam of from 1,000 to 10,000 candles. The Scots 18″ facet reflector with piped-wick lamp, according to Stevenson's rough observation from the sea, was worth perhaps two-thirds of an 18″ metal reflector, say 1,000 candles along the axis. At Sangrain's lights, the concentration by the spherical reflectors was so slight that it might be disregarded, so one need only multiply the number of wick flames visible to the seaman by their candlepower, to arrive at a total of perhaps 30 candles. Bordier-Marcet's *fanal sidéral* was valued at 35 to 70 candles. There is insufficient basis to calculate the useful effects of Rogers's and Lewis's unsatisfactory lens lights.

It should be repeated again that all these figures are offered as giving only a general impression of the candlepowers of the old reflectors. More definite figures might be obtained by experiment with such of the apparatus as has been preserved: on interpreting them it must be borne in mind that the horizontal divergence needed to be larger for fixed lights than for revolving lights.

Lenses and refraction

When a ray of light from a source or focus o falls on the plane surface of a plano-convex lens as shown in diagram 185d, it is deflected both on entering the glass and

The concentrative property of the lens was known in England before 1658. In that year the English edition of Porta's book declared that 'a convex lenticular chrystal kindleth fire most violently'. In 1685 Samuel Hutchinson received Parliamentary protection for his convex glass lights fitted in hand-lanterns. Craftspeople such as lace-workers assisted their eye-tiring work at night with glass spheres or bottles filled with water to concentrate light from candles or lamps. About 1790 similar methods were tried for street-lighting in London.

A London optician seems to have been the first person with the idea of utilising the refractive properties of glass for navigation lights, but the account of his offer about 1757 to construct a lantern for the Eddystone incorporating his ideas does not disclose his method of carrying it out. According to Smeaton, who assured Trinity House that the idea was worthless, he intended to 'grind all the panes of glass for the lantern to circular segments so that it should form a sphere of 15′ diameter'.

Construction and efficiency of lenses

The plano-convex lens, with flat surface set next to the lamp, was the only type of lens used for lighthouses before 1820. Three individuals fitted it at lighthouses: Thomas Rogers at 2 in England and at from 6 to 10 in Ireland, George Robinson at 2 in England and Winslow Lewis at some 50 in the United States. Stevenson experimented with Robinson's type but did not fit it. In each case the lens was a solid piece of glass. William Hutchinson made one of hollow glass filled with brine but it was too fragile. Rogers's lenses were the largest, $21\frac{1}{2}''$ in diameter, $5''$ in thickness and $19''$ in focal distance. Lewis's were $9''$ in diameter and from $2\frac{1}{2}''$ to $4''$ in thickness. Robinson's were half-spheres, $4\frac{1}{2}''$ in diameter and set $2\frac{1}{8}''$ from the focus. All were used with reflectors.

When viewed from the front along the line of axis, they appeared to be complete circles like the reflectors.

None of these lenses as fitted gave a satisfactory light—either because they were made of thick coarse glass or were of inferior design and setting.

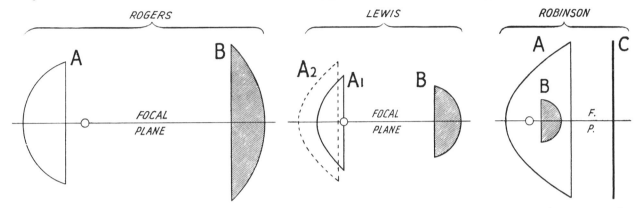

189. Diagram showing the reflector-lens lights of Rogers, Lewis and Robinson drawn to the same scale, Robinson's Flamborough reflector being $21''$ in diameter. The extreme diameters of Lewis's reflectors are indicated at A1 and A2. Reflectors are marked A, lenses B, and a red glass sheet C

E. ACTUAL OPTICAL APPARATUS

SWEDEN

The shape and material of the reflectors in use about 1680 at Örskär and Landsort (the oldest Swedish lighthouse of which records are preserved) are not known.

On 1st June 1681 a proclamation of Charles XII granted to J. D. Braun a patent for the use of cast-steel reflectors for sea-lights. It declared that the heirs of Van der Hagen, who had permission to erect a lighthouse at Landsort, had begun to use such reflectors and thereby had infringed Braun's invention. The patent prohibited the use of the invention without his consent, on penalty of confiscation of the reflectors and a fine of 200 dalers, payable half to Braun and half to the church of Carlskrona. Silver-plating was not invented then.

It is not clear whether the value of the invention lay in the use of the parabolic curve or of cast-steel, or in its application to sea-lights. The value of the patent would be extremely small if it applied only to Swedish lighthouses, so few in number.

Reflectors at Örskär 1736

An inspection on 4th August 1736 disclosed that 6 metal reflectors of 1 ell or $23\frac{1}{2}''$ diameter were in use, and may have been installed in 1687. From the mention of their diameter one might suppose that they were spherical or parabolic but the record of 2 lamps at each reflector shows that the concentrative advantage of either curve had been cast away: a second lamp was added on the mistaken assumption that more light would be emitted by substituting 2 lamps for 1.

Reflectors at Örskär 1738

A reference in January 1738 to the adoption of the parabolic line or curve for the 5 cast-steel mirrors of $32''$ diameter to be made in Stockholm seems to have been the first mention of parabolic reflectors for lighthouses in Sweden or elsewhere, but it is disconcerting to learn that from 2 to 6 lamps were supplied to each reflector as this suggests that the advantages of the parabolic curve, which required only one flame at the focus of each, were again not understood. Perhaps the lamps were of such low power that a number seemed necessary or their exfocal arrangement was required to increase the horizontal spread of light. Norberg drew attention to this faulty arrangement on an inspection of the lighthouse in May 1768 when he found 2 lamps serving each reflector. He observed also that the reflectors were inclined wrongly to the perpendicular, that the surfaces were corroded from smoke and oil and that the apparatus lacked proper care.

Reflectors at Korsö 1750

Polished brass mirrors were fitted here in 1750 but particulars are not known.

Reflectors at Utö 1753

Mirrors may have been used here: particulars are lacking. This lighthouse is important historically as its light was the first to be exhibited and then eclipsed for short periods, but it was not occulted in the modern sense.

Oscillating lights at Korsö 1757

The eclipsing arrangement at Utö may have given rise to the idea of waving or oscillating lights: such was the appearance of Korsö lighthouse to the seaman, to whom the timing of the flashes from the four reflectors would vary according to his direction from it. The shape of the reflectors was not stated but, considering their purpose and as Norberg had been satisfied with his test of a parabolic reflector with a candle, there can be little doubt that he made the reflectors parabolic and placed one lamp at the focus of each or perhaps at the coincident foci of each pair. See figure 54.

Improved oscillating light at Örskär 1769

The principle of oscillating or varying a light by introducing intervals of darkness was carried to a further stage by Norberg when he fitted at Örskär 4 gilded reflectors of 30″ diameter, each with one lamp, and added another reflector later, to produce a light described as very good and powerful. The engineer Hilmer Carlsson stated in 1944 that each reflector was attached by a pivot to a stationary frame and had bearing pins at top and bottom so that it could be rotated to show its light-beam through a sector of 60°. According to his tentative reconstruction, the 5 parabolic reflectors were arranged in a circle in the lantern 60° apart and facing outwards, and attached to a horizontal circular bar which was moved to and fro by clockwork. The seaman received light from not more than one reflector at a time and from 4 lamps constantly, an arrangement which at that date might justify the contemporary opinion of its excellence. Had the 5 reflectors been arranged always to show light in the same direction, while they were being turned by the bar, the candlepower would have been 5 times greater and the assessment of the value of the light would have been more justified.

Revolving reflectors at Carlsten 1781

The novel apparatus which Norberg fitted here consisted of 3 oil lamps with 6 gilded parabolic reflectors of about 24″ diameter described as *burning-mirrors* which were set on a rotating axle with a dip of $\frac{1}{2}°$ to allow for the height of the lantern above sea-level. A lamp incorporating an oil container was set in front of each pair of reflectors at their coincident foci, an efficient and economical arrangement. The occurrence of unequal intervals between the flashes was due to the frames, which screened reflected rays from the end and the beginning of successive flashes. Light from two or more lamps was seen constantly. Three mirrors and 3 lamps were added in 1784 in some unknown manner; probably they were smaller mirrors set between the frames supporting the backs of the original reflectors. The mirrors were re-gilded occasionally as in 1796. The lamps burned herring-oil until 1819, then unrefined hemp-oil, and rape-oil later. In 1820 an argand lamp was purchased from England and, as it gave satisfaction, the original lamps were replaced in 1823 by more argands, their oil containers being covered by sheep-skin.

Norberg described his apparatus as arranged round a vertical shaft, turned by a perpetual screw operated by clockwork contained in a brown-painted wood-and-iron frame or case. Brass bearings held the ends of four polished spindles—the main axle with large wheel, rope-drum and winding-up wheel; the second and third axles with wheels and pinions; and the fourth axle with ratchet-wheel driven by the pendulum and connected to the shaft carrying the mirrors. The rope passed over an oak pulley at the ceiling, down to a lower pulley and up again to the ceiling where it was fixed. The weights were 10 lb. and 19 lb. of lead. See figure 168.

The efficiency of the apparatus was proved by its service until 1836. It is unlikely that the original flash had a candlepower exceeding one-third of that of one of the 1790 Scilly reflectors with its argand lamp.

FRANCE

Bitry's reflectors 1727

The flat iron plates set over the coal fire of Cordouan by Bitry seem to have been the first reflectors used at French lighthouses: the soot deposited upon them from the beacon fire rendered them useless for their purpose of increasing the light. See figure 125.

Sangrain's reflectors c. 1777

Spherical mirrors had a value for lighthouses when incorporated in the design of catadioptric apparatus between say 1850 and 1900, perhaps adding 15 per cent. to the candlepower. In perfect condition they might add 50 per cent. to the light distributed over a large vertical angle as in a room, hall or street, but Sangrain's mirrors could do little in directing a lamp's light-rays towards the horizon. He supplied spherical reflectors of various sizes to the French lighthouses between 1777 and 1805. He made circular cuts in the 4 sides of his lighthouse reflector to give space for the lamp and remove it from the stream of corrosive smoke and to make it fit closer to its neighbours. He set them usually not in a circle round the inside of a lantern but on the faces of 3- or 4-sided iron frames that were jacked-up by the keepers after they lighted the lamps. The thin metal of which the reflectors were made distorted readily and the strenuous and frequent cleaning occasioned by the use of smoky lamps soon removed their delicate films of silver. See figures 126 and 190.

Stevenson visited French lighthouses in September

Illuminants and Optical Apparatus

1824. His notebook contains a description of Sangrain's apparatus as fitted at Chassiron: 'The lightroom is about 8′ in diameter and the parapet 10′ in height, the glazed part 6′ in height. There are two tiers of reflectors . . . 16 in number; the lower ones measure about 18″ in their longest dimensions over the lips and the upper ones 15″, so that they form zones of different dimensions. The reflectors are cut with 4 great lips for the burner and junctions at the sides. The burners have fountains with flat wicks 1¼″ in breadth and stand or occupy a *focus* (if such it may be called) of 6″ in breadth. After the lamps have been trimmed and lighted the reflecting apparatus is raised by a winch to the lantern. When any lamp is to be trimmed or snuffed the keeper mounts up by a ladder with some difficulty.'

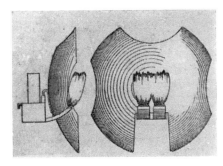

190. Sangrain's spherical reflector with two burners as fitted in French lighthouses *c.* 1780 (Allard)

Lenoir's reflectors 1790

Lenoir's reflectors seem to have been of excellent construction. They weighed 100 lb. each and were too heavy for the light clockwork machines provided to revolve them, so they moved round in jerks. Each had a reflecting area of 5·6 square feet whereas 1·8 square feet was the area of each English 18″ diameter reflector of 1790. Lenoir formed his mirrors of steel faced with 3 or 4 leaves of silver: the Cordouan Commission of 1793 found this thin coating had disappeared in the 3 years' use, being worn away by removing daily the deposit of soot from Quinquet's chimney-less lamps. Lack of silver on these reflectors may have contributed to Fresnel's criticism of Cordouan light in 1822.

In 1824 Stevenson saw Lenoir's reflectors at l'Ailly and observed: 'There are 6 reflectors measuring 30″, ranged 2 and 2, the one above the other. The copper is about ¼″ in thickness, the plating is roughly executed—the nail points appear through the inside of the reflectors and they are in some parts deficient in silver—the whole being strong and massive but coarse and ill-finished. Yet we must have seen this as a good light about 16 or 18 miles off when approaching this port [Havre]. The revolving machinery is in a wooden glazed case and is very strong.' This improved machinery had been evolved by Wagner of Paris at the instigation of Fresnel.

Bordier-Marcet's reflectors 1808–33

According to tradition all types of reflectors constructed by Bordier-Marcet were of beautiful workmanship.

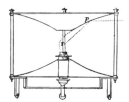

191. Elevation of Bordier-Marcet's *fanal sidéral* which emitted light equally round 360°

Figure 191 shows the *fanal sidéral* in elevation. This example rotated on 3 wheels in a small lantern for cleaning. At the centre was a flame from which a ray striking the reflector at p was emitted parallel to the focal plane. The apex of the parabolic curve is also indicated by dots.

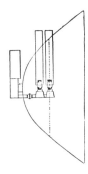

192. Sectional elevation of Bordier-Marcet's *fanal à double effet* which emitted one beam of light from 2 reflectors of different focus

Figure 192 shows the *fanal à double effet* in sectional elevation. The dotted line marks the junction of the two reflectors: the outer lamp is set at the focus of the outer reflector and the inner lamp at that of the inner.

Stevenson saw his *fanaux à double effet* at La Hève in 1824: 'The lighthouse towers have each 12 reflectors in two tiers. They measure 30″ over the lips and have 2 focusses. . . . The frame is strong and substantial, constructed with a rack and pinion by which the whole is elevated and depressed at pleasure (the keeper said) for the purpose of taking the reflectors out of the sun's rays. It was also convenient for enabling him to light the lamps. Each reflector has of course 2 burners, which are so short that the wick serves only 2 nights. The reflectors are of brass $\frac{3}{16}$″ thick, coated with tinning like silver; the burners of tinplate. 60 grammes of oil serve a lamp for one hour.'

To complete the record of Bordier-Marcet, his *fanal à double aspect* must be referred to. It emitted 2 beams of light in opposite directions by setting the outer portions of 2 parabolic reflectors back to back round a lamp. Each had its apex cut away. One opening was covered by a reflector of a longer focal distance which gave the benefit of a smaller divergence. Figure 193 shows the arrangement of reflectors with revolving mechanism. The black centres are the backs of reflectors reinforcing the opposite beam. Although the *fanal* appeared to utilise a large proportion of the light from only 6 lamps it was not put into use.

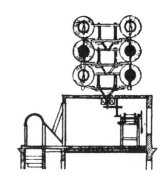

193. Elevation of Bordier-Marcet's revolving *fanal à double aspect*

THE BRITISH ISLES

Reflector at Harwich before 1790

Particulars are unknown of the brass reflector which was in use at the enclosed coal fire at Harwich between 1790 and 1809. Probably it was fitted before 1772; if so, it was the earliest reflector at a British lighthouse. If kept highly polished, it may have increased by a fraction the varying light from the glowing coal fire.

Hutchinson's reflectors c. 1772

In 1801 the largest of the reflectors attributed to Hutchinson was observed by Stevenson to be at Bidston; this tower was built later than the others at Liverpool and was perhaps the most important of the lighthouses at that port. The reflector had a diameter of 13½' and a focus of 4'. The size and the arrangement of the mirror-glass pieces set in plaster on the shaped wooden frame have not been recorded; Hutchinson's illustration of a reflector of say 3' diameter shows a radial arrangement in rings like the reflector at Walney. His smallest reflectors were built up of soldered tin plates. See figure 194.

The wick of the Bidston reflector had a breadth of 14" and it was spun specially from common cotton thread ¼" thick. On snuffing the lamp every 3 or 4 hours, the keeper drew the wick through the burner tube with long pincers and cut it with a pair of shears in one hand; with a box containing water in the other, he collected the snuffings—so avoiding the risk of fire.

When Hutchinson last described his huge reflectors, he conceded that a facet reflector of 3' diameter and 12" focus gave a stronger light proportionally than his reflector of 12½' diameter. Stevenson made a similar observation and estimated that the oil consumed by the 14" wick of the Bidston reflector would serve 30 argands and that 7 of Robinson's reflectors in use at the English lighthouses would give as good a light.

Drummond, who may have seen the Bidston reflector in use, declared in 1830 that a volume of smoke arose from its lamp that completely intercepted the light from the upper part of the reflector.

Ezekiel Walker's reflectors c. 1776–95

Particulars are not recorded of the facet reflectors which Walker designed for Hunstanton about 1776 but it can be supposed that Smith's mirrors were generally of the same type. A Cumberland journal of 1788 described Walker's work on reflectors and mentioned the developments in Scotland; this description may have led

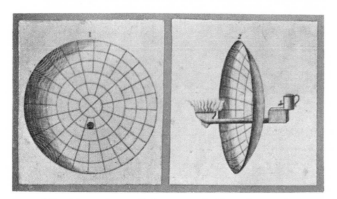

194. Hutchinson's small facet parabolic reflectors in 1777

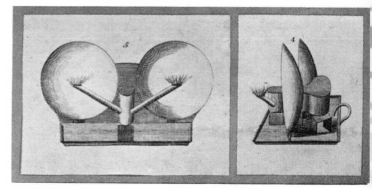

195. Hutchinson's small metal parabolic reflectors as fitted at Point Lynus before 1790

to the fitting of reflectors at the harbours of Maryport and Whitehaven and at Walney island.

In 1795 Walker drew up instructions for making reflectors. To the inner surface of a parabolic shell of plaster he fixed, by a cement of copal varnish and white lead, pieces of Dutch mirror-glass $\frac{1}{2}''$ long and tapering slightly in width. They were arranged in long rows commencing horizontally at the centre. His focus was $3''$. Five cotton strands passed out of a metal tube from the back of the reflector to form the wick. He preferred to lay wide facets horizontally near the focal plane. Like Smith he did not consider it necessary to make reflectors of metal or to adopt the argand burner.

Reflectors at Lowestoft 1777–84

The Trinity House Minutes refer to the spangle light. They record that in June 1778 several Elder Brethren embarked in their yacht to view it from the sea; they noted that 'the new light' was preferable to the coal fire but decided to invite navigators' opinions on 'the usefulness of a reflected light'. In July a letter with many signatures appended, presumably those of seamen, declared the light to be 'constant, certain and regular' and seen at a greater distance than the coal fire. In August Captain Denham of the *Friends' Adventure* of Shields reported that he saw it from 5 leagues off as a bright, steady, clear light and preferable to any he had seen. In October the local agent put out to sea on two nights and saw the spangle light from distances between 4 and 5 leagues. He recommended that 34 of its burners should be lighted in the summer and 40 in winter, but the Brethren decided that 50 burners 'on the side next the sea' should be lighted and the opinion of navigators then obtained. The navigational value of the light came from the direct rays of the many lamps. See figure 59.

In February 1779 a small reflector was ordered to be fixed on a *triangle* or beacon for the low front light. In September a Mr. Smith was paid £6. 5. 0 for a plated reflector, lamp and fountain; in November a Plate Glass Company received £13. 0. 0 for 32 polished panes of glass $15\frac{7}{8}'' \times 14''$ for the new lantern.

Gradually it was recognised that the spangle light was inefficient: no doubt it was out-shone by Mr. Smith's reflector in the low light. In May 1780 the Brethren ordered the 'Great Reflector' to be taken down and sent to London and replaced by a new reflector.

In January 1783 the lightkeeper noted that the oil consumed in the previous quarter was 288 gallons and that 140 gallons remained in store. Pugh & Son were ordered to send a supply by the first vessel sailing for Lowestoft. The oil was unsatisfactory and in July 1784 Pugh sent one barrel of spermaceti-oil and one of whale-oil—the keeper was to mix the two half and half, and report the result. In October 1783 he noted the 'great light' burned 15 pints of oil using 51 burners with wicks $3''$ long. The use of so many burners or lamps at the two

lights would indicate that parabolic reflectors were not fitted, or the lamps would have been fewer.

Casquets and Portland reflectors 1779–82

According to a Minute of June 1779 the Elder Brethren ordered 3 copper lamps and reflectors for the Casquets. The order seems strange not only because the lighthouse was apparently still under private control but also because with only one reflector fitted at each of the 3 towers the lighting would be inadequate; each reflector, if parabolic, would illuminate a sector of only some 15°, while about 360° required to be lighted. It may be that the 3 reflectors were wanted merely for a trial or as an addition to the existing coal fires.

In April-May 1780 the Brethren ordered reflectors and oil lamps for Portland instead of coal; details were not stated. In August 1781 James Lukin received £10. 18. 0 for supplying a metal reflector, brass lamp and *Bason*, perhaps an oil reservoir. In 1782 the agent or supervisor reported that he could not buy seal-oil at Poole under £34 per ton of 280 gallons: he was ordered to lay in a stock at that price as soon as the Newfoundland ships arrived. In July Pugh & Son were ordered to send 1 ton of seal-oil and 14 lb. of cotton.

Smith's reflectors 1786

In June 1786 Thomas Smith informed John Gray the Town Clerk of Edinburgh whose mezzotint portrait, after the picture by Raeburn, was dedicated to the Royal or Honourable Company of Golfers and who was the first Secretary to the Northern Lighthouse Trustees: 'I have constructed two small reflectors and lamps with a view to demonstrate by experiment what has been only laid down in theory.' No details were noted of this parabolic apparatus or of the model which he submitted at the Trust's first meeting in August. It is probable that he carried out most of Ezekiel Walker's ideas for his early reflectors but that as he was an experienced lamp-maker his lamps were of his own design. Those which he made later differ from other makes in having separate tubes to hold the wicks and in showing small bright flames. In 1802 the keeper at Portpatrick was instructed to set each wick to project $\frac{3}{16}''$ from the orifice, 'if less, the rays will not fill the reflector'; and to test the flames by holding a piece of white paper immediately over them. If they were of the right length and if the draught were satisfactory the paper would not be discoloured: few oil lamps without chimneys would pass this test. Strands of cotton were twisted loosely to form the wicks. In 1787 a keeper was told to 'fill each hole with 2 or 3 threads according to the grist [thickness] of your cotton, taking care that your different wicks be neither too strait [tight] in the hole to prevent the oil from coming to feed the flame nor too slack, else they will be too ready to sink'. Evidently the lamps were altered before 1803 when a keeper was informed 'on no pretence whatever will you reduce the size of the wicks below 14 threads'.

Illumination of Early Lighthouses

The inside diameter of one of Smith's later parabolic reflectors was 17½″. It was formed of facets of mirror-glass 1/16″ thick set on plaster upon a foundation of copper or brass, each 1/32″ thick. To ensure sufficient accuracy of reflection, about 350 facets were arranged in horizontal rows in the upper part and circularly in the lower quarter. There were 28 rows of facets with 5 to 21 in a row. The largest facet measured 1 3/16″ horizontally and 11/16″ vertically. The horizontal arrangement suited the small flames in giving the divergence required. The lamp could be slipped back from the reflector and removed for cleaning. The pipes holding the wicks gave a spread of the flames to 1½″. The outer orifice of each pipe was set and cut at an angle. See figure 196.

196. Smith's facet parabolic reflector in 1787

In 1787 Smith instructed the keeper at Kinnaird Head 'in frosty weather to have oil near a fire and not to fill lamps until they are to be lighted: or oil will congeal and not come forward in the pipes'. He was to attend the light-room twice or thrice nightly 'to help any of the lights that might be turning down', to remove all inflammable materials from the wooden lightroom, to remain in it in stormy weather and if a lantern pane should be blown in, 'to shut up the space immediately with one of the tin blanks left with you for that purpose and in the morning replace it with one of the spare panes'. In cleaning the reflectors he should first take off any oil, then 'rub them with a soft linen rag and Spanish white or finely-powdered chalk till they are perfectly bright: this must be strictly adhered to, or a great part of the effect of the light will be lost'.

Smith's charge for reflectors was small. In 1789 he supplied 9 reflectors at 3 guineas each with spare chimneys at 1s. 3d. and lamps at 1s. to the Sailor Fraternity or Trinity House of Dundee for Buddonness lights, with a cistern to hold half a ton of oil for £3. 10. 0. In June 1793 he charged the same rate for 36 reflectors for Cumbrae lighthouse. In March 1804, following his son-in-law's recognition of the superiority of the metal

reflectors used in England, he supplied silver-plated reflectors for a fixed light at Inchkeith island at 15 guineas each.

Facet reflectors at Trinity House—date unknown

About 1933 two facet reflectors were discovered in the Trinity House workshops, of which the history is not known: neither their place of use nor date—perhaps 1787–8. Their shape was parabolic with diameter 18″, focus 4″ and depth 7″. The burner to carry the wicks had an opening 1 1/8″ wide at the end of a 3/4″ pipe carried through the reflector to a rectangular metal reservoir at the back, 8½″ broad, 6″ long and 2″ deep. The 632 facets about ½″ high and 1 3/16″ broad were inserted in plaster in 42 rows with from 5 to 20 facets in each. The burner or lamp could not be removed for cleaning. The reflector was set on thin metal sheeting and had a short chimney. Some scratches on a facet of one reflector are illegible except for a date 1817.

Robinson's reflectors c. 1788

Rogers mentioned that he was associated in business with Robinson from 1788 to 1792 when they were supplying lighthouse apparatus to Trinity House, and one can assume that both men were engaged in the Trinity House tests of 1788–90. After 1792 Robinson and his assistant and successor Robert Wilkins were the sole suppliers of parabolic reflectors and lamps to Trinity House until after 1845, and they supplied many such apparatuses for private lighthouses in England and abroad.

Stevenson noted in 1801 that Robinson's reflectors were of excellent manufacture, of copper with a fused lining of silver, thicker than used in France. Their diameter is mentioned variously as 18″ and 20½″ with a focus about 3″. In 1804 Robinson charged Stevenson £97 for 6 'strong silver-plated high polished parabola reflectors 21″ diameter and 6 Japand Lamps with brass burners'. The lamps were argands described as *spiral*.

The reflectors which Robinson fitted at Flamborough in 1806 measured 20 5/8″ in diameter, 8 3/4″ in depth and 3 1/4″ in focal distance. Circular panes of red glass were set 5 3/4″ beyond the lips. The Elder Brethren agreed to Stevenson sending to Flamborough in December 1809 two prospective lightkeepers for the Bell Rock, for training under their keeper. On instructions from Robinson the reflectors were never removed from the revolving frame but daily were 'scoured and cleaned where they stand, for fear of any accident happening', with dry rouge sprinkled on a chamois skin. Every 3 weeks they were rubbed with turpentine and florence oil. A circular sweep was made: 'on no account rub from the edge to the centre'. Every 2 months the lamps were taken down and washed and their glass chimneys were cleaned daily with turpentine. New wicks were fitted every 2 to 3 days and daily in winter. The cotton threads of the wicks were more open in the weave than those used in Scotland, so took up the oil more readily and gave a better flame.

292

Robinson was not without rivals in London. At the private lighthouse of Dungeness in 1818, Stevenson found parabolic reflectors in use which had been obtained from Howard in Old Street, London. When bought about 1802 they were thicker in silver but cheaper than Robinson's. But by 1818 much of the silver was cleaned off and the copper base exposed.

Rogers's lenses and reflectors c. 1788

The light fitted by Rogers at Portland in England in 1788–9 is of particular interest as being the world's first use of a lens at a lighthouse—the system of illumination by lenses and prisms that has been adopted for most sea-lights today. The following details come from contemporary sources. Like all makers of reflectors and lenses, he supplied apparatus of different dimensions, which is confusing.

a. Hutchinson's observations 1791

In 1791 Hutchinson stated that Rogers brought one of his lights (lens, reflector and lamp) to Liverpool 'to compare with reflectors made with plain pieces of looking-glass which it surpassed greatly' at 3 of the Mersey lighthouses. He added that they 'tried the effect of small lenses with small reflectors which proved the advantage of the principle . . . could not get large lenses made here, but got some blown in the form of a plano-convex, like a bottle, and filled it with strong brine to prevent their being broke by frost, which answered the purpose to magnify the light, but the heat of the blaze of the lamp and reflector broke them'.

Hutchinson hoped to give Rogers's lenses a practical trial but seems to have doubted their suitability for the Mersey where not only was visibility required for a considerable range but light for ships in the channels must 'diverge to each side as much as necessary, to let them see when they are out of a fair way, which is most important, for ships in a fair way are in no danger in comparison with those that are out of a fair way'.

The lamp with a wick of 3″ diameter which Rogers used in his lights was of more practical interest to Hutchinson, who carried out promising experiments with the lamp and a metal reflector of 18″ diameter. In advance of his times, Hutchinson appreciated the value of obtaining an illuminant of considerable intensity in a marine light and observed that the strength of reflected light would be 'in exact proportion to the brightness and intensity of the luminous body'. He found that Rogers's patent lamp 'greatly exceeded all others in that important point'.

b. Stevenson's observations 1801

Stevenson saw Rogers's lens and reflector light at Portland lighthouse in 1801: he sketched its outline and noted that the lenses were inserted in alternate panes of the lantern and that the purpose of using them was to offer a distinction of the lighthouse from others.

c. Inspection by Scots foreman 1812

There is no doubt that Rogers's reflectors and lamps were not constructed well. His apparatus fitted in 1797 at South Rock was unsatisfactory: about 1804 the machine was sent 'to Dublin by a car and was repaired there'. In June 1812 George Carr, the lighthouse superintendent, reported that the keeper 'has been complaining of it this quarter back and had to help it by hand at certain times but now it will not go'. After repair it went out of order again in July. In August one of Stevenson's foremen visited the lighthouse at the request of the new Irish Lighthouse Board, who wished to improve the light. He reported as follows: 'This machinery was first intended to make one revolution in one minute, but at present it will not do it in 2 minutes, and the keeper is obliged to be almost continually at it, driving at one of the wheels which has a pin on it for that purpose. There are in this Lightroom 10 Reflectors of common plated metal about 15 inches diameter.' They had been made so carelessly that he could not say if they were parabolic or spherical, and because of the use of coarse cleaning materials little reflecting quality remained. 'The Lamps are of a kind of argand burner about 2 inches diameter . . . the whole forms a most contrasting appearance to the Northern or English Lighthouses. . . . It is not considered to be of any use to have Cylinders [glass chimneys] upon the Lamps . . . the whole of the upper part of the Reflectors . . . is in one minute after they are Lighted entirely black with smoke and the Lightroom immediately filled. . . . There is always a large quantity of Coal Ashes lying on the floor to dry up the Snuffing of the Lamps and any oil that may fall from the Lamps or otherwise.' He reported direct to Dublin that it would be useless to supply a new apparatus until the lighthouse was better kept, as to which the superintendent could not direct the keeper. Control had passed from Rogers a year previously and Halpin had not had time to establish a new system of management.

But Rogers's lights were esteemed in earlier years: a private letter of 1803 from Ireland refers to Hook as an excellent light and to Howth as 'well kept by the contractor'. The writer, who was not a seaman, was judging their excellence in clear weather.

d. Trinity House test 1829–30

Pressure from 1826 by Lieutenant Drummond of the Ordnance Survey on the British Lighthouse Authorities to adopt his system of obtaining an intense light from jets of oxygen and hydrogen impinging on a ball of lime— a system which proved unsuitable for lighthouses, though up to 1914 his *lime-light* (this was the origin of the term) was of much value for magic-lanterns and in theatres— led to experiments in 1829–30 at Trinity House with his light, Rogers's lens, Robinson's reflector and Fresnel's lens.

Of Rogers's lenses of 20″ diameter, 5″ thickness and 19″

focus Drummond wrote in 1830: 'from the imperfection of form and the badness of material, the light transmitted by them appears by our late experiments to be about one-third of that of the reflectors [Robinson's of 21″ diameter] now in use, while their divergence is so small, that at $1\frac{1}{3}°$ on each side of the axis they cease to be visible. With a view probably to remedy these defects, a somewhat extraordinary arrangement was adopted, viz.—the addition of parabolic reflectors behind the lenses. It is true that by this means some addition is made to the direct light of the lens, and, what is of more consequence, the divergent light is increased so that at an angle of about 3° with the axis, it is equal to about thirteen times the light of an argand. So far therefore the reflector, though but a small portion of it comes into use, contributes to the effect of the lens; but the converse experiment does not appear to have been tried, viz.—how far the reflector was improved by the lens placed before it; otherwise it would quickly have been perceived that the effect of the reflector alone was about double the united effects of the reflector and lens; while at the same time its effective divergence was also greater, being about eight times that of the combined lens and reflector, at an angle of 3° on either side of the axis.' His criticism applied to reflectors that were parabolic, not spherical. He seems not to have appreciated that horizontal divergence depended on the breadth of the flame and the focal length of the optical apparatus. He stated that Rogers's lens light at North Foreland, managed by Greenwich Hospital, 'remains a solitary example of a method which cannot be too soon abandoned, more especially since the remedy is so easy,—merely to remove the lenses, and leave a free and unobstructed passage to the light of the reflectors'.

Drummond's observation that parabolic reflectors were set behind the lenses indicates that Trinity House had substituted them for spherical reflectors at Portland. Perhaps Rogers's blown-glass reflectors were fitted there and were too fragile, but it is most likely that his smoky lamps with flames of 3″ diameter were unsatisfactory. Doubtless Robinson's metal parabolic reflectors and argands, which were the standard equipment of Trinity House, were substituted with no disadvantage to the seaman and with much advantage in maintaining the lighthouse.

In 1834 Drummond recollected the same experiments. He referred to the lens as 'consisting of one solid piece of glass, very thick and very bad. The result of this arrangement was entirely to destroy the effect of the reflector; and in fact, it was absolutely putting a shade before a very good light. In ordinary cases a window of the lantern is of thick clear plate-glass; but here, instead of the plate glass, they put a lens in front of each, which destroyed the parallelism of the beam of light from the reflector, and entirely injured its effect. The reflector, it is true, did not interfere with the action of the lens; but from the thickness and badness of the glass and other causes of an optical nature, the effect of the lens was far inferior to that of the reflector when unobstructed by the lens.' Again it is clear that Drummond did not appreciate Rogers's use of the lens combined with a spherical reflector and a lamp with a broader flame: if he had tested the lens with the multiple-wick lamp used by Fresnel a powerful light would have been forthcoming. He referred to about 15 lenses at North Foreland as costing £40 to £50 apiece, which seems too high a price even if it included the reflectors and lamps.

e. Rogers's reflector curve

Contemporary accounts of Rogers's system do not specify the curve used for his reflectors but Hutchinson's omission of the word *parabolic* (a curve which he could identify at a glance), his statement that the reflectors were blown, his likening of the arrangement to a magic-lantern and his belief that the resulting divergence would be too small to serve the navigable channels at Liverpool, all point to Rogers's original reflectors being spherical: Drummond's mention of the substitution of parabolic reflectors at Portland seems to clinch that deduction.

Reflectors at Walney 1792–1804

The reflectors 31″ diameter, $4\frac{1}{2}$″ deep and about 15″ focus which have been preserved are exceptionally flat. A wooden frame shaped to a parabola was coated with a thin layer of plaster into which 721 pieces of mirror-glass were pressed, with a circular piece of 4″ diameter in the centre. They were arranged radially in 12 rings $1\frac{3}{4}$″ deep, each consisting of 60 facets of from $\frac{1}{4}$″ to $1\frac{3}{4}$″ in width. The wood surface became distorted by damp so that many facets were out of alignment. The lamps were completely separate from the reflectors.

Captain Richard Walker's revolving parabolic reflectors were installed in 1792 and William King, who may have made them, repaired reflectors in 1802. Fire destroyed the lighthouse completely in December 1803 but it was re-built and put into operation in March 1804. King again repaired reflectors in 1814, during the annual discontinuance of the light from the end of May to the beginning of September. Possibly the existing reflectors were made by King in 1804 and repaired in 1814. Discontinuance of the light was unusual in Britain and seems to have been in breach of the patent conditions.

Stevenson's reflectors c. 1810

The instructions given by Robinson to the keepers at Flamborough not to disconnect the lamps and reflectors while cleaning prevented the reflecting surfaces from being polished satisfactorily and so dulled the light emitted. To avoid any inefficiency from lack of polish, Stevenson drew down the lamp and thereby exposed the whole surface of the reflector to the attentions of the keeper. A locking device ensured that the lamp returned exactly to the focus. Minor improvements included a small tray below the burner to trap surplus oil and a tiny *frost lamp* which was lighted in cold weather to warm the main lamp, thus to assist combustion 'when oil was liable to turn thick'. To ensure accuracy

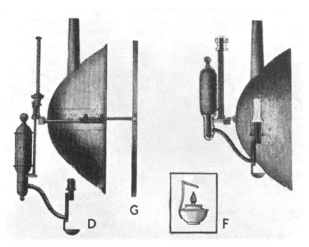

197. Robert Stevenson's metal parabolic reflector with frost lamp F in 1810

Stevenson had the reflector curves drawn by Professor Leslie and their moulds made by the optician Adie.

Figure 197 shows Stevenson's 25″ diameter parabolic reflector weighing 11½ lb. with a brass reservoir holding 24 oz. of oil, sufficient to last 24 hours. A ¾″ argand lamp is shown both withdrawn for cleaning and set at the focus. The *frost lamp* F was hung over the drip cup D an hour before sunset in cold weather. A sheet of red glass for a coloured beam was set at G.

This type of optical apparatus—an argand lamp with wick under 1″ diameter and either a 21″ reflector for fixed lights or a 25″ reflector for revolving lights—was supplied from 1810 to 1880 by Robinson, Wilkins, Milne and other makers for many Scottish, Irish and British Colonial lighthouses. When improved apparatus was installed at 3 Scottish lighthouses between 1836 and 1842 the original sets were sent complete—reflectors, lamps and machine to rotate the reflector frame—to lighthouses newly-built in Newfoundland. The apparatus of Inchkeith of 1816 was re-erected at Cape Spear in 1836, that of the Isle of May of 1816 went to Harbour Grace and that of the Bell Rock of 1811 went to Cape Bonavista in 1843. At those new situations they gave long service: in 1870 two were listed as being in excellent condition, renewal of the machinery and re-plating of reflectors not having been necessary. In 1861 Sir George Airy, the English Astronomer Royal, inspected lighthouses in Britain and France in the course of a Parliamentary investigation of the British Lighthouse Services, and noted this design of reflector and lamp as the best that he had seen.

Lenses at Flamborough c. 1809

On their visit of instruction to Flamborough lighthouse in December 1809, the Scots lightkeepers recorded that the lenses fitted in the lantern were half-spheres of 4½″ diameter, the centre of the plane surface being set 2⅛″ from the focus and close to the chimney of each lamp. They intercepted a large proportion of the rays otherwise lost from the front of the flame but only 5 per cent. of the rays from the reflector, of which the lamp would have obstructed a portion: so the lenses had little effect upon the light. They were held in brass rings.

SPAIN

Cadiz reflectors c. 1795

In 1793 the French Minister of Marine stated that reflectors were giving satisfaction at sea-lights in Spain. Perhaps he referred to a revolving light which a list of 1829 suggested had been established in 1795 at the tower of St. Sebastian at Cadiz. Three horizontal rows of 4 reflectors were placed parallelly on an axle turned continuously by clockwork: in 3 minutes it produced short eclipses and flashes. The description is contradictory and obscure: one might suppose, among alternatives, that there was one revolving face of 12 small reflectors. Particulars of the reflectors and their country of origin were not mentioned.

UNITED STATES OF AMERICA

Lewis's reflector and lens c. 1812

Lewis's lights, which consisted of an oil lamp with a metal reflector behind and a lens in front, were described in 1889 by A. B. Johnson of the United States Lighthouse Service: 'The reflector was of a thin sheet of copper, commonly segments of a sphere, plated over with a slight film of silver, though the copper was so thin that the compression between the arms of its iron supports materially altered its form, and its silvered concave surface had much the grain and lustre of tinware, and would reflect no distinct image. The patentee of 1812 made no pretension to a knowledge of optics as now understood, and his reflectors came about as near to a true paraboloid as did a barber's basin. The lamp, roughly constructed on the principle of Argand's fountain-lamp, burning from 30 to 40 gallons of oil per year, had a three-quarter inch burner, and was attached to a circular iron frame in front of the reflector. Before

295

the lamp was a so-called lens, of bottle-green glass, shaped like the bull's eye let into ships' decks, from $2\frac{1}{2}$ to 4 inches thick through the axis and 9 inches in diameter, which was supposed to have some magnifying power. The apparatus was enclosed in a massive wrought-iron lantern, glazed with panes 10 by 12 inches in size. The effect of the whole was characterized by one of the reporting inspectors as making a bad light worse.' Another observer noted the lens as a plano-convex mass of coarse striated glass mounted in a copper rim and weighing over 8 lb.

Lewis's lamps were not argands and they lacked chimneys. To burn satisfactorily they had to be screwed back in cold weather and forward in warm weather, thus were rarely in focus. Johnson and other critics were mistaken in supposing that the reflector of this catadioptric system should be parabolic; it was so at the South Stack where there was some excuse for fitting the small lens of $4\frac{1}{2}''$ diameter as it obstructed only 5 per cent. of the light-rays from the $20\frac{5}{8}''$ parabola and endeavoured to concentrate rays escaping in front. Lewis's lens of $9''$ obstructed 33 per cent. or 100 per cent. of the reflected rays respectively from his $16''$ or $8\frac{1}{2}''$ reflectors which should have been spherical as Rogers realised. So the navigator received rays passing through Lewis's lens and few, if any, of the rays that had struck his reflector.

Lewis fitted his lenses and reflectors usually to give fixed lights but he may have fitted them as revolving lights at the following lighthouses: Charleston, Wood island, Gay Head, Watch Hill and Point Judith.

APPENDIX

THE BELL ROCK LIGHTHOUSE:

ITS DESIGNER AND CONSTRUCTOR

APPENDIX

THE BELL ROCK LIGHTHOUSE: ITS DESIGNER AND CONSTRUCTOR

Although the Commissioners of Northern Lighthouses, who employed Thomas Telford, John Rennie and Robert Stevenson in connection with the Bell Rock lighthouse, put upon record in 1850 that to Stevenson 'is due the honour of conceiving and executing the great work of the Bell Rock lighthouse', statements appear in the Press every few years ascribing that work to Rennie. This is due to the re-issue without correction of the 1874 edition of Samuel Smiles's *Lives of the Engineers*.

Stevenson's Account of the lighthouse

The Bell Rock lighthouse was lighted on 1st February 1811. In Minutes of January 1811 and July 1812 the Northern Lighthouse Board directed Robert Stevenson to prepare an Account of the work 'from the commencement to the conclusion of the undertaking' under the direction of a committee of three of their number including the Solicitor-General who was a member of the Government, and they authorised the expenditure of £400 towards the cost. The Account, a large volume of some 250,000 words, was published in 1824. It detailed exactly how the three engineers were connected with the lighthouse from its inception to its completion. About 1829 the Board placed in the tower a marble bust of Stevenson which they had commissioned from the sculptor Samuel Joseph.

Sir John Rennie's assertion

In 1848 Sir John Rennie published an Account of the building of Plymouth breakwater in which he asserted for the first time that his father, who died in 1821, had 'designed and built' the Bell Rock lighthouse. Stevenson's sons denied this in correspondence with Sir John which was published in the *Civil Engineers' and Architects' Journal*. In July 1850 Stevenson died and, in recording their appreciation of his services as their engineer, the Commissioners took the opportunity to deny Sir John's claim and attributed the work to Stevenson in the words quoted already. As they were familiar with the history of the lighthouse and as the majority of the Board were sheriffs or county judges whose business it was to sift evidence, it might be expected that the opinion of so informed and almost judicial a body would have been accepted as conclusive. But in 1854 Sir John published a History of harbours in which he described the Bell Rock lighthouse and affirmed that 'the design was prepared by the late Mr. Rennie; that no modifications were introduced without his sanction

and consent; and that from first to last he was responsible for the success of the undertaking'. Without mentioning the Commissioners' opinion, Sir John supplied his own version of the construction of the lighthouse to Smiles who published it in the first edition of his book. Again the Stevensons set out their denial in the same Journal. In an edition of 1874 or earlier Smiles reproduced a letter from John Rennie to a friend in which he said: 'the original plans were prepared by me and the work was visited by me from time to time' The letter was dated 12th March 1814.

It was chiefly on that quotation and on Minutes by the Commissioners of 3rd and 26th December 1806 appointing his father *chief engineer* for the work, that Sir John based his assertion. He seems not to have questioned critically the circumstances or implications of the appointment or what part his father actually took in the operations. Perhaps the Stevensons were remiss in not countering his statements more fully: they considered that their denial and the main facts which they quoted were ample to refute Sir John's assertions.

While it is the case that Rennie supplied one coloured drawing, visited the Rock and had a responsibility for the part which he played, the fuller facts are that his one outline sketch was not carried out, that he never visited the Rock while the lighthouse was being constructed and seems never to have set foot in the tower, and that his responsibility was hardly even that of a consulting engineer at the present day: correspondence shows that his sanction or consent was never asked for or given to any modification of the plans, which were made entirely by Stevenson.

Appointment of Rennie and Stevenson

After the Commissioners had decided that the lighthouse should be constructed of stone, Stevenson reported to them on 15th November 1806 as to preparations for the work and pointed out that 'stone is the principal material that requires consideration'; certain Scottish quarries produced stone that might not be durable while others supplied blocks not sufficiently large. At that time Rennie wrote to Stevenson saying that he was about to visit Scotland and as Stevenson desired to have the authority to consult him if necessary during the building of the lighthouse he arranged for the Commissioners to invite him to attend a meeting at which the supply of stone should also be discussed. The meeting took place in Edinburgh on 3rd December;

the Commissioners' Minutes mention that they considered 'the different reports on the subject, particularly on the kind of building to be adopted' and that they re-affirmed that the lighthouse should be built of stone and 'that the same shall be erected under the direction of John Rennie Esq., whom they hereby appoint chief engineer for conducting the work. . . . He was requested to furnish the Commissioners with plans.' As he intended to travel to Perth, he was also 'requested to visit' quarries and report. Stevenson was 'authorised to proceed along with' Rennie and to set up a workyard at Arbroath. During their travels and discussions, Rennie evidently decided not to comply with the request to furnish plans or to accept the sole appointment as minuted; for a Minute of the Commisioners of 26th December noted that 'Messrs Rennie and Stevenson, having in terms of last Minute . . . examined the different quarries, they presented a joint report in the following terms . . .'. Their joint report dealt with many points which they had discussed and stated that 'a plan of the lighthouse similar to what is proposed is handed in', but the plan has not been preserved. The Minute continued: 'Mr. Rennie proposed to the meeting that Mr. Stevenson should be appointed assistant engineer to execute the work under his superintendence and mentioned to the Commissioners that the mode of re-imbursing him [Stevenson] for his trouble and the risk attending the business which was customary in similar undertakings and what he knew would be most agreeable to the Board of Treasury, would be to allow him a certain percentage upon a limited sum of expenditure with such a sum at the conclusion of the work as they may choose to fix. And the Commissioners agree to the appointment of Mr. Stevenson as assistant engineer under Mr. Rennie. . . .' There is no mention of payment to Rennie.

Rennie's position

The Minutes of 26th December 1806 do not indicate whether Rennie and Stevenson would continue to act jointly in preparing plans and reporting. However, it seems that Rennie's position became nebulous in that the extent and value of his services could not be estimated and assessed in advance: he assumed a position which was somewhat that of a consulting engineer at the present time. All that he did after that meeting is clear: he supplied an outline sketch of a tower which was not carried out, in correspondence with Stevenson he offered a suggestion occasionally but no direction or instruction, on 3 occasions he visited Arbroath and sailed out to the vicinity of the Rock, and after each of these visits he wrote a letter to the Commissioners reporting that the work was going well and recording little else than what Stevenson had done and what he proposed to do, which indeed they knew already. It is of course usual for a consulting engineer to make such routine reports but it is surprising that Rennie, who took a keen interest in the lighthouse, never saw or apparently endeavoured to see the artificers at work on the tower or a stone laid upon it at any stage of its construction between July 1808 and July 1810.

Plans of the lighthouse

On 13th February 1807 Rennie wrote to Stevenson asking: 'Have you procured a proper assistant for the Bell Rock?' and telling him that although on returning to London at the end of 1806 he had been working night and day at his business, 'I have sketched out a new plan for the lighthouse and I trust this will give you satisfaction'. Evidently his purpose was to offer a compromise on the diameter of the base of the tower and its other dimensions, about which they had differed in opinion as mentioned in the *Civil Engineers' Journal*. He signed the plan *London Feby 21st 1807 John Rennie* and sent it to Edinburgh. It was a coloured elevation of a tower like the Eddystone; but the proposed interior and the method of construction were not indicated. It is reproduced in figure 199. This was the only plan or drawing that Rennie supplied for the Bell Rock. Stevenson departed from it entirely, as in designing the base and the upper part of the tower. That Rennie supposed that his drawing guided Stevenson is borne out by his letter to the Commissioners of 29th October 1807 after he saw the foundation pit marked out on the Rock: 'As to the construction of the lighthouse, I submitted a plan to your consideration in the month of February last. According to this plan the works are proceeding: plans of each course of stone have been made.'

A letter to the Commissioners' Secretary shows that Stevenson returned to Edinburgh on 26th March 1807 from a visit to the granite quarries near Aberdeen where he had given the quarriers 'the sizes and numbers of stones wanted for the first five courses and given them moulds for their directions'. He had spent 8 days at Arbroath and journeyed by horseback. As the external curves and the shapes of the 235 granite stones of the total of 586 blocks comprising these lower courses could not have been determined without fixing the curve for the complete tower, the final design of the tower must have been settled before Stevenson set out for Aberdeen in the beginning of March. There is no record of any design having been sent by him to Rennie for comment nor did Rennie refer to any when he forwarded his abortive sketch to Edinburgh on 21st February. If this sketch had reached Stevenson before his departure for Aberdeen the shortness of the interval after its receipt precludes the possibility of his final design being sent to London and comment received from Rennie before the Aberdeen quarriers received instructions in the middle of March.

A letter from Rennie to Stevenson dated 3rd December 1807 confirms that Stevenson made the plans and carried them out without reference to Rennie: 'I shall be very glad if you would send me the drawings of the different courses of stones that I may fully study them. I should also like to have a drawing of the Beacon with the building on its top for lodging the workmen.' Rennie acknowledged the receipt of Stevenson's drawings on 21st January 1808.

Modifications of design

Some 30 letters from Rennie to Stevenson from 1807 to 1809 establish the facts that on no occasion did Rennie give instructions or directions to Stevenson or to anyone else in connection with the work and that Stevenson alone was in complete control of the design and the construction of the tower. The diagrams printed by Sir John in 1854 show many radical differences between his father's outline design of 1807 and the tower as completed; Stevenson made all the plans on his own responsibility. Except for the base diameter which was a compromise, they rendered Rennie's plan a piece of scrap paper.

Rennie's visits to the work

The 3 occasions on which Rennie visited Arbroath and saw the artificers cutting the stones and then sailed out to the Rock were in October 1807, December 1808 and October 1809. In 1807 he landed on the Rock on the last day of the working season with his son George, who became a well-known engineer. They viewed the beacon and watched the artificers excavating the foundation of the tower while tools and implements were being removed from the Rock. In 1808 the tide seems not to have fallen sufficiently to allow Rennie to land: probably the 3 completed courses were awash and the boat unable to approach closer than a quarter of a mile. In 1809 operations had already ceased on 25th August when the solid portion was completed. Unless Rennie's description of the wave action on the tower—from its outline presenting 'comparatively small obstruction to the roll of the waves which played round the column with ease'—was mere hearsay (as was much of his letter of 12th December 1808), he saw the tower from a distance about high-water when the Rock was covered. It is scarcely possible that a sea rough enough to provide an adequate test of the wave-action which he described would have abated sufficiently, even 5 hours later, to enable him to land when the tide fell. On none of these 3 occasions was the building of the tower in progress.

Rennie frequently asked for news of the work; on 24th June 1807, 'I shall be happy to learn from time to time how matters proceed' and on 25th July 1808, 'I shall be glad to hear of your further progress'.

Responsibility

The Commissioners' Minutes of 26th December 1806 put on Rennie the responsibility of superintending Stevenson's execution of the work, but the unique circumstance of the site being at sea added the prospect of delays in boating to the week required to carry mail by horse coach between Arbroath and London and evidently made supervision impracticable, for Rennie never attempted to direct Stevenson. Their correspondence showed him as taking up the position of an engineer interested in the unusual work of a fellow-engineer and sometimes ready with a suggestion but punctilious in leaving every decision to be taken by Stevenson. His opinions and views, as also to a lesser degree those of many people of various qualifications and experiences, were of great value to Stevenson who often expressed his appreciation of their discussions, particularly in December 1806 when solutions were being sought of problems which neither man had faced before.

If any mishap occurred, Rennie's responsibility was limited to the advice he gave to the Commissioners and his reports and letters including his outline sketch of 1807, also to the plans by Stevenson which he saw before construction, namely, those forwarded in January 1808 on which he offered no comment.

In responsibility, Rennie often bracketed himself with Stevenson, as in references to *our* work. On 15th September 1808 he pointed out 'the discredit that a failure, if even trifling, should bring upon us'. But even that remark did not induce Stevenson to order a large quantity of lead—Rennie tried in two letters to persuade him to do so—to cover the 3 completed courses as protection from the coming winter's storms. In assuming the part of a consultant he offered suggestions for Stevenson to accept or reject without comment. In 1809 Stevenson contemplated fitting a brass ladder between the rock and the entrance door, and on 20th February Rennie wrote: 'No doubt a ladder such as you mention would be of great use but I confess I am not inclined to advise anything being done that will occasion holes being cut on the outside of the tower. Would not a rope ladder be quite enough?' Stevenson accepted this advice but some years later fixed his intended brass ladder without detriment to the tower.

Rennie and Stevenson

During the progress of the work Rennie did not take credit for it. On 29th October 1807 he wrote to the Commissioners: 'On the whole I feel confident that this work will be brought to a successful conclusion within a reasonable period. The knowledge which has been acquired [by Stevenson] by the operations of the last season, impresses me with additional confidence in the practicability of the work, though confident from the commencement that with proper care and attention such a work might with certainty be completed'; and on 12th December 1808 he wrote: 'As there was little swell, I was enabled to form a tolerable judgement concerning the perfection with which it [the masonry] is executed and this I have pleasure to say is very favourable'. On 2nd October 1809 he expressed the opinion that the lighthouse when finished 'would be found to be the most perfect work of its kind'. Clearly, on each of these

3 occasions he was fulfilling the part of a consulting engineer reporting not on his own work but on that of another engineer.

Rennie wrote the following letter to Stevenson from London dated 7th September 1807:

'*Dear Sir*

I was this day duly favoured with yours of the 2nd and it gives me much pleasure that the alterations I suggested in the manner of dovetailing the stones in the courses of the Bell Rock Lighthouse can be so easily accomplished. If you could send me a rough sketch of the mode in a letter p. return of Post I will be obliged. I propose to set out for Scotland on the 15th and expect to be there about the end of the month. My Journey will rather be a circuitous one—as I have Boston, Hull, etc. etc. to take in my way.

I propose myself much pleasure in the viewing of your operations. This will be heightened if in the interim you can bargain with old Neptune to favour us with a quiet sea while I am on board the floating light—I hate your rolling seas—if ever I am to have a Provost Paton's breakfast afterwards. However, my good Sir, we are so tossed and tumbled about in the great Theatre of life, that it must be taken rough and smooth as it comes in our way.

I rejoice to find that you have been so successful in landing some stones on the Rock, it forms a pleasing presage of future success—but for God's sake do not lose the Smeaton. *Poor old fellow, I hope he will now and then take a peep of us, and inspire you with fortitude and courage to accomplish a work which will if successful, immortalise you in [the] annals of fame. With such perseverance as yours I entertain no doubt of final success. Do as much as you can in preparing the foundation this year. I wish this had been next year for I fear we shall not have soon such another season.*

I have just heard that Copenhagen was taken on the 24th. There are no official dispatches but it is generally believed over at the Treasury—from whence my information [?arises.]

God help you and best wishes for your success,

Dear Sir
Sincerely yours
JOHN RENNIE

Robt. Stevenson Esq.
on board the floating light
Bell Rock
Arbroath. N.B.'

When this letter was quoted to Sir John Rennie, he dismissed as 'a mere joke' by his father the reference to the accomplishment of the work by Stevenson.

Samuel Smiles and lighthouses

In his books Smiles gave a correct and interesting general view of the works of the early British engineers but in details he was not always accurate. Of lighthouses, he had no personal knowledge and he had been misinformed on many points, as when he stated that the lighthouses established by the Northern Lighthouse Board before 1800 'consisted of coal fires in chauffers'. Again as to the Bell Rock, he was not aware that in 1800 Stevenson recommended that the tower should be built of stone and proposed a new design for the stone floors which, according to Professor Playfair in 1802, was 'likely to prove perfectly secure and has the advantage of being far more easily constructed than Mr. Smeaton's'. Rennie opposed the design in 1805 and approved it later.

According to Smiles: 'During Mr. Rennie's lifetime various notices were published, claiming for Mr. Stevenson the sole credit of having designed and erected the lighthouse. At this Mr. Rennie was naturally annoyed; the more so when he learnt that Mr. Stevenson was about to write a book without communicating with him on the subject.' It is curious that Rennie who lived 10 years after the lighthouse was finished did not correct what he considered was wrong: the idea of the book originated with the Commissioners. On this point, Sir John wrote: 'Mr. Stevenson took care not to publish his book until after my father's death so that he had no opportunity of answering it, which no doubt he would have done . . . even Mr. Stevenson's book establishes sufficient to prove that the Bell Rock Lighthouse was designed and carried into effect under Mr. Rennie's superintendence.' Sir John set his complaint in vague general terms and he failed to point out one inaccuracy in the book to justify his assertions.

Rennie's letter of 1814

The letter of 1814 which Smiles printed about 1874 was occasioned by the successful completion of the Bell Rock tower, which immediately brought employment to Stevenson as a civil engineer to an extent that surprised Rennie and cut into the professional business which he divided with Telford in Scotland and for which he was training two of his sons. He had expected that Stevenson would confine his activities to lighthouses and the purpose of the letter was to complain of his launching into general practice as a civil engineer as well. Probably on a grumble from his friend Huddart whose health was failing, he mistakenly complained that Stevenson had claimed for himself the invention of 'applying coloured glass to lighthouses of which Huddart was the actual inventor', whereas what Stevenson suggested was that the credit for the coloured Flamborough light should go to Milne. In letters to his friends Rennie seems to have tended to disparage his fellow-engineers. This was his attitude as regards Smith and Stevenson in his letter of 1814; and in a letter to Stevenson on 3rd November 1806 he wrote of Telford, whose bridges and other engineering works are appreciated so greatly: 'He has no originality of thought and has all his life built up the little fame he has acquired upon the knowledge of others which he has generally assumed as his own.' In 1806 Telford recorded his belief that his business actually benefited from Rennie's openly-declared hostility to himself, which was shown also by Sir John Rennie many years later.

Sir John Rennie's diagrams

In his History of harbours of 1854, Sir John took the extraordinary step of producing under the title of *original design* for the Bell Rock lighthouse an elevation section of a lighthouse which was evolved by himself.

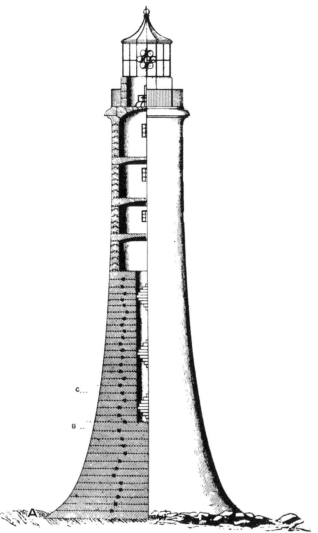

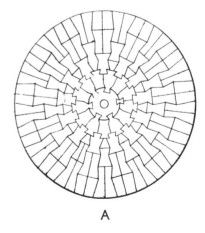

199. This is the only plan or sketch made by John Rennie in connection with the Bell Rock. His tower measured 89′ 6″ from rock to parapet. The plan is dated Feby 21st 1807

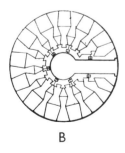

B

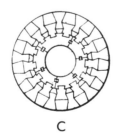

C

A

198. Under the title of 'Original Design' of the Bell Rock lighthouse, Sir John Rennie published in 1854, as showing fuller details of his father's design of 1807, this half-sectional elevation with cross sections. In fact, Sir John himself prepared the elevation and took the cross sections from Stevenson's plans. (Cross section A represented the 1st entire course; the levels of B and C are marked on the elevation.)

It combined his father's outline of 21st February 1807 and his own idea of what its interior might have been like. This concocted drawing is shown in figure 198.

He showed 5 cross-sections of the stone courses designed by Stevenson but instead of indicating their levels on a drawing of Stevenson's tower which he reproduced, he marked them on his own composite elevation, thus crediting his father with Stevenson's designs.

Summary

If despite the Northern Lighthouse Commissioners' attribution of the Bell Rock lighthouse to Stevenson, anyone should still suppose that Rennie—who produced only one plan or sketch (which Stevenson did not adopt), who never saw a stone laid on the tower and probably never set foot in it, and who never took a decision or issued instructions or directions to anyone about the plans or the operations—either designed the lighthouse or built it as his son declared, he should notice the amounts received from the Lighthouse Board by the three engineers. Telford received £77 which covered one visit to the Rock and his preparation of evidence to support the Parliamentary Bill of 1803. Rennie received £440 and Stevenson £4,052. 16. 0 along with his salary as engineer of the Scottish lighthouses. When it was put to Sir John Rennie in 1862 that the extent of the responsibilities of the three engineers might be judged from these sums, he wrote: 'This goes for nothing, for it too frequently happens that those who are least entitled to it get best paid.' Evidently he was unaware that his father not only received from the Commissioners the exact sum for which he asked but also advised them what they should pay to Stevenson.

Rennie's account for the Bell Rock lighthouse covered the following professional work as a consulting engineer: in 1805 visiting the Rock and the South Rock lighthouse and reporting to the Commissioners that he concurred in the proposal to erect a tower of stone; in 1806 supporting Stevenson's evidence in Parliament, meeting the Commissioners, visiting quarries with Stevenson and reporting and submitting a plan of a lighthouse jointly with him; in 1807 sending the outline sketch plan that was not carried out; in 1807, 1808 and 1809 visiting Arbroath and the Rock or its vicinity and after each visit reporting to the Commissioners on the state of the works; and from 1806 to 1809 having discussions and correspondence with Stevenson.

The fee of £440 which Rennie charged would fairly cover that consulting work by such an eminent engineer.

Rennie's opinions and advice were exceedingly useful to the Commissioners and to Stevenson, but he did not design or build the lighthouse or request payment for doing so.

Stevenson's account of £4,052. 16. 0 included £315 for his work before Telford and Rennie were consulted. Other details are not recorded but a percentage payment for carrying out the work would amount to not less than £2,100, *i.e.* 5 per cent. on say £42,000. The balance included the additional sum which Rennie recommended the Commissioners to pay 'at the conclusion of the work as they may choose to fix' and covered Stevenson's extensive preliminary work between 1803 and 1807 and his preparation of the plans which were carried out.

All Sir John Rennie's statements will be found in Smiles's book and the other books and journals that have been mentioned.

INDEXES

A

VARIETIES OF SEAMARKS AND LIGHTHOUSE EQUIPMENT, AND LIGHTING SUBJECTS

Structures (*cont.*),
  lever, 31, 274
  piles, 54, 127, 241
  reinforced, 167, 221
  swape, *see* lever
  twin towers, 36
  vierbotes, 26
  vippefyr, 41, 78, 245
  vuurboeten, 40
  wave-swept, 88

Tests, 18, 49, 63, 66, 79, 82–3, 190, 193, 196, 198–9, 244, 273, 283–6

Varieties of lights,
  catadioptric, 67, 279
  catoptric, 279
  dioptric, 279
  eclipser, 182
  fanal à double aspect, 76, 290

Varieties of lights (*cont.*),
  fanal à double effet, 76, 78, 243, 283, 289
  fanal sidéral, 76, 79, 243, 284, 289
  spangle, 56–7, 291
  and see Characters

Wrecking, *see* False lights
Wreck-markings, 49
Wreck statistics, xxiii, 189

B

DESIGNERS AND CONSTRUCTORS OF SEAMARKS AND LIGHTHOUSE EQUIPMENT, SEVERAL BEING CONCERNED ONLY INDIRECTLY

Adie, 295
Aldini, Giovanni, 84
Allen, Joseph, 133
Alexander, Daniel, 4, 142, 231–2
Anderson, 157
Angell, Justinian, 106
Arago, D. J. F., 83, 90, 278
Argand, Ami, xxiii, 61–3, 75, 196, 278, 283
Avery, David, xxiii, 138–40
Augier, 36

Batten, Sir William, 104
Bayley, Captain, 108
Beusher, François, 33–4
Bitry, 195, 288
Blackett, 142
Borda, Chevalier, 63, 197–8
Bordier-Marcet, J. A., xxiii, 76, 78–9, 243–4, 283–6, 289–90
Boulton and Watt, 77, 284
Braun, J. D., 287
Bushell, 97

Champion, 83
Chatillon, Claude, 30–1, 35
Clarkson, James, 157
Clayton, Sir John, 106–8, 133, 257, 259
Le Cocq, Thomas, 137
Cotton, Captain, 84, 232
Crispe, William, 140
Cunningham, Alexander, 38

Dashwood, Francis, 47
Dominique, 34
Douglass, Sir James, 126, 130, 149
Drummond, Lieutenant, 280, 293–4

Ewing, James, 156

Faraday, Michael, 246
Farish, Richard, 141
Le Fevre, 283
De Foix, Louis, xxiii, 31–5
De Foix, Pierre, 33
Fonnereau, Thomas, 141
Franklin, Benjamin, 18, 74
Fresnel, Augustin, 68, 85, 91, 244–5, 278

Gardiner, 42
Gedy, John, 25
De Godyton, Walter, 22
Greenside Callum, 169, 240
Groves, J. P., 41, 274

Hagen, 42, 287
Halden, 51
Halpin, George, senior, 242, 284
Hamblin, Robert, 138–9
Holland, John, 120
Hopkinson, John, 282
Howard, 235, 293
Howard, Sir Edward, 98
Huddart, Captain, 77, 84, 302
Hunter, 62
Hutchinson, Samuel, 286
Hutchinson, William, xxiii, 51, 55–6, 67–8, 165, 190, 273, 279, 284–6, 290, 293

Jallier, 197
Jessop, Josiah, 122
Jupp, R., 143

Killegrew, Sir John, 100–2
King, William, 144, 294
Knight, John, 105

Lange, 278
Langridge, Charles, 134
Lenoir, xxiii, 83, 91, 197, 199, 244, 289
Leslie, Professor, 295
Lewis, Winslow, xxiii, 77, 80, 249–50, 287, 295–6
Life, Nathaniel, 136
Lukin, James, 291
Lutwige, Thomas, 136

McKay, 159
Mathieu, 83
Meldrum, Sir John, 99, 100–2
Meunier, 278
Milne, 295
Milne, Benjamin, 77
Le Moyne, 63
Muletin, 63

Norberg, Jonas, xxiii, 49, 50, 279, 281, 287–8
Norcutt, 117–19
Nordquist, *see* Norberg
Norman, William, 137

Oaky, James, 225

Palmer, James, 165
Peckston, T. S., 84
Pellet and Green, 80
Penseron, Pierre, 52
Phillips, John, 54, 126–9
Pickernell, J., 63
Polheimer, Anders, 70, 275–7
Porta, 283, 286
Puttock, John, 23

Quinquet, 62, 196–7

C

SEAMARKS: ACTUAL AND REPUTED

(L.V. denotes a Lightvessel or Lightship)

Indexes

308